THE NATIONAL
GEOGRAPHIC TRAVELER
GREECE

THE NATIONAL
GEOGRAPHIC TRAVELER

GREECE

Mike Gerrard

Contents

How to use this guide 6–7 About the author 8
History & culture 9–48 The regions 49–336 Travelwise 337–390
Index 391–397 Illustrations credits 398

Page 1: Bronze detail, Thessaloniki
Pages 2–3: Kefalonia harbor
Left: Santorini at sunset

How to use this guide

See back flap for keys to text and map symbols

The *National Geographic Traveler* brings you the best of Greece in text, pictures, and maps. Divided into three main sections, the guide begins with an overview of the country's history and culture. Following are nine area chapters with featured sites selected by the author for their particular interest. Each chapter opens with its own contents list.

The regions and sites within the areas are arranged geographically. Some areas are further divided into smaller areas. A map introduces each region, highlighting the featured sites. Walks and drives, plotted on

their own maps, suggest routes for discovering an area. Features and sidebars give intriguing detail on history, culture, or contemporary life.

The final section, Travelwise, lists essential information for the traveler—pre-trip planning, special events, getting around, and emergencies—plus a selection of hotels, restaurants, shops, activities, and entertainment.

To the best of our knowledge, all information is accurate as of the press date. However, it's always advisable to call ahead when possible.

Color coding

154

Each region is color coded for easy reference. Find the region you want on the map on the front flap, and look for the color flash at the top of the pages of the relevant chapter. Information in **Travelwise** is also color coded to each region.

Ancient Agora Museum

- ▲ 50 B2
- ✉ Adhrianou 24
- ☎ 321 0185
- 🕐 Closed Mon.
- 💲 $$
- 🚇 Metro: Monastiraki

Visitor information

Practical information for most sites is given in the side column (see key to symbols on back flap). The map reference gives the page number of the map and grid reference. Other details are address, telephone number, days closed, entrance charge in a range from $ (under $4) to $$$$$ (over $25), and nearest public transport. Other sites have information in italics and parentheses in the text.

TRAVELWISE

PELOPONNESE — Color-coded region name

ANDRITSAINA — Town & area name

🏨 **THEOXENIA HOTEL** — Hotel name & price range
$

ANDRITSAINA — Address, telephone & fax numbers
TEL 0626 22219

The only hotel of any size in this mountain village. Facilities are basic but so are prices, and the rooms are clean, have ensuite facilities, and phones. — Brief description of hotel

🛏 28 🔧 🚭 🚫 No credit cards — Hotel facilities & credit card details

🍴 **O YIORGIS** — Restaurant name & price range
$

MAIN PLATEIA — Address & telephone number
TEL 0626 22004

The center of this mountain village is a perfect setting for this simple taverna. The food is staple hearty fare such as grilled chops and beef dishes. — Brief description of restaurant

🚭 🚫 No credit cards — Restaurant facilities & credit card details

Hotel & restaurant prices

An explanation of the price bands used in entries is given in the Hotels & Restaurants section (beginning on p. 347).

REGIONAL MAPS

Airport

Drive start point

Important point of interest

Map reference

Important featured town

Road number

Point of interest

- A locator map accompanies each regional map and shows the location of that region in the country.
- Adjacent regions are shown, each with a page reference.

WALKING TOURS

Building outline

Red numbered bullets link site on map to descriptions in the text

Featured site (in bold) on walk route

Start point

Walk route

Direction of walk route

Point of interest not on walk route

- An information box gives the starting and ending points, time and length of walk, and places not to be missed along the route.
- Where two walks are marked on the map, the second route is shown in orange.

DRIVING TOURS

Start point

Red numbered bullets link site on map to descriptions in the text

Important featured town

Road number

Line of route

- An information box provides details including starting and finishing points, time and length of drive, and places not to be missed along the route, or tips on terrain.

THE NATIONAL
GEOGRAPHIC TRAVELER

GREECE

About the author

Mike Gerrard is an award-winning travel writer (Travelex Travel Writers Award, Outdoor Writers; Guide Awards for Excellence in Photojournalism and Features; and the British Guild of Travel Writers award for "Best U.K. Feature") who first visited Greece in the late 1960s and fell in love with the country at first sight. He has been back every year since, sometimes several times, and has written guides to Athens, the Greek mainland, the Greek islands, and Corfu. His travel journalism has appeared in newspapers and magazines worldwide, including *The Times* in London and *The Washington Post*. To research a piece for *The Times* he tried being a Greek waiter for a week on the island of Zakynthos and, as a result, he now gives bigger tips.

History & culture

Minoan mural from 1600 B.C.

Greece today

WHAT IS GREECE? GREECE IS THE PARTHENON, STANDING ABOVE ATHENS, a monument to the country's ancient history. Greece is also deep blue skies and turquoise seas, and white houses stacked like cubes on a hillside above a harbor, enticing modern tourism to the islands. But Greece is much, much more than those things. It is a country with a unique culture, a unique language, a landscape that is among the least explored in Europe, and a people who are the most hospitable in the world.

Of course many visitors have time to see only the tourist centers and can't explore off the beaten track. Even so, they will still find that special quality encountered nowhere but in Greece. No one's heart can fail to be lifted on arriving in the country's busy capital and finding the skyline dominated not by sky-scrapers but by a building over 2,500 years old—and not merely old but one of the most beautiful ever constructed. The first sight of the Parthenon, no matter how familiar it is from postcards and prints, will fill you with excitement.

A brief visit allows you to take in some other of Greece's highlights, such as the treasures of the National Archaeological Museum (one of the very few national museums that does not contain foreign works), and a trip to the ruins of Delphi, one of the most magical sites in the world. A leisurely cruise through the islands might take you to the Old Town of Rhodes, and the harbor that the Colossus of Rhodes allegedly bestrode, and to the reconstructed ruins of the Royal Palace at Knossos on Crete, the center of the mighty Minoan civilization. There will also be time for one of the greatest and simplest pleasures that Greece has to offer—a delicious meal outdoors at the water's edge, and at a price as cheap as you'll find in any Western country.

Those who have longer to spare will be torn between idling the days away on one tiny island, getting to know the local people—who will be as interested in you as you are in them—and exploring several islands to see how they subtly differ. Rent a car to explore the mainland and you will be made welcome in towns where few tourists venture. You can plan to see the great classical sites such as Delphi and Olympia first thing in the morning or last thing in the afternoon, and will probably have these atmospheric places

virtually to yourself. Go walking in the mountains, visit the lakes and other places that only the Greeks know about, and you will truly feel yourself to be a privileged traveler in this special land. Take plenty of film for your camera, because everywhere you turn, you'll see charm, beauty, and vivid local color.

GREEK CHARACTER

Although it has become a cliché to describe a country as being "a land of contrasts," it is certainly true that the Greek character is full of contrasts. On the one hand, Greeks think nothing of cheating their own government—in fact it is seen as something of a national sport—and even pulling a fast one on their next-door neighbor, yet the vast majority are wonderfully honest in their dealings with strangers. Regular visitors will tell you of countless experiences of Greek honesty: When bags have been left behind in a restaurant and dutifully handed in to the owners; when wallets have been dropped and someone has come running after to return it without thought of reward; when a busy bar owner has said "come back and pay tomorrow" when rushed off his feet.

That is not to say that the entire Greek nation is made up of angels. There are thieves in Athens, yet nowhere near as many as in other Western capitals, and there are waiters who will try to shortchange you, or add up the bill in their favor. But for every one of those there are ten Greeks who would willingly pay for your meal rather than see you cheated.

There is a Greek word *xenoi*, which is one of the first things you must understand when visiting the country. It is a word with a dual

Brettos is one of the tiniest and most colorful bars in Athens.

meaning, which cannot be translated by a single English word. Xenoi means both "stranger" and "guest" simultaneously. A stranger is automatically a guest in their country, their town, their home. Visit a Greek home and you will experience a hospitality that can be overwhelming. Admire a painting on the wall and you may find yourself taking it away with you as a gift. Walk in the country and you might be given fruit to eat by a farmer, or beckoned to someone's house for a drink or a slice of bread and cheese.

The Greeks love nothing more than a good argument. This is, after all, the birthplace of philosophy and discourse, and still today in *kafenion* (cafés) throughout the land you will find men arguing ferociously, slamming the table and gesticulating wildly. It might be about the next elections, or it could just as easily be about the price of honey or fish these days. The discussions always seem more violent than they are, as if about to boil over into a fist fight, but that is merely the Greek passion for argument.

Greece is a male-dominated society, which is why it will be men and not both sexes sitting in cafés putting the world to rights. Cafés are male places, where few Greek women would care to venture. That is not because they are insalubrious places, just that it is not the custom. Foreign women can venture in alone or with company and will not feel threatened, as the Greeks make exceptions for visitors. There is still a vast chasm between the role of women in a city like Athens, where it is common to see them in positions of authority and men seem comfortable with this, and in rural Greece, where the sex roles are still very firmly defined and the woman's place is in the home.

FAMILY
It is in the home where the women wield the power. No man would admit it in public, where he plays the strutting head of the household, yet Greek women are fearsomely strong characters. The family is vitally important to the Greek people, particularly in rural areas. Children live at home until they

A windmill against an azure sky is an enduring image of the Greek islands, though few operational mills remain.

are married. Even when married, the couple may live with one set of parents until they can afford a house of their own. When one grandparent dies, the other moves in with the rest of the family, as it would be unthinkable to allow an elderly person to live alone.

You will see very few beggars outside Athens, and those that you do see are most usually Albanian or other Balkan immigrants who have come into Greece illegally. Greek families look after their own. People with mental or physical disabilities can find themselves shunned, however, as if bringing some kind of shame on the family. It is fairly common for them to be put into a home, although within the broader family of, say, a village, you will often see someone with mental disabilities provided with a simple job such as sweeping the street and treated like any other member of the society.

RELIGION
Religion and family are very much tied together. About 97 percent of Greeks are Greek Orthodox, although not necessarily devout. Most practice their religion to a certain extent, attending weddings, christenings, and funerals. Sunday morning services are a focal point and a time when communities get together. The services are interminably long, and few Greeks attend the whole three hours or so that a service lasts. They call in for a while, then leave, have a chat outside the church, and maybe go back later if they feel like it. Visitors are quite welcome at the services as, like the Greeks themselves, services are both casual and formal at the same time.

FEAST DAYS & FESTIVALS
There are numerous feast days around Greece, as every saint's day is celebrated in every church named after that saint…and there are a lot of saints and a lot of churches in Greece. When the local saint's day is celebrated, you can expect fireworks—often literally—as well as parades, parties, shows, and maybe a day or two when the stores will be closed.

Most Greek celebrations revolve around the church and are occasions for eating, drinking, dancing, and music. A feast often starts on the eve of the day itself with a church service, and afterward there may be a huge meal, frequently followed by music and traditional dancing. The next day they often see no reason not to do it all over again. Festivals often involve parades, the scale depending on the size of the place, but they usually include children, bands, and dance groups. After the parade there is another huge communal meal and more music and dancing as the spirit takes them. The Greeks like to party and need little encouragement to make sure the celebra-

tions go on as long as possible. The visitor will always be warmly welcomed to join in.

For dates of public holidays, see page 344.

A RELATIONSHIP WITH THE SEA

Greece has always been a maritime nation, and much of its past wealth has come from shipping dynasties, of which the Onassis family is probably the best known. It was inevitable that a country which includes about 2,000 islands should develop a knowledge of the sea. Travel by ferry is as natural to a Greek islander as using a train or plane in other countries. Despite that, many Greeks do not make good sea travelers. While visitors head for the sun decks, most Greeks make straight for the lounge, where they find space to lie down and often look the worse for wear when the journey is over.

Fishing is a mainstay of many Greek towns and villages, in the islands or along the country's rugged coastline. Most fishermen

The Goat Dance of Skiros, in the Sporades, is a noisy and dramatic pre-Lenten festival with pagan origins.

work individually rather than as part of a large fleet, catching enough for their family, the local market, and any restaurants they might supply. Most fishing takes place at night, and during the day a characteristic sight is fishermen by the harbor mending their yellow nets. You will no doubt see some of them pounding octopuses against the rocks to tenderize them before taking them to a local restaurant or home to the family. And don't be surprised when you come across a clothesline with raggedy-looking handkerchiefs—look closer and you'll see tentacles.

RURAL GREECE

Greece is very much a rural country and until the advent of tourism its economy was as dependent on agriculture as on fishing and

the shipping trade. The overwhelmingly predominant crop is olives. Not only are olives and olive oil prime exports, but also the Greeks themselves consume more olive oil per capita than any other country in the world.

Olive groves dominate the landscape. To give an idea of the scale of things, the single island of Corfu has an estimated three million olive trees. There are other crops, of course, including tobacco and cotton in Thrace. Almost every household in the country has its

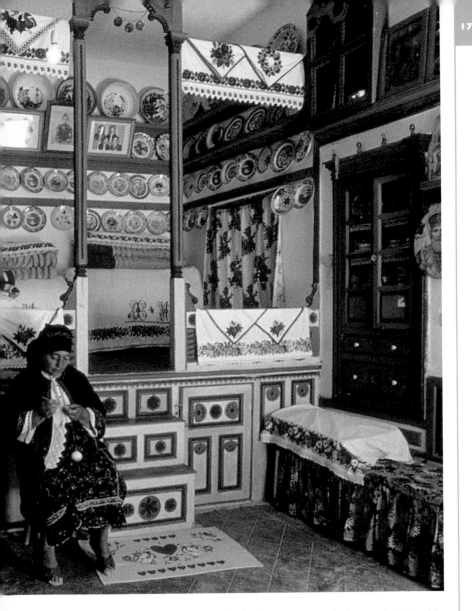

gnarled but abundantly fruitful olive trees and its vine-covered patio, and even the smallest family might well produce enough grapes to make its own wine.

This is not to claim that Greece is the epitome of a rural idyll. By the standards of Western Europe it is a poor country, and many people hold down two or even three jobs just to survive. Greece's rural past has been thrown into conflict with some aspects of the modern world. Farming here has been naturally

On Karpathos, a single-room dwelling with embroideries and artifacts preserves the traditional way of life.

organic and the land maintained with care. However, the gains to be made from tourist development are creating environmental conflicts. Short-term gain may be long-term loss. Nowhere is this better illustrated than with the turtles nesting on Zakinthos (see pp. 334–35). ■

Food & drink

GREEK COOKING IS STEEPED IN 3,000 YEARS OF HISTORY AND, DUE TO ITS geographical location, combines Eastern and Western cuisines with good, simply prepared food that is delicious. Eating out is one of the highlights of any visit to Greece.

So how come? The answer lies in the locations and the people. On the islands, food is enhanced by a glorious setting where your table is right by the water while you sit under the stars on a warm summer evening, looking out across the sea. In cities, the lively atmosphere and natural exuberance of the people provide for an entertaining dining experience.

Greek food is best when kept simple. Take a cut of lamb, or a fish caught just that morning, grill it slowly over charcoal, serve it with a slice of lemon and a crisp salad, and nothing tastes as good.

Greek wine has improved immeasurably in the last few years, and where once there was little choice, now Greek wines are winning international competitions. Retsina, the unique resin-flavored white wine, accounts for only 15 percent of domestic wine sales.

DINING HABITS

Greek restaurants prepare many dishes in the morning, keeping them warm for lunch and dinner. Greeks like dishes that are not too hot, but which you may regard as lukewarm. The answer is to have something that must be cooked fresh, like souvlaki (skewered lamb).

In common with other Mediterranean peoples, Greeks tend to eat late. Lunch is usually available from about 1 p.m., earlier in holiday resorts, although you won't find many Greeks eating before about 2 p.m. In the evening most restaurants open at about 7 p.m., but that is mainly for the benefit of visitors; the Greeks themselves will not get going until 9 p.m. or later. When the meal is finished they go to a café for a cup of coffee and maybe a slice of cake, as Greek restaurants have limited dessert menus.

Popular hors d'oeuvres include dips such as *taramosalata* (cod's roe pâté), *tsatsiki* (yogurt and cucumber), or a mixed dish of different items, known as *meze*.

The most famous Greek dish is probably moussaka, which is layers of potato, ground meat, and eggplant, often with a béchamel topping. It is mouthwateringly light and delicious. Fish is widely available, and menus should state whether the fish is fresh or frozen. (See p. 386 for the most common fish, and their Greek names). Meat is widely available, with lamb being the most popular. But you will find chicken, pork, and beef as well.

HAVING A DRINK

The preferred Greek apéritif is ouzo, an aniseed-based drink that turns milky when mixed with water. Greeks prefer to drink it straight, but it is always served with a glass of water to help cleanse the palate. After dinner, people often move on to a café for a Metaxa, which is a brand-name synonymous with brandy. It is usually available in 3-star, 5-star, or 7-star varieties, the last being the smoothest. Another strong after-dinner drink is *raki*. This is like Italian grappa, and can range from the rough to the smooth. But be warned, it always has a high alcohol content.

Many Greeks drink beer with a meal instead of wine, and there is usually a choice of two or three types. The most popular European beers are Amstel and Heineken, both light lager-type beers suited to a hot climate. The major Greek brand is called Mythos, which has a slightly nutty taste.

Be careful how you refer to coffee. What you might elsewhere describe as Turkish coffee is here called Greek coffee. It is very concentrated, and served in a small cup without milk but with a glass of water. It is normally served with sugar already boiled into the coffee, when it is known as a *metrio* (medium). If you want extra sugar ask for a *glyko* (sweet); coffee with no sugar at all is a *sketo*. If you want an American-style cup of coffee, ask for a Nescafé. Greeks also love a frappé, a refreshing, cold milky coffee served in a tall glass. ■

Family and food form an important part of tradition, and Greeks have a healthy appetite for both.

History of Greece

THERE ARE SEVERAL PLACES THAT CAN CLAIM TO BE THE CRADLE OF
civilization but Greece can certainly claim to be at least the cradle of European
civilization. It is a country in which the arts developed and flourished alongside
philosophy, architecture, and democratic politics. Of its capital, Athens, it has been
written that "wherever you set your foot, you encounter some memory of the past." And
that was said by the Roman writer Cicero (106–43 B.C.).

STONE AGE

In many countries the Paleolithic period,
dating roughly from 2.5 million B.C. to about
9000 B.C., provides the richest and most
fascinating archaeological pickings. Yet in
Greece comparatively little has been found
from this period. This apparently late start
makes the sudden flourishing of culture in

Greece from about 3000 B.C. onward appear
all the more extraordinary.

The oldest significant Greek find from the
Stone Age is a single pre-Neanderthal skull
discovered in a cave 30 miles (50 km) southeast of Thessaloniki. The cave of Kokkines
Petres (Red Stones) also contained remains of
prehistoric animals, and was found not by

archaeologists but accidentally by villagers from nearby Petralona in 1959.

It is known that there were settlers in Greece as early as 200,000 B.C., probably coming from the Middle East, and these were concentrated in northern Greece, and on the fertile plains of Thessaly. Three caves farther west in the Louros Valley in Epiros have produced evidence to indicate that they were inhabited about 40,000 B.C. The oldest known farming communities in Greece, and therefore in Europe, have been dated to about 7000–5000 B.C., again in Thessaly and Macedonia, where remnants of pottery and mudbrick houses have been found. The earliest settlements on the island of Crete— for example, the tombs found in the Cave of Trapeza, high on the Lesithi Plateau)—and

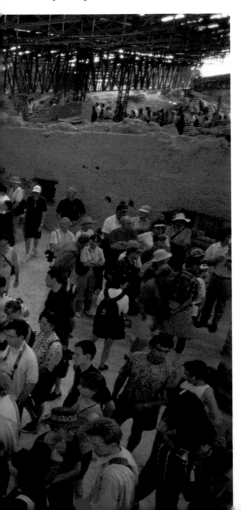

on some of the Aegean islands, have also been dated to this period, with indications that trade between the communities was flourishing. The ancient past of Greece looks set to keep scholars occupied well into the future.

MINOANS

The Cycladic culture flourished from about 3200 B.C. onward in the islands of the Cyclades group in the Aegean. Large numbers of statues and figurines dating from about 2800 B.C. onward have survived, mostly found in burial tombs. These graceful and elegant creations with their deceptively simple, stylized lines and smooth pale marble curves have influenced many 20th-century artists and can still cause gasps of admiration in anyone seeing them for the first time, knowing they are almost 5,000 years old.

Greek culture truly flourished for the first time, however, with the Minoan civilization. It owes its name to the English archaeologist Sir Arthur Evans (see pp. 288–89), who excavated the Royal Palace at Knossos on Crete and named the civilization which created it after Minos, the legendary king of Crete. (Scholars now believe that *minos* was the title, like king, rather than an individual's name.)

The first palace at Knossos was built around 2000 B.C., and its vast scale is a vivid pointer to the wealth and power of the people who created it. At that time Crete dominated trade in the Eastern Mediterranean, as strategically placed then as it was during World War II. There were other Minoan cities at Argos, Tiryns, and Mycenae, all close together in the Peloponnese on the Greek mainland, as well as on Rhodes, on Kithera (off the southern coast of the Peloponnese), and in the Cyclades. The civilization reached its peak at around 1500 B.C., by which time trade in pottery, wine, oil, jewelry, and other goods was flourishing in places such as Egypt and the Middle East.

Evans believed that it was the mighty eruption on the island of Santorini in 1500 B.C., and the resultant tidal wave that washed

Akrotiri on Santorini was a Minoan city covered by volcanic ash in the 16th century.

ARCHAIC GREECE ca750–500 B.C.
- ▨ Greek city-states, 750 B.C.
- ▨ Greek influence
- ● Colonizing community
- • Colony
- – – Trade route

0   400 miles
0   400 kilometers

ATLANTIC OCEAN

IBERIA

SPAIN

TARTESSUS

GALLIA

Massalia   Spina

SCYTHIA

BLACK SEA

Sinope

ILLYRIA

ITALIA

THRACE
MACEDONIA

PHRYGIA

Evia
Megara   Phocaea
Achaea   Andros
    Paros   Naxos   Miletos
Syracuse   Corinth   Thira

CILICIA

ASSYRIA

NUMIDIA

MEDITERRANEAN SEA

Cyrene

Naucratis

AEGYPTUS
EGYPT

The Athenians' struggle for supremacy with the city state of Sparta led to the bitter Peloponnesian War in 431 B.C., a conflict pitting Greek against Greek that would rage for 27 years. Spartan supremacy was ensured by significant naval victories at Syracuse in Sicily, and Aegosopatamia, on the Dardanelles.

Adriatic Sea

ITALY

•Neapolis

•Taras

MAGNA

GRAECIA

SARDO
(SARDINIA)

Tyrrhenian Sea

Ionian

Lipara •
Mylae •   •Messana
      •Rhegium
Himera•

•Selinus   *SICILY*

Catana•
Syracuse ✕
413   •Syracuse

CLASSICAL GREECE ca500–323 B.C.
- ▨ Athens and Delian League
- ▨ Independent allies of Athens
- ▨ Sparta and Peloponnesian League
- ▨ Neutral Greek states
- → Athenian allies' offensive
- → Spartan allies' offensive
- ✕ Major battle, Peloponnesian War
- ✕ Major battle, Persian wars

TUNISIA

Present-day political boundaries and names shown in gray

0   100 miles
0   100 kilometers

Warfare & empire

The fifth century B.C. was a time of glory and strife in Greece. Athens was entering its "Golden Age" in 495 B.C., with the development of a lasting political structure as well as a flourishing arts scene (see p. 28). At this time the Greeks, at the head of the Delian League, triumphantly fought off attacks from the Persians, following up the famous victory at Marathon in 490 B.C. with further success at Mycale and Plataea in 479 B.C.

Ionic column

ILLYRIA

MACEDONIA

• Epidamnus

• Apollonia

ALBANIA

• Corfu

EPIROS

GREECE

Sea

MACEDONIA

Sindos • Thessaloniki

Spartolus ✕ 429 ✕ CHALKIDIKI
430-32

THESSALY

Olpae ✕ 426
Thermopylae ✕✕ 480

Artemisium ✕ 480

BOEOTIA

Delphi •

Aegitium ✕ 426
Plataea 431 ✕

ACHAE
Plataea 479
Corinth •

PELOPONNESE

Olympia •

Mantinea ✕ 418

Vasses •
ARCADIA

MESSENIA

Sphacteria ✕ 425

• Sparta

LACONIA

THRACE

Amphipolis ✕ 422

Aegospotami ✕ 405

Cynossema 411 ✕

• Troy

Assos •
Agia
Paraskevi •

Aegean Sea

SKIROS

EVIA

Delium ✕ • Eretria
Thebes 424 ✕ • Lefkadi
Megara Marathon 490
Salamis ✕ Vravron
480 ✕ ATTICA
Piraes • Lavrion
Tenea Athens •

PAROS

Byzantium •

Cyzicus
✕ 410

TROAS

TURKEY

TROAS

AEOLIS
Arginusae ✕ 406

LESVOS

• Phocaea

IONIA

Notium 406
• Ephesus

SAMOS

Mycale ✕ 479
• Miletos
Lade 494 ✕

• Halicarnassus

PERSIAN EMPIRE

• Dilos

• Rhodes

RHODES

CRETE • Knossos

The period 750-500 B.C., sometimes known as the Archaic Age, was characterized by considerable emigration from Greece—the spread of an empire. Colonies grew up to the west around the shores of the Mediterranean, and east along the coast of Turkey, boosting trade and spreading Greek culture far and wide. In the wars that were to follow, eastern colonies sided with Athens to form the Delian League, while western colonies remained neutral.

MEDITERRANEAN SEA

over Crete, that brought a premature end to the Minoans. In fact their civilization ended in about 1450 B.C., but his theory has so strong a hold that the Santorini eruption is often dated to 1450 B.C. because of it.

We do not know for sure why the Minoan civilization ended.

Above: A stone fragment with Linear B script
Opposite: The massive 13th-century B.C. Lion Gate guards the entrance to the palace at Mycenae.

It may have been a revolution by the people themselves against the overly powerful priests and rulers, or it may have been some kind of natural disaster. Or maybe there was an invasion by an unknown power, or even by the Myceneans. What we do know is that the Myceneans became the dominant people in the Aegean.

MYCENEAN AGE
Work by the German archaeologist Heinrich Schliemann (see pp. 112–13) revealed that the city of Mycenae was founded in about 2100 B.C. It was settled by some of the waves of migrants who were then passing into Europe from the Indian subcontinent, but quickly fell under the control of the Minoans, whose center of strength was at Knossos on

Crete. Due to the mix of myth and history conjured up by Homer (see pp. 330–31), Schliemann believed that he had located the burial place of the legendary king of Mycenae, Agamemnon.

There are some things we can be sure of. Thanks to the existence on clay tablets of fragments of writing referred to as Linear B (which was also found at Knossos) we know that the Myceneans spoke an early dialect of Greek. We also know that by about 1400 B.C. when the Minoan civilization had declined, for whatever reason, the Myceneans came into the ascendancy and took over the wealth, trade, and control of the Eastern Aegean, which the Minoans had previously enjoyed.

There is no question that Myceneans possessed that wealth and power. At Mycenae itself many gold and silver objects were found, some of incredible beauty and obviously of enormous value, the best of these being among the highlights of the collection at the National Archaeological Museum in Athens (see p.78). In addition, the Myceneans controlled several other cities, such as nearby Tiryns, Pilos on the west coast of the Peloponnese, and even as far as Troy in western Turkey.

The site at Tiryns, just a few miles south of Mycenae, also contained a large palace complex, with grand halls and huge entrance gates. Until Evans uncovered the Minoan palace at Knossos, the site at Tiryns was the best-preserved example of such a "royal palace" known to exist.

Fact and fantasy start to mingle with the story of the Battle of Troy. It was Homer in the *Iliad* who told how Agamemnon, king of Mycenae, took his troops to Troy and was among the heroes of the ten-year siege of that city. Troy eventually fell to the Greeks, thanks to the ruse of the wooden horse. Agamemnon returned to Mycenae in triumph, bringing with him the Trojan princess Cassandra.

There certainly were powerful Mycenean kings at Mycenae, but whether one of them was named Agamemnon is another matter, and whether it was his death mask that

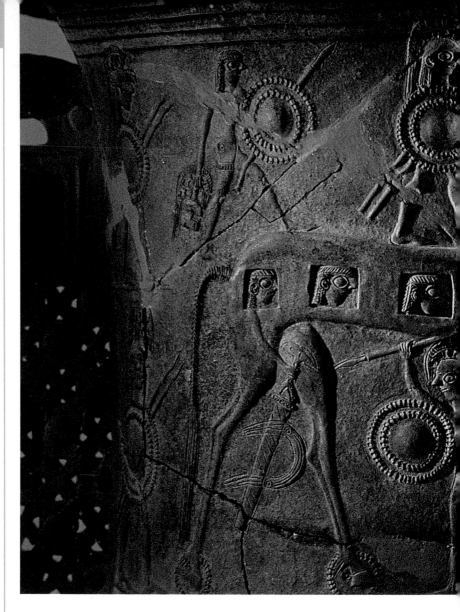

Schliemann found is highly debatable. The tale goes that Agamemnon and his troops, ready to sail for Troy, were delayed by strong winds. In order to overcome them Agamemnon sacrificed his daughter to the goddess Artemis. The king also appears in the *Oresteia* by Aeschylus (see p. 106). The play tells how, after Agamemnon had returned home from Troy with Princess Cassandra, he was killed in his bathtub by his wife Clytemnestra and her lover.

Although strong, the Mycenean culture was comparatively short-lived, flourishing for only 200 years. Its power waned in about 1200 B.C., and, as with the Minoan decline, no one yet knows why. It may have been wiped out by some natural disaster, or by the arrival of a new enemy—the Dorian tribes from the north.

DORIAN AGE

The collapse of the Mycenean civilization was the beginning of ancient Greece's

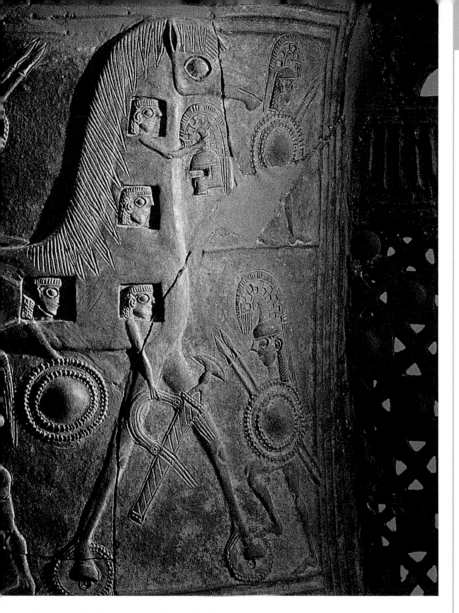

"Dark Ages." There were several factors behind this, not least of them the invasion by the Dorian people from northern Greece in about 1200–1100 B.C. They entered the Peloponnese and occupied Corinth, then moved in and took control of Mycenae, Sparta, and Argolis.

The Dorians were a warlike people, but they lacked the culture that had made the Minoans and Myceneans so great. The Dorians simply suppressed the beliefs of the people they conquered in lands that in time included most of the Greek mainland, Crete, the Dodecanese, parts of southern Italy, Sicily, and into the Middle East. Despite this, the sea trade that had made previous rulers so rich dwindled under these ruthless people.

Greece has always depended on its maritime trade, right through to the shipping dynasties of the 20th century, so with its disappearance the country suffered badly. Trade over land had always been difficult because of the mountain barriers of the north and the constant disputes with the Turkish people to the east. The sea was vital. Under the Dorians, the Greeks lost not only their trade but also communication by sea with their immediate neighbors, and cultural exchanges suffered as much as commerce. The people became inward-looking and had to rely on farming to survive.

It is easy to imagine how difficult that time must have been. Even today Greece is not a rich country; it relies heavily on the finance generated by tourism and maritime trade and the money sent back to Greece from Greeks settled overseas.

CLASSICAL GREECE

Out of the darkness there eventually came light, and the first signs of what was to become the greatest period in Greek history. Because Greece had been so insular, people focused on their own communities, and this led to the emergence of the city-states from about the ninth century B.C. onward. They functioned totally independently of each other, forming alliances, trading, and going to war just like separate nations.

Eventually the two strongest city-states to emerge were Athens and Sparta. Sparta had been a Dorian stronghold, and from descriptions of its harsh and militaristic way of life it is easy to see where the word "spartan" came from. The Athenians were much more cultured, and by the fifth century B.C. all male Athenians who were not slaves had the vote. The importance of this, at such an early date, can be appreciated when you consider that as recently as the second half of the 20th century there were countries where citizens did not have the vote.

Athens also had military might, as victories over the Persians at Marathon, Mycale, and Salamis showed, and it was this city rather than Sparta that flourished in the sixth and fifth centuries B.C., the era we know as Classical Greece.

This was also known in Athens as the Golden Age of Pericles. Pericles (circa 495–429 B.C.) was an Athenian statesman who

introduced revolutionary ideas and encouraged the arts and architecture. During his reign the Parthenon was built, drama flourished (see p. 106), and many democratic ideas were introduced. Pericles initiated the idea that people who worked for the state should be paid for their labor, that free male citizens should have the vote, and that the citizens should decide who governed them. The word "democracy," so close to the heart of all Americans, derives from the Greek *demokratia*—control by the people.

The arts also flourished in Athens at this time, with dramatists such as Aeschylus and Aristophanes (see p. 106) to the fore. Poetry was already established, notably in the works of Sappho (see pp. 238–39). The great philosophers Socrates, Plato, and Aristotle were pushing back the boundaries of debate.

Rivalry between Athens and Sparta continued and resulted in the Peloponnesian War of 431–404 B.C. Sparta had long dominated the city-states of the Peloponnese, and together they launched attacks on Athens, with Sparta victorious in 404 B.C. In the following year the Athenians revolted and threw the Spartans out of Athens, returning to their cultured and independent way of life.

Alexander the Great defeated the Persian king Darius III in 334 B.C.

But there was another threat on the horizon, one that would come not from the Peloponnese, but from the opposite direction: Macedonia to the north.

ALEXANDER THE GREAT & THE MACEDONIAN EMPIRE

In 382 B.C. at Pella, then the capital of Macedonia, Philip II was born and would be crowned king of Macedonia in 359 B.C. He himself became powerful enough, but his son, Alexander the Great, changed the face of that part of the world forever (see pp. 30–31).

It was obvious from the nature of Greece at that time, with its warring city-states, that it was vulnerable to outside attack, although not even the might of the Persian army had been able to take control. The Greeks had always somehow managed to raise enough forces to repel any potential invaders, only to return to internal fighting afterward. Philip II and Alexander were going to be attackers of a very different order, as Greece—and the rest of the civilized world—was about to discover.

Philip II had been a prisoner in Thebes at a time when it was the most powerful of the

Greek city-states. He observed the workings of their army, and on his return home he adopted Theban military tactics. Macedonia then centered on the fertile plains north of Athens; it was an independent but vulnerable kingdom inhabited by Greek-speaking people. Philip II pulled the Macedonians together, then began to attack neighboring territories, both in the east toward Chalkidiki and on into Thrace, and to the south toward Athens. He at first made a peace pact with Athens, but it did not last long and in 338 B.C. in the Battle of Chaeronia, he defeated the combined armies of the Athenians and his old role models, the Thebans.

In 336 B.C. Philip was assassinated as he prepared to invade Persia, and it is uncertain whether Alexander had a hand in this. Philip was buried at Vergina, between Pella and Mount Olympus. The discovery of his royal tomb in 1977 was one of the greatest archaeological finds in 20th-century Greece. His intact skeleton and the golden treasures buried with him are now on display in the Archaeological Museum at Thessaloniki. Philip was without question one of the most powerful rulers of

A Byzantine-style mosaic gleams down from the ceiling of Nea Moni convent on Hios island.

his time. His power, however, was nothing compared with that of his son.

Alexander was only 20 when his father was assassinated and, as the new ruler of a newly powerful small empire, he was naturally very vulnerable. He did what many great rulers before and since have done: He killed any potential enemies in his own camp. He regained control of Thessaly, which had rebelled against the Macedonians, did the same against Thrace, and then again, in ruthless fashion, against Thebes, burning the city to the ground and imprisoning its luckless inhabitants.

With these swift, strong, and brutal actions, Alexander quickly established himself as a powerful ruler of the then Greek world. He took command of the Macedonian troops, and in 334 B.C. led an army of some 35,000 across the Hellespont (now the Dardanelles).

Although outnumbered, they defeated the Persian army, allegedly with the loss of only 110 of their own men. Alexander treated the Persians as mercilessly as he had treated the plotters in his own camp and the rebellious Greek states. His leadership inspired his men, and although frequently outnumbered, they continued to defeat the Persians and pushed on into the Middle East and Egypt.

Though he had by this time complete control of the Eastern Mediterranean, Alexander was still not satisfied and headed for India, where he won more victories but at the cost of great numbers of men. He was back in Babylon in 323 B.C., turning his attention to more conquests, when a fever laid him low. He died 11 days later.

It is said that Alexander had a vision not merely to conquer the world but to unite East and West in one large, harmonious empire.

Certainly the cities he founded were all civilized and cultured places, and he fervently spread Greek culture and language while taking an interest in the cultures of the lands he conquered. Had Alexander lived, the empire would undoubtedly have expanded even farther, but it was almost inevitable that upon his death no one man could take his place and keep the empire together.

ROMAN GREECE

With the death of Alexander, his empire quickly disintegrated, some of the remoter places claiming their independence while three separate areas were still nominally under Macedonian control: Egypt, Persia, and Macedonia/Greece itself. The consequent break-up produced a series of wars and resulted in loss of power for the individual Greek city-states. This so-called Hellenistic Period lasted from the death of Alexander in 323 B.C. right up until a new power emerged. This was the Roman Empire.

The king of Macedonia was now Philip V but his army was nowhere near as strong as its predecessors, and it was defeated in a battle against the expanding Roman might in 200 B.C. Within less than ten years Rome had taken control of what had been Macedonian Greece, but within this territory the Greek city-states such as Athens, Sparta, and Thebes were allowed to maintain their independence. It was a situation that could not last. The city-states were effectively run by Rome anyway; although they joined forces and rebelled against Roman rule, their disparate nature could never be a match for a combined Roman force. In 146 B.C., the Roman Empire took control of the city-states, removing their independence and creating instead a new Roman province called Macedonia.

Apart from the loss of independence, the change was not too detrimental to Greece. The people were allowed to retain the Greek language, and Roman culture boosted rather than diluted Greek culture. Christianity was introduced and became the dominant religion. Under enlightened emperors such as Hadrian, Athens was reborn as a center for the arts, architecture, and politics. Hadrian's Arch, Hadrian's Library, and the Theater of Herodes Atticus in Athens are but a few examples of Rome's positive influence on Greek life. Compared with the later Turkish occupation, it was virtually a return to the Golden Age.

EASTERN (BYZANTINE) EMPIRE

By the fourth century A.D., the Roman Empire had lost much of its power and had grown so big that it was divided into two, the Western Empire with its headquarters naturally in Rome, and the Eastern Empire, ruled from the "new Rome," modern Istanbul.

Emperor Constantine the Great (circa 280–337) moved the capital of the Eastern Empire to the site of the ancient Greek city of Byzantium, which became Constantinople, which in turn became Istanbul. Work on building the city began in 326, and was completed four years later. It was at first a blend of Greco-Roman culture, but the shift of the empire's center eastward meant that there was an inevitable increase in oriental influence on life there. Byzantine culture became a blend of Roman Christian and Greek culture with the exoticism of the east.

The focus emphatically shifted from Athens to Constantinople, which blossomed as Athens had done during its golden age. Anti-Greek feeling developed, resulting in the eradication of all traces of the old Greek paganism, the closing of the Oracle at Delphi (regarded as the center of the world by the Greeks), and the ending of the Olympic Games, that representation of the Greek spirit. Greece became of little account, and when parts of it were invaded by Slavonic tribes it was of no great concern to what was now referred to as the Byzantine Empire.

Constantinople resisted all attempts to capture it by outside forces, and the empire lost little of its territory at this time. The Byzantine Empire continued long after the Western Empire had disappeared, invaded by Goths in 476. The Byzantine Empire remained a force for almost 1,000 years, until the Crusaders captured Constantinople in 1204. Many Greeks to this day believe that at some time in the future, Istanbul will return to being Greek Byzantium (a notion that does nothing to help the precarious Greek-Turkish relationship). Given what happened next on Greek territory, such strength of feeling is understandable.

Between the end of the Byzantine Empire

and the arrival of the Turks, the Greek people were subjected to waves of other invasions, notably during the Crusades. The Normans arrived on Corfu in 1081 and proceeded to establish themselves there and on the mainland, while in the early 13th century the Venetians and the Franks also occupied large parts of Greece. This resulted in two centuries of squabbling for supremacy, settled only when Turkey took over the vast majority of Greek territory in 1453.

TURKISH OCCUPATION

The Greeks still resent the long period when they were ruled by the Ottoman Empire and when a mosque was built inside the Parthenon, which was itself left to decay. Furthermore, it was during this period that Lord Elgin, then British ambassador at Constantinople, obtained the Elgin Marbles (see p. 53) from the Turkish rulers and shipped them back to Great Britain.

Constantinople fell into Turkish Muslim hands in 1453, the year the Greeks regard the occupation as beginning, even though it was a few more years before the Turks began to infiltrate what is modern Greek territory. When they did, it was with a vengeance. Most of Greece fell into their hands, bar the Ionian islands off the western coast, the Cycladic islands in the Aegean, and small parts of Crete and the mainland.

This was a time of mixed fortunes for the Greeks. Some did well, where the Turks effectively handed over control to a local chieftain, happy that he should make his fortune, as long as he paid his dues to Constantinople and subdued the local populace. In other areas, where a tyrannical Turkish ruler was imposed, entire towns and villages were slaughtered if they offended him. While this was going on, Turkish culture was being introduced, and it lingers on in places such as Ioanina, the capital of Epiros, in Thessaloniki, and of course in Thrace, the Greek region closest to Turkey.

The Turks kept control of their empire quite comfortably for over 300 years. Only toward the end of the 18th century, and into the beginning of the 19th, did moves toward forcibly regaining independence begin to be made.

WAR OF INDEPENDENCE

Several events spurred the fight for independence. One such occurrence was on Crete in 1770 when the Russian Orthodox Church came to the aid of its Greek Orthodox brothers in a failed attempt to overthrow the Turkish government. Not long after came the French Revolution, which encouraged ordinary Greeks to believe that they, too, could overturn tyrannical rulers.

In 1821 the War of Independence proper began. On March 25 at the Monastery of Ayia Lavra, just outside Kalavrita near the north coast of the Peloponnese, Archbishop Yermanos of Patra first hoisted the Greek flag in defiance of the Turks. The monastery is now a place of pilgrimage on that same date each year, to celebrate the start of the fight to throw out the Turks. After centuries of subjugation, the fight would be won before the decade was out.

There was support for the Greek cause throughout Europe, and volunteers made their way to Greece to fight alongside the resistance movement. Many of these came from Germany, but the figure who attracted most attention was the English poet, Lord Byron (1788–1824). That a young English nobleman and celebrated author should side with the cause of the ordinary Greek people was a terrific boost. Byron even gave his life for the cause, although not in battle: He died of a fever.

The impact of his death was immense. Britain, France, and Russia all then sent official aid to the Greek forces, while the Turks had recruited the help of their fellow Muslims, the Egyptians, with the promise that they would be handed Crete and other parts of Turkish territory if victorious. The end of the war came about after an accidental naval encounter in Navarino Bay, off the southwest coast of the Peloponnese. The Turkish-Egyptian navy was annihilated, and when soon afterward the mighty Russian Bear declared war directly on Turkey, the Turks capitulated over Greece and agreed to the country's independence. When this was officially formalized in 1830, under the guarantee of Britain, France, and Russia, it was an act of immense importance to the Greek people.

Young citizens don traditional dress and join in the fun of an Independence Day parade.

POST-INDEPENDENCE
& THE BALKAN WARS

Although the Greeks had won their freedom, this was not the start of a peaceful period for the new nation. For one thing, when the various parties involved drew up the boundaries for the new Greece, the result was a long way from being what the people had hoped for. The large regions of Epiros and Macedonia on the mainland remained in Turkish hands, as did the islands of the Dodecanese, while the Ionian islands off the western coast became a British Protectorate. The Greeks had every right to feel that justice had not been done.

Sadly the result was internal conflict, which eventually erupted into a full-blown civil war in 1831, when the former resistance leader and the new country's first president, Ioannis Kapodistrias, was assassinated by two fellow Greeks. The Western powers quickly stepped in again and in 1832 turned Greece into a monarchy under an imposed ruler, King Otto I, who came from Bavaria. Otto was only 17 years old and proved to be a poor choice. The newly liberated Greeks, optimistic

for their future, had a double complaint: They had been given a territory much smaller than the present Greece, and Otto handed key positions of power to fellow Germans. Greece appeared to have exchanged one oppressor for another.

In 1862 Otto faced a revolt by his army and civilians alike, and was officially deposed with the cooperation of the Western powers, who provided a replacement in King George I, from Denmark. Greece's second king proved a much better and more popular choice. He returned to the people land that had been seized by the Turks—something Otto had resisted doing—and he pressed further Greek territorial claims against Turkey. By 1878 Thessaly and part of Epiros had been regained as Greek territory.

Further inroads into what was still Turkish territory were much less successful. In 1895 the Cretans revolted against their Ottoman rulers. The revolt was only partially successful. In 1898 Crete was given a high commissioner on behalf of the European powers. The island was eventually reunited with Greece in 1913.

Macedonia proved to be a greater problem.

In 1917 Greece attacked Turkish forces in Macedonia, and was overwhelmed by the resultant retaliation, disaster being averted only by the intervention of the other European powers pressing Turkey to desist.

BALKAN WARS

The First Balkan War took place in 1912–13,

Constantine I (R. 1913–17, 1920–22) regained the throne for a short period before a second abdication in favor of his son.

a complicated catalog of alliances and old enmities. Greece was not the only country to claim Macedonia from the Turks, as its northern neighbors (Romania, Serbia, and, most of all, Bulgaria) also had their territorial eyes turned toward it—with some historical justification. In addition, the Macedonian port of Thessaloniki was a vital trade route into the Mediterranean. An uprising by Bulgarians living within Macedonia resulted, bizarrely, in the Greeks offering to come to the aid of the Turks, sending forces into western Macedonia. As the fighting intensified, and Turkey sent in troops with a view to getting

rid of all the warring parties, the latter united and Turkey was defeated by a combined force of Greek, Bulgarian, Serbian, and Montenegrin armies. Greece reclaimed parts of Macedonia, and Turkey finally ceded Crete to the Greeks.

Hot on the heels of the First Balkan War, a second war in the region erupted that same year, 1913, but lasted only a month. This time Greece and Serbia allied against Bulgaria, which was no match for them.

Greek involvement in World War I was equally complicated. Prime Minister Venizelos was keen to support the British side, but King Constantine I, who was married to the sister of the German kaiser, insisted on neutrality. Venizelos went from Athens to Greece's second city, Thessaloniki, and set up a government in opposition. Unsurprisingly, the British and the French recognized Venizelos' government.

All appeared to be going well for Greece, as its troops under Venizelos fought on the side of the Allies and the king was forced to abdicate, handing the throne to his son Alexander. After the war, Greece reclaimed Thrace from the Bulgarians and Turks, and also islands in the Aegean that Turkey had continued to occupy.

Venizelos, however, made one claim too many. Instead of settling for what Greece had been given, he also staked a claim to the territory of Smyrna on the Turkish Aegean coast, which was indeed mainly inhabited by Greeks. In 1919 Greek troops landed there. Initially they made inroads, but the Turks under their powerful and forward-looking new leader, Kemal Ataturk, fought off the Greeks and drove them out of Smyrna. They also slaughtered the remaining Greek population and destroyed the city.

The result of all this was that Ataturk had the upper hand, and the infamous "Exchange of Populations" took place in 1923. Turkey, a vastly bigger country than Greece, received about 400,000 Turks back from Greece to their Muslim homeland, but in return about 1.3 million Greeks living in Turkey were forced to leave. This immediately added about 25 percent to Greece's existing population—for the most part poor, dispossessed refugees, who settled largely in the suburbs of Athens and in the slums around its port of Pireas.

They may have added to the music and culture of Greece, but their arrival had a devastating effect on the economy, which took a long time to recover given the general state of world affairs in the 1920s and 1930s.

WORLD WAR II & THE GREEK CIVIL WAR (1945–49)

It is said that Greece's entry into World War II began with a single word: *Ochi*—No. This was allegedly the response by Greek Prime Minister General Metaxas (1871–1941) to the request from Mussolini to allow Italian troops to pass through Greece. Mussolini's ultimatum was delivered on October 28, 1940, and Metaxas's curt reply to the Italian foreign minister in Athens propelled Greece into the war. That response is commemorated every year on October 28, a public holiday known as Ochi Day. It's a good story, but in fact the response would have been delivered in French, the language of diplomacy, and is thought to have been "*C'est la guerre*"—It's war.

War it was, and despite initial resistance in the mountains of northern Greece, Italian troops eventually moved down from Albania and, with naval support from Germany, had occupied Greece and most of its islands within little over six months. By this time General Metaxas was dead, and the king and his government were in exile.

Greece suffered terribly in the war, and the full horrors of the years of occupation have never been fully told. About half a million Greeks died of starvation, many of them on the streets of Athens, and some of these appalling stories are depicted in the War Museum in Athens (see p. 71). Many more were the victims of atrocities, and the dreadful events that took place are still remembered by the older generation.

The Greek Jewish population suffered terribly, and in some towns and cities where there had been only a small Jewish population, it was completely wiped out. Even in Thessaloniki, which at one time had the largest Jewish population in Europe, their numbers were reduced from 60,000 before the war to a few hundred afterward. In all, 87 percent of Greek Jews were killed.

In other places the war had less of a direct impact, especially on some islands where the

occupying Italian forces were not far removed in temperament from the Greeks themselves and a working relationship was established.

The Greek resistance was focused on the National Liberation Front (EAM, its Greek initials), which worked alongside the British secret services against the occupying forces. There were some successful heroics, but sadly,

One-time Chief of General Staff Ioannis Metaxas rose to become Prime Minister of Greece in 1936.

too, the Communist-dominated EAM was divided into two warring factions fighting for control of a peacetime Greece. When the war ended for the rest of Europe in 1945, it only plunged Greece into a bitter civil war, which lasted until 1949. One side of that story is told in the book *Eleni* by American-Greek author Nicholas Gage, which recounts the dreadful events in his family's village in the mountains of northern Greece.

The dispute arose when the British occupying forces formed an interim government with the EAM. The British wanted to see a return of the monarchy and tried to reduce

Greek partisans, noted for their fierce tenacity, celebrate liberation in 1944.

the influence of EAM, which went down badly with the men who had been risking their lives for Greek freedom.

In 1946 a right-wing government was elected, and in 1947 a vote was taken in favor of reinstating the monarchy. By this time the Communists were marginalized, with the help of significant U.S. support for the right-wing government. EAM found itself again fighting a resistance movement, but this time against fellow Greeks and their allied support. The conflict was every bit as bloody as more recent Balkan wars. Eventually the right-wing forces emerged with a precarious victory.

All these events may have taken place over half a century ago, but it is always wise to be circumspect if starting to discuss the war and its aftermath in Greece. For some people the memories are as vivid as yesterday.

THE COLONELS

It is hardly surprising that after the turbulence of the last few centuries, followed by a series of wars large and small in the first half of the 20th century, Greece did not immediately settle down to a period of peace and stability.

In the 1950s Cyprus became a trouble spot, where Greek terrorists were active on an island governed by the British but which they felt was territorially Greek. The granting of independence to the island was a compromise solution that would prove to have disastrous consequences.

In the 1960s a series of changes in leadership, both politically and in the monarchy, led to increased divisiveness. Greece, for all its history of resistance fighters and a frequent sense of anarchy, has traditionally had a right-wing ruling party. The more moderate rule by Prime Minister George Papandreou (1888–1968) was seen as far too liberal by many, and run-ins with the monarchy over who should have control of the army (among other things) resulted in Papandreou resigning in 1965.

This strong character was followed by several ineffectual leaders, and on April 21, 1967 a right-wing military junta led by a group of colonels seized control of the country. It was the kind of rule more familiar to Central American republics: mass arrests, torture, disappearances, martial law, news censorship, and clampdowns on civil liberties. After the moderate Papandreou, the country was now ruled by a hard-line right-winger, Colonel George Papadopoulos (1919–1996). King Constantine II (born 1940) was exiled after a failed attempt to overthrow the junta.

The Colonels brought about their own downfall, however, in attempting to seize control of Cyprus. Instead of succeeding, there was a counter invasion by Turkish troops who took over 40 percent of the island, where they remain to this day. The Greek army mutinied against its own leaders. The Colonels had already demonstrated their ruthlessness at home when they killed a number of students demonstrating against the regime at the Athens Polytechnic on November 17, 1973. No one has ever established the number of students killed that day (still commemorated in Greece), but the Polytechnic still bears the bullet holes, as the nation bears the scars of the Colonels' junta.

AFTER THE COLONELS

Once democracy was returned to Greece, the country entered a much more stable and prosperous period, which included a huge boom in tourism and membership in the European Union.

After the defeat of the Colonels, former Prime Minister Constantine Karamanlis returned from his exile in Paris and won a good majority for his New Democracy party (Nea Dimokratia) in the first democratic elections. However, one of his defeated rivals, Andreas Papandreou (1919–1996), the son of George Papandreou, with his new PASOK Socialist party, played a center stage role in Greek politics for the next two decades. Karamanlis held a referendum on the monarchy, and a sizable majority of the people voted against the return of the exiled king.

Karamanlis himself had seven years of power before PASOK and Papandreou were voted overwhelmingly into office in 1981 to form the first left-wing government in Greece in almost 50 years. Papandreou embarked on a campaign of populist reforms, including equal rights for all, increases in pensions, the right to have a civil marriage in a church-dominated society, and other similar measures. However, the cost of some of those reforms meant that the economy suffered, so Papandreou

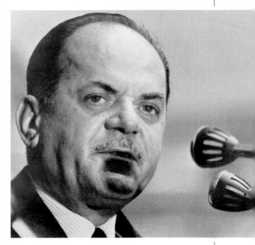

George Papadopoulos was himself ousted from power in the military coup of 1974.

did not enjoy universal popularity. PASOK promised removal of U.S. air bases and withdrawal from NATO, but these promises were never fulfilled.

Two elections in 1989 proved inconclusive and provided only coalition governments. Then in spring 1990, the New Democracy party was returned with the slenderest of majorities. This swing back to the right lasted less than four years, and in October 1993 Andreas Papandreou returned as prime minister at the age of 74.

Within two years Papandreou's health had deteriorated to the extent that he had to resign, and with his death in 1996 Greece lost one of its most prominent politicians of the 20th century. Since then, PASOK has stayed comfortably if not overwhelmingly in government, helped in no small way by Papandreou's legacy. Relations with Turkey, and in particular over the Turkish occupation of Northern Cyprus, remain a burning issue. ∎

The arts

IT IS INEVITABLE THAT GREEK ARTISTS WORKING TODAY, IN WHATEVER fields, will be dwarfed by the achievements of their predecessors. It is almost impossible for any kind of creative artist to throw off the shackles of history, of Greek myths and legends, of the long shadow cast by centuries of Orthodox religion. Most artists at some stage, be they writers or painters or jewelers, will explore that heritage in their own work, albeit by giving it a modern interpretation.

VISUAL ARTS

Ancient Greece excelled at sculpture. Greek statues often combine power and strength with grace and agility. The first statues were produced in the Archaic Period, about the eighth and seventh centuries B.C. when trade with Egypt was flourishing. Egyptian statues were brought to Greece and at first merely imitated. You can see the similarities: upright bodies, arms by the side, hands held rigidly attached to the body. Soon, however, the pupils were excelling their tutors. Within a century of the first Egyptian statues being copied, the Greeks were adding their own flourishes, giving the bodies some movement and making them much more realistic. Back in Egypt, the statues remained exactly as they had always been.

To see the developments in Greek sculpture, take a stroll through the centuries in the National Archaeological Museum in Athens (see pp. 78–81), where a knowledgeable guide will talk you through the ages and take you to the highlights of the collection. Some of the greatest Greek work is not in its homeland, of course. In addition to the thorny question of the Elgin Marbles (see p. 53), the Louvre alone boasts both the Venus de Milo and the Winged Victory of Samothrace.

The issue of the Elgin Marbles is important to Greece because temple friezes such as these are not merely works of art in themselves but integral parts of the temples for which they were made. The finest sculptors were hired, and friezes were usually complete narratives, working their way around the temple, depicting such legends as the Battle of the Gods and Giants, which adorned the Siphnian treasury at Delphi.

Vase painting was another traditional Greek skill, which also often told a story, and many fine examples reside in museums throughout the country. This art is especially important, as it tells so much about the lives of the ancient Greeks. The most striking style is the combination of red and black colors. At different periods either the figures or the background would be carved from the clay, and the rest of the scene painted in black or dark brown. Vase painting was at its height in the fifth century B.C., when it attracted the best artists, who all wanted to work in this new, exciting medium. It could be said to have laid the groundwork for the representational art that was later to flourish throughout Europe.

In the more modern visual arts, one area where Greece is very strong is that of photography. Greece has often been said to have the best light in the world for photography, with the clarity of the Aegean and its deep blue skies and blinding white houses inspiring its photographers to explore their land most thoroughly and effectively. Greek traditions are captured by the native photographer's lens in a way that the traveler passing through can never hope to attain. Young photographers to watch out for include Nick Apostolopoulos (born 1955), whose sports photography has won a Fuji Award, and Andreas Zacharatos (born 1961), whose award-winning work varies from jazz in Athens to rural landscapes.

Greece has not had an abundance of painters of international renown. Its one artist known throughout the world was dubbed El Greco, The Greek, when he went to Spain. Domenikos Theotokopoulos, El Greco (1541–1614), was born in Iraklio on Crete but did his greatest work in Italy and Spain, and is more accurately thought of as a Spanish artist.

The renaissance of buildings in Athens, including the Syntagma Metro station, provides bold new space for public art.

A Greek artist whose work is well worth investigating is the naïve painter, Theophilos Hadzimichalis (1873–1934), known as Theophilos. He was a prolific worker and examples of his work can be seen in many places, including the Folk Museum in Athens and in the house in which he lived, now a museum, just outside Mitilini on Lesvos (see p. 237). He was an eccentric, prone to wearing traditional Greek costumes, often penniless, and prepared to paint murals on taverna walls in exchange for a meal or a drink. Though unsophisticated, his work has a vibrancy and energy that leaps from the canvas.

Limited reconstruction at sites such as Delphi shows the scale of original buildings.

ARCHITECTURE

If there is one artistic skill that, quite literally, towers above all others in Greek history it is that of architecture. Take one look at any of the better-preserved temples, such as the Parthenon or the Temple of Aphaia on Egina, and you know that ancient Greek craftsmen were masters.

Greek temples were originally influenced by Egypt, but quickly took on a style and grace all their own. This was in part due to the building materials available. While the Egyptians worked in stone and created a somber grandeur from it, the Greeks were using limestone and, later, marble to create structures of grace and light.

If anyone knows anything at all about Greek architecture it is that there are two main 'orders' or types of columns, Doric and Ionic (even if you cannot always remember which is which). The name Doric comes from the Dorians (see p. 26), and is most easily identified because the columns do not stand on a base. They rise straight from the floor and are usually closer together than in the Ionic style, giving a more claustrophobic feeling. The style spread throughout Greece and into southern Italy and Sicily, and an outstanding example—though imagination will be required to appreciate it today—is the Temple of Zeus at Olympia (see p. 128).

The Ionic style comes not from the Ionian islands off the west coast but from Ionia, the ancient name for western Asia Minor, where modern Turkey now is. Ionic columns are

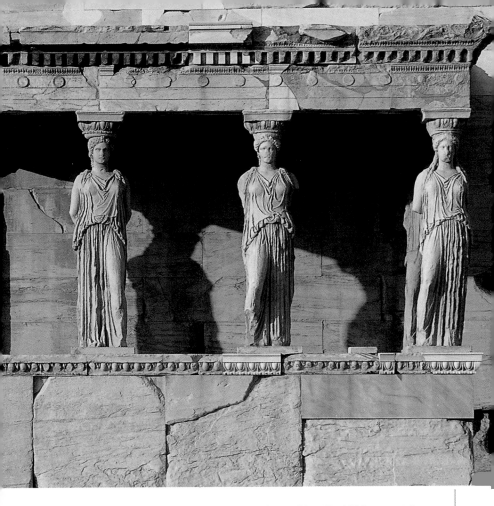

Copies of the original six graceful caryatids, each well over 6 feet (2 m) high, support the southern portico of the Erechtheion, facing the Parthenon in Athens.

placed farther apart and are also generally narrower than Doric columns, creating a greater sense of space on temple frontages. They are also usually placed on a small base, and their capitals are more ornate than the plain Doric style. Good examples are at Ephesus in Turkey, in the area where the name originated, and on the Erechtheion on the Acropolis in Athens.

The most famous piece of Greek architecture in the world, the Parthenon on the Acropolis, combines both Doric and Ionic columns. To get a fuller sense of its original beauty, see the small-scale model in the National Archaeological Museum in Athens. To understand some of the drudgery needed

to create that beauty, look at the displays about its construction in the Acropolis Study Centre (see p. 57).

If the workers provided the 90 percent of perspiration that is needed to produce great works of art, then it was the architect Pheidias who provided the 10 percent of genius or inspiration that is also required. Pheidias was the great sculptor of his day, and he is also known to have produced the statue of Olympian Zeus that stood at the center of Olympia and the giant statue of Athena Nike that served as the centerpiece of the Parthenon itself.

Temples became churches, and the other great aspect of Greek architecture, visible

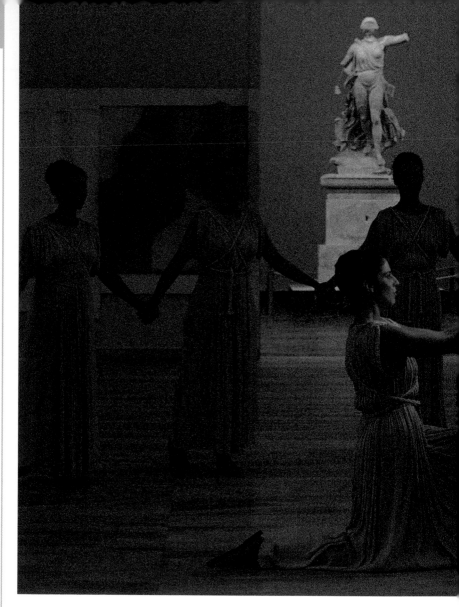

from the tiniest rural village to the very center of urban Athens, is the Byzantine church. These red-tiled buildings may be big or small, but all have certain elements in common.

The altar in a Byzantine church is always to the east, and always concealed behind the screen known as the iconostasis. In front of this there are three main aisles, and above the central aisle, in the largest open part of the church, is the main dome. This is invariably decorated with a painting of Christ

Pantokrator, or Christ All Powerful, gazing down unremittingly on the congregation. Another icon of Christ will usually be found over the main door to the church, to greet you as you enter. The interiors of Byzantine churches are always elaborately decorated with mosaics and friezes, the walls hung with icons and votive offerings—a real assault on the senses, especially during services when the air is filled with the smell of incense and the sound of holy chanting.

A flame brought from Olympia is used to light the symbolic torch of the Olympic Games at the National Archaeological Museum in Athens.

A look at Athens today may leave you wondering what became of Greece's glorious architectural heritage, and it is true that few modern buildings stand out. Some of the finest were influenced by German architects in the 19th century, notably Ernst Ziller. Among other buildings, Ziller was responsible for the magnificent 1896 Olympic Stadium.

MUSIC

Greece is one of the few countries in the world that has not succumbed to Western pop music. Turn on a radio at random and you can almost guarantee that the first music you hear will be distinctly Greek. It may be modern Greek pop music, but it will still have that unique sound born of the *bouzouki* (the mandolin-like stringed instrument that epitomizes Greek music) and the influences of Asia, with definite echoes of Indian music.

That's not to say that young Greeks are not aware of the latest rock bands and trends. They are. And you will have no trouble finding indoor and outdoor discos, outdoor rock concerts in summer, and clubs where blues, rock, and jazz are just as good as back home. But young Greeks grow up with the music of Greece in their blood…and certainly in their ears, for wherever you go in Greece you will hear music: in tavernas and bars, on ferries, in buses, escaping through the windows of houses and cars.

Every region, every island has its own folk music, although not much of it is truly native as the imported oriental influences are ubiquitous. Everywhere you will come across official music and dance festivals (the two are virtually inseparable in Greece), as well as impromptu sessions when the chairs are

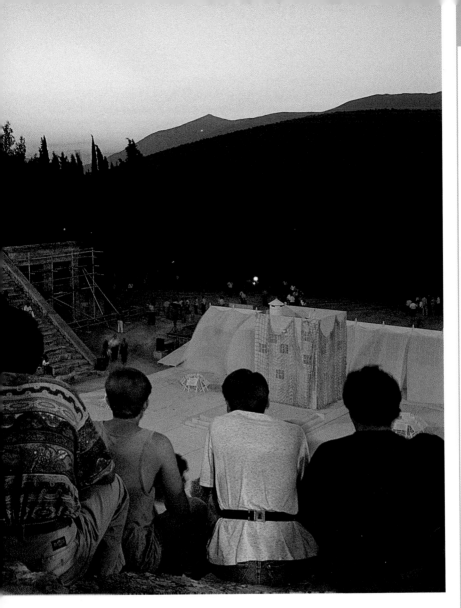

The restoration of theaters such as Epidavros has brought classical Greek drama to life for thousands of visitors.

pushed back and the mood of the music simply takes over.

Rembetika is the blues of Greece, with a blend of jazz. As with those types of music, it is created from various influences yet combines them all to produce a style that is unique. No one is sure where the name came from, but the music came to Greece with the exchange of populations that took place in 1923 (see pp. 34–35). Greeks who had been living in Turkey—most of them born there—brought back with them the distinctive oriental music that was popular in cafés and bars. The people who returned were for the most part desperately poor, many of them forced to live in primitive conditions around Pireas, the port of Athens. Here drinking dens grew up where musicians and singers would meet, their music expressing the poverty of their lives and their feelings of alienation. In this way the Greek blues was born.

Rembetika lives on, just like the blues in America, because it expresses heartfelt feelings that are both particular to a certain class of people and at the same time universal. If you want an insight into the Greek soul, seek out one of the rembetika clubs in Athens and spend an evening watching and listening. If you do not understand the words, you will understand the sincere sentiments being expressed. Be prepared for a late night, too.

The most famous Greek musician of contemporary times is undoubtedly Mikis Theodorakis (born 1925), best known for his soundtrack music for the 1965 movie *Zorba the Greek*. No one will get through a visit to Greece without hearing either the title track of *Zorba* or that of another famous Greek movie, *Never on a Sunday,* whose music won an Academy Award for composer Manos Hadjidakis (1925–94). Theodorakis's music —at least in those days—was known as Entechno. This has nothing to do with modern Techno music but is a fusion of the folk and rembetika styles that produced a new type of music with a more contemporary feel without losing the sounds of the past.

Theodorakis studied at the Paris Conservatoire, but became critical of the Greek classical musical establishment—and, in fact, the Greek establishment generally. When the Colonels came to power in 1967, two years after *Zorba's* success had made Theodorakis a Greek musical hero, he was imprisoned and his music was banned for being subversive.

Greece has produced a composer of international standing in Iannis Xenakis (born 1922). Also an architect, he worked as assistant to the innovative French architect Le Corbusier (1887–1965) from 1948 until 1960. Xenakis's work shows a corresponding interest in the mathematical and harmonious elements in music. He founded the School of Mathematical and Automatic Music in 1966. He sometimes works with Greek themes, such as providing music for a production of the *Oresteia,* but Xenakis has lived in France since the late 1940s, and became a French citizen in 1965.

LITERATURE

The influence of Greece on the literature of the world has been profound and the past resonates down through the centuries. Modern literature has its roots in Homer (see pp. 330–31), and those roots still nourish the literary tree. Arguably the greatest novel of the 20th century was *Ulysses,* by the Irish writer James Joyce (1882–1941), who based the plan for his complex and experimental book on Homer's *Odyssey.*

It could be said that the Greeks invented travel writing too, as the first such book was *Hellados Periegesis* (Description of Greece) by the historian and traveler Pausanias, who lived in the second century A.D. and provided this guide for Roman visitors to Greece's classical sites. It is as useful today as it was then, as indeed are many books by historians that give us literary accounts of life in ancient Greece, notably the *Histories* by Herodotus (circa 484–425 B.C.) and the *History of the Peloponnesian War* by Thucydides (circa 460–400 B.C.).

Herodotus has been called the Father of History, and his book is regarded as the first major work of nonfiction, slightly predating Thucydides. It includes sections on the Persian Wars (490 and 481–479 B.C.) but also illuminates life in those days with accounts of legends, customs, beliefs, traditions, and everyday events that bring the period vividly alive once again.

The value of Thucydides's book is immense for several reasons, not least because of the chronicle it gives of the war itself. Though Thucydides participated in the war as an Athenian commander, he also saw the value of recording events, and of trying to give an objective rather than partisan account. He interviewed combatants and quotes the speeches of the leaders in a manner that serves as a template to this day.

The great Greek poets from Homer to Elytis are dealt with elsewhere (see pp. 238–39), as are the great dramatists Aeschylus, Sophocles, and Euripides (p. 106) and modern novelist Nikos Kazantzakis (see p. 283). But Greece has

The eight-stringed *bouzouki,* a long-necked mandolin, traditionally accompanies singing and dancing in Greece.

many other fine writers, less known to the outside world simply because of the language they write in. The enterprising Athenian publisher, Kedros, has published a superb series called "Modern Greek Writers," translating its works into English for the first time.

Greek writers still grapple with the big themes, as shown by Dido Sotiriou (born 1909)

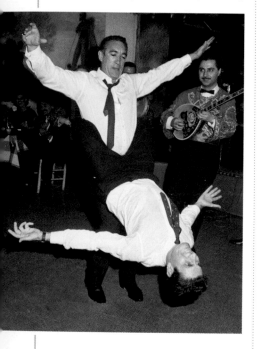

Anthony Quinn captured the exuberance of Greek folk dance in the movie *Zorba the Greek*.

in her novel *Farewell Anatolia*. A bestseller in Greece since it was published in 1962, the book recounts the forced exchange of Greek-Turkish populations in 1923. Its publication in a Turkish translation in 1970 was welcomed as providing a greater understanding of the suffering on both sides, and in 1990 the author was awarded the highest literary award in Greece, the prize of the Academy of Athens.

Eugenia Fakinou (born 1945) is another female writer whose books deal with what it means to be Greek. Her first novel, *Astradeni*, has been in print since it was published in 1982. It tells a tale familiar to many Greeks, of

a family forced by circumstance to leave its island home to move to Athens in search of a better life. The young girl who tells the story, Astradeni, depicts the changes with the bold, simple gaze of a child.

Petros Abatzoglou (born 1931) has written several novels and collections of stories, but for an outsider perhaps the most interesting is *What Does Mrs. Freeman Want?* It gives the Greek perspective on a pair of English tourists, who come to soak up the sun while the book's narrator observes them and soaks up the ouzo.

CINEMA

Movies as varied as *For Your Eyes Only, Shirley Valentine, The Magus,* and *Boy on a Dolphin* have all been shot in Greece. Several Greek movies have won Academy Awards in various categories including, not surprisingly, music.

First and foremost must be *Zorba the Greek,* made by director Michael Cacoyannis in 1964 and starring Anthony Quinn in the title role. The first notable modern Greek movie had been four years earlier with *Never on a Sunday,* which picked up five Oscar nominations, including best director for Jules Dassin, who also starred in the movie, and best actress for Melina Mercouri. It won an Oscar for best song—the irresistible title tune written by Greek composer Manos Hadjidakis.

The most distinguished contemporary Greek moviemaker is Theo Angelopoulos, born in Athens in 1935. He first came to prominence in 1974 with *Traveling Players,* which told the story of a group of actors moving physically through Greece but also temporally through Greek history. Angelopoulos's 1986 movie, *The Bee-Keeper,* also tells of a journey through Greece, this time a retired schoolteacher transporting his bees on a truck and forging a relationship with a young hitchhiker along the way. Its feel for Greece's landscape, people, and history make it a movie that should not be missed by anyone seeking to understand the country.

Angelopoulos won the Palme d'Or at Cannes in 1998 for his 11th movie, titled *Eternity and a Day.* Not only was this the most prestigious award that any Greek moviemaker had ever achieved, it was also a sure sign of the renaissance underway in Greek moviemaking. ∎

Athens is like a friend you accept despite his or her faults. See the Parthenon rising above the city, or glimpse the treasures inside the National Archaeological Museum, and you will forget the noise of the busy city streets.

Athens

Ceremonial guard, or *Evzone*

Athens

ATHENS IS STEEPED IN HISTORY AND ALTHOUGH YOU HAVE SEEN PICTURES of the Acropolis, you cannot fail to be impressed by this architectural wonder at the heart of the busy modern city. You will want to visit the Parthenon but don't overlook the other ancient sites and excellent museums here. Then take a break from culture and shop in the Plaka district, the old but touristy part of town below the Acropolis—or just wander. Regular visitors know that the streets of Athens are full of wonderful treasures.

Almost five million people—nearly a quarter of the entire Greek population—live within the greater Athens area. This is a busy metropolis whose main problems are an excess of traffic and, in summer, the consequent *nefos* (smog). Fortunately, the government is introducing measures to curb the traffic and its pollution, including pedestrian areas (still a novelty in Greece) and restrictions on driving into the downtown area. Things will slowly improve.

The agreement to hold the 2004 Olympic Games in Athens has been a great incentive for change. Suddenly all those half-completed projects that had been lingering for years have come to fruition—Syntagma subway station and Omonoia Square are good examples. These changes and others, such as the steady expansion of the Metro subway system, also help to combat the old problem of pollution.

Ironically, the nefos is a result of Athens' attractive location, with hills on three sides trapping the smog—a situation similar to that in Los Angeles. The Aegean Sea lies to the south, beyond the port of Pireas, which merges with Athens. The two are connected by a subway, and anyone who feels that central Athens is busy should try spending some time in the bustle and chaos of Pireas. Little wonder that the sleepy islands appeal so much!

But spend some time in Athens, and its charms start to surface. Many cities are described as being like collections of small villages, but Athens is a Greek village magnified. Human touches are everywhere: flowers in pots on balconies, neighbors chatting, people doing each other favors, an old lady stopping for a few minutes in church.

The very existence of the churches in Athens shows that this is an unusual city, a city still on a human scale. Tiny Byzantine chapels force the modern traffic to detour around them, when in other cities they would long since have been demolished. The homogeneity of the population in Athens, its very Greekness, is also extraordinary. There are scatterings of other nationalities, such as Americans or Albanians, but without the pockets of foreign neighborhoods that you get in almost all major capitals. When you are in Athens you could be in no other city in the world. ■

Acropolis

Acropolis

🅰 50 C2

☎ 321 0219 (museum:
323 6665)

💲 $$

🚇 Metro: Monastiraki

**Visitor
information**

✉ Athens Tourist
Information H.Q.,
Amerikis 2, P.O. Box
1017, 105 64

☎ 331 0562 or
331 0565

AKRO POLI MEANS "UPPER CITY," AND MANY GREEK TOWNS have their acropolis. Athens has the most famous one in the world. Capped by the tall columns of the Parthenon, the Acropolis (or Akropoli) is one of the most beautiful constructions made by man. Whether you see the Parthenon in daylight when approaching from the airport, or from your hotel balcony or roof, illuminated at night, or up close when you visit, it dominates the city center, a constant reminder of the golden age of ancient Greece.

You can reach the entrance to the Acropolis by walking up one of the two approaches to the western end. The more atmospheric is through the Plaka district where you spot occasional handwritten signs directing you up the steep streets. Local storekeepers are used to being asked directions as the route is not always obvious. The only approach from Dionysiou Areopagitou, a street recently pedestrianized for visitors, is easier to follow.

Evidence of a settlement on the southern slopes of the Acropolis dates the first habitation in Athens to about 3000 B.C. The buildings that remain date mainly from the fifth century B.C., when ancient Athens reached its pinnacle during the Golden Age of Pericles (see pp. 28–29). Pericles hired the finest workmen of the day, including the master sculptor Pheidias. He was the main artistic director of the **Parthenon,** a temple and the first building to be raised on the site. The great architect Iktinos was probably responsible for its overall design and construction.

It is now well known that the Parthenon has no straight lines in its construction, the apparent symmetry created by gently tapering columns and steps. The building is designed using repeated ratios of

9:4, for such aspects as the gap between columns in relation to the width of a single column, or the width of the building in relation to its height. Originally the focus of the building was a 40-foot-high (12 m) golden statue of the goddess Athena, after whom the city is named. A model of the Parthenon as it would have looked then can be seen in the National Archaeological Museum (see pp. 78–81).

The building took nine years to construct, was finished in 438 B.C., and is made from marble quarried locally. Flecks of iron in the marble give the building its wonderfully warm golden glow in evening light.

For the last few years the Parthenon has been roped off to prevent visitors from destroying the precious marble. The sheer number of feet and hands of those who come to admire, and not vandalize, has had to be curtailed. The skyline is usually marred by the sight of a crane, but this is vital reconstruction and preservation work, as in places some of the marble has cracked and needs to be bound together.

Several other buildings on top of the Acropolis are worthy of a closer

The mighty Acropolis, topped by the pillars of the Parthenon, still dominates the modern city.

Elgin Marbles

In 1801 Thomas Bruce, the Earl of Elgin, was British Ambassador to the Porte, the Turkish government then in control in Athens. The Acropolis was in a sorry state, and the Turks were using some of the antiquities as building materials. Lord Elgin was permitted to remove some of the stones and sculptures, but far exceeded his remit and sold his acquisitions to London's British Museum in 1816. The most famous of these, friezes from the Parthenon, are known as the Elgin Marbles.

The Greeks continue in their concerted campaign to get these back to their rightful home in Athens, something which may one day come to pass. ■

look. To the right soon after you enter, is the small **Temple of Athena Nike,** added in 427–424 B.C. to celebrate victories by the Athenians in their wars with the Persians. Athena Nike means Athena of Victory. (The Parthenon was dedicated to another aspect of the goddess: Athena Promachos, Athena the Champion.) In 1686 the temple was destroyed by the Turks then occupying Greece. It has been reconstructed twice, most recently in 1936–1940.

The Turks wreaked havoc on the Acropolis, building a mosque inside the Parthenon, which was left to fall into ruin before parts

Temple of Rome and Augustus

Sacred Way

Erechtheion, an Ionic temple built in 421–395 B.C. and partially reconstructed in 1827. The famous caryatid pillars are on the side that faces the Parthenon.

Site of the Old Temple of Athena

Enhanced by deep fluting, the marble columns of the Parthenon were built in sections.

The statue of Athena Promachos by Pheidias commemorates victory over the Persians

of it were sold off to Lord Elgin (see p. 53). They also used the building as a weaponry store, which resulted in further damage when the arsenal exploded.

Over to your left as you approach the Parthenon is the **Erechtheion,** added between 421 and 395 B.C. It is said that the first olive tree in Athens sprouted here when the goddess Athena touched the ground with her spear. An olive tree has been kept growing here since 1917 as a symbol of this.

The building includes the Porch of the Caryatids, where the supporting columns have been sculpted in the shapes of six maidens. Those now on the site are copies: Five of the originals are in the Acropolis Museum, the other was looted by Lord Elgin. The **museum** is at the far end of the site, and has an impressive collection, but some of it may be removed to the much newer **Acropolis Study Center (Kentro Meleton Akropoleos),** which is open but still being built, to the south of the Acropolis (see p. 57). ■

The Pantheon served as a church and a mosque, losing its marble roof in the explosion of 1687.

The Propylaia was built about 437 B.C. as the main gateway to the site.

Destroyed in 1686, the Temple of Athena Nike was last reconstructed in 1935.

Pinakotheke, or art gallery

Monument of Agrippa

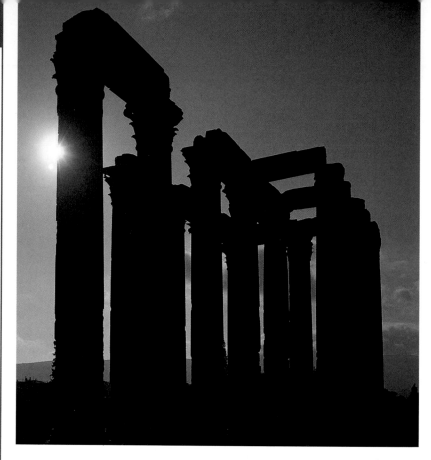

Standing over 350 feet (107 m) tall, the Temple of Olympian Zeus, southeast of the Acropolis, was the tallest in Greece.

South of the Acropolis

THE APPROACH TO THE ACROPOLIS FROM THE SOUTH side (the usual route if you arrive by bus) is a walk up a modern pathway that snakes up through trees and behind the most prominent building on the southern slopes, the Herodes Atticus Theater.

Herodes Atticus Theater

- 🅰 50 C2
- ✉ Leoforos Dionysiou Areopagitou
- 🕐 Only open for special performances
- 🚇 Metro: Theseion

Unlike the Acropolis buildings, the **Herodes Atticus Theater (Teatro Irodou Attikou)** dates from the Roman period and was built in A.D. 161–174 by a businessman from Marathon with the grand name of Tiberius Claudius Atticus Herodes. The theater, restored in 1955, seats 5,000 people and is still used during the Athens Festival from June to September.

Farther along below the Acropolis, the unrestored **Theater of Dionysos (Teatro Dionysiou)** provides a great contrast to the grand-looking Herodes Atticus Theater next door. Bear in mind that what you see are only the remains of a large complex, which seated 17,000 spectators at its height. The original Greek theater, built in 342–326 B.C., was much expanded during the Roman period.

The Dionysos was used for a multitude of purposes—most notably for gladiatorial fights and annual drama contests. When you look at the stage here, you are looking at the place where drama was born. This is where Sophocles and Aristophanes first had their works produced—although not on the remains that stand today, which date from Roman times. Among those remains are marble thrones for dignitaries, and marble flooring put in by Emperor Nero in the first century A.D. Walk back toward the rock of the Acropolis to see the unusual chapel of the Lady of the Caves, inside a cave in the rocks.

Cross the road from the Theater of Dionysos to one of Athens's newest cultural attractions, the **Acropolis Study Center (Kentro Meleton Akropoleos).** This former army barracks is rapidly becoming a place where visitors can appreciate and scholars can study the Acropolis, which is visible from its upper floors. It was the brainchild of Greece's Minister of Culture, former actress Melina Mercouri (1922–1994). She envisioned a place where the Elgin Marbles would one day be shown in a setting that did justice to their splendor, beneath the Acropolis.

On display already are reproductions of the Parthenon friezes, and by being able to look closely at them, visitors get some sense of their magnificence and grand scale. Other displays show how these and other structures and carvings on the Acropolis were produced: How the great slabs of marble were quarried and brought to central Athens, how the huge columns were carved and then carefully erected, and the fine tools used by the master craftsmen. A scale model shows how the study center will look when completed, although visitors are likely to be picking their way past a partial building site for some time yet.

West of the study center is the hilly park known as the **Pnyka.**

The entrance is almost opposite the Herodes Atticus Theater, and here you can enjoy the **Acropolis Sound and Light Show** *(tel 322 1459, closed Nov.–March, $$).* Few visitors realize that the seating is in the actual place where the Assembly of Athens used to take place in the days of Pericles, when 18,000 people would gather to hear the city's finest speakers, and to debate issues affecting the city.

Life wasn't always so gloriously democratic, however, as a sign pointing to the "Prison of Socrates" indicates. This somewhat shabby-looking place claims to be the site where the philosopher Socrates (circa 470–399 B.C.) was imprisoned after his arrest for "corrupting the youth of Athens" with his radical teachings. He was sentenced to death and obliged to drink deadly hemlock, but this actually took place in a prison on the site of the Agora. His imprisonment in a cave on the Pnyka is most likely a piece of folklore. ■

Theater of Dionysos
🅰 50 C2
✉ Leoforos Dionysiou Areopagitou
💲 $
🚇 Metro: Syntagma

Acropolis Study Center
🅰 50 C2
✉ Makrygianni 2-4
☎ 923 9381
🚇 Metro: Syntagma

Pnyka
🅰 50 B2
🚇 Metro: Theseion

A carving at the Theater of Dionysos shows signs of corrosion by weather and pollution.

North slopes of the Acropolis

Ancient Agora museum

- 50 B2
- Adhrianou 24
- 321 0185
- Closed Mon.
- $$
- Metro: Monastiraki

VISITORS WHO APPROACH THE ACROPOLIS FROM THE northern side may seriously doubt the validity of the handprinted signs, arrows, and scribbling on the walls that directs them to one of the most significant historical sites in the world. There are no prominent official signs pointing the way as you might expect, but continue up steps, past postcard sellers and cafés, and you'll reach the Acropolis.

Follow the signs and you will eventually get there, but you could miss one of the most delightful parts of Athens: **Anafiotika.** This quaint area is like an authentic, self-contained little village in the heart of the city. It nestles between the Plaka area and the rocks of the Acropolis. The dazzling white-washed houses with brightly painted blue doors give the impression that you are in a village in the Cyclades. The roar of the traffic is left behind, and the paths are so narrow that there is scarcely room to squeeze through.

The people who first lived here came from the island of Anafi, in the Cyclades. They were brought to Athens by King Otto soon after he ascended to the Greek throne in 1832. He wanted a palace built by the country's best craftsmen and was assured that the workers on Anafi were the best that money could buy. He commissioned them to construct his palace. When they realized they would be based in

Alfresco dining beneath the plane trees in the Plaka

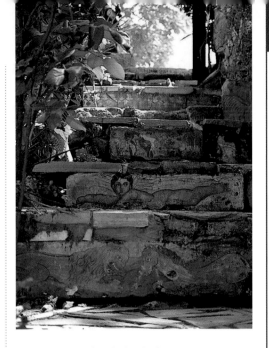

Athens for several years, they re-created their island home right here at the foot of the Acropolis. Don't leave Athens without seeing this charming side of the city.

AGORA

As you walk down from the Acropolis to the north, the large site of the **Ancient Agora,** or market-place, spreads out below you to the left. After the Acropolis itself and the National Archaeological Museum, this is the next essential visit for those interested in the city's history. The area was originally a cemetery, and many tombs are still visible, but it began to be used as a market place around the sixth century B.C. It expanded to become the center of Athenian life for several hundred years, packed with stalls and shops, and crowds just as talkative as modern Athenians.

Two major buildings on the site merit close attention: the **Temple** of Hephaistos (Hephaisteion) and the Stoa of Attalos. The Temple is clearly visible above the trees in one corner of the Agora, looking like a miniature Parthenon. It is also known as the Theseion, a name given to the surrounding area of Athens, (including the nearby sub-way station). The temple was built in 449–444 B.C., so it predates the Parthenon. In fact it marked the start of the city's development that became known as the Golden Age. Hephaistos was the god of many things, including fire, art, and met-allurgy, and the temple was built in the metalworkers' quarter of the city. It rivals the Parthenon as one of Greece's best-preserved temples.

On the far side of the Agora is the **Stoa of Attalos (Stoa Attalou).** A *stoa* is a roofed colonnade, and this two-story building is unique in Athens, as it is the only one that has been fully restored. Reconstruction of such buildings is a thorny subject, as some people prefer to see them left just as they were found. There is no doubt that this restoration was splendidly carried out, in 1953–56,

Unexpectedly delicate paintings enhance the steps to a sunken gar-den in Anafiotika.

Temple of Hephaistos

🅰 50 B3
✉ Pelopidha/Eolou
☎ 324 5220
🕐 Closed Mon.
💲 $
🚇 Metro: Monastiraki

by the American School of Archaeology in Athens, generously funded by John D. Rockefeller, Jr.

The Stoa was first built in the second century B.C. by Attalos, king of Pergamon, but was burned to the ground in A.D. 267. Inside it today is a small but fascinating museum, with a collection that brings to life the people and society of the Agora. It includes a wide range of artifacts, from a child's toilet to important historical items, such as one of the voting machines that citizens used to elect the city's officials.

ROMAN FORUM

Just over 100 yards (100 m) east of the Ancient Agora is the interesting but less impressive Roman Forum, also known as the **Roman Agora,** or marketplace. It was originally an extension of the earlier Greek Agora, and was built by Julius Caesar (*R.* 59–44 B.C.) and Emperor Augustus (*R.* 44 B.C.– A.D. 14). While it looks scruffy in comparison with other sites nearby, it contains one of the most unusual and distinctive Athenian landmarks, the **Tower of the Winds (Naos Aiolou).**

The marble tower was built in the second half of the first century B.C., to the design of a Syrian astronomer named Andronikos of Kyrrhos. The tower stands 39 feet (12 m) high and measures 26 feet (8 m) across, and its Greek name is *Aerides,* which means "the Winds." Its Pentelic marble glows as golden as the Parthenon itself under the last rays of the setting sun. It has eight sides and several functions.

Each side faces one of the eight main compass points, and a decorative frieze at the top of each represents one of the eight winds of mythology. The North Wind, for example, is Boreas, warmly clad and with billowing cloak; his brother Notos, the South Wind, brings rain,

which he pours from a pitcher of water. Another brother is Zephyros, the West Wind, scattering flowers, while the Northeast Wind, Kaikias, brings hailstones. Beneath Boreas and Apeliotes (the East Wind), small holes allow some light into the tower. All eight sides once had a sundial below the friezes.

The tower also originally had a water clock, driven by a stream of water which flowed down from the Acropolis. All that remains today is a water channel on the floor inside. The water was let into a cylinder at a predetermined rate, and the time could be told by examining the level of the water as it slowly filled the cylinder.

The tower may also have been used as an early planetarium, with a device inside for recording the movements of the sun, the moon, and the five planets that were known and visible at that time.

The other notable building within the Roman Forum is the **Mosque of Fethiye Tzami,** built in 1458 and therefore the oldest in Athens, but today only in use for storage. Another Islamic building stood opposite what is now the public entrance to the Roman Forum. This was a *medresse,* or school, where Muslim students were taught the Koran. It later became a prison, and a tree in the grounds was used for public hangings, but the building was almost completely destroyed after the prison closed down.

At one time **Hadrian's Library (Vivliothiki Asriianou)** stood on the edge of the Roman Forum, but it is now separated from the site by several streets. It was built around A.D. 132 by Emperor Hadrian, mainly to house his vast collection of books, the extent of which can be gauged by the fact that this was the largest building he erected in Athens. The library had a pool and a garden surrounded by a walled courtyard 400 by 270 feet (122 m by 82 m), and containing no less than 100 columns. There is not much to see there now apart from the remaining East Wall, but archaeologists have been working on the site for some years, and visitors should eventually be able to enter the library. A notable feature will be the recesses in the stone where the books—in the form of rolled-up manuscripts—were stored. ■

The pepperpot Tower of the Winds found new purpose in the sixth century as a chapel, and survived when structures around it were allowed to fall into ruin.

Monastiraki

CENTERED ON THE SQUARE OF THE SAME NAME, Monastiraki is one of the most vibrant and exciting shopping areas of Athens. This Greek flea market with its shops and stalls sells everything from holy icons to old copies of *Playboy*. Bordering the pleasant, pedestrianized Plaka district (see p. 64), Monastiraki is a rough and ready hubbub of activity.

For the last few years **Monastiraki Square (Plateia Monastiraki)** has been not at all reminiscent of the peaceful monastery that once stood on this site and gave the place its name. The chaos has been created by extensive work to improve the Metro (subway) station—one of the city's busiest. Barriers have blocked much of the square, and the resultant crush of people only adds to the cacophony. But this is a temporary state.

If you walk westward away from Plaka you enter the exotic world of the **flea market.** Hundreds of shops of all kinds line the main street and the many side streets, and are to be found up and down staircases, along alleys, and in small squares. Naturally enough, many of the first shops you encounter are aimed at the visitors who spill over from the Plaka and venture into the labyrinth, but the farther you get the more varied the shops become. If you want to find a genuine Greek coffeepot or a traditional *bouzouki,* this is the place to come. There are shops selling clothes, CDs, books, videos, antiques, junk, paintings, postcards, musical instruments, electrical appliances, kitchen equipment—you name it. If you can't find it in Monastiraki then it probably doesn't exist in Athens.

Shopping here has the flavor of a Middle Eastern bazaar. The shopkeepers will try to coax you in, but usually in a jovial way and without too much pressure. Pickpockets can be a problem, so be as vigilant as you would be in any crowded place.

The biggest crowds and best spectacle are on a Sunday morning, when the market expands to take in the main road, Ermou, as well as every inch of the side streets, extending as far as the Kerameikos cemetery and beyond. The crowds can be so intense that everything comes to a halt in a human traffic jam. It is all very good-natured, with the occasional scene of Greek drama thrown in.

Try to visit the cemetery of **Kerameikos,** but if you are in a hurry then Sunday morning is not the best time. The name comes from the potters of the ancient city. Keramos was the patron deity of potters: hence, ceramics. The cemetery is a peaceful haven, with much greenery and wildlife within its small area. It first served as a burial ground as long ago as the 12th century B.C., and many old tombs still remain, most notably along the central "thoroughfare" known as the Street of the Tombs. Take a look, too, at the incredibly moving grave inscriptions in the site's small museum.

Walk back along Ermou away from Keramikos, past Monastiraki Square, and you reach another, much more peaceful and graceful square known as Cathedral Square —Plateia Mitropoleos. There are in fact two cathedrals here, the little and the large. The **Little Mitropolis (Mikri Mitropoli)**

Monastiraki
- 🚇 50 B3

Kerameikos
- 🚇 50 B3
- ✉ Ermou 148
- ☎ 346 3552
- 🕐 Closed Mon.
- 💲 $
- 🚇 Metro: Theseion

to the right is a charming, tiny church dating back to the 12th century and dedicated to Agios (St.) Eleftherios. Its cave-like interior is usually lit by the glow of votive candles, and it exudes an air of peace and spirituality. Outside delicate carvings grace its walls. Next door is the **Great Mitropolis (Megali Mitropoli),** which is Athens's cathedral, constructed in the middle of the 19th century over a period of some 25 years. Note the detailed and colorful mosaics stretching above the impressive entrance. The cathedral is used today on formal occasions, such as the funerals of distinguished Athenians.

Next door to Monastiraki, north of Ermou and west of Amerikis, **Psirri** is one of the most up-and-coming areas of the city. For many years the district was a rundown warren of small workshops, builders' merchants, and hardware stores. Today it has been transformed and is brimming with fashionable bars and restaurants, smart new shops, ouzeries, and cafés. It is a great place to head for a night out. You could start the evening with an apéritif in a sidewalk café—they avoid the worst of the Athenian traffic as the streets are narrow and lead nowhere. If you venture into the restaurants, however, you may need your phrase book with you, as most menus are only in Greek. If you want to know the latest news on Psirri, then the district even has its own website (in English as well as Greek, see p. 343), which tells you how fashionable it is! ■

Modern temples to the passion for shopping dwarf a Byzantine church in Monastiraki.

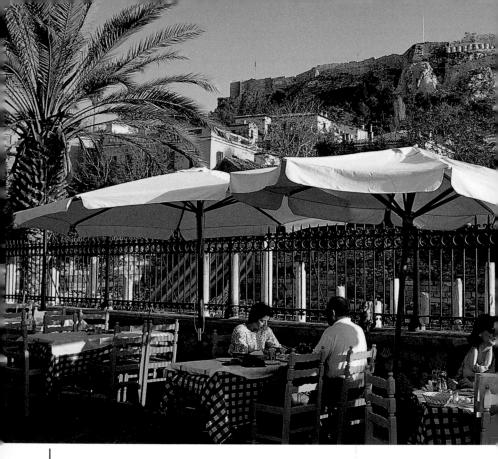

Museum of Popular Instruments

🅰 67
✉ Diogenous 1–3
☎ 325 0198/4119
🕐 Closed Mon.
🚇 Metro: Monastiraki

Kanellopoulos Museum

🅰 50 C2
✉ Panos/Theorias
☎ 321 2313
🕐 Closed Mon.
💲 $
🚇 Metro: Monastiraki

Plaka

PLAKA IS THE WARREN OF STREETS THAT MEANDER TO THE north and east at the foot of the Acropolis. It is the prime visitor area of Athens, and you will be surrounded by picture postcards, souvenir shops, and restaurants trying to attract your custom. Many of the buildings are old and beautiful. The streets are mainly pedestrianized, there are some good eating places, and the atmosphere is lively, day and night.

The area expanded in the 19th century, and was home to many well-to-do Athenian families. They built grand neoclassic mansions, several of which have been turned into museums or stores and can therefore be enjoyed both inside and out.

An essential stop on a stroll round the area is the **Museum of** **Popular Instruments (Mouseio Ellinikon Mousikon Organon),** housed in a mansion that was built in 1842. Its courtyard is used in summer for outdoor concerts. Inside on three floors are some of the 1,200 or so musical instruments amassed over the years by the Greek musicologist Fivos Anoyanakis (born 1915). It is a museum that is both fascinating and fun, telling the story of Greek music in an entertaining manner. Headphones allow you to listen to many of the exhibits being played. In one wing is the museum gift shop, which has one of Athens's best collections of Greek traditional music on CD.

Another mansion, dating from 1884, houses the **Kanellopoulos Museum (Mouseio Kanellopoulos).** Inside is a collection of ceramics, statues, jewelry, and general art and craft work built up by Athenian collectors Paul and Alexandra Kanellopoulos. Exhibits cover the years from the third century B.C. to the 19th century A.D., ranging across civilizations (Minoan, Mycenean, Roman, Persian, Egyptian, and Phoenician). Items include exquisite jewelry, and erotic vases, and the museum makes a good stopping-off point on the way up to or down from the Acropolis.

The other principal museum in Plaka that all visitors should try to see is the **Museum of Greek Folk Art (Mouseio Ellinikis Laografias).** It is somewhat chaotic, and crammed in—rather like Athens itself—but like the city it is fascinating, with intriguing nooks and crannies. The five floors contain a wealth of material, and there is usually an additional temporary exhibition to see.

Highlights include examples of the work of the primitive painter Theophilos (see p 40), including an entire painted room transported from a house on the island of Lesvos. Displays of work by, and costumes of, the Sarakatsani nomads are here too (see p. 159), alongside a large collection of other folk costumes covering most of the island groups and the main regions of the Greek mainland. For anyone interested in embroidery or clothing generally, the museum is a must. A small shop sells

samples of work as well as books on the folk arts.

Sampling the food is the other essential ingredient of any visit to Plaka. Almost half the premises seem to be tavernas, bars, or cafés, with a number of eating places distinguished by someone standing at the doorway trying to persuade you inside. As a general rule, it is best to avoid such places. The better restaurants appeal to locals year-round, so they have no need to pay someone to fill their seats—their reputation does it for them. There are several basement restaurants in Plaka, which are very basic affairs but with good value and lots of fun, and their walls often covered with lively murals by local artists.

Plaka wakes up slowly, but it is the perfect place for an outdoor lunch or an evening's entertainment, starting with a stroll, taking in a typical Greek meal, moving on to some music, and ending late with a coffee and a brandy in the warm night air. ∎

Pleasures of the Plaka: dining with a view of the Acropolis (above) and shopping (right)

Museum of Greek Folk Art
- ⬛ 50 D2
- ✉ Kydathinaion 17
- ☎ 322 9031
- 🕐 Closed Mon.
- 💲 $
- 🚇 Metro: Syntagma

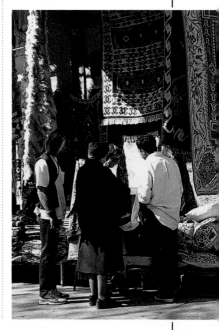

Walk: Plaka highlights

Plaka's shops, restaurants, and nightlife make the district one of Athens's most popular with visitors. It also has some fine churches and examples of neoclassic architecture, with several of these mansions now housing museums. This short walk takes in a variety of Plaka's many delights.

From **Syntagma Square (Plateia Syntagmatos) ❶** (see p. 68), face away from the Parliament Building at the top, walk across to the far left corner, and turn left along the right-hand side of Filellinon, the one-way street taking traffic away from the square. Walk a little way along here until you see the **Church of St. Nikodemos (Agios Nikodimos)** on the left (also known as Agia Triada). This is the main Russian Orthodox Church in Athens, built in the 1850s, although there has been a church on this site since 1031. Almost opposite the church, turn right, where you see a sign for the folk art museum.

The street you enter, Kydathinaion, is one of the main Plaka streets, and it starts to get busy just beyond the **Church of St. Sotira (Agia Sotira)** on the right. This is the main church of the Plaka district, and dates from the late 11th or early 12th century. Note the fountain in the courtyard, for a long time the

Shops in the lively Plaka district remain open well into the evening, ready to entice late diners.

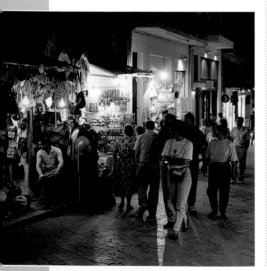

only source of water in this area. On your left is the **Museum of Greek Folk Art (Mouseio Ellinikis Laografias) ❷** (see p. 65), and farther along on your right the **Hellenic Children's Museum (Elliniko Paithiko Mouseio,** *tel 331 2995),* worth seeing if you have children with you since it is more of an activity center than a traditional museum.

Continue down Kydathinaion a short way and look on your right for the street named Geronta. At the far end of Geronta is the **Center for Popular Arts and Traditions (Kentro Laikis Technis kai Paradosis,** *tel 324 3887)* **❸;** you may wish to make a detour to see the collection of Greek folk art inside this Plaka mansion. Further down Kydathinaion is the intersection with Adrianou, but cross over and walk up Thespidou Street. On the right you will find the **studio of George Savakis,** a Plaka artist who has painted many murals in the local tavernas as well as scenes of Plaka life. You can buy an original as a distinctive souvenir.

Return to Adrianou, go left and walk down into the heart of the Plaka. After about 300 yards and beyond a small intersection, look on the left for the small stepped street called Mnissikleous. Walk up here and take the first right onto Diogenous. At the far end of this

- ⓜ See area map p. 50
- ► Syntagma Square
- ⬌ I mile (1.5 km)
- ⏱ 30 minutes
- ► Monastiraki Square

NOT TO BE MISSED

- Museum of Greek Folk Art
- Center for Popular Arts and Traditions
- Museum of Popular Instruments

Locals and visitors pursue their different purchases side by side in Monastiraki Square.

street on your right is the mansion that now contains the **Museum of Popular Instruments (Mouseio Ellinikon Mousikon Organon) ❹** (see p. 64).

Continuing along Diogenous brings you out at the **Roman Forum ❺** (see p. 60). Turn right and walk around the Agora, and just about opposite the entrance take a

right turn down Eolou. Pass the bottom of Adrianou on your right and take the next left onto Pandrossou Street, another of the Plaka's shopping streets. This will bring you out in **Monastiraki Square (Plateia Monastiraki) ❻**, on the edge of the Athens **flea market** (see p. 62), where there is a Metro station. ∎

The former royal palace became the Vouli in 1935.

Syntagma Square
(Plateia Syntagmatos)

SYNTAGMA IS THE HEART OF ATHENS. THE NAME MEANS Constitution Square and the Greek Parliament Building, or Vouli, stands here. Built as the royal palace, it was completed in 1842, and King Otto I proclaimed Greece's first constitution from its balcony.

Syntagma Square
🅰 50 D3
🚇 Metro: Syntagma

In front of the **Vouli** and marking the boundary of the square is the Tomb of the Unknown Soldier. Its permanent guard, Greek soldiers known as *Evzones*, are there in their colorful traditional costumes of red beret, dark tunic in winter or red vest in summer, short white kilt over white leggings, and red wooden shoes adorned with huge pom-poms. The best time to visit is at 11 a.m. on Sundays for the main Changing of the Guard ceremony, but if you can't make it, you can see the guards change on the hour in an elaborate routine.

Along one side of the square, the **Grande Bretagne Hotel** is normally used by dignitaries who might be visiting the Parliament, and by other celebrities. Over the years guests have included actress Elizabeth Taylor, composer Richard Strauss, and Sir Winston Churchill.

Syntagma has at last returned to its full glory, after years of construction works saw much of the square barricaded off while the new subway station was completed. This was finally opened in January 2000 (see p. 77), allowing Syntagma to become once again the kind of central plaza Athens deserves. It is surrounded by stores and offices, but there are also cafés. Kiosks at the bottom end of the square have the latest editions of most major overseas newspapers, so you can relax with a coffee and catch up with events back home. You will find a McDonald's here as well. ∎

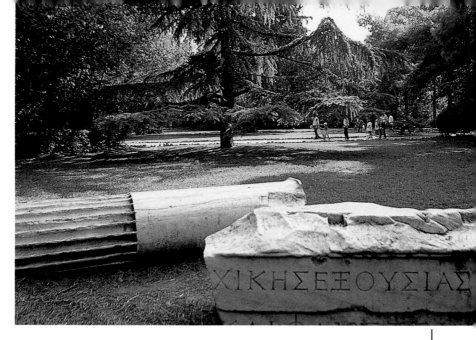

National Gardens

Ancient tumbled marble provides cool seating in the shady National Gardens.

THE NATIONAL GARDENS (ETHNIKOS KIPOS) ARE LAID OUT beside the Greek Parliament Building, formerly the royal palace, making a peaceful and shaded retreat. Created in the 1840s, the gardens are still a focal point in Athens, with the modern Presidential Palace right behind them. They are also known as the Royal Gardens, because they were created at the same time as the palace.

The gardens were the creation of Amalia, wife of King Otto I. The queen brought no less than 15,000 seedlings from Italy to landscape the grounds.

At 40 acres (16 ha), the National Gardens are not quite big enough to get lost in but still a good size to explore, with plenty of park benches if you want to relax or enjoy a few moments of solitude. It's a popular spot with working Athenians who come here to eat a sandwich at lunchtime or read the daily paper. You might see nannies with babies in strollers visiting one or other of the children's playgrounds. The gardens also have a children's library, with books in several languages—worth knowing about if you're traveling with a family and encounter a rainy day. Small ponds in the gardens are filled with terrapins, which can be observed sunning themselves on rocks, or resting with their tiny heads peeping out above the surface of the water. There are some larger animals in a small, somewhat unappealing old-style zoo near the center of the gardens.

Graceful marble statues line the footpaths, and there are fountains and quiet cafés. At the south side, a grand 19th-century building called the **Zappeion** is now a conference center, but was originally built as an exhibition hall by Greek-Romanian cousins, Evangelos and Konstantinos Zappas. The café alongside it makes a good place to take a break. ∎

National Gardens
- 🅰 50 D2
- ✉ Leoforos Amalias
- 🚇 Metro: Syntagma

Icons such as this depiction of the Crucifixion can be highly stylized yet remain remarkably vivid.

Benaki Museum
(Mouseio Benaki)

ANTOINE EMMANUEL BENAKI (1873–1954) WAS A GREEK cotton trader from Alexandria, Egypt. He spent much of his vast wealth amassing a varied collection of historical artifacts, now displayed on several floors of the neoclassical mansion that was once his family home. Benaki's collection, built up over a 35-year period, reflects his eclectic tastes, ranging from the third century B.C. to the early 20th century. He eventually donated it to the Greek state on condition that it be put on public display in a museum.

Benaki Museum

🅰 51 E3
✉ Vasilissis Sofias/ Koumbari 1
☎ 361 1617
🕐 Closed at time of writing, phone to confirm
💲 Phone to confirm
🚇 Metro: Syntagma

The eclectic collection is ordered roughly chronologically, starting with statues dating back to the fifth century B.C. On the second story artifacts from the Greek islands and Asia Minor have pride of place.

Greek culture and crafts feature on the third floor, including jewelry, wooden carvings, ceramics, and a sizable collection of Greek costumes. There are also Mycenean jewelry and many religious items, such as early Gospels, church vestments, and some exquisite icons. Lord Byron's desk is a star exhibit (see p. 32).

Another major piece, which combines both beauty and grandeur, is the reception room taken from a 17th-century Egyptian palace.

Paintings on the fourth floor include work by El Greco. One of the earliest paintings is from the third century A.D.; it's a delicate and wonderfully lifelike portrait of a young man painted onto linen by an Egyptian artist.

The museum reopened in 2000 after many years of closure for renovation, creating more display space for the collection. Don't miss the delightful rooftop snack bar. ■

War Museum
(Polemiko Mouseio)

THE WAR MUSEUM CATCHES THE EYE AS YOU WALK ALONG Vasilissis Sofias because outside is a display of Greek military equipment, including tanks that date back to World War I and several fighter planes, including a venerable Tiger Moth. Steps lead up to the exhibits, so that you can inspect their interiors.

War Museum
- 51 E3
- Leoforos Vasilissis Sofias 22/Rizari 2
- 729 0543
- Closed Mon.
- Metro: Syntagma

War has always played a major part in Greek history, from as far back as the Trojan Wars almost up to the present day. This museum is one of the few good things to come out of the warlike rule of the Colonels in 1967–1974. It was intended to reflect glory on themselves and the army, but the propaganda element is minimal and the museum has become an unlikely attraction— well worth allowing a few hours to look around.

Inside, over several large floors, the theme of war is given the broadest possible interpretation, and the exhibits are arranged chronologically. Military conflict in ancient times is represented in the displays by copies of dramatic carvings from the Temple of Vasses (see p. 127) and other statuary. The vast collections of rifles, swords, and other weapons might lack variety, but your imagination will surely be stirred by exhibits such as models of Greek castles and fortified towns. Other models show the reenactment of significant battles from Greek history—and there are certainly plenty of those to draw on.

From more recent times there are displays covering the War of Independence, including interesting exhibits showing the role of the Greek Resistance heroes. There are also very moving accounts of the way Greece was affected by World War II, especially on the streets of Athens, and in the bloody Civil War that followed it. ∎

The streamlined body of a modern fighter jet stands outside the museum.

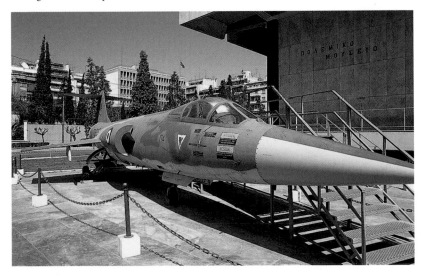

National Gallery
(Ethniki Pinakothiki)

National Gallery

🅜 51 F3

✉ Vasileos
Konstantinou 50

☎ 723 5857

🕐 Closed Tues.

Ⓜ Metro: Syntagma

THE NATIONAL GALLERY OF GREECE IS HOUSED IN A modern building a short walk down Vasilissis Sofias, near the intersection with Vasileos Konstantinou and close to the Hilton Hotel. It has a sculpture garden as well as extensive indoor displays.

The gallery houses the finest collection of paintings by Greek artists, dating mainly from the 18th to the 20th centuries.

Greece has never, as a nation, had money to invest in major works of art, so the gallery relies largely on the work of local artists, few of international renown.

An advantage of this concentration on the work of Greek artists is that you can learn a great deal, in one go, about the talent that exists within Greece. Many of the paintings are conventional landscapes of Greece, and some of these historic views are fascinating if you have visited areas such as Meteora or the smaller islands. In among the ordinary are some extraordinarily vivid works: Look for the name of Nikos Hatzikyriakos-Ghikas, who signs himself "Ghika," one of Greece's most prominent modern artists. The work of Greece's primitive school, as typified by Theophilos (see p. 40), is also well represented here.

There are works on display by important artists such as Cézanne, Breughel, Caravaggio, Picasso, Braque, Rembrandt, and Dürer, but they are on the whole smaller and lesser-known works such as engravings and sketches. The most famous Greek painter is, of course, El Greco (see p. 38), and five good examples of his work are displayed in the gallery.

Unfortunately the gallery is frequently closed while temporary exhibitions are being prepared or removed, as the main rooms are usually inaccessible when the temporary galleries are being worked on. However, the temporary displays can be excellent, including touring exhibitions by major artists, and displays that concentrate on specific aspects of Greek art, such as theater design or Byzantine art. ■

Byzantine Museum
(Vizantino Mouseio)

Byzantine Museum

⬛ 51 E3
✉ Vasilissis Sofias 22
☎ 721 1027
🕐 Closed Mon.
$ $
🚇 Metro: Syntagma

THE BYZANTINE MUSEUM IS A SMALL AND SPECIALIST collection. Even if you are not an enthusiast for this style of religious paintings, the attractively planted museum grounds are worth a visit in their own right.

The museum, near the National Gallery, is housed in a villa built in the 1840s and owned by the French Duchesse de Plaisance (1785–1854). The duchess fell in love with Greece as soon as she visited it. She had this Florentine villa built in what were then the suburbs of Athens, and went on to become one of the leading lights of Athens society life.

The villa was converted into a museum in the 1930s, and the collection is spread over the main house and other buildings, around a delightful courtyard filled with flowers and orange trees. The fountain in the center has been copied from one that can be seen on a fourth-century mosaic housed in the monastery of Dafni, to the west of the city center. It is a beautiful and relaxing spot.

The bulk of the collection is made up of religious icons, many of them well preserved and vivid in their depictions and colors. The whole collection spans some 1,500 years and takes in work not just from Greece but also from Greek communities around the world. There are also Bibles and ecclesiastical items on display, alongside statuary, embroidery, and mosaics.

Among the highlights of the collection is a mosaic icon from the 13th–14th centuries showing the "Visitation to the Virgin Mary." Another unusual icon from the same period shows St. George; it's double-sided, with gold on one side, silver on the other.

At the far end of the museum grounds, two impressive sites are housed in the same building. One is the reconstruction of an early Christian basilica, from the fifth century, and alongside it is a completely re-created Byzantine church of the 11th century.

Although much of the information with the exhibits is only available in Greek, this is a collection that can be appreciated by skimming—looking for the jewels that catch your eye. ■

The fresh, glowing colors appear undiminished on this icon of St. Michael, over 600 years old.

Kolonaki

51 E3

**Museum of
Cycladic Art**

51 E3

✉ Neofytou Douka 4

☎ 722 8321 or
714 9706 (shop)

🕐 Closed Tues. & Sun.

$ $

🚇 Metro: Syntagma

Kolonaki & Lykavittos

AS YOU APPROACH THE DISTRICT OF KOLONAKI FROM
Syntagma, you are aware that you are entering a more upscale area of
Athens. There is an increasing number of galleries, antique shops, and
fashion stores, as well as far more well-dressed young people,
frequently posing in sidewalk cafés with their mobile phones, and
ladies with their lapdogs. The hill of Lykavittos can be seen from
everywhere in central Athens, and a visit there is a must.

KOLONAKI

If you walk toward Kolonaki along
Neofytou Douka you will come
to the splendid **Museum of
Cycladic Art (Mouseio
Kykladikis kai Archais
Ellinikis Technis),** one of the
city's most important but lesser-
known highlights. This modern
museum, opened in 1986, houses a
collection of art from the Cycladic
islands (see pp. 244–259) that
dates back 5,000 years. It was
originally amassed by Greek
shipowner Nikolas Goulandris, and
donations from other specialists

**Belltower at the
summit of
Lykavittos**

have made this the finest such
collection in the world.

There are vases and glassware,
as well as other sculptures in the
museum, but it is the extensive
range of Cycladic figurines that
steals the show. The best works,
however, were produced at the
height of the Cycladic civilization—
about 3000–2000 B.C.

The Cycladic figures—statues
and face masks—are known for
their graceful simplicity and are
wonderfully displayed here, with
subtle lighting bringing out every
nuance of their shape and texture.
You will immediately see how the
figures inspired modern artists,
including Spanish artist Pablo
Picasso (1881–1973) and British
sculptor Henry Moore (1898–
1986), but most notably the Italian
painter and sculptor Amedeo
Modigliani (1884–1920).

If you feel tempted to buy a
copy of one of the works, the well-
stocked gift shop has some excellent
reproductions.

The collection is extensive
enough to cover four floors, and in
1992 a new wing was opened in
the nearby Stathatos Mansion,
connected to the original museum
by an unusual covered glass walkway. The new wing has some
rooms with period furniture to
show what the mansion was like
when built in 1885; others contain
overspill from the main museum,
some with the Greek art owned by

the Athens Academy, and there's also space for temporary exhibitions.

The **American School of Classical Studies (Gennadeion)** is also in Kolonaki. It opened in 1926 and is of interest mainly to scholars for its vast archive of some 24,000 books. However, the attractive neoclassic building is open to the general public and worth seeing for the landscape paintings on the walls, including some by English poet Edward Lear (1812–1888), and the collection of items that once belonged to Lord Byron (see p. 32).

LYKAVITTOS

The dominant feature of this part of town is the hill known as Lykavittos, or Lykabettos. At 909 feet (277 m), this is the highest hill in Athens and naturally provides superb views over the city. The best are toward the Acropolis and beyond that to Pireas and the Aegean Sea—and even to the island of Egina if the air is clear.

Lykavittos can be reached on foot or by **cable car.** The walk to the top is pleasant but tiring, the path zigzagging through scented pinewoods, While you don't have to be super-fit to undertake the walk, you might think twice in the height of summer. The cable car leaves from the top of Plutarchou Street and is in operation until after midnight in the summer, reflecting the popularity of the spot for locals and visitors alike.

At the top of the hill is the whitewashed 19th-century chapel of **Agios Georgios,** or St. George. (His feast day is celebrated on April 23, and ceremonies are well worth attending if you happen to be in Athens at the time.) Near the chapel a restaurant—a little overpriced—offers some of the best views in the city, particularly when the Parthenon is illuminated at night. There is also a café partway down Lykavittos, for a restorative coffee or glass of ouzo.

On the far side of the hill from Kolonaki the modern, open-air **Lykavittos Theater** stages some of Athens's biggest concerts—everything from classical music and dance to modern rock bands. ∎

Well-to-do Athenians congregate at the cafés on Kolonaki Square.

American School of Classical Studies
- 🅰 51 F3
- ✉ Souidias 54
- ☎ 723 6313
- 🕐 Closed Aug.
- Ⓜ Metro: Syntagma

Lykavittos
- 🅰 51 E4

Cable car
- 🅰 51 E4
- ✉ Aristippou/ Plutarchou
- 💲 $
- Ⓜ Metro: Syntagma

Around Omonoia Square

PLATEIA OMONOIAS MEANS HARMONY SQUARE, WHICH
must rank as one of the greatest misnomers in the city. It is the
second most important square in Athens after Syntagma Square, but
unlike Syntagma, where traffic circles the square in a one-way system
with a large pedestrian area in the center, Omonoia is simply where
six main roads intersect, with several minor roads also feeding traffic
into the maelstrom. However, work on the new Metro line was
recently completed and Omonoia is beginning to look like its old,
more harmonious self. There are fountains in the center and seating
that looks down Athinas to the Acropolis.

Omonoia Square
🚇 50 C4

Omonoia is like Athens itself: Your
first impressions are likely to be of
an overwhelmingly noisy and
polluted place. Yet once you get
used to the noise and the crowds, a
different picture starts to emerge. If
you do a complete circuit of the
square you will pass newsstands
where the world's press is available
and vendors sell lottery tickets, fast
food, cheap watches, smuggled cig-
arettes, and much more. There are
also busy cafés where you can soak
up the real Athens atmosphere. And
as a landmark for negotiating the
city, Omonoia can't be beat.

If Syntagma is the European face
of Athens, then Omonoia is quite
definitely the Balkan/Middle
Eastern face. It is loud and bustling,
full of traders and cheap goods, and
emphatically full of life.

At night the square becomes
Athens's equivalent of an older
Times Square or London's Soho.
Illegal immigrants cluster in
Omonoia and surrounding streets,
selling imported goods or fake
designer gear. If you are very
careless, you might find someone
taking advantage of you, but by
and large the area is safe because

it is so busy. There are always plenty of people about, even late into the night. You will see a few sleazy movie theaters showing erotic movies in the streets just off the square. At night Omonoia also becomes the red-light district. However, this is so low-key that many visitors might not even notice it.

One of the liveliest places is a few blocks down Athinas, heading south from Omonia Square—the **Central Market (Kentriki Agora).** The market is housed in a 19th-century building of glass and metal, and although it is the city's main meat and fish market, many other goods are on display, too. If you are interested in seeing the fish that are hauled in daily from the waters of the Aegean, then this is the place to come. Even if you have no wish to buy, you can observe Athenian housewives and restaurant owners bargaining for the best cuts of meat and the freshest fish.

The Central Market is busy from early in the morning through the afternoon. In the evening it livens up again as there are several ouzeries (where you can sample a variety of ouzos along with snacks) and *rembetika* (see pp. 45–46) music clubs in this area.

If you plan a picnic or you're taking a trip to the islands and want to stock up for the ferry ride— Greek ferries always provide basic snacks, but little more—this is the place to come. You will find cheeses and olives, bread and fruit, fresh herbs and spices, along with flowers and vegetables. If you are looking for a souvenir, there are nuts and ouzos. In short, if you can eat it, then you'll find it here.

Athinas itself is an unofficial employment exchange. In the early morning you may see painters and decorators standing with their buckets and ladders, hoping to pick up a day's work. They add yet another shade to a colorful area. ■

Freshly caught octopus for sale in the Central Market

Athens Metro

Athens remains one of the few European capitals not to have an extensive subway system. With its traffic and pollution problems, it is also the city most in need of one. For years its citizens and visitors have made do with a single line running north–south, but at last an east–west line has been added.

The two meet at Omonoia, but the showcase is stylish Syntagma Square. Antiquities found during tunneling are on display in the museum here. They represent a big problem in the building of the subway, as ancient sites which had to be excavated were uncovered. Even on the modern Metro, you are traveling through ancient Greece. ■

National
Archaeological
Museum

 50 D5

✉ Oktovriou 28/
Patission 44

☎ 821 7717

🕐 Closed Mon. before
12:30 p.m.

💲 $$

🚇 Metro: Omonoia

National Archaeological Museum

(Ethniko Archaiologiko Mouseio)

THIS COLLECTION OF THE BEST TREASURES FROM GREEK civilizations down the centuries forms the core of one of the world's great museums. If you do only two things in Athens, one should be to see the Parthenon and the other to visit this awesome collection of artifacts. To see it properly, plan to visit the museum twice, as there is too much to take in on one long visit. If time is limited, take a guided tour; these are available in several different languages by inquiring in the reception hall. Alternatively, follow the description below to see some of the highlights.

A slender-necked amphora from about 750 B.C. was discovered in Athens.

The museum is arranged in chronological order. The most impressive display, in **Room 4,** is from Mycenae, uncovered by archaeologist Heinrich Schliemann in 1874 (see pp. 112–13). The golden burial mask believed by Schliemann to be that of King Agamemnon (it in fact predated the Trojan War by 200–300 years) is here. It is an exquisite object, and surrounded by other rich finds from the royal tombs at Mycenae, including a stunning silver wine vase (*rhyton*) in the form of a bull's head, with horns of pure gold.

The majesty of some of the larger works is overpowering, none more so than in **Room 15** where a huge bronze figure of the sea god **Poseidon** is about to throw a trident (some believe it is not Poseidon but Zeus preparing to throw a thunderbolt). The expression on his face has enabled experts to date the statue to about 460–450 B.C.

Room 21 houses the more delicate but equally famous combination of two bronzes, known as the **"Jockey Boy."** The powerful horse and its tiny male rider may or

may not have been intended as one work, but the result is dramatic and full of movement. The figures were found, like the bronze of Poseidon, in the sea off Cape Artemision and date from the second century B.C.

Also, don't miss the **"Youth of Antikithera"** in **Room 28,** a 6.5-foot (2 m) high bronze statue of a nude young man that combines delicacy and power. Both lifelike and larger than life, it was found in the waters off the small island of Antikithera in 1900 and dates from the Hellenistic period.

There is something splendid to see in almost every room, so two visits are recommended if time allows. **Room 30,** the Hellenistic Sculpture Room, for example, has a rudely exuberant statue from the first century A.D., depicting the gods **Pan and Aphrodite.** He clearly has lascivious designs on the naked goddess, while she preserves her modesty with one hand and wields a shoe in defense in the other one. The same room also has the remnants of a colossal cult statue of Zeus, found in 1916, and some delicate plaques of dancing girls from the Theater of Dionysos (see pp. 56–57).

Downstairs in the museum, exhibit space is given over to temporary displays. They are almost always worth checking out, as there have been some impressive shows put on here in recent years. Nearby, at the foot of the main staircase, are two of the private collections that have been given to the museum: the Eleni Stathatou Jewelry Collection and the Karapanos Collection. The latter includes many artifacts from the site at Dodoni, near Ioanina in Epiros (see pp. 162–63), including lead tablets containing questions for the oracle there. The jewelry collection includes beautiful work in turquoise, silver, bronze, and glass, ranging in time from the Bronze Age to the Byzantine era.

Signs in the museum are generally good. Many exhibits are labeled in both Greek and English, although some of the smaller objects—and there are thousands of these—may be unlabeled or have information just in Greek. For that reason, to get the most from your visit it is worth buying one of the inexpensive guidebooks on sale in the reception hall.

Coin enthusiasts will want to see the **Numismatic Museum.** This was formerly housed in an annex of the National Archaeological Museum but was recently moved to separate premises, which are interesting in their own right. The 1878 mansion containing the collection was originally the home of Heinrich Schliemann, and so became known as the Palace of Troy. The museum's collection of 600,000 coins ranges from Ancient Greece through Roman and Byzantine periods right up to the present day. ■

Numismatic Museum
- ✉ Venizelou 12
- ☎ 364 3774
- ⏱ Closed Mon.
- $ $
- 🚇 Metro: Syntagma

Every line of the "Jockey Boy" statue suggests speed and movement.

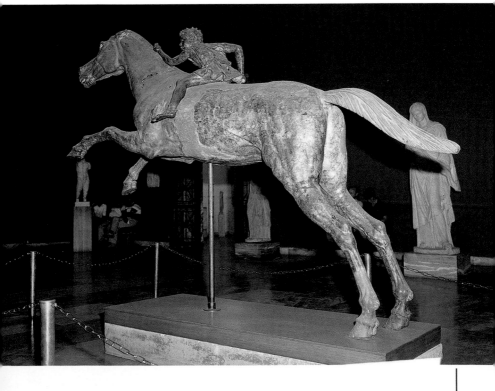

Left: The outstanding bronze from Artemision of Poseidon, in the act of throwing a weapon (see p. 78)

Eleni Stathatou Jewelry Collection (see pp. 78–79)

Access to second floor

Karapanos Collection (see p. 79)

Poseidon statue, Room 15

"Jockey Boy" statue, Room 21 (see pp. 78–79)

Golden Mask of Agamemnon (see p. 113) and Bull's Head rhyton (see p. 78), Room 4

Main entrance hall, with access to gift shop, café, and rest rooms

Entrance

Right: A stylized Assyrian bronze of horse and (female) rider offers a contrast to the fluid "Jockey Boy."

Second floor

First floor

Pottery

Temporary & other exhibits

Temporarily closed

Classical Sculpture

Hellenistic & Roman Sculpture

Mycenaen Art

Neolithic Art

Archaic Art

Non Exhibition

Courtyard, with access to gift shop and café

Youth of Antikithera statue, Room 28 (see p. 78)

Pireas

FOR MANY VISITORS, PIREAS IS ALL THAT THEY SEE OF Athens, as they fly into the airport then take a ferry straight to one of the islands. Yet Pireas has a cosmopolitan character and charm of its own, along with handsome public buildings, chaos, and traffic and noise—all you expect of a busy harbor. It has been a major port since about 500 B.C. and is still one of the largest in the Mediterranean.

Pireas

🅰 87 C2

Tourist information

✉ Diikitirio Building, Zea Marina, 185 04

☎ 452 2586 or 452 2591

Archaeological Museum

✉ Harilaou Trikoupi 31

☎ 451 8388

🕐 Closed Mon.

💲 $

Ⓜ Metro: Pireas

Naval Museum of Greece

✉ Akti Themistokleous

☎ 451 6822

🕐 Closed Mon.

💲 $

Ⓜ Metro: Pireas

At the southern end of the subway line connecting with central stations Monastiraki and Omonoia, Pireas is easy to reach from downtown Athens.

If you are looking for a ferry, make sure you know the departure point first, and allow yourself plenty of time to find it. The layout of Pireas can be confusing, because of the indentations made by the various harbors, and it is easy to become disoriented. Kentriko Limani is the main ferry port, with upscale shops and restaurants close by. Different harbors serve different parts of Greece, and some are a long way from each other and from the Metro station.

The bustle of life here was well illustrated in the 1959 movie *Never on a Sunday,* which starred Melina Mercouri as a local prostitute. This side of life is also described in some of the *rembetika* songs (see pp. 45–46), which originated here and can still be heard in the late-night clubs that flourish in the back streets, a world away from the tourist areas of central Athens.

Pireas has its cultural highlights too, with a small but rewarding archaeological museum, and a naval museum. The prize exhibits in the **Archaeological Museum** were all found in the harbors around here. In 1930 a collection of stone statues was discovered in a sunken ship used to transport the pieces from a Greek workshop to Italy. In 1939 the harbor also yielded up huge, magnificent

bronze statues of Artemis, Athena, and Apollo.

The **Naval Museum of Greece (Nautiko Mouseio Elladhas)** overlooks the Zea Marina Harbor and is easily recognized by the old submarine that stands at the entrance. Greece has an illustrious maritime history, and this collection of over 2,000 items covers a great deal of it, from the early days of the elegant triremes with their three levels of rowers, to the lone fisherman with his little caïque, and the vast luxury liners of shipping dynasties. The whole story is told in a rich mix of paintings, photographs, maps, flags, uniforms, artifacts, and fascinating scale models of ships and boats.

Part of the Naval Museum is made up of the remains of the so-called Long Walls, or Legs, barriers constructed between 493 and 456 B.C. as fortifications for the harbors, but largely destroyed in 86 B.C. The walls, which also connected Pireas with Athens, were begun by the Athenian statesman and soldier Themistocles (circa 523–468 B.C.), and were enhanced by Pericles in the Golden Age of Athens when Pireas was already a major port.

Pireas has a number of upscale restaurants, especially around the harbor of **Mikrolimano,** where luxurious yachts tie up beside fishing caïques. Fresh fish is the dish to have, but it won't be cheap. The harbor makes a great place for an alfresco lunch, and is especially popular on Sundays, or for a romantic evening meal, with a view of the bobbing yachts, the twinkling lights, and the blue Aegean Sea beyond. ∎

Greece's biggest port, Pireas has harbored boats since ancient times.

More places to visit near Athens

If you are based in the heart of Athens, you might like to explore farther afield. It might take some effort to get to these places by a combination of subway, bus, taxi, or ferry, but each is worth seeing.

ELEUSIS

Who has not heard of the Elysian Fields? Here they are, at what was one of the world's most sacred sites in the sixth century B.C. It is not very Elysian today—instead it's an industrial suburb, but it once marked one end of the Sacred Way that ran from here to the Parthenon. Only foundations of the site remain, but models and artifacts in the museum at the site help to create a picture of the unusual sect that worshiped at Eleusis. Little is known about the cult except that up to 30,000 people gathered here to attend its rituals, and the cult lasted for 2,000 years, having been established as early as 1500 B.C.

✉ Gioga/Iera 1 ☎ 554 6019 $ $$ 🚌 Bus: A16 or B16

KAISARIANI MONASTERY

Look southeast from downtown Athens and you will see the slopes of Mount Hymettus, about 3 miles (5 km) away. A bus or taxi ride brings you to the 11th-century monastery of Kaisariani. The main attractions here are the frescoes. Some of these date back as far as the 12th century, but most are from the 16th and 17th centuries.

The monastery is still inhabited and open to visitors. Forest fires have scarred the hills around Athens, but the landscape here is lush and green, thanks to the River Ilissos. The river once supplied Athens with fresh water, and the spring at its source was named after the emperor Hadrian. It is called the Imperial Spring, and the Greek word for imperial is *kaisariane*.

☎ 723 6619 $ $ 🚌 Bus: 234

KIFISSIA

The suburb of Kifissia is at the northern end of the Metro line, and well worth a day's exploration. It is a prosperous and fashionable area, with a slightly cooler climate even though it is only 906 feet (276 m) above sea level. The **Goulandris Natural History Museum** *(Levidou 13, tel 808 6405)* is worth exploring for its vast collection of Mediterranean plants, but Kifissia is also simply a pleasant area to stroll around and enjoy the parks and the grand old mansions.

Tourist Police ☎ 808 1464/808 1465
🚇 Metro Kifissia

PAIANIA

Beyond Kaisariani about 11 miles (18 km) east of Athens stands the village of Paiania. Known as the birthplace of Demosthenes (284–322 B.C.), the Athenian statesman who was said to be the greatest Greek orator of them all, its main attraction today is the unusual Vorres Museum: Ian Vorres is the name of the owner. He exhibits traditional Greek folk art alongside contemporary works in renovated buildings, with a delightful sculpture courtyard.

Also accessible by road from the village is the Koutouki Cave, with a guided tour through its strangely-shaped stalactites and stalagmites.

Vorres Museum ✉ Diadochou Konstatinou 1 ☎ 644 2520 🕐 Closed Aug. **Koutouki Cave** ☎ 644 2108 $ $$

SALAMINA

The Argo-Saronic islands (see pp. 220–25) are undoubtedly the most popular places for one-day trips from Athens, yet the largest of them is almost unknown outside Greece. It sits closest to Athens in the Bay of Salamis, and is probably neglected by visitors because of its very proximity to the city. Many Athenian commuters choose to live here, and although the main town and the port are fairly unattractive, Salamina has several small, quaint fishing villages, a 17th-century monastery, some beautiful old mansions, and a small beach resort at Selinia.

It was in this bay that the Battle of Salamis took place in 480 B.C., when a large Persian fleet was defeated by a smaller but speedier Greek fleet. The fast-moving Greek triremes were able to maneuver quickly among the bulkier Persian warships and inflict great damage.

🅰 87 B1 ⛴ Ferry from Pireas ■

The city's glories lie at the center of Athens, but a short distance out there are more treasures—isolated ruins and temples, beaches, Greek village life—accessible to anyone prepared to explore.

Around Athens

Sun-weathered shutters, Attica

Around Athens

MOST VISITORS TO ATHENS SEE ONLY THE DOWNTOWN AREA BEFORE moving on. Yet it is easy to get a fuller Greek experience simply by traveling a few miles to explore the areas immediately around the city. You will have to pass through the apparently endless, sometimes industrial, suburbs first, but the reward is the chance to have some classical sites all to yourself, particularly if traveling out of high season.

It can be unnerving to drive in central Athens since, despite attempts to cut vehicle numbers downtown, the volume of traffic is still high and signs are poor. If you wish to see Attica (the region around Athens), it is better to rent a car at the airport, on the eastern edge of the city, and head straight off from there. Many of the best attractions are easily reached by public transportation, and it is surprisingly inexpensive to rent a taxi by the day.

A short trip out to Akra Sounion, where there is one of the most gloriously located temples in Greece, is an absolute must. Many Athenians go out there to watch the sun set and enjoy a drink with a view out over the beautiful blue Aegean. The coast that runs from Pireas to Akra Sounion also has the closest beach resorts to Athens—not as peaceful and beautiful as beaches on the islands, but a reasonable escape from the

stresses of city life. Farther afield, places such as Marathon will spring to life when you realize you are standing where that historic battle took place (see p. 92). And simply wandering around places like Marathon and Vravron gives you a very different perspective from the hustle and bustle of the capital. ■

Area of map detail

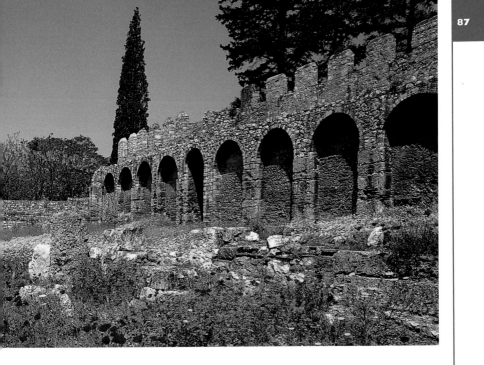

Wildflowers bring color to the
UNESCO-listed monastery ruins at
Dafni, on the outskirts of the city.

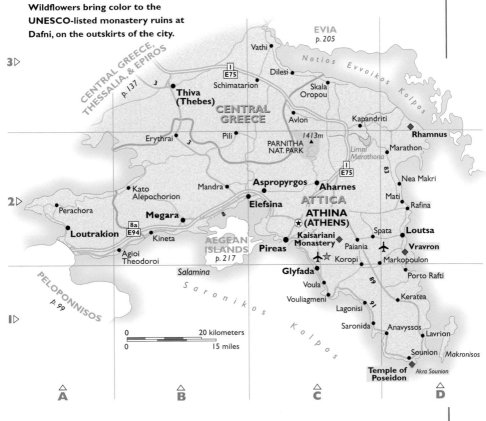

EVIA
p. 205

Vathi

Dilesi

Skala
Oropou

E75

Schimatarion

Thiva
(Thebes)

CENTRAL
GREECE

Avlon

Kapandriti

CENTRAL GREECE,
THESSALIA, & EPIROS

p. 137

3

Notios Evvoikos Kolpos

Rhamnus

Erythrai

Pili

PARNITHA
NAT. PARK

1413m

*Limni
Marathona*

Marathon

Kato
Alepochorion

Mandra

Aspropyrgos

Aharnes

E75

83

Nea Makri

Perachora

Elefsina

ATTICA

Mati

Rafina

Megara

ATHINA
(ATHENS)

Spata

Loutsa

8a
E94

Kineta

Kaisariani
Monastery

Paiania

Vravron

Loutrakion

AEGEAN
ISLANDS
p. 217

Pireas

Koropi

Markopoulon

Agioi
Theodoroi

Salamina

Glyfada

89

Porto Rafti

PELOPONNISOS

p. 99

Saronikos

Voula

Vouliagmeni

Keratea

Lagonisi

91

Saronida

Anavyssos

Lavrion

Kolpos

Sounion

Makronisos

Temple of
Poseidon

Akra Sounion

0   20 kilometers
0   15 miles

A   B   C   D

Akra Sounion

🗺 87 D1

Temple of Poseidon

🗺 87 D1
☎ 0292 39363
🕐 Closed Mon.
💲 $

Akra Sounion & the east coast

ATHENS IS BLESSED WITH BEACHES ON ITS DOORSTEP AND beautiful islands just a short boat ride away from Pireas. Visitors should do what the Greeks do and head for the beach playgrounds in the suburbs as summer temperature soar. You'll be in good company as everybody wants to cool off, and it reveals a different side to the capital more famous for its classical sites.

For a day out from the city, the first major resort to the east, less than 30 minutes from downtown Athens, is **Glyfada,** which merges with **Voula** to the south.

While neither is the peaceful beach resort you might hope for, if you are traveling with children and they want a day on the beach, this strip of the Apollo Coast will provide them with sea, sand, and entertainment, and parents can enjoy a seafood lunch at a waterfront restaurant. Flight noise from the airport can be a drawback.

As you head south along the coast and farther from Athens, the resorts are quieter and more spread out. Whether you travel along here by bus or in a rented car, there is no mistaking the magnificent spectacle of the temple that stands proud on the 200-foot (60 m) headland of Akra Sounion.

The **Temple of Poseidon** on the headland was built in 444 B.C. out of gray marble mined just a few miles away in the quarries at Agrileza. Of the original 34 columns, 15 are still standing to their full height, one of them bearing the initials of the British Romantic poet, Lord Byron (see p. 32). Byron visited the site in 1810 and carved his signature on the column nearest the entrance; unfortunately you won't be able to get close enough to see. The remains of the temple are now roped off to prevent further damage by the thousands of people who come here every year.

The temple stands on the remains of an even older building, thought to have dated back to 490 B.C. The present temple is dedicated to the god of the sea, Poseidon, and there could be no more fitting setting for it than this cape overlooking the Aegean Sea. The temple may have been designed by the same (unknown) architect responsible for the elegant Temple of Hephaistos in the Agora site in Athens (see p. 59).

Sounion is famous for its impressive sunsets, which give breathtaking vivid blood-red and fiery orange colored skies, the stuff of many a postcard. There is a café here, so you can enjoy the sunset in comfort. Below the promontory is a beach with accommodations, if you choose to stay. Your best chance for avoiding the crowds in this lovely spot is to be here first thing in the morning.

The largest island near the cape is Kea, one of the smaller Cycladic islands and the closest of that group to Athens. Look west toward the setting sun to see the island of Egina, in the Argo-Saronic group (see pp. 220–25). Beyond it you should be able to see the east coast of the Peloponnese.

Heading north from Cape Sounion up the east coast of Attica brings you to **Lavrion.** This small town may not look prosperous today, but without its existence there would be no Athens as we now know it. Huge silver mines here helped to finance the building of Periclean Athens; they also provided the wealth that paid for the powerful Athenian navy that defeated the Persians and established Greece as one of the great maritime nations. The mines closed in the 19th century, and a small mineralogical museum in Lavrion tells their story.

Farther up the coast is the more attractive—and today more prosperous—resort of **Porto Rafti.** Its lively fishing harbor, good restaurants, and bars make

The Temple of Poseidon promises spectacular sunset views.

Lavrion
87 D1

Porto Rafti
87 D1

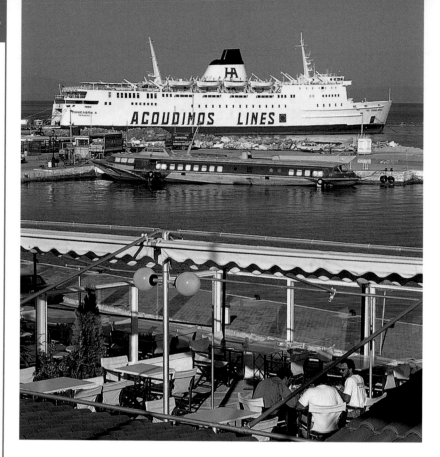

Rafina is the main harbor for both ferries and fast hydrofoils to the islands.

it a popular weekend retreat for Athenians.

Just off the coast in the harbor—one of the finest in Greece—is the island that gives the port its name: Rafti. There is a huge marble statue of a seated woman here, made in Roman times and used over the years as a safety beacon for ships. It is known as "the Tailor" (*raftis* in Greek) because it is thought that the statue's hands (one arm is now missing) once held a pair of scissors. It is also possible that the missing arm once held either bunches of fruit or sheaves of wheat, as a symbol of fertility. It was from here that the first fruits from the mainland were sent every year to the sacred island of Dilos (see p. 251).

Markopoulon
🗺 87 D2

Koropi
🗺 87 C2

If you head inland to **Markopoulon** instead of taking the coastal road to Vravron (see p. 96), you will find yourself in a busy market town that prospers thanks to its fertile setting and proximity to Athens. Vineyards spread out around the town. Several tavernas provide an authentic Greek lunch (you'll find no tourist menus here), and plenty of bakeries sell the local bread, for which Markopoulon is widely known. There are also some small chapels that you can visit. Ring the bell for admission or ask the first person you see how to find the key-holder.

A diversion slightly farther west takes you to **Koropi,** which is even bigger and also noted for its extensive wine production. Koropi is particularly famous for its production of retsina, the unique white wine of Greece that is flavored with pine resin. The resin was originally introduced into the winemaking process in ancient times as much for its preservative qualities as its flavor. On the southeast outskirts of the town is the church of the Metamorphosis Sotiras, which dates back to the tenth century and is therefore one of the oldest churches in Attica.

RAFINA
The port of Rafina, on the eastern coast of Attica, about a 40-minute bus ride from central Athens, is likely to increase in size and importance over the next few years. A new international airport is being built east of the city, which will mean that many tourists will find it more convenient to head for Rafina, rather than Pireas, the traditional gateway to the Greek islands. Rafina already serves the islands of Evia and the northeast Aegean, and many more islands in both the Cyclades and Dodecanese groups.

The heart of the town is the old fishing harbor, which remains wonderfully picturesque but has been enhanced by the addition of many excellent seafood restaurants, most with rooftop terraces overlooking the boats bobbing in the water below. Here you will find Athenians escaping the city's pace, especially on weekends, and demanding the best fresh fish—it can get very crowded down here on weekends.

Around the harbor you will also find the main ferry departure points; away from the city center, coastal development serves as a reminder that Rafina is a popular resort in its own right. There is no shortage of affordable hotels, places to swim, and watersport facilities. Several small beaches lie either side of the resort, and the coast is dotted with vacation villas for Athenian residents. Beyond beaches, little remains from the old settlements that have always existed here.

Inland from the harbor and slightly uphill is the large main square, where you can escape the noise of the harbor and feel you are in any Greek town, with children playing while grandmothers watch them. How long Rafina will retain its charms once the new airport is in full swing remains to be seen.

To the north of Rafina is another resort, **Mati,** slightly quieter and without the bustle of busy ferries.

From the slopes behind Mati a fabulous view takes in the Bay of Marathon. Nearby is a good bathing beach, Agios Andreas. If you are taking a ferry to or from Rafina, where hotels can be fully reserved well ahead, it is worth thinking about staying at Mati and taking a taxi to or from Rafina. ∎

Rafina
🄰 87 D2

Mati
🄰 87 D2

There's no delay in distributing the catch of the day in Rafina's old harbor.

Marathon

THE WORD "MARATHON" HAS PASSED INTO THE LANGUAGE of the world, and while the approximate story of how a Greek village came to give its name to a long endurance race is well known, the details of that story may be less familiar.

It was a great honor for the 11 Plataian casualties to be buried in the mound at Marathon. Men who fell in battle were normally buried by their families.

In 490 B.C. the Athenians were under attack and heavily outnumbered by the Persian army. No exact figures are available, but it is estimated that as many as 25,000 Persian troops were fighting 10,000 Athenians. The Athenians had their backs not to the wall but to the pass of Thermopylae in the mountains on the east side of Athens, defending it from the enemy who had been thus far victorious in their progress through Greece. Persian warships brought their army ashore here, and they thundered onto the Plain of Marathon and toward the outnumbered Greeks.

The people in Athens knew that their fate was being decided by soldiers on the plains of Attica, and waited anxiously for news of the battle. The Athenians duly fought for their lives and defeated the Persian armies. The heroic nature of the victory is indicated by the fact that some 6,400 Persians are thought to have been killed, while the Athenians lost only 192 men.

News of the remarkable victory was carried back to Athens by one of the soldiers, Phedippides, who ran all the way from Marathon to the Acropolis in his full armor. After relaying the information he promptly died on the spot from his exertions.

The present-day marathon race of 26 miles 385 yards (42.195 km) commemorates that brave feat, and each October the Athens Open International Marathon is run over the probable route the soldier took—minus the full armor—and ends in the Panathenaic Stadium.

What we know of the Battle of Marathon comes from the Greek historian Herodotus, who recorded the events some 50 years after they occurred. The Athenian dead were buried under a simple earthen mound only 33 feet (10 m) high but 590 feet (180 m) in circumference. Its very simplicity makes it all the more striking. The **burial mound** is about 2.5 miles (4 km) south of the modern town of Marathon, down a road that is off to the right if you are heading toward Marathon itself. The site was originally marked by a gravestone that showed a soldier fallen in battle. This can now be seen in the National Archaeological Museum in Athens (see pp. 78–79), with a copy on display at the site.

If you continue toward Marathon, a left turn takes you to the **Archaeological Museum.** Well worth seeing, the small collection displays items found on the field of battle and on the estate of the wealthy arts patron Herodes

Marathon

🗺 87 D2

Archaeological Museum

☎ 0294 55155

🕐 Closed Mon.

💲 $

Atticus (A.D. 101–177), who came from this area. The finds include statues, urns, gravestones, an unusual bronze mirror, and part of the memorial erected by the Greeks at the time to celebrate the victory at Marathon. There are also vases from the Mound of the Plataians.

Behind the museum you can climb to the **Mound of the Plataians,** discovered in 1970. Allies of the Athenians, the Plataians joined in the Battle of Marathon. They lost 11 of their own soldiers, including a 10-year-old boy. The dead Plataians are buried here in this mound.

Marathon itself is a fairly ordinary small town, worth a stop if you need to buy provisions but otherwise unremarkable.

A short drive to the west of Road No. 83 takes you past the impressive **Lake Marathon.** The reservoir owes its existence to a marble dam that was built in 1925–1931 to trap the waters coming down from the Mount Parnitha range; until the 1950s it was the main water supply for all of Athens.

If your interest in the historical significance of this place has drawn you here, you can round off your visit by heading for some pleasant small beaches along the coast, the best being at Skhinias. If you merely want to cool off with a dip in the Aegean, you can walk from the burial mound to the coast and find some small stretches of beach to relax on. ■

The athletic grace of long-distance runners is captured on a vase dating from 470 B.C. Much of what we know of sport in ancient Greece comes from such vivid records.

Drive: Exploring Attica

The region of Attica that surrounds Athens offers visitors a picture of Greece in miniature. It has high hills, beach resorts, small villages, old churches, and a number of interesting classical sites.

Taking in the best of Attica's attractions, this route begins at the airport and leads you safely away from Athens's chaotic traffic. It winds along the coast and finishes at Halkida, the gateway to Evia; anyone who wishes to return to Athens could do so at Marathon, which would shorten the route and the time slightly.

The current **Athens airport** has two terminals, the west one for Olympic Airways flights and the east one for other airlines. If you're leaving from the east terminal, turn right and head east along Vouliamegni toward Akra Sounion. After a few miles the road joins the main Highway 91. Bear right onto this road and follow the signs. From the west terminal, turn right onto the highway, then take the first U-turn and head east along the coast road to Akra Sounion.

Vouliagmegni ❶, just south of the suburban sprawl of Athens, is a popular beach resort and escape from the city. This scenic route is slower than if you use the main highway, but it seems a shame to miss driving along the coast, with the Aegean Sea on your right-hand side, a welcome sight after either a long flight or a few days in Athens. Soon the impressive sight of the ruined **Temple of Poseidon ❷** (see pp. 88–89) comes into view, on top of Akra Sounion and visible from miles away. It takes less than an hour to drive from the airport all the way to the temple.

Having visited the cape, return to Highway 91 and turn right. Almost immediately, the road changes its number to 89. It heads north now, sticking to the Attica coast before veering inland through the fertile interior toward the small town of **Markopoulon ❸** (see p. 90). Here you can stretch your legs and stock up on provisions, if you like.

On leaving Markopoulon, retrace your route to Highway 89 and turn left. Almost immediately, turn right onto Highway 85, which brings you—after about 12.5 miles

(20 km) and another pleasant section of coastal driving—to the port and resort of **Rafina ❹** (see pp. 92–93). If you follow the signs for "Ferries" you should be able to find somewhere to park near the harbor, where you can enjoy a lunch or dinner in one of the many waterside restaurants.

Return to Highway 85 and continue north to the smaller resort of Nea Makri, passing vacation homes and villas along the way. At Nea Makri, join Highway 83 and turn right toward **Marathon** (see p. 92). Watch for the sign after about 2 miles (3 km) for the **burial mound ❺** (Tymfos Marathona). A few miles after that is the **Archaeological Museum.**

From the town of Marathon, continue on the winding Highway 83, until you reach the village of Agios Stefanos. Here a right turn will take you to the main Athens–Thessaloniki highway, which is known as Highway 1 but also, confusingly, in certain places as the E75.

Turn right onto the main road and, after about 25 miles (40 km), look for a right turn marked for Evia and **Halkida ❻** (see pp. 208–209), the main town and entrance point for the island of Evia, reached across a bridge from the mainland. Alternatively, when you join Highway 1 you can turn left, which returns you to central Athens. ∎

Ⓜ See area map p. 87

▶ Athens airport

⟳ 120 miles (190 km)

⏱ 3 hours

▶ Halkida

NOT TO BE MISSED

- Akra Sounion
- Markopoulon
- Marathon burial mound & Archaeological Museum
- Rafina

6 Halkida (Chalkis)

Thiva (Thebes)

1/E75

Waiting for sunset, Akra Sounion

Limni Marathona
Kaledzi

Parnitha
1413m

83

Marathon
Archaeological Museum

5 Tymfos Marathona

Agios Stefanos

83

Nea Makri

**Left: Memorial to the
fallen, Marathon**

1/E75

1109m
Pendeli

Korinthos
(Corinth)

Mati

8A

ATHINA
(ATHENS)

Rafina

4

Spata

Loutsa

1026m
Imitos

Peania

Pireas

85

START

SALAMINA

Koropi

3

Glifada

Markopoulon

Voula

Vouliagmeni

1

Keratea

Varkiza

Lagonisi

89

The busy harbor, Rafina

Saronida

91

Thoriko

Anavyssos

Lavrion

Kato
Sounion

Saronikos Kolpos

Akra Sounion
2 Temple
of Poseidon

0   20 kilometers
0   10 miles

Rhamnus & Vravron

THE CLASSICAL SITE OF ANCIENT RHAMNUS IS ONE OF the most remote and, for this reason, also one of the most appealing in Attica. While not as isolated, Vravron (also known as Brauron) is well worth allowing time to explore thoroughly. Lying about 5 miles (8 km) northeast of Markopoulon, it incorporates a sizable archaeological site and an interesting museum, as well as a modern village. The site and museum are close to each other, and the village is only a few hundred yards away if you want to walk.

Rhamnus
- 87 D3
- ☎ 0294 93477
- 🕐 Closed Mon.
- 💲 $

RHAMNUS

You will need a rental car or a taxi to get you to Rhamnus, since there are only a few buses a day from Athens to the nearest village, Kato Souli, and from there it is a long walk to the site.

Once at the site, however, you will be glad you made the journey and will possibly even have the place to yourself. You might wonder why it is kept open, with so few visitors, but archaeologists have been working here since 1975 and only a small part of the area is open to everyone. It is hoped that at some time in the near future, when the archaeological work is complete, more of the site will be opened up to the public and access improved.

Largely overgrown by nature in an appealing way, the remains at Rhamnus are scattered over a hillside above the sea. Wandering through the ruins you are accompanied by butterflies and lizards that scuttle into cracks in the stones. The name of the site comes from a prickly shrub that grows in this area, called *ramnos* in Greek.

There is in fact very little to see, so it helps to know something about the background to the site in order to appreciate it for more than just its tranquility and as an idyllic picnic spot. It is known that Nemesis, the Greek goddess responsible for dispensing good or bad luck to us mortals on earth, was worshipped here. (The gods always eventually got their revenge on those who had broken the law or had offended them, hence the modern expression "to meet your nemesis.")

Some of the Persian forces are said to have landed here before their defeat at Marathon, a defeat sometimes blamed on their theft of a marble block from the **Temple of Nemesis,** on which they intended to commemorate their victory over the Athenians. What remains today are mainly foundations, but the sixth-century B.C. Temple of Nemesis can be clearly identified.

VRAVRON

Unusually, Vravron is located at the foot of a small hill rather than on top of one. On the crown of the hill is a pretty little Byzantine chapel dedicated to St. George—**Agios Georgios.** The village and site are in a marshy valley surrounded by agricultural land. It is an attractive area with abundant wildlife. The people are welcoming, as they are not yet overrun by visitors.

The story of this site is a fascinating one. Its main focus is the mysterious **Sanctuary of Artemis,** of which only the foundations remain today. Artemis is the Greek equivalent of the Roman goddess Diana, the

Part of the colonnaded stoa at Vravron, famous for its quiet setting daughter of Zeus and the twin sister of Apollo. She was the moon goddess, as well as the goddess of childbirth and of the harvest, of hunting and of wildlife, especially bears. She was worshipped here at Vravron, where every four years a festival would take place that involved mysterious rituals in which young girls would dress as bears and dance. Aristophanes refers to the dance in *Lysistrata*, but as with many of these ancient Greek cults, such as the one that centered on Eleusis (see p. 84), we still do not know exactly what took place or why.

In his play *Iphigenia at Tauris*, Euripedes (see p. 106) relates events at Vravron. Iphigenia, the daughter of Agamemnon and Clytemnestra, was held responsible for a strong wind that prevented the Greek ships from sailing to Troy prior to the Trojan Wars. The wind was sent in retribution for the killing of one of the wild animals that Artemis protected, probably a bear. Agamemnon agreed to the sacrifice of his daughter on the altar of Artemis at Vravron so that the ships could set sail.

According to Euripedes, the goddess spared Iphigenia because she would not allow her altar to be stained by human blood, and substituted a deer for the sacrifice instead. Iphigenia went on to found the sanctuary here, dedicated to Artemis.

Vravron

🔺 87 D2
☎ 0299 27020
🕐 Closed Mon.
💲 $

**Archaeological
Museum**

☎ 0299 27020

🕐 Closed Mon.

💲 $

In other versions of the story, Iphigenia was sacrificed. Her alleged grave was discovered here, south of the stoa (a colonnaded building) and next to the remains of the building known as the **Sacred House,** where the priestesses of the Artemis cult stayed during the festivals.

By the fourth century B.C., the area here flooded, and the communities that had arisen all disappeared. The village of Vravron eventually reestablished itself, but it was not until 1946 that work began on uncovering the site of ancient Vravron, work that continued until 1963.

These excavations uncovered the remains of a temple from the fifth century B.C. as well. Located

you will see anywhere in the world. The structure dates back to the fifth-century B.C. Other evidence from the site points to the existence here of stables, a gymnasium, and other buildings, but these have not yet been properly uncovered.

The nearby **Archaeological Museum** displays finds from the site and elsewhere, and is intriguing despite its comparatively small size. It includes a scale model of the temple that gives a vivid impression of how the site must have looked in its prime; it's worth the effort to see.

Among the more important exhibits is a decorated stirrup jar from about 1200–1000 B.C. that was found in the late-Mycenean cemetery at Perati. A beautifully

Her companion deer clearly identifies the goddess Artemis on this carved relief.

next to the temple is a **stoa,** which may be even older. Inscriptions discovered within the structure describe it as "the Parthenon of the Bears." Other finds made there, such as stone couches, indicate that some of the rooms in the building were utilized as dining rooms and dormitories.

Next to the stoa are the remains of one of the oldest stone bridges

detailed statue that has been dated to the fourth century B.C. depicts a young girl clutching a rabbit. Several other statues and busts date from the same period, and there is a fascinating collection of pottery and jewelry. A votive relief of Artemis, from Vravron, also dates from the fourth century B.C. It shows the goddess seated, welcoming pilgrims of all ages. ∎

The shape of the Peloponnese is imprinted on people's minds as the shape of Greece, with its three "fingers" of land projecting into the Mediterranean and separated from the rest of Greece by the Corinth Canal.

Peloponnese

Olives are a Greek staple.

The 16th-century Bourtzi tower marks the entrance to Methoni's harbor.

Peloponnese

MANY VISITORS CHOOSE TO RETURN AGAIN AND AGAIN TO THE MASSIVE peninsula of the Peloponnese (Peloponnisos), and it is an area with enough variety to invite weeks or even months of exploration. The landscape is impressively wooded and mountainous, and around its edges are wonderful beaches, as fine as any on the Greek islands. It has some of the most important archaeological sites in the world—Epidavros, Mycenae, and Olympia to name only the best known. There are also cosmopolitan old towns such as the former Greek capital, Nafplio, as well as unspoiled mountain villages where you might be the only visitor.

The name goes back into ancient history, as this is the "island of Pelops." Pelops was the son of Tantalus, one of the sons of Zeus. When the gods came to dine at Tantalus's home, he killed his son and boiled him in a cauldron to feed to them—he wanted to see if the gods truly were omniscient. They were, and they restored Pelops to life, punishing Tantalus by leaving him hanging from a tree, with a raging thirst and hunger. Every time he tried to drink or eat, the water and food

moved away from him, although both were "tantalizingly" close.

The Peloponnese has played a central role in more recent history, too. This was the heartland of the War of Independence in the 19th century, where the Greek flag was first raised in defiance of the Turks, and where the capital was based before it was moved to Athens.

It is not quite an island—a narrow isthmus, just 3.5 miles (6 km) wide, joins the Peloponnese to the mainland, yet in resorts

CENTRAL GREECE, THESSALIA, & EPIROS
p. 137

AROUND ATHENS p. 85

SARONIC ISLANDS p. 220

Rion
Egio
Diakopton
PATRA
1926m
Panachaikon
Kato Achaia
Paralia
Nea Manolas
Dervenion
Kalavryta
Kiaton
Corinth Canal
2224m
2341m
Erymanthos
Aroania
Kyllini
2376m
Lechaina
Kastanea
Korinthos
Korinthos (Corinth)
Andravida
Labeia
Akrokorinthos
Sofikon
Kyllini
Gastouni
Dafni
Nemea
Amaliada
Mykinai (Mycenae)
PELOPONNISOS
Olympia
Levidion
Argos
Tiryns
Epidavros
Akra Katakolon
Lagkadia
74
1980m
Lygourion
Pirgos
Nafplio
Tolo
Andritsaina
Karitaina
Tripoli
Kranidion
Ermioni
Galatas
Kyparissiakos Kolpos
Vasses
Astros
Portochelion
Figaleia
Megalopolis
Argolikos Kolpos
Spetses
Idra
E55
1935m
Kyparissia
Messene
Meligalas
Sparti (Sparta)
Leonidion
Filiatra
Mavromati
Gargalianoi
Kyparission
Messini
Chora
Kalamata
Mystras
Gerakion
Nestor's Palace
2404m
Sfaktiria
Kardamyli
Pilos
Skala
Methoni
Stoupa
Sapientza
Koroni
Molaoi
Schiza
Kelefa
Githio
Akra Akritas
Areopolis
Boza
Monemvasia
Spilia Dirou
Lakonikos Kolpos
Elika
Mezapos
Kotronas
Elika
Neapolis
Kita
Vatheia
Elafonisos
Gerolimin
Akra Maleas
Akra Tenaro (Cape Matapan)
Kithira
Karavas
Agia Pelagia
Kithira

0   50 kilometers
0   30 miles

Kyparissiakos Kolpos

Messiniakos Kolpos

Taygetos Oros

Parnon Oros

Argolis

Alfeios

E65
E55
39/E961
E55/E65
Mani

4▷
3▷
2▷
1▷

△A   △B   △C   △D

such as Koroni and Methoni, with their busy tavernas and long, sandy beaches, you could believe yourself on an Aegean island. In the interior, however, the older traditions of mainland Greece linger, with a mountain scenery that appeals to walkers and nature lovers.

Historians will never want to leave. Aside from the famous sites already mentioned, there are lesser-known but equally exciting treasures to discover, such as the Byzantine ruins of Mystras coiled around a hillside, and the rock at Monemvasia, which has an entire village hidden from the mainland. Allow plenty of time to explore the Peloponnese. ■

Athens

Area of map detail

Corinth

THE CORINTH (KORINTHOS) CANAL IS ONE OF THE GREAT sights of Greece. With luck, you might be there when a ship is being steered between the narrow, sheer walls, which stretch away in the distance to link the Gulf of Corinth with the Aegean Sea.

Emperor Nero (A.D. 37–68) first mooted the idea of cutting a canal through the narrow isthmus to enable ships to sail from Italy into the Aegean without having to go around the Peloponnese. He performed the first symbolic excavation in person, using a silver shovel, but the task was never completed. Ships would continue to sail up the Gulf of Corinth, then unload their cargoes and have them carried down the 3.5-mile (6 km) road to a ship waiting on the far side, rather than risk the stormy circuit.

It was not until 1893, after a total of 12 years' work, that the 75-foot (23 m) wide **Corinthos Canal** was finally cut through, enabling boats to sail directly to Pireas. The canal is still used, although less these days, as super-tankers cannot squeeze through.

A few miles beyond the canal is **modern Corinth (Korinthos)** which detains few visitors except as a convenient refueling stop. It is mainly an agricultural service town, although it is interesting to note that it is a center for the Greek currant industry; the word "currant" actually derives from Corinth.

The main attraction here is the site of **ancient Corinth,** which perches on a hill 1,854 feet (565 m) high, 4 miles (7 km) away to the southwest, sandwiched between the main roads to Patras and Nafplio.

Ancient Corinth comes to life as you walk around the well-preserved remains of its center, dominated by a fifth-century B.C. Temple of Apollo. With its massive Doric columns, this was one of the buildings that the Romans left when they redeveloped the city as their provincial capital in 44 B.C.

The city was once home to 300,000 citizens and 460,000 more people who were slaves—about the population size of modern Dallas. The smaller buildings are the ones that speak of the history: the remnants of shops, houses, and administrative buildings. The **Peirene Fountain** was a gift from Herodes Atticus, the wealthy Athenian, patron and friend of the Romans, and the spring beneath it still supplies water to the modern town of Corinth.

The **Archaeological Museum** on the site has a good display of remains found there. Some lovely mosaics, mostly dating from the second-century A.D. Roman period, are a good indication of the city's wealth at that time. Domestic vases, pottery, and jewelry give the collections a more human scale.

Overlooking the lower city from the hilltop 2.5 miles (4 km) away was **Akrokorinthos,** or Upper Corinth. Its walls and spectacular views are the chief reasons to visit. When you see the position the city commands, you realize its immense strategic importance and why it has been refortified by every wave of invaders, notably the Venetians, the Franks, and the Turks. The walls run for about 1.25 miles (2 km) around a 60-acre (24 ha) site, where you can find the remains of chapels, mosques, houses, fortifications, and the still working Turkish Fountain of Hatzi Mustafa. ∎

Corinth
* 101 C4

Ancient Corinth & Archaeological Museum
* 101 C3
☎ 0741 31207
$ $$

Akrokorinthos
* 101 C3

Until the 13th century, smaller ships were hauled on rollers between the Gulf of Corinth and the Aegean Sea. Now the canal makes that journey much easier.

Epidavros

THE ANCIENT THEATER AT EPIDAVROS (OR EPIDAURUS) IS one of the most wonderful sites in all of Greece. Renowned for its perfect acoustics, the theater is still used for modern performances during the Athens Summer Festival. Few people can resist testing the acoustics on their friends at the back of the theater, so be prepared to make your speech!

Epidavros

101 D3

0753 22009

Museum closed Mon.

$$

Because much of Epidavros appears overgrown, many visitors do not take the trouble to explore it, leaving after a quick visit to the theater. Yet there are signs leading you to the various remains, and if you arm yourself with a map, and can pay a prior visit to the museum, you'll thoroughly enjoy your exploration.

The **theater** was built during the fourth century B.C., and has 55 rows of seats able to hold 14,000 people. The stage is 65 feet (20 m) in diameter. It is hard to believe that the theater lay buried and undiscovered until modern excavations started here in the late 19th century. It was finally restored in 1954, and it is worth noting that the first 34 rows of the auditorium are all original. Audiences look out across the site of Ancient Epidavros to the mountains beyond. If you are fortunate enough to have a chance to see a performance here, don't hesitate to take it.

AROUND THE SITE

There is more to Epidavros than the theater, which was not built purely for aesthetic reasons or to celebrate the art of drama. The site was dedicated to the god of healing, Asklepios, the son of Apollo. He learned his skills from the centaur, Charon, and so gifted was Asklepios at healing that he was thought to have the ability to bring people back from the dead. But they were proven wrong when he was killed himself by a thunderbolt from

Zeus, who feared that Asklepios was becoming too powerful.

There was a **temple** at Epidavros dedicated to Asklepios, which contained a statue of the god made out of gold and ivory. While little of the temple is visible today, Epidavros is undergoing long-term excavation work and may eventually be revealed as an even more important site than it is already known to be.

People brought their health problems to Epidavros, where medical practitioners were based, and the **museum** on the site contains examples of the medical instruments used at the time. Drama played a part as a kind of catharsis (purging) in some of the healing processes recommended in those days. The museum also contains records of cures alleged to have taken place here, as well as more conventional

Craftsmen continue to renovate and restore the site.

vases and statuary recovered during the excavations.

There are also the remains of guesthouses, a bath, and a gymnasium, showing that physical exercise was as important in some cures at that time as it is today. The Greeks were firm believers in a healthy mind in a healthy body. This small nation gave the world not only the greatest philosophers but also the Olympic Games and the Father of Medicine, Hippocrates.

Another important building on the site is the circular **tholos,** designed by the same architect, Polykleitos, who was responsible for the theater. The purpose of this building is not certain. It may have housed the sacred serpents used in some rites, or may even have been a place where some of those rites were carried out. One theory suggests that it worked as shock

therapy for the mentally ill, who were made to crawl through the concentric passages inside, until they found themselves in the central area in pitch darkness, surrounded by snakes—treatment guaranteed to produce a shock if not a cure!

Near the tholos and about 400 yards (365 m) northwest of the theater are the remains of the fifth-century B.C. **stadium;** some of the seating and the starting and finishing lines for races are visible. It would have been used during the major festival in honor of Asklepios, held every four years. ■

The back row is about 74 feet (23 m) high off the ground.

Side gates, or paradoi, were the stage entrances.

The theater's main stage, or orchestra, had an altar at its center.

The reception hall, or skene, provided additional staging for the actors.

A promenade divided the upper and lower seating levels.

36 sets of steps gave access to the tiers of seats.

Greek drama

Ancient Greece was the birthplace of modern drama. The fifth century B.C., known as the Golden Age of Pericles (inspired by the Athenian statesman Pericles), was a time when the arts, architecture, and politics all flourished in Athens, with the dramatic arts high on the agenda.

The very word "drama" derives from the Greek verb for "to do," and the dramatic form developed in the sixth century B.C. from an acting out of stories or songs. It is thought that drama derived from a choral tradition, when choirs would sing hymns in honor of the gods—but hymns that included some kind of narrative or story. Somehow a choral leader named Thespis (hence, "thespian") stepped out from the chorus and began to make the hymns more dramatic and active.

The chorus remained an essential part of early Greek plays. They were a group of observers who interpreted and commented on the action as if the audience could not understand it for themselves. The plays were written in verse, and alternated the performance of scenes with choral interjections. Gradually, as the art developed and the possibilities of drama were explored, the chorus became less important.

The works of many of the playwrights from those early days are still performed all around the world—and during the summer season in an original setting at the magnificent old theater at Epidavros (see pp. 104–105), as well as in Athens at the Herodes Atticus Theater (see p. 56).

Three writers dominated the developing drama of tragedy: Aeschylus, Sophocles, and Euripides. Aeschylus (ca 525–456 B.C.) introduced a dramatic feature that might seem simple now but was revolutionary at the time: a second character on the stage. Until then all plays had been monologues, the telling of tales in the Homeric tradition. Now poetry and drama began to mingle. Aeschylus drew on his experiences as an Athenian soldier (he fought at the Battle of Marathon in 490 B.C., for example) in plays such as *The Persians* and *Seven Against Thebes*. The best-known of his seven works that have come down to us are *Prometheus Bound* (the only surviving part of an original trilogy of plays) and the *Oresteia,* a complete trilogy about the doomed family of Agamemnon.

One of Aeschylus's great rivals was Sophocles (ca 496–405 B.C.), another Athenian tragedian. He introduced a third character into his dramas and started to play down the commentary role of the chorus. Sophocles wanted to let the action speak for itself. The greatest of his seven major surviving works is undoubtedly *Oedipus, the King,* a masterwork from any age of drama, let alone from an art form still in its infancy.

The third towering figure of those days is Euripides (ca 480–406 B.C.), who devised much more intricate plots and allowed his characters to speak a more natural dialogue. The technique brought him much criticism at the time, but it was a breakthrough in the development of drama. His more famous works include *Medea, Electra,* and *The Bacchae,* all of which are still performed today. Euripides was an early example of an artist whose works became even more popular after his death than when he was alive.

Many humorous and satirical plays were being written at this time as well. Another Athenian, Aristophanes (ca 450–385 B.C.), was the outstanding playwright in this genre. Humor usually has the shortest of shelf lives, but the plays of Aristophanes, including *The Birds* and *The Frogs* (in which he spoofs his fellow dramatist Euripides), are still per-formed all over the world. Aristophanes's most famous comedy, with a theme that has been borrowed down the ages, is *Lysistrata,* in which the women refuse to make love to their men until the men agree to stop making war.

The dramatic art was treated as seriously in historic times as it is today, and the first work of literary criticism, *Poetics,* was written by Aristotle in the fourth century B.C. ∎

Micaela Esdra in Euripides's The Bacchae. Punished by Dionysos for denying his divinity, Agave unknowingly kills her son.

Nafplio, Tiryns, & Argos

Nafplio

🅰 101 C3
Visitor information
✉ Tourist Police
☎ 0752 28131

Palamidi Fortress
☎ 0752 28036
💲 $

NAFPLIO IS THE MOST DELIGHTFUL TOWN IN ALL OF THE Peloponnese. Much of its charm stems from the medieval architecture of its old town, dating from the second Venetian occupation (1686–1715), not to mention its looming castles and watery vistas. Less well known than Mycenae, but much of it better preserved, Tiryns is worth visiting for an hour or two. One of the earliest inhabited towns in Greece, Argos has some remains worth investigating.

NAFPLIO
There are several reasons for visiting Nafplio, not least the town's location by the water with views across a gulf to the mountains of the eastern Peloponnese. The narrow streets and pristine white-washed houses of the old town

Rooftop view over Nafplio

are reminiscent of a Greek island, and it has excellent restaurants. Nafplio's appeal is enhanced by two high fortresses dominating the low buildings of the town. You can reach the **Palamidi Fortress** either by climbing up 999 steps, which is not for the fainthearted, or by an easier but longer route by road. The spectacular views from the top make the effort worthwhile. The main fortress is Venetian and dates from the 18th century, although inside the primary walls there are remains of three smaller fortresses to explore.

The **Its Kale fortress**, whose name is Turkish for Inner Castle, is slightly less dramatic. This was the site of Nafplio's original acropolis, and several castles have stood here over the centuries. There are very few remains to see now, but it is a pleasant place for a short stroll. Another good walk leads around the headland on which Its Kale fortress stands.

On an islet in the bay is another, smaller fortress known as the **Bourtzi.** Built in the 15th century, at the time of the Venetian occupation, it owes its importance to the deceptive waters here. They look deep, but in fact there is only one navigable passage into Nafplio. The Bourtzi guards could block this by stringing chains across from the islet to the town. Among the fortress's various functions over the years, it was the home of the town's executioner until 1930 and later a luxurious hotel. At the moment it simply stands there, empty and undeniably picturesque.

Nafplio's museums are all worth a visit for different reasons. On the main square, Plateia Syntagmatos, is the **Archaeological Museum** *(tel 0752 27502, closed Mon., $)*, housed in an elegant 18th-century former Venetian warehouse. The highlight of its collection is a suit of bronze armor that has survived virtually intact from Mycenean times (about 1500 B.C.). Many items here were found at the nearby sites of Tiryns (see this page) and Mycenae (see pp. 114–15).

The **Folklore Museum** in Nafplio is one of the best in the country. Run by the Peloponnesian Folk Foundation, it has excellent and extensive displays of colorful traditional costumes from all over the region, which are well explained in both Greek and English. There are also interesting displays of old photographs, many showing folk traditions. A wide collection of farming and domestic artifacts provides a lot of information about the rural life of the region. Lovely examples of local handicrafts, made by those who keep the folk traditions alive, are sold in the first-rate gift shop.

The **Military Museum** is full of authentic weaponry and documents. There is a large collection of moving—and occasionally harrowing—photographs, portraying the impact of World War II on Greece. There is also an interesting collection of artifacts relating to the War of Independence, with which Nafplio is closely linked. In fact, the town served as the capital of a newly independent Greece from 1829 to 1834.

Although originally from Corfu, Greece's first president, Ioannis Kapodistrias (1776–1831), lived in Nafplio and also died

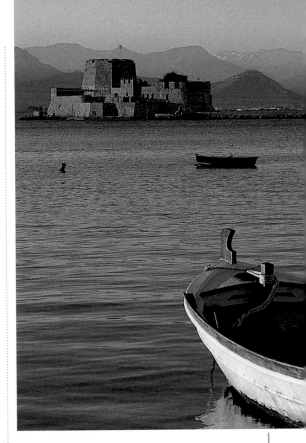

there, assassinated outside the church of **Agios Spiridon** by two villainous chieftains from the Mani region of the southern Peloponnese. You can see the bullet holes on the wall of the church. Three years later, in 1834, Athens was made the new capital of modern Greece.

TIRYNS

At the time of the Mycenean civilization (about 1400–1200 B.C.), Tiryns stood on the shores of the Aegean guarding Mycenae and neighboring Argos from attack. It may even have been the main port for Mycenae. Since then the sea has retreated, leaving Tiryns stranded a few miles inland, and easily reached off the Athens road 2 miles (4 km) west of Nafplio.

Topped with a gun emplacement, a sturdy polygonal tower dominates the Bourtzi fort in Nafplio.

Folklore Museum
✉ Vasilissis Alexandrou I
☎ 0752 28947
$ $
🕐 Closed Tues.

Military Museum
✉ Leoforos Amalias 22
☎ 0752 25591
🕐 Closed Mon.

Tiryns

🅰 101 C3

Royal Palace

☎ 0752 22657

🕐 Closed Mon.

💲 $

Argos

🅰 101 C3

Archaeological Museum

✉ Plateia Agiou Petra

☎ 0751 68819

🕐 Closed Mon.

💲 $

Homer described Tiryns as having mighty **walls,** and these are still the first thing you really notice in the town. The remains of the walls—rebuilt in the 13th century B.C.—are 2,300 feet (700 m) in length, up to 26 feet (8 m) wide, and 33 feet (10 m) high, although they originally stood twice this high. The site is much better preserved than Mycenae but lacks the resonance of the royal tombs, and because of this has not been as well excavated or cared for. Some parts are off-limits to visitors, as much to protect people from accidents as to protect the remains from damage.

Arriving at the site is impressive: You climb the entrance ramp that any attackers would have had to negotiate, with its sharp turn at the top. The thick gateway here, which would have matched the famous lion gate at Mycenae, has not worn so well, and its distinctive carvings have not survived.

Little remains of the **royal palace,** aside from foundations. However, with a floor plan, available from stores in modern Mycenae (don't wait until you get to the site), it is possible to make out sections such as the royal apartments. A bathroom is easily distinguishable, its floor made up of one immense flat stone. The stone staircase that leads down to a postern gate has survived, virtually intact, for almost 3,000 years.

ARGOS

The town of Argos is at a crossroads, where the Nafplio–Athens and Tripoli–Athens roads meet, and is a changing place for those traveling by bus. It has all the facilities you might want, such as banks, stores, post offices, and gas stations, and a good archaeological museum that tells the story of the town's more illustrious past.

The **Archaeological Museum,** close to the main square, has finds from both Mycenae and Tiryns. The best of these are now in the National Archaeological Museum in Athens (see p. 78), but Argos can boast a bronze helmet and breastplate that date to Mycenean times and

A narrow vaulted passage runs through the massive stone walls of Tiryns.

excellent collections from the later Roman period.

The importance of Argos in historic times can be seen at the site of **Ancient Argos,** which is only a short walk from the center of town along the road that leads to Tripoli. The principal attraction is the theater, which is bigger than Epidavros and one of the largest in Greece, with steeply ascending seating for 20,000 spectators. It was built toward the end of the fourth century B.C. but was twice modernized by the Romans. The site also has the remains of a Roman bath, a Roman theater, an aqueduct, and large drainage channels, which indicate the size and importance of the settlement that grew up here.

Above the site a path leads to the fortress where the original acropolis of Argos was situated before being replaced by a castle in medieval times (although some of the walls date back to the sixth century A.D.). It is a steep climb, so if you have a car you may prefer to take the circuitous road instead. At the top you are treated to breathtaking views to the Aegean, north toward the Gulf of Corinth, and south across the hills of the Peloponnese. ■

National flag

The distinctive blue and white flag of Greece seems ideally suited to this country of deep blue skies and almost blindingly bright whitewashed houses. The two colors have been Greek colors for centuries, although the modern design was adopted only in 1833, when Otto of Bavaria was made the first king of an independent Greek state (see p. 33). Before this, the flag was a simple white cross on a blue background, a design that was adopted again between 1975–78 and which is still occasionally seen.

The nine horizontal stripes on the flag are highly significant. They represent the nine syllables of the motto of the freedom fighters who fought against Turkish rule in the War of Independence: *"Eleutheria i thanatos!*—Freedom or death!"

Over the years the shade of the blue stripes has changed from light to dark and light again. The flag you see today was finally settled upon on December 21, 1978.

Greece is a country with a keen sense of patriotism, and you will see the flag flying everywhere, all year round. ■

Heinrich Schliemann

German-born archaeologist Heinrich Schliemann (1822–1890) devoted his life to pursuing the treasures hidden in the Greek earth. If at times he let his theories override the evidence, he was still a great enthusiast who discovered many of Greece's finest ancient treasures—even if they were not always exactly what he believed them to be.

Schliemann was an intriguing man. After making his business fortune partly as a military contractor in Germany, Holland, and Russia during the Crimean War, he became a U.S. citizen while living in California in 1850s. He moved to Greece at age 46 to devote the rest of his life to archaeology. More specifically, he had been fascinated since childhood by the works of Homer, and their mingling of myth and history. Did such places as Troy and the Palace of Odysseus actually exist? Schliemann resolved to find out.

He began by looking for Troy, scene of Homer's *Iliad*. In 1870 he began digging at Hissarlik, close to the Turkish Aegean coast, which he had identified as the probable location of the city. He found evidence of several cities having existed on the site, and declared that the second earliest of them, where there were traces of burning, was Homer's Troy. It is now known that if, in fact, Troy was located there, it was one of the later levels that Schliemann had already dug through and destroyed in the process of excavation. Whatever the truth of the find—it has never been established for sure, and

probably never can be—Schliemann certainly uncovered an important historical site.

From Troy he moved in 1874 to explore at Mycenae (see pp. 114–15). He was seeking the tombs of the ancient Mycenean kings and was determined to find the tomb of Agamemnon, to prove that this character actually existed. Schliemann uncovered a stunning golden burial mask, and confidently announced to the king of Greece in a famous telegram: "I have gazed upon the face of Agamemnon." In fact, later dating established that it could not have been Agamemnon, even if the king had been a historical rather than a legendary character. Schliemann never let the opinions or evidence of experts divert him from his own strongly held views.

It was inevitable that Schliemann would move on to Ithaca, to look for historical evidence of the existence of Odysseus and his palace, and other sites described in Homer's *Odyssey*. It was equally inevitable that he would find something that he identified as those sites, but again there is still no absolute proof that he was right. He did further important work at Tiryns, near Mycenae, and also hoped to excavate at Knossos on Crete, another location mentioned by Homer, but he could not agree to the price being asked for access to the land.

Despite his great knowledge and enthusiasm, Schliemann was perceived by other archaeologists as an amateur and an upstart. Nevertheless, it cannot be denied that he uncovered large and significant sites that other archaeologists had missed. ∎

Although the formal education of Heinrich Schliemann (opposite, left) ended at age 14, he went on to make extraordinary archaeological discoveries. His Greek wife, Sophia, is shown (center) wearing gold jewelry from Mycenae.
Above: Schliemann believed this gold death mask to be Agamemnon's; in fact it dates from the 16th century B.C. and so is too old to be his.

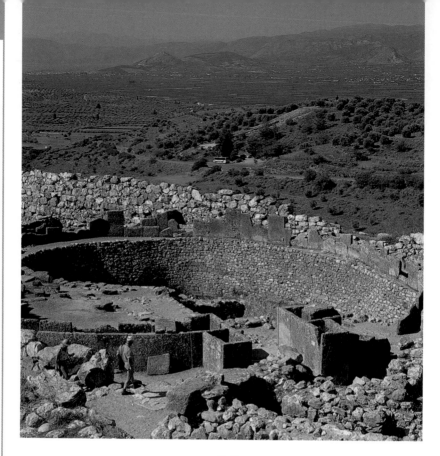

Mycenae

WITHOUT DOUBT, MYCENAE (MYKINAI) IS THE MOST
important historical site on the Peloponnese. Its popularity means
that at the height of the tourist season it seems as if everyone is
visiting it at the same time. But, join the crowd! The ruined complex
lies just over a mile (2 km) outside the modern village of Mycenae,
which straddles the Nafplio–Athens main road, and is clearly signed.

Mycenae
🗺 101 C3
☎ 0751 76585
💲 $$

The first thing you see as you
approach, on your left, is the
Treasury of Atreus. This
beehive tomb is an impressive
structure, especially considering
that it was built without a scrap of
mortar. Pass down a long corridor
into the main tomb, where the
acoustics are startling. Try speaking
aloud to experience this yourself.
Take a look, too, at the hefty lintel
over the entrance door, which is
26 feet (8 m) long and weighs
almost 120 tons.

The great palace of Mycenae was
known as the House of Atreus after
the ruler of that name, the son of
Pelops (who gave his name to the
Peloponnese, see p. 100). Greek
dramatists tell the grisly story of the
curse on the House of Atreus.
Atreus's wife was seduced by his
brother, Thyestes. In revenge,
Atreus murdered two of Thyestes's

sons, boiled them, and served them to their father at a banquet. He then showed Thyestes the severed heads of his sons, to let him know what he had eaten. From then on, Atreus and his descendants—who included Agamemnon, Menelaus, and Orestes—were cursed by the gods.

The Treasury is often referred to as the Tomb of Agamemnon, and although it was indeed a royal burial tomb, there is no evidence to support this attribution. The spot that Schliemann (see pp. 112–13) believed to be the tomb of Agamemnon is at the main site, farther along the road. The Treasury dates to the 14th century B.C. and so would have been used before the time of Agamemnon.

The first thing to strike visitors arriving at the main site is the famous **Lion Gate,** the carved lintel which straddles the entrance at the top of the approach. Built in the 13th century B.C., it is 12.5 feet (3.75 m) wide at the base and almost 11 feet (3.5 m) high. The lions may have been the symbol for the royal Mycenean household; the same design was also found on a seal discovered at the site. Note the grooves in the floor, which were made by chariots, and the holes for bolts at the side to keep the doorway firmly shut when required.

When you pass through the gate, to your right are the circular remains of the **royal tombs.** In Grave Circle A, as it is known, six graves were discovered, containing a total of 19 bodies. This is where Schliemann found the glorious golden burial mask that he believed was buried with King Agamemnon. In all, 30 pounds (14 kg) of gold in the form of masks, jewelry, crowns, and other items were discovered here, and this treasure haul is one of the major attractions at the National Archaeological Museum in Athens (see p. 78).

You need to use a certain amount of imagination, and maybe have a map, to make the most of a visit to the rest of Mycenae. There are plenty of foundations to see, and the picture that emerges is of a large royal palace, with huge walls, and an extensive community living

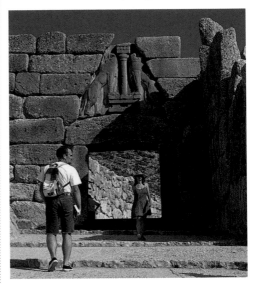

just outside the walls and serving the royal court. The walls themselves were up to 46 feet (14 m) thick, and were called the Cyclopean Walls, as people later could not understand how they had been built, if not by the one-eyed giants known as the Cyclops.

The royal palace was destroyed by fire in 1200 B.C.; the burn marks can still be seen on the foundation stones that remain. A century later, the site was abandoned and left to decay until its rediscovery by Schliemann in 1874. As you wander around today—and the ruins farther from the Lion Gate are likely to be much less crowded on busy days—you can see the remnants of bedchambers, royal apartments, baths, a grand reception hall, and a throne room. ■

A pair of lionesses supports a central pillar on the magnificent Lion Gate.

Monemvasia

Monemvasia

[N] 101 C1

Visitor information

[✉] Tourist Police

[☎] 0732 61210

IT IS ASTONISHING THAT THE NAME OF MONEMVASIA is hardly known outside Greece, because it is one of the most extraordinary towns in the whole country. The result is that it remains delightfully unspoiled. Those who venture here can regard it as a special place that few other visitors see.

A network of paths and tunnels zigzag up the steep cliffs above town.

A huge mountain of a rock stands offshore, linked to the mainland by a single stretch of road. This is Monemvasia, known as the Gibraltar of Greece. When you approach it for the first time you may feel that, yes, it is an impressive sight—but once you have seen it, what then? Well, then you walk or drive across the road to the entrance; if you drive, be prepared to leave your car outside.

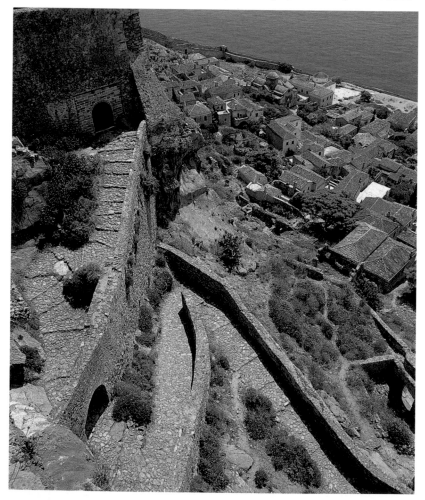

The name Monemvasia means "single entrance." To discover the secrets of this remarkable island you must walk through the single doorway, as into a medieval castle. The doorway is only wide enough to accommodate a loaded donkey.

ENTERING THE TOWN

As you pass through that entrance, you feel that you are stepping back into the 15th century, when Monemvasia was a busy Byzantine city of some 50,000 people. Today its permanent population stands at a mere 50, leaving it full of ghosts and echoes of the past. A few of the old houses have been renovated and turned into hotels, and a handful of others are now restaurants and gift shops. But development has been on a very small scale, and the atmosphere remains unique. The hotels are small, so if you want to stay in the old town and experience the full flavor of Monemvasia, then make reservations. There are also several small, simple hotels in the modern town across on the mainland.

The rock became an island when it was severed from the mainland by an earthquake in A.D. 375, and the old town was founded when the first road was built in the sixth century. It became a vitally important port, controlling the passage of ships traveling around the southern Peloponnese between Italy and Constantinople. With its one entrance and sheer sides, the rock was virtually impregnable, and the only time it fell was in 1821 during the War of Independence, when Turkish occupiers were trapped here and besieged by the Greeks. After five months, the people inside were reduced to eating grass, rats, and even, it is reputed, each other, before they surrendered.

Dining on the island today is, you'll be glad to know, more sophisticated. Whether you visit by

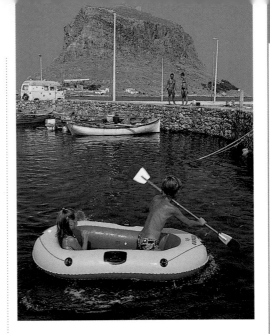

day or in the evening, allow time to wander through the streets—not just the main streets but the back streets, where crumbling churches and houses create a picture of what life used to be like here.

Immediately on your left as you go through the entrance gate is the house where the respected Greek poet Yannis Ritsos (1909–1990) was born. At the far end of the village, look for the church of Panagia Chrysafitissa. Its original date is uncertain, but it was restored by the Venetians in the 18th century. Its bell hangs from an acacia tree. Close by is the larger church of Agios Nikolaos, built in 1703. All this is in what is known as the **lower town.**

The approach to the **upper town** at the very top of the rock is by a zigzag stone path that leads to another entrance, still with its original iron gates. All that remains of the upper town, however, is the 13th-century church of Agia Sofia, which stands alone at the very top of the site. Make the effort to reach the top because the views along the coast are very impressive. ■

Monemvasia gives nothing away to tourists passing by on its landward side.

Mani

OF THE THREE PENINSULAS THAT JUT SOUTHWARD FROM the mass of the Peloponnese, the central "finger" is the Mani. Its tip at Akra Tenaro (also known as Cape Matapan) is the southernmost point of the Greek mainland—and the legendary entrance to Hades (Hell). Even without such associations, you know that when you enter the Mani you are entering a special region. The landscape becomes much more barren and rugged in the Lower Mani, where you will start to see the distinctive stone tower houses that hint at the violence of life here in the past.

The remoteness of the Mani meant it was always a place of escape or refuge, and the families who settled here in the 15th century became very clan-like, fighting bitterly for the best areas of land. The Nyklian family were dominant. At first they alone had the right to build onto their properties the characteristic tall, square stone towers, which were used for both defense and attack. The taller the tower, the easier it was to fire down on enemies through the narrow slits of windows.

Eventually other families began to build towers, each trying to build as high as possible. If one family offended another, or killed someone, then a feud began, heralded by the ringing of church bells and a retreat by the respective families

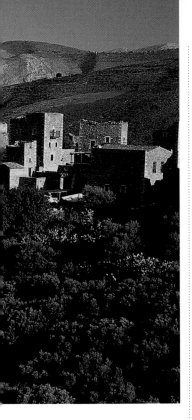

into their towers. Such feuds often lasted for years and down generations, as the sense of honor was great. There was no difficulty in keeping the tower houses supplied—women were protected and could continue to bring food into the towers for their men. The only hiatus in the feuding came at harvest time, when a truce was called. A feud could only be ended by total annihilation or capitulation by one party. The last recorded feud of this kind took place in 1870 at Kita, and was stopped only by the intervention of the Greek Army.

Kita is one place where the tower houses survive, and there are also several clustered dramatically together in the village of **Vatheia,** in the very south of the Mani. But you will see others as you travel around, sometimes just a single tower in an isolated village.

There is much more, however, to the Mani than feuds and a barren landscape. Several delightful fishing villages welcome visitors in summer, such as **Stoupa** and **Kardamyli.** In a churchyard just outside the latter is the grave of British travel writer and novelist Bruce Chatwin (1940–1989), who loved the area.

AROUND THE MANI

The northern region, known as the Outer Mani, is dominated by the mountain range of **Taygetos,** a defiant spine of rock climbing to a height of 7,885 feet (2,404 m). The lower slopes offer wonderful walking, as well as a scenic backdrop of pine forests, but to venture farther, seek advice from local guides.

The main town of the Inner Mani, the more southerly half of the peninsula, is **Areopolis.** This town provides all the facilities you might want, including a few hotels, but it is not the best place to be based for any length of time. On the coast a few miles south of Areopolis is one of the region's main attractions, the **Spilia Dirou,** or Diros Caves. You can combine a 30-minute boat ride into the underground cave network with a short exploration on foot of the Alepotripa Caves. Both have dramatic stalactites and stalagmites. Those in the Diros Caves are enhanced by the echoey, damp atmosphere and the striking reflections in the water.

The main town on the east coast of the Mani is **Githio,** actually the capital of the whole area but very different from it in style. It is a busy and prosperous little port, with several good restaurants around its attractive harbor. With the remains of a Roman theater, beaches on its outskirts, and a choice of accommodations, it is a good place to relax while you make forays into the unique Mani region. ∎

Kardamyli
🗺 101 B2

Areopolis
🗺 101 C1

Spilia Dirou
🗺 101 C1
☎ 0733 52222
💲 $$$

Githio
🗺 101 C2
Tourist information
✉ 20 Vass. Georgiou, 232 00
☎ 733 24484

A drive around the Mani

You could spend several days exploring the Mani, discovering its unique culture and a landscape that is harsh but compelling. In spring the wildflowers add dashes of color, yet in winter it can be austere. This drive takes in the highlights if time is limited, and can be done in half a day—but allow a full day if possible. It begins in the main west-coast town of Areopolis (see p. 119) and ends in Githio, the principal town on the east coast.

Flowers brighten the hills near Areopolis.

Before you set off, make sure you have a full tank as there are few gas stations in this quiet area. From **Areopolis ❶** head south on the unnumbered local road following the signs for the **Spilia Dirou ❷** (Diros Caves, see p. 119). These caves are 5 miles (8 km) south of the town. Follow the signs and turn right, just past a left turn. (You will emerge here after a circular tour of the Inner Mani, see p. 119.) The caves are 2.5 miles (4 km) down the road. They are worth visiting, but you will need plenty of time, especially in high season when waiting time increases and you can enter the caves only on the organized boat tour.

Return to the main road and continue south, avoiding any turns; most of these will eventually return you to the main road anyway, as they are either dead-ends or loops through villages.

On this western part of the route, known as the Shadowed Coast, look for **tower**

houses, and also consider stopping in any of the villages you pass through, many of which have beautiful old Byzantine chapels.

One circular detour you should take is about 6 miles (10 km) beyond the turnoff for Spilia Dirou, where you come to an intersection. Here you turn right toward Agios Giorgios and on to the village of **Mezapos ❸**. From Mezapos a short walk gives you a view across the sea to the 13th-century Byzantine fortress at **Tigani,** or "frying pan" (named for its shape). If you continue driving along this road you will circle around and rejoin the main road, where you turn right to resume your original drive route.

When you reach the village of Alika, look for a right turn marked for **Vatheia ❹**; take this to look at the cluster of stone tower houses that dominate this otherwise tiny settlement. Here you must turn around and retrace your route back to the main road, unless you want to drive on to the southern-most tip of the Mani and admire the hill of Akra Tenaro at closer quarters.

At the main road turn right again to continue along the only road, which swings north and takes you up the east coast of the Inner Mani. You travel through several remote villages and past some quiet beaches —pleasantly off the beaten track. The road eventually swings left and back across the peninsula to rejoin the main west coast road south of Areopolis.

Turn right here and the road becomes Highway 39, which you follow all the way back across the peninsula. The route passes to the south of the Taygetos Mountains, winding up and over until, after about 15 miles (25 km), you arrive at the small port of **Githio ❺** (see p. 119), the main settlement on the Mani's eastern coast. ∎

A DRIVE AROUND THE MANI

See area map p. 101
► Areopolis
◄► 70 miles (110 km)
🕐 2 hours
► Githio

NOT TO BE MISSED
- Spilia Dirou
- Mezapos
- Tigani
- Vatheia

0   10 kilometers
0   6 miles

Githio
5

Chosiari

Lakonikos Kolpos

39

Areopolis
1

START   Pirichos

Spilia
Dirou   2   Chimara

Pirgos Dirou

Kotronas

Triantafillia

Chalikia

Mezapos
Tigani   3   Agios Georgios

Kokkala

Kita

Gerolimin   Tsikkalia

Alika

Vatheia   4

Marmari

Akra Tenaro (Cape Matapan)

Formidable tower houses characterize the Mani.

Curtains of stalactites, Diros Caves

Majestic Mystras dates from Byzantine times.

Mystras

A WANDER AROUND THIS MAGICAL RUINED BYZANTINE city is sheer delight. Its setting is spectacular, with a hill rising from a plain at the edge of the Taygetos Mountains, which thrust down into the Mani. Atmospheric ruins sprawl over the top and slopes of the hill, with enough remaining to give a good idea of what it must have been like for the 42,000 people who lived here in the 15th century.

Mystras

101 C2

0731 83377

$$

The city was founded in 1249 by the Franks, who had taken control of Greece at the start of the 13th century. It owes its existence to Guillaume II de Villehardouin, who planned Mystras as the third of his strongholds in this region, alongside Monemvasia and Tigani in the Inner Mani. He saw Mystras as a replacement for nearby Sparta, which lies in the plain. Mystras fell to the Byzantines in 1262, but the

new town that grew up in and around the fortress began to flourish. It developed as a notable center of artistic excellence, attracting painters from as far afield as Italy and Constantinople.

There are two entrances to the site. Approaching from Sparta, you first come to the lower entrance. The second entrance is at the top of the hill, and both have parking. There is no particular advantage to

Above right: Looking over the rooftops of Mystras to the plains below

either of them, although if you don't enjoy a lot of climbing you might wish to explore the lower slopes first, before driving up to the top and looking around there. Whichever you choose, a map is essential to make sense of the labyrinth of paths, and even so you can't avoid some doubling back.

If you begin at the bottom and turn right you come almost at once to the **Mitropolis,** the cathedral, which dates to 1309, making it the oldest church in Mystras. Inside are some 14th-century frescoes and, conspicuous on the floor, a stone with the Byzantine double-headed eagle carved into it. On this spot the last Byzantine Emperor, Constantine XI Paleologus, was crowned in 1443.

Beyond the Mitropolis is the convent of **Pantanassa,** whose few nuns are the only people still living in Mystras. They sell refreshments and their own handicrafts at busy times of the year. Not surprisingly, the church of this working convent is the best preserved of all in Mystras. Built in 1365, it was the last to be constructed in this hillside walled town.

Turn left at the bottom entrance to reach the **Perivleptos Monastery.** The church here has particularly fine 14th-century frescoes around the dome which, in accordance with Byzantine convention, carries an image of Christ Pantokrator.

KASTRO

The dominant feature at the top of the site is the castle, or Kastro, though first you come to the Palace Chapel of Agia Sofia with its stunning marble floors. Below here it is possible to walk around the castle keep, which gives wonderful views over the ruined city. This dramatic spot is where the German writer and scientist Goethe (1749–1832) set the meeting between Faust and Helen of Troy in his famous play, *Faust*.

In addition to the Kastro, there is also the **Despots' Palace.** The first Byzantine rulers here were the Despots of Morea, Morea being the name of this whole region of Greece. The palace has survived well over the centuries but has been closed for extensive renovations for several years. One wing dates from the original Frankish days; another was added in the 14th century. This section includes a throne room that was used for the coronation of several Byzantine kings. ■

Medieval pilgrims
on their way to
the Holy Land
stopped off at
the Methoni
fortress.

Messenian peninsula

THE TOWNS OF KORONI AND METHONI STAND LIKE TWIN
sentinels on either side of the Messenian peninsula in the south-
western Peloponnese. Once known for their fortresses, they are better
known today as beach resorts. The rest of the region has a range
of minor but interesting archaeological sites.

Koroni
101 B2

Methoni
101 B2

The two towns were known as the
"eyes of Venice," as their respective
forts kept close watch over the shipping movements between Italy and
Greece. The castle at **Koroni** was
begun in 1206 and its imposing
walls still stand, now sheltering the
convent of Timiou Prodromou and
some private houses. It is a charming place to wander around in the
evening. The town below the fort,
an attractive jumble of houses,
dates only to circa 1830. Its main
appeal for vacationers is the magnificent mile-long sandy beach.

Contemporary with the fort
at Koroni, the Methoni fortress juts
out into the sea, with water on

three sides. A moat protects the
fourth side. It is a forbidding
stronghold, conveying a feeling of
abandonment as you walk around
inside the walls and see the remnants that are still standing. In contrast to the inhabited fortress at
Koroni, in Methoni you find only
the ruins of houses, a cathedral, a
Turkish bath, and some underground passages.

Methoni also has a good beach,
and is altogether a much busier
resort than Koroni. Yet at its heart
are still the attractive whitewashed
houses, with their colorful
bougainvillea and hibiscus flowers
trailing from the balconies.

NESTOR'S PALACE

In Homer's *Odyssey,* as the hero Odysseus is endeavoring to make his way home to his palace on the island of Ithaca, his son Telemachus visits the palace of King Nestor to try to get news of his father. Here Telemachus is bathed by Nestor's daughter, Polycaste. Naturally, a bathtub has been found on this site, alleged to be that of the palace of King Nestor, and adding substance to the legend.

An early visit to the **Archaeological Museum** located in the nearby village of **Chora** is recommended. Finds from the palace are on display here with good explanations and help to make more sense of your visit to the site itself.

At first sight the remains of this Mycenean palace are not particularly impressive. Yet it has much of interest, and the small scale of the palace helps bring alive the people who lived here.

The bulk of the site consists of foundations little more than a few inches high, yet with the aid of a plan it is possible to rebuild the palace in your mind. The task is made easier by its fabulous setting, on top of a promontory overlooking the sea and olive groves.

Nestor's Palace was only discovered in 1939, and so has not been subject to the over-enthusiastic interpretations of the likes of Heinrich Schliemann. Exploration continues, using the most modern archaeological techniques. One of the most exciting finds so far was several hundred tablets inscribed with the script known as Linear B, which Sir Arthur Evans had also found at the Minoan site at Knossos on Crete, thereby proving a link between the Minoan and Mycenean civilizations. Ironically the tablets were preserved by being baked in the very fire which destroyed the palace around 1200 B.C.

Nestor's Palace
- 101 B2
- Closed Mon.
- $

Archaeological Museum
- Chora
- 0763 31358
- Closed Mon.
- $

Messene

101 B2

Megalopolis
101 B3
Closed Mon.

Taking it easy on
the beach at
Koroni. Fishing
boats are usually
hauled up for
repair and
repainting in the
winter.

MESSENE

Ancient Messene is said to have
been built in a mere 85 days in
369 B.C. as the brand-new capital
of the Messenian people. This
westernmost of the Peloponnese's
three peninsulas is named after
them. Like other sites, it owes its
appeal to its location as much as
to what has actually survived here.
It is found just outside the village
of Mavromati, on the slopes of
Mount Ithomi (2,600 feet/800 m)
at the northern end of the peninsula, and is referred to as Ithomi
on road signs.

If you are driving, take the
road to Meligalas to pass through
the huge and dramatic Arcadia
Gate, part of the original city walls.
Some 5.5 miles (9 km) of wall
have so far been unearthed, and
excavations at the site are ongoing.
You can see the foundations of a
temple to Artemis here, along with
the remains of the Acropolis on
top of Mount Ithomi, and a
fountain in the Sanctuary of
Asklepius, which still provides
water to the modern village.

MEGALOPOLIS

Farther north on the road towards
Tripoli are the ruins of ancient
Megalopolis, the Big Town, on the
edge of the modern town that
retains that name. Little of the
town remains, but to get some
impression of its former glory,
know that the theater here could
easily seat some 20,000 people,
making it bigger than the theater at
Epidavros and even the Theater of
Dionysos in Athens.

Megalopolis was built at about
the same time as Messene, in the
years 371–368 B.C., and by the same
person, the Theban leader
Epaminondas. His aim was to have
a series of defensive cities to keep
the Spartans at bay. However,
Megalopolis never prospered, and
even today it has an abandoned air.
Its overgrown state makes a welcome contrast to sites where everything is mapped and labeled. ■

Andritsaina & Vasses

Old mountain towns like Andritsaina seem almost untouched by the modern world.

HEADING NORTHWEST FROM MEGALOPOLIS, A WINDING road leads up into one of the most picturesque and unspoiled mountain settlements in all of Greece: Andritsaina. On its way the road passes Vasses and its temple, one of the most dramatically situated in Greece. Andritsaina was an important market town during the Turkish occupation and is still a focal point for life in the smaller, isolated villages around, with old men whose eyes have seen a great deal of history now sitting in cafés to watch the world go by.

There are places to stay overnight here if you don't mind something simple, but most visitors make only a brief stop before heading out on an even more remote road, high into the mountains, to see the **Temple of Vasses,** also known as Vassae or Bassae. This is one of the most isolated and impressive classical sites, standing at a height of 3,711 feet (1,131 m), with little around it to distract the eye.

The temple was dedicated to Apollo and built by the Figalians, the local people, as thanks for protection from a plague. The site of ancient Figalia was west of here,

scattered around the modern village of Figalia. Vasses is one of the best preserved temples in Greece, in an even better state of preservation than the Parthenon. At one time it was thought that it might have been designed by Iktinos, the architect responsible for the Parthenon. Now it seems likely that it predates those buildings and was probably completed by 425 B.C.

It will be even more impressive when Greece raises the money necessary to restore the temple. Until then it must remain protected from the elements by a vast tent, although even this creates a novel experience. ∎

Andritsaina
◮ 101 B3

Vasses
◮ 101 B3

Olympia

THE MODERN OLYMPIC GAMES DATE BACK ABOUT A
hundred years, but the original games in ancient Greece were first
held nearly 3,000 years ago and took place every four years for more
than a millennium. A visit to the actual stadium where those games
were held—and where the Olympic flame to herald the start of the
modern athletic contests is lit—is, for many, a dream come true.

Ancient Olympia

🅰 101 B3

☎ 0624 22517

💲 $$

Visitor information

✉ Tourist Police

☎ 0624 22550

The first official competition took
place in 776 B.C. The subsequent
history of the games is dealt with
on pages 132–33, but no factual
relating of history can capture the
magic felt by most visitors when
they walk down the entrance
tunnel, beneath the third-century
B.C. arch and out into the arena at
Ancient Olympia. You can still
hear the roar of the crowds, echoing
down across the centuries.

You see much more of the site
before reaching the stadium itself,
however, revealing what a vast
complex it was—the equivalent of
today's modern Olympic villages.

At the center of the site was the
Temple of Zeus, constructed in
the fifth century B.C. when the

games were in full flow. Only the
bases of the columns remain,
although some fallen columns have
been left in sections where they
crashed to the ground, helping to
give a picture of the place not only
in life but also as it fell into decay.
The significance of the site at
Olympia is evident from the fact
that this temple was the same size
as the Parthenon in Athens, and
was built at roughly the same time.

The temple contained a huge
statue of Zeus, which was made
in the group of buildings whose
foundations are in front of the
temple, on the side away from the
stadium. One of these buildings
is marked as the **Studio of
Pheidias,** the sculptor who crafted

the statue. Across the path from here are the remains of the **Leonidaion,** the guesthouse used for distinguished visitors.

Behind the Leonidaion is the **Bouleuterion,** the meeting house where the equivalent of the modern International Olympic Committee would gather. It was also where the athletes swore to uphold the Olympic rules, in front of another imposing statue of Zeus. From here the athletes made their way into the stadium, passing rows of statues portraying past athletes who had broken the rules. Paid for by fines levied on these disgraced athletes, the statues recorded each rule breaker's name as well as that of his father and his hometown. Cheaters were not taken lightly.

There was also, naturally, a section where the heroes of the games were honored. Close to the modern-day entrance is another building worthy of note. The **Temple of Hera** is much smaller in scale than the Temple of Zeus. Dating from the seventh century

B.C., it was rebuilt in the sixth century B.C., making it almost as old as the games themselves.

ARCHAEOLOGICAL MUSEUM

Opposite the site of Olympia, its modern museum houses finds from the site. The collection is one of the finest in Greece, ranking alongside the museums in Athens and at Delphi. Pride of place in the main hall goes to the sculptures and friezes that adorned the Temple of Zeus. Tools from the workshop of Pheidias are displayed in another room, along with the cup that bears his name and which helped identify the location of his workshop. Displays on a more human scale include items used in the games themselves, such as discuses, part of a starting block, and the stones used by the weightlifters.

One of the most beautiful finds on the site is the Nike of the sculptor Paionios, a marble statue from the fifth century B.C. This Goddess of Victory stood at one corner of the Temple of Zeus.

A double row of columns marks the boundary of the square sports arena, or *palaestra.*

Archaeological Museum
☎ 0624 22529
Ⓢ $$

Only the foundations of the third-century B.C. gymnasium remain.

Exedra of Herodes Atticus, an elaborate drinking fountain, dates from A.D. 160.

The Temple of Hera is one of the oldest temples in Greece.

Philip II of Macedonia began the Philippeion, a circular memorial.

Wrestlers, boxers, and other athletes could train and relax in the Palestra, or arena.

Roman villa

The gold-and-ivory statue of Zeus was made in the Studio of Pheidias.

Important foreign guests and officials stayed in the superior accommodations of the Leonidaion, built in the fourth century B.C.

A superb sixth-century B.C. relief of wrestlers shows how athletes competed nude.

The Terrace of the Treasuries displays statues of Zeus funded by athletic fines.

Spectators sat on wooden stands in the stadium to watch the main events

The Bouleuterion was built in the sixth century B.C. as an Olympic Council chamber.

Processional Way

An earthquake destroyed the Temple of Zeus 1,100 years after its construction in the fifth century B.C.

The entrance to the stadium, built in the third century B.C., was originally vaulted.

The Olympic Games

Only a brief look at the history of the Olympic Games will explain why the Greeks were disappointed not to host the Games in 1996, having to wait now until 2004. The original Olympic Games were first held in 776 B.C., regarded as the first datable event in Greek history. The modern Olympic Games were revived in 1896.

They took place in Athens in a stadium built to replicate an original stadium known to have stood on the same site and described in the second century A.D. It would have been fitting to hold the 100th anniversary of the modern games in that same elegant stadium, for symbolic reasons.

When they first began in Olympia, the games were no more than local sprinting races. Later, events such as horse racing and wrestling were added, as well as poetry and music contests. The competitors began to come from farther afield.

In the games held in 720 B.C. it was decided that athletes should compete in the nude, and for this reason female spectators were banned. Nevertheless, crowds of some 20,000 would gather on the raised terraces overlooking the track in Olympia, which has survived to this day and is imbued with a great sense of history and magic. It is still the place where the Olympic flame is kindled every four years, using the rays of the sun, and from where the flame is conveyed to herald the new competition. During opening ceremonies, the Greek team leads the procession of competing nations in honor of their ancestors.

A museum in the town of Olympia tells the full story of the games, both ancient and modern. The first modern Olympics were held among only 13 nations, with just nine sports represented and a grand total of 42 events. Today, some 186 nations are affiliated with the International Olympic Committee (IOC), which is based in Lausanne, Switzerland.

The games have been held every four years since 1896, with exceptions because of war in 1916 (when they were due to be held in Berlin), 1940, and 1944. Politics are now inseparable from the Olympic Games. About one-third of the competing nations,

including the United States, withdrew from the Moscow Olympics of 1980, protesting the Soviet invasion of Afghanistan. It was almost inevitable that the USSR would withdraw from the 1984 Olympics in reprisal, which were held in Los Angeles (the host nations are decided six years ahead).

The 1936 Olympic Games in Berlin were also controversial. Adolf Hitler's belief in white supremacy was challenged by the African-American athlete Jesse Owens, who won four gold medals.

In 1972 in Munich, 13 Israeli athletes were murdered by Arab terrorists. Despite such problems—and there were equivalent controversies right back at the very start of the games—more countries want to take part each year, and the Olympics continue to be one of the biggest events on Earth. ∎

Above: Alabama-born Jesse Owens (1913–1980) is regarded as one of the greatest Olympic sprinters, winning gold medals for the 100 meters, 200 meters, broad jump, and 4 x 100 meter relay in 1936. Left: A view of the first revival of the Olympic Games in 1896, held in Athens, gives a snapshot of how the events have changed—as well as sporting fashion. The athletic dress of the time now looks cumbersome, and the spectators few when compared with the millions worldwide who had access to the Sydney Olympics of 2000.

Patra

THE LARGEST CITY IN THE PELOPONNESE AND THE THIRD largest in Greece, Patra (or Patras) is chiefly attractive to visitors for its port, which allows access to other areas. It is the second largest port after Pireas, with connections to Italy and to several of the Ionian islands, as well as train connections to Athens and bus connections to many parts of the Greek mainland. From just outside Patra at Rion, a short ferry ride transports you across the Gulf of Corinth to northern and western Greece. A bridge to speed up the journey is under construction.

Patra

🗺 101 B4

Tourist information

✉ Peloponnese & West Central Greece H.Q., Filopomenos 26

☎ 61 620353 or 61 621992

Nevertheless, if you decide to spend a night here, there are plenty of hotels and enough diversions to keep you amused for a few hours. The downtown is at **Plateia Psila Alonia,** where sidewalk cafés invite you to sit and watch the drama of everyday street life unfold. At the southern end of the waterfront is the large Byzantine-style modern church of **Agios Andreas** (St. Andrew), built in 1979 on the spot where the saint is said to have been martyred. You may be surprised to find that inside is the head of the saint, which was returned to Patra from Rome in 1964.

The most attractive part of Patra is the **upper town,** around the slopes of the ancient acropolis where the **castle** now stands. The castle is mainly Byzantine but has been added to by everyone over the years. The ruins are in a pleasant park and worth the climb. From here you can see north across the Gulf of Corinth, south to the mountains of the Peloponnese, and across the Ionian Sea to the islands of Zakinthos and Kefalonia. A few blocks south of the castle is the Roman **Odeion** (theater), which has been restored so that it can now be used for modern performances. ∎

More places to visit in the Peloponnese & Kithira

KALAVRYTA

Few foreign visitors make the journey to
Kalavryta, about 20 miles (32 km) southeast
of Patra, but to the Greeks it is a place of
pilgrimage. In 1821 at the **Monastery of
Agia Lavra,** about 4 miles (6 km) outside
Kalavryta, the Archbishop of Patra raised the
Greek flag in defiance of Greece's Turkish
occupiers, signaling the start of the War of
Independence. The small mountain town is
likely to be filled with Greek visitors at any
time of the year, but on the anniversary of that
event, commemorated every March 21, you
will be unable to move.

The monastery itself had to be rebuilt after
World War II. In a terrible act of reprisal, the
occupying Nazi forces killed the entire male
population of Kalavryta—1,436 men and
boys—then burned down the town and, in the
ultimate act of contempt, also burned down
the monastery where the rebellion had begun.
A mural in the reconstructed town commemorates that event, and one of the clock towers
on the main church remains forever fixed at
2:34 p.m., the time of the massacre.

The journey to Kalavryta can be one of
the most uplifting travel experiences in
Greece. A **rack-and-pinion railway** runs
from the coastal town of Diakofto, on the Gulf
of Corinth, and climbs slowly for 14 miles
(22.5 km) along gorges, by cliff faces, through
woods and 14 tunnels, alongside rivers, and
across bridges, bringing you through breathtaking scenery to Kalavryta at 2,480 feet (756 m).
🅜 101 B4 ☎ 01 513 1601 for railroad
timetable details 🆂 $

Not a trip for the fainthearted, the
vertiginous Kalavryta railway winds along
the mountain side.

KITHIRA

Kithira is an island that sits on its own at the
foot of the Peloponnese and is awkward to
reach. There are daily flights from Athens, and
in summer several ferries or hydrofoils per
week from the Peloponnese. Outside the short
peak season of June–September, the ferry
service is very limited, and cancellations are
frequent because of the notoriously rough seas.

In part Kithira owes its fortunes, or lack of
them, to those rough seas. The difficulty of
negotiating these waters was a prime reason
for the opening of the Corinth Canal in the
late 19th century (see p. 102). Before then,
boats would call at Kithira regularly, bringing
welcome trade and income. With the opening
of the canal, that trade ceased almost completely. Since then the island's population has
fallen to about 3,000 people. Although few visitors reach the island there are numerous
attractions—and you'll have them all to yourself if you're lucky.

The capital is **Chora.** Whitewashed buildings cluster on a hillside above the harbor,
leading up toward the domineering walls of a
hugely impressive **fortress,** which seems
almost as big as the town again. The castle was

KALAMATA

With its busy airport, and the biggest city in
the southern Peloponnese, Kalamata is more
often a place to set out from than a place to
stay. It has long been famed for the quality of
its olives and olive oil, however, which are
exported around the world. Visitors should
certainly try to buy some locally. The most
attractive part of the city is around the **castle,** with the Archaeological Museum close by.
🅜 101 B2 **Tourist information**
✉ Aristomenous & Poliviou 6
☎ tel 721 86868

begun by the Venetians in the 13th century and expanded in the late 15th century—you can see the date of 1503 inscribed there. Within its walls is the church of the Panagia Myrtidiotissa, with a straight drop to the sea behind it, and a view of the islet of Avgo, one of several places claiming to be the birthplace of Aphrodite. Inside the castle there is also a very small **Archaeological Museum** *(Kastro, Chora, tel 0735 31739, closed Mon.).*

Below Chora is the harbor-cum-resort of **Kapsali,** which is as close as the island gets to a developed resort. It has an adequate beach of of pebbles and sand, but to get to the best sandy beaches you will have to explore. Public transportation is limited by the lack of visitors, and you really need to rent a car or make use of the taxi service to get around. There are excellent beaches at Diakofti on the east coast, Limiona on the west, and Plateia Ammos in the very north.

To get to Plateia Ammos, you pass through the beautiful unspoiled hill village of **Karavas,** from where a road leads down to the island's main port at **Agia Pelagia.** Several hotels here cater for the travelers who might need to stay overnight before moving on. Farther south again is the site of the island's former capital at **Paleochora,** now deserted. Its ruins stand 650 feet (200 m) above the sea—a haunting place, and an essential visit if you are on the island. A thriving Byzantine town with some 72 churches, Paleochora had been the island capital since 1248. Although the town was designed to be invisible from the sea, the renowned pirate Barbarossa attacked and destroyed it in 1537, killing many of its occupants and taking a further 7,000 captive. Today only half a dozen churches survive among the ruins.

🄰 101 C1

OFF KITHIRA

Elafonisos is the Greek islands' nearest approach to a desert-island paradise. It has some glorious, long, white sandy beaches and just one village with two small pensions, open only in the summer months.

Andikithera, halfway between Kithira and Crete, is even more remote, with fewer than 200 inhabitants, some ruins, a few beaches, and two villages where accommodations are primitive and scarce. This is definitely a place to get away from it all— but rough seas might mean it's some time before you get back.

🄰 101 C1

PILOS

Boats bob and fishermen mend their nets in this appealing harbor—familiar scenes in the Greek islands. The attractive town of Pilos, on the west coast of the Peloponnese, makes a good base for a few days or even longer. Waterfront restaurants serve the freshest of food, and one end of the harbor is dominated by the castle, built originally by the Turks in 1572 but added to by the Venetians and the French. Parts of the structure are run-down, but, with the beautiful church of Agios Sotiros within sitting its walls, the castle is a good place to explore.

Pilos commands the southern entrance to Navarino Bay (Ormos Navarinou), which is almost sealed off from the rest of the Ionian Sea by Sphaktiria Island. It was in this bay that one of Greece's most significant sea battles took place. On October 20, 1827, a fleet of 26 Greek and allied warships approached the bay, where 82 Turkish and Egyptian ships were waiting. The intent was to negotiate, but an Egyptian ship supporting the Turkish fleet fired a cannon, after which a full-scale battle took place. No fewer than 51 Turkish ships were sunk, while the Greeks lost none. The resulting dominance of the waters was in no small way responsible for Greece winning its independence from Turkey in 1828.

🄰 101 B2

SPARTA

The word "spartan" has passed into the language to denote the tough and austere regime for which Sparta's (Sparti's) soldiers were renowned in the days when the site rivaled Athens as one of Greece's main city-states. Although it is a thriving city today, there is little to detain you for more than an hour or two as you track down the scattered remnants of the past. These include a theater and some temple remains, with a small **Archaeological Museum** *(Dionysiou-Dafnou, tel 0731 28575, closed Mon.).*

🄰 101 C2 ■

This part of the Greek mainland, which stretches from the mountains of the north to the Gulf of Corinth and from the blue Ionian Sea in the west to Macedonia in the east, is the most diverse and exciting region of the country.

Central Greece, Thessaly, & Epiros

Modern icons for sale

Central Greece, Thessaly, & Epiros

IF YOU HAD TO CHOOSE A SINGLE AREA OF GREECE THAT ENCAPSULATES all that is best about the country, it would have to be this central region. Modern beach resorts such as Parga dot the west coast, and important historical remains, such as those at Dodoni, are found farther inland. In Delphi, the region also has the most important historic site outside of Athens. The lakeside town of Ioanina (see p. 162) is incredibly popular with Greeks but often overlooked by visitors. Its setting, beside a deep lake and with a backdrop of mountains, is breathtaking.

This is a mountainous region, including the dramatic Pindos range and the Parnassos farther south, both favored by avid walkers in search of fresh air and unspoiled beauty. The Pindos Mountains include an area known as Zagoria, where villages built of stone and slate are linked to each other by centuries-old paths cut out of the harsh surroundings.

This region also has the magnificent Vikos Gorge, which is the second longest in Europe after the Samaria Gorge in Crete (see pp. 300–301), but visited by a few hundred people rather than thousands every day. East of here you climb high into the Pindos, where the roads may be blocked by snow in winter but in summer give access to awesome scenery and very special mountain villages—including appealing Metsovon, home to some of Greece's last remaining nomads.

Across these mountains and back down in the plains of Thessaly (Thessalia), you find a place unlike any other in the world. This is Meteora, appearing like a landscape by Salvador Dalì, where ancient monasteries cling to the tops of rocks that thrust up out of the plain.

Heading east to reach the coast again, you find the picture-postcard scenery of a Greek idyll, complete with sandy beaches, fresh fish, and overwhelmingly friendly people. It's all there on the Pilion peninsula, the legendary relaxing place of the Greek gods and a favorite with modern Greek vacationers. It is, however, still something of a secret to foreign visitors. A week—or preferably several—spent here will give you the feeling of having discovered the "real" Greece. ∎

Arachova hugs the foothills of Mount Parnassos.

MAKEDONIA & THRAKI

p. 169

3/E65

2917m
Olympos

6/E92

Elasson

Stomion

Meteora
Kalabaka

Tirnavos

E75

1978m
Ossa

Zarkos   6/E92

Larissa

Trikala

Pineios

Kanalia

Athens

Area of map detail

Pyli

T H E S S A L I A

Makrinitsa   1551m

Agios
Ioannis

Tsagkarada

Karditsa

Farsala

Volos   Vizitsa

Mileai

Limni
Tavropou

Kastania

Neo Monastiri

Pagasitikos
Kolpos

P i l i o n

Domokos   3/E65

Almyros

Trikerion

Platania

O r o s

Sourpi

Agia
Kiriaki

1726m
Othrys

Fragkista   2315m   Makrakomi
38/E952

Lamia

S>ercheios

Glifa

EVIA
p. 205

Acheloos

Texniti Limni
Kremaston

Karpenision

C E N T R A L
G R E E C E

27/E65

Vorios Evvoikos Kolpos

E75   Arkitsa

Agrinio

Evinos

2510m

3   PARNASSOS
NAT. PARK

Parnassos

Malesina

Limni
Trichonida

Lidorikion

Amfissa

2457m
Corycian Cave

Kifisos

5/E55

Messolongi

E65   Galaxidion

Delphi   Arachova

Livadia

Nafpaktos

Osiou
Louka

Aliartos   3/E962

Adirrion

Thisvi

Thiva
(Thebes)

Gulf   of   Corinth

Korinthiakos   Kolpos

C

PELOPONNISOS
p. 99

D

E

AROUND ATHENS
p. 85

Gulf of Corinth

THE SPECTACULAR DRIVE ALONG THE NORTHERN SHORE of the Gulf of Corinth (Korinthiakos Kolpos), looking across the blue waters to the mountains of the Peloponnese, is one of the best in Greece. Behind you rise the imposing Parnassos Mountains. The road heading west, when it joins the coast beyond Delphi, links a series of appealing little coastal towns, all delightful stop-off points.

Gulf of Corinth
🅰 139 D1

Galaxidion
🅰 139 D1

Archaeological & Nautical Museum
✉ Mouseio 4
☎ 0265 41558
💲 $

The first of these is **Galaxidion,** its houses radiating from a headland and painted in white and pretty pastel colors. The dome of the church is clearly visible as you approach the town, in pride of place on the headland, and dedicated to Agios Nikolaos, patron saint of sailors. The fine 19th-century mansions that line the waterfront—along with many good tavernas—indicate the importance of shipping to the town. To learn about Galaxidion's past, visit the **Archaeological and Nautical Museum,** which has a small but interesting maritime collection.

The next town of note as you head west along the coast is **Nafpaktos,** which is also built around a headland, this time crowned by a 15th-century **Venetian fortress.** Take a walk to the top for views along the coast

Throwing flour is part of the pre-Lenten fun on "Clean Monday" in Galaxidion.

and across the gulf. The castle walls extend to the sea and around the harbor, with one of the old gates leading to the town's beach.

The medieval Venetian name for Nafpaktos was Lepanto, and this was the scene of the last major sea battle to be fought with ships propelled primarily by oars, in 1571. The Battle of Lepanto was between the Turks, who occupied Greece at that time, and an attacking fleet made up of a Christian Alliance from several European nations. The Turks lost the battle but did not lose Greece. One notable casualty was the Spaniard Miguel de Cervantes Saavedra (1547–1616), the author of *Don Quixote,* who lost his left hand in the fight.

From Nafpaktos it is a short drive southwest to **Andirrion,** from where the ferries leave for the short sail across the Gulf of Corinth to Rio, just outside Patra on the Peloponnese side. A road bridge is also under construction. The main reason for visiting Andirrion is to explore the remains of the Franco-Venetian castle that stands guard over this stretch of water—known to the Greeks as the Little Dardanelles—and matches another castle on the far side.

Beyond Andirrion the road swings inland and crosses a slightly flatter landscape as it heads for the marshes and saltpans that surround the town of **Messolongi.** This is where Lord Byron died of a fever, and his statue stands in the town's **Garden of Heroes.** Beneath the statue, erected in 1881, is buried the poet's heart.

Close to the garden is the **Gate of the Exodus,** through which you'll probably pass on your way in or out of Messolongi. In 1826, two years after Byron's death, the town was besieged by Turkish forces. In a desperate bid for freedom, an

Nafpaktos
🗺 139 C1

Messolongi
🗺 139 C1
Visitor information
✉ Tourist Police
☎ 0631 27220

Lord Byron in Greece

"Mad, bad and dangerous to know" was the description given to British poet Lord Byron (1788–1824) by one of his lovers, Lady Caroline Lamb. The sixth Baron Byron also had a memorable love affair with Greece, and it was while traveling there that he wrote one of his most famous works, *Childe Harold's Pilgrimage.* He felt so strongly about the country that in January 1824 he joined Greek rebels fighting the Turkish rulers in the War of Independence. In only three months he was dead, after contracting a fever in Messolongi, then much more swampy than it is today. A statue in the town commemorates the poet, and scarcely a Greek city exists without a Byron (Vyronos) Street somewhere. ■

estimated 9,000 men, women, and children broke out through the gate, leaving their fellow citizens to destroy the town rather than let it again fall into Turkish hands. The rebels fled into the hills, but they were caught and every one of them killed. The bodies of those people left behind are also buried in the Garden of Heroes, under a small, plain mound near Byron's statue.

Byron died at a house on Odos Levidou that was destroyed during World War II. A memorial garden marks the spot. There is a small **museum** you will want to visit if you are especially interested in the War of Independence; its collection includes an original copy of the patriotic poem by Solomos that became the Greek National Anthem, "Hymn to Freedom." ■

The gleaming mosaics with somber saints' faces at Osiou Louka date from the 11th century.

Osiou Louka

THE MONASTERY OF OSIOU LOUKA (BLESSED LUKE) STANDS alone in an olive-filled valley surrounded by mountains, just a few miles down a side road off the Athens–Delphi road. The saint to whom it is dedicated was a Greek hermit, not the more famous Gospel-writer. He died in A.D. 953 and is buried in a crypt at the monastery. The chapels here are among the best examples of Byzantine architecture in Greece, and contain some of the finest preserved frescoes in the country. Despite its isolated position, Osiou Louka is usually busy, not just because of the frescoes or reverence for St. Luke, but because it makes a convenient second stop on one-day trips from Athens to Delphi.

Osiou Louka
- 139 D1
- 0261 24088
- Closed Mon.
- $

St. Luke was probably born in Delphi in A.D. 896, to parents who had fled from Egina to escape the Saracens. Known to be spiritual and somewhat other worldly even as a very young child, Luke left home in his teens to seek solitude. He gained a reputation as a healer, and was soon credited with miraculous cures. Eventually Luke settled in the nearby village of Stiri, and the first church on the site of the monastery was built between 941 and 944 and dedicated to St. Barbara.

By this time Luke had also developed an apparent gift for prophecy, and among his predictions was one that Crete would be liberated by an emperor named Romanos. In 961, eight years after Luke's death, Crete was taken from its Arab rulers by the Byzantines under Emperor Romanos, and in that same year, in recognition of Luke's prophecy, Romanos built a larger church alongside that of St. Barbara.

The first thing to greet you when you arrive at Osiou Louka is a glowing gold mosaic of the saint on an arch over the entrance gate into the monastery proper. The church built by Romanos has been replaced by one built in 1020, known as the **Katholikon.** It is an awesome experience to enter the tall building, with its marble walls, and see the light slanting in from high windows onto the ancient frescoes, some of which date back to the original building of the church at the start of the 11th century. However, many of the frescoes were repainted after an earthquake in 1659 damaged the monastery.

The finest of the mosaics is reckoned to be *The Washing of the Apostles' Feet,* which is in the narthex high up to your left as you enter the main, western door. It is a striking work, not only for the bright gold and other colors that remain, but for the very human expression on the faces of the Apostles. It helps to have some binoculars with you to get a good look at this and the other exquisite mosaics.

Beneath the Katholikon is the crypt containing the body of St. Luke; the entrance is at the side. More frescoes dating back to the 11th century are here, although it is difficult to fully appreciate them as the light is kept low, both out of reverence to the remains of the

saint and also to help preserve the frescoes.

In an unusual arrangement, the smaller church of the **Theotokos** (the God-Bearing, referring to the Virgin Mary) is connected to the larger church. The Theotokos is thought to have been built in the years 997–1011, so it is slightly older than the Katholikon. Its mosaics are easier to see, most being on the floor, although there are some wall frescoes. Note, too, the elaborate exterior brickwork.

The monastery has outbuildings that can be explored, as well as a museum containing finds from the site, and shops indicating the popularity of the place for pilgrims. Don't miss the terrace, which gives wonderful views across farmland and groves of olives and almond trees to the Elikonas Mountains beyond.

Only a handful of monks still live here, and the daily round of visitors is a necessary interruption to their monastic life. Lucky indeed is the visitor who arrives here to find the tranquillity that the monks themselves seek out, and can perhaps share it with them, if only for a while. If you want to enjoy the place in as peaceful a way as possible, arrive early or late in the day to avoid the crowds. If that is not possible, don't avoid it—it is still a magical place at any time. ■

Icons

Icons have become universal in our modern world, but the specific meaning goes back to the Greek *eikon*, meaning an image of a person. In some churches that is all it is: an image or depiction of the saint or other holy person. In Eastern Orthodox religions like the Greek Church, however, the image itself is sacred. When you visit

churches and see worshippers kneeling before an icon, or kissing it, they are communicating directly with the person portrayed. Icon painting in Greece goes back to the earliest days of Christianity and continues to this day. Greeks still buy them, both large ones for the home and small ones for their cars, and they make unusual souvenirs. ■

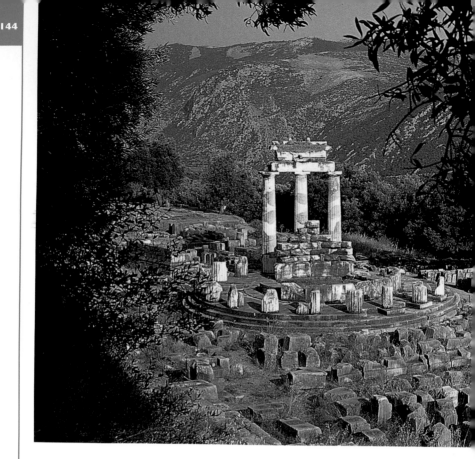

Delphi

THE ANCIENT GREEKS CONSIDERED DELPHI THE CENTER
of the world, and to the modern visitor looking to travel beyond
Athens, it should be the center of any itinerary. The site lies on the
southern slopes of the Parnassos Mountains, looking out over a wide
valley filled with olive trees that falls away towards the coast. Even
without the wonders of the ancient site, it would be unforgettable.

Delphi
- 🗺 139 D2
- ☎ 0265 82312 (site & museum)
- 🕐 Open daily
- 💲 $$

Visitor information
- ✉ Tourist Police
- ☎ 0265 82220

At no time of year is Delphi empty
of visitors so, if you have your inde-
pendence and are not reliant on an
organized tour, it is worth staying at
least one night in either modern
Delphi or the next village along,
Arachova. This will ensure that you
can be at Delphi early in the
morning or toward the end of the
day, and enjoy its marvelous sights
in relative peace.

When you visit Delphi you are
part of a tradition that goes back
over 3,000 years. In the 12th cen-
tury B.C., the first pilgrims began to
come here to seek advice from the
Pythia, the most famous oracle of
the ancient world. They continued
to do so in large numbers until the
fourth century A.D. The traditional
time to visit was on the seventh
day of the month, when anyone

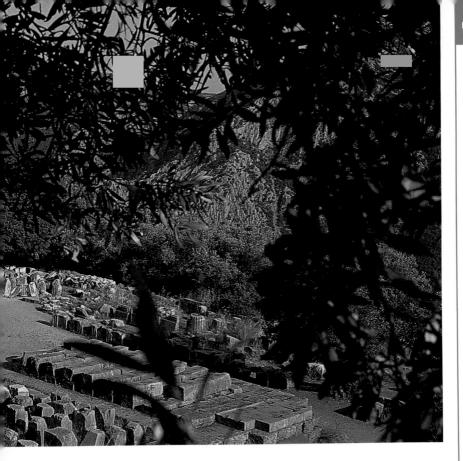

could ask questions of the oracle for guidance on matters large or small. From tablets and fragments that have been found here and at other oracles, it can be seen that concerns through the ages have changed little. People wanted to know if their partner was faithful, whether they could trust a friend, or whether to take up a particular offer of work.

The oracle was not one particular person, but a woman (usually over age 50) deemed to have been given the powers of prophecy by the god Apollo. The Pythia was attended by priests, who interpreted her prophecies. It is thought that when called upon to prophesy she might have gone into a drug-induced trance, resulting in utterances that needed a great

deal of translating, so making the priest's job a vital one.

The **Rock of the Sibyl,** which stands on the spot where she was consulted, is marked to one side of the paved **Sacred Way.** This path leads up through the site to the remains of the **Temple of Apollo,** which dates from the fourth century B.C. (an earlier building is known to have existed here in the sixth century B.C.). The temple was discovered by French archaeologists exploring here only in 1892, and since then six of the temple's fallen Doric columns have been re-erected to try to give a sense of the grandeur of the building.

Above the temple is the **theater,** which has survived remarkably from the fourth century B.C., when it was built to hold 5,000

The beautiful rotunda, or tholos, in the Sanctuary of Athena was a fourth-century B.C. shrine.

The reconstructed Treasury of the Athenians, on the Sacred Way, was built about 490 B.C. in thanks for the Greek victory at Marathon.

The Delphi senate met in the Bouleuterion.

Treasury of the Athenians

The first oracle stood at the Rock of the Sybil.

Siphnian Treasury

Sikyonian Treasury

Sacred Way

The monument to the king of Argos was built in 369 B.C.

spectators. Beyond the theater, where comparatively few visitors have the time or the inclination to venture, is the **stadium.** This is one of the best examples of its kind in Greece, with much of the seating surviving, including the seats for the VIPs. It held 7,000 people and was used every four years to hold the Pythian Games, which were similar to the Olympic Games.

The **museum** at Delphi is an essential part of the visit. Its treasures, for its size, rival those found on the Acropolis in Athens. The most famous and impressive exhibit is a bronze statue known as "The Charioteer," dramatically placed at the far end of the central corridor. Commissioned to commemorate a notable chariot victory in the Pythian Games in 478 B.C., it was found during excavations in 1896. The life-size statue is apparently top-heavy, but this is the sculptor's trick of perspective,

as the statue was intended to be perched high up on top of its chariot and only seen from below.

The second major exhibit is the sculpture known as "Three Dancing Girls," which it is thought would have been the support for a tripod on which the Pythia would sit to prophesy. Give yourself time to appreciate the museum's many treasures to the full. ■

The Temple of Apollo was built in the fourth century B.C.

The theater, rebuilt by the Romans, offers the best viewpoint over the site.

Meeting hall

Stoa of Attalos

"The Charioteer" wears the victor's headband, his eyes of enamel and colored stones.

Sacred Way

The Sacred Way was the paved route to the sanctuary of Apollo, once lined with statues and treasuries.

Entrance

Parnassos Mountains

BEHIND DELPHI RISE THE DRAMATIC PARNASSOS Mountains. Their highest point is the 8,061-foot (2,457 m) peak of Mount Liakoura, or Wolf Mountain. You are unlikely to see wolves today, as roads make the top easily accessible, and skiers, hikers, and mountain bikers now flock here. The nearby peak of Gerontovrachos, or Old Man's Rock, looms slightly lower at 7,989 feet (2,435 m).

Parnassos National Park

⛰ 139 D2

Much of the area is protected as **Parnassos National Park,** established in 1938. This makes it one of the first national parks in Europe and, with the one around Mount Olympus, the oldest in Greece. It is dominated by forested slopes of Cephalonian fir. Between the trees there are beautiful meadows, colored with alpine flowers in the spring. Only the occasional wolf makes a visit these days, when driven down by especially harsh conditions in the mountains farther north, but there are foxes, badgers, squirrels, and even wild boars. The Parnassos Mountains are home to several species of vulture and eagle, including golden eagles. On a hot day you may well see eagles or is especially known for its cheeses and its robust wine. The roadside stores are also filled with the woolen rugs known as *flokates,* excellent for keeping out the cold mountain air in winter.

From Arachova it is easy to make forays into the lower slopes of the Parnassos range, either by hiring a local guide or simply arming yourself with a good map. As with any mountain walking, however, always keep a watchful eye on the weather, which can change quickly. Let someone at your hotel know where you are going and when you expect to be back.

DELPHI

The modern village of Delphi is another good base, not only for visiting the classical site (see pp. 144–47), which is within walking distance, but for venturing into the mountains. Hotel and restaurant prices are a little higher than at Arachova.

If you are based in Delphi a popular walk leads up to the **Corycian Cave**, which was once the scene of frenzied orgies when it was held to be sacred to Pan, the god of fertility. Today you will need a flashlight, not for illuminating any such activity but rather to see the stalactites and stalagmites inside the cave and to read the inscriptions carved into the walls. Check local conditions before setting off, and note that the cave is not usually accessible between Nov.–April.

From December to April the ski season is in full swing here. The main center is at **Fterolakkas,** a 15-mile (24 km) drive from Arachova. Here you will find a restaurant and a chairlift to take you up to 6,200 feet (1,900 m), from where a ski lift takes you higher up the slopes. The snow gives way to a colorful carpet of wildflowers in spring. ∎

Arachova
139 D2

Delphi
139 D2

vultures circling in the thermals high above, where the ancient site of Delphi backs up against the cliff.

ARACHOVA

Despite being just 7 miles (12 km) from Delphi, and right on the main Athens–Delphi road, this delightful mountain village is little affected by tourism. Beyond the souvenir shops lining the main road the traditional life of Arachova goes on, as you will see if you spend a night or two there and join the local people in their evening *volta,* or watch the men packing into the cafés in the early evening to loudly discuss everything under the sun.

Away from the main road you find narrow streets of traditional houses, and the tavernas serve hearty mountain food. The region

Volos

⚑ 139 E3

Tourist information

✉ Thessaly Region H.Q., Plateia Riga Fereou, Volos

☎ 0421 23500 or 0421 36233

Archaeological Museum

✉ Athanasaki 1

☎ 0421 25285

🕐 Closed Mon.

$ $

Makrinitsa, a traditional village, clings to the mountain slopes.

Volos & the Pilion peninsula

TRADITION HOLDS THAT THE PILION PENINSULA IS WHERE the Greek gods used to go to enjoy themselves by relaxing, eating, and drinking. Today it's where modern Greeks go to do the same, joined by an increasing number of discerning visitors. The region's highlights include beaches, unspoiled mountain villages, forests, good walking, orchards, and abundant fruit and vegetables that make for a unique and excellent cuisine.

In Greek mythology the Pilion was home to the centaurs, those creatures who had the upper torso and head of a man and otherwise the body of a horse, and were known for their lusty, drunken ways. The exception was the wise and good centaur Chiron, who was tutor to the young Jason. In later life Jason undertook a quest for a famous trophy, the Golden Fleece, in order to claim his rightful kingdom. He set off on the heroic quest with his company of Argonauts from **Volos,** the city that marks the gateway to the Pilion.

Volos is now an industrial city and a major port from where visitors head into the Pilion itself. The principal reason to linger in Volos might be to visit the **Archaeological Museum,** an excellent example of its kind, with the best of the treasures from two nearby archaeological sites, at Dimini and Sesklo.

Leaving Volos, enter the green and densely wooded Pilion, where your first port of call, depending upon which route you take, may well be **Makrinitsa.** This mountain village was founded in the 13th century by refugees fleeing from Constantinople. Its steep streets and protected status mean that you will have to leave your vehicle outside the village and proceed on foot. Several traditional mansions have been well restored, and some of these are now available as hotel accommodations. There are also a number of old churches to explore, and a monastery, as well as a wonderful view over Volos and the bay on which it stands.

Vizitsa is a similar village farther south in the Pilion, and should also not be missed. Vizitsa, too, has mansions restored for use as guesthouses and a few eating places for those lucky enough to stay there. It can be busy during the daytime, but at night it is more like the peaceful, traditional mountain settlement it has always been.

To reach Vizitsa, turn off the road at the larger village of **Mileai,** where there are more attractive old mansions, as well as churches to visit and the small Mileai **Folklore Museum.** The village is connected to Volos by a steam train on summer weekends, offering an exhilarating way to enjoy some of the Pilion's lovely scenery.

If you're looking for a beach head for **Agios Ioannis,** an attractive small resort at the end of a steep zigzagging road coming down from Pilion's hills. It has a good beach with water sports and several restaurants serving Pilion cuisine for an evening meal overlooking the water.

South from Agios Ioannis is the inland village of **Tsagkaranda,** sprawling over a wide area yet keeping a distinctly village feel. Its main claim to fame is the biggest and oldest plane tree in Greece, reputedly a thousand years old and with a massive trunk 59 feet (18 m) in circumference. This whole area is covered in forests of plane and oak, with apple and cherry orchards, and whitewashed houses, their terraces draped in vines.

Farther south still is a small bump at the end of the peninsula, called Trikerion. It is much quieter than the rest of the Pelion. The beautiful fishing village of **Agia Kiriaki** is everything you ever dreamed a Greek fishing village could be. Boats are still made here by traditional methods in the boatyard. Although there's no beach, just a few rooms to rent and a few places to eat, the village still makes an idyllic location to spend a few days. It is connected by road and tracks to the even more peaceful hilltop village of Trikeri. Regular boats leave in summer for the Sporades, if you wish to move on into the Aegean. ∎

Exploring on horseback. The Pilion was the home of the mythological centaurs, half man and half horse.

Mileai
🏔 139 E3

Folklore Museum
✉ Mileai
☎ 0423 86602
🕐 Closed Mon.–Tues. & Nov.–March
💲 $

Meteora

Meteora

⬜ 139 C4

☎ 0432 22649

🕐 Varies with monastery & season, so check ahead. All closed 1–3 p.m.

$ $$

METEORA IS ONE OF THE MOST EXTRAORDINARY PLACES in the world. The name means "rocks in the air," which is a simple and accurate description. A series of sandstone rocks rise from the surrounding plain of Thessalia like tall lumps of clay on a potter's wheel. They were formed some 30 million years ago beneath the sea, and it was the pounding of the water on the sandstone that created these weird Daliesque shapes, left high and dry when the sea retreated.

A primitive chair lift offers a perilous alternative to climbing hundreds of steps.

**Opposite:
The much-photographed Roussanou Monastery was founded about 1288.**

Reaching for the sky as they do, it is hardly surprising the rocky pinnacles were seen as places of religious retreat, and their inaccessibility led to their use by hermits seeking spiritual solitude. The first was probably a man named Barnabas, who moved into a cave on one of the rocks in A.D. 985. A colony of hermits seems a contradiction in terms, but that is what developed around the several rocks that form Meteora, until a monastery was eventually founded in 1336.

That first monastery was the **Megalo Meteoro,** begun by a monk named Athanasios on a pinnacle 1752 feet (534 m) high. Athanasios came here from Mount Athos (see pp. 188–89), and his hermit's cave can still be seen

outside the entrance to the monastery. Other monks and monasteries followed, until at one time there were 24. Today only 13 monasteries remain, of which six are open to the public. To give the remaining monks and nuns some solitude, all six do not open at the same time. Check locally for the current opening hours, as they can change at short notice.

How did the monks build these monasteries on top of sheer cliff faces? It was only in recent times that paths were cut into the rocks to create greater access for people, and at the **Monastery of Varlaam** you can still see the winch formerly used to haul both supplies and visitors up in a basket at the end of a rope. One theory is that kites were flown over the rocks, trailing strings tied to light ropes, which in turn were used to haul up stronger ropes to build the first rope ladders to the summits. No one knows for sure, but what was created is absolutely amazing.

Visiting the monasteries is easiest by car. The nearest accommodations are in the village of Kastraki, or slightly farther away in the town of Kalambaka. From here you can walk to the nearest monastery, **Agia Triada,** in about 30 minutes. Or you can take one of the several daily buses to the farthest monastery, **Metamorphosis,** and walk or get a later bus back again. ■

Metsovon
🗺 138 B4

Tositsa Mansion
✉ Tositsa
☎ 0656 41084
🕐 Closed Thurs.
💲 $

Averoff Gallery
✉ Off central square
☎ 0656 41210
🕐 Closed Tues.
💲 $

Metsovon

TO TRAVEL FROM THE PLAINS OF THESSALY INTO THE
western region of Epiros (Epirus) involves a drive over the highest
road pass in Greece, which is 5,599 feet (1,707 m) high and often
closed in winter. Nearby is the lovely mountain town of Metsovon,
full of character and atmosphere, reflecting the independent spirit
of the people who live high in these hills. Some are settled Vlach
nomads (see pp. 158–59), although a few hill dwellers retain the old
nomadic lifestyle.

Metsovon is very much on the
tourist trail, as it is a ski resort in
winter and popular with walkers in
summer, but it has lost none of
its charm. It has developed a
distinctive and hearty cuisine
including strong sheep's cheeses,
game, and robust red wine, and
there are plenty of restaurants in
the town offering you a chance to
try it. Stores sell wine, honey, and
cheeses—great for gifts or a picnic
lunch. Other souvenirs reflect the
cultivation of arts and crafts in
the area, especially in embroidery,

silverware, and in the carving of
wooden shepherd's crooks, which
are carried by almost every old
man in the town. Some older men
still wear their traditional dark blue
or black pleated costumes, not
unlike the kilted outfit of the Greek
army, complete with their pom-
pommed shoes.

Metsovon has flourished for
many years, thanks to judicious tax
benefits under the Ottoman rule
because of its position at the head
of this vital mountain pass.

Merchants prospered under
these favorable conditions, and
some of their grand mansions can
still be seen; one such, the **Tositsa
Mansion,** is open to the public.
The Tositsa family was prominent
in Metsovon and a famous benefac-
tor, not just locally but across
Greece. The family *archontiko*
(mansion) has been preserved as
a museum, to give visitors an
indication of the sumptuous
lifestyle. Three floors are elegantly
laid out with expensive furniture,
rugs, silverware, jewelry, and
local folk costumes. Entry to the
museum is via guided tour, offered
every half hour.

The Averoffs were another
wealthy and influential local family.
The **Averoff Gallery** displays
the collection of 19th and 20th-
century art built up by writer
and politician Evangelou Averoff
(1910–1990). ∎

**Snow-clad in
winter, the hills
around Metsovon
offer wonderful
hiking in the
summer.**

Pindos Mountains

THE PINDOS IS ONE OF THE MIGHTIEST MOUNTAIN RANGES in Greece, stretching from its northern borders west to the Ionian Sea, south to Metsovon, and east into Macedonia. The range encompasses two national parks, the second longest gorge in Europe, and some of the highest mountain peaks in the country.

One area of the Pindos is protected in the **Vikos-Aoös National Park,** which was created in 1973 and covers the area around the Vikos Gorge. The larger **Pindos National Park** was created in 1966, in part to protect the Balkan and black pines that have covered these mountain slopes for thousands of years. This park technically belongs in the Macedonia chapter, but the Pindos Mountains pay no heed to regional boundaries. Here you find Greece's remaining wolves and bears (see p. 156), as well as deer, wild boar, wildcats, and chamois. There are snakes too, such as the dice snake and the nose-horned viper, so watch out if walking in the more remote areas. When not watching the ground, scan the skies for signs of the many birds of prey that survive here, including the goshawk, Egyptian vulture, golden eagle, imperial eagle, and griffon vulture.

Fed with spring meltwater from the Pindos range, this braided river fills its wide riverbed.

Pindos Mountains
 138 B4

Konitsa

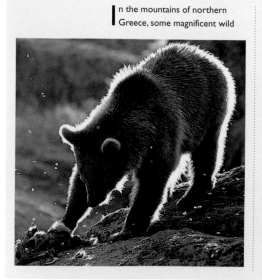 138 B4

These are rugged and potentially dangerous mountains, so if you have never done any serious mountain walking, do not venture into the Pindos without a guide, and never go out on your own. The peaks are covered in snow from October until May, longer in severe winters, and when the snows melt the waters come cascading down the rivers. Paths normally easy to follow in midsummer can become dangerous.

The ultimate challenge for experienced trekkers is **Mount Smolikas,** which at 8,459 feet (2,637 m) is Greece's second highest peak after Mount Olympus. To reach the summit requires several days, good preparation, and either your own camping equipment or reservations for the mountain huts that provide shelter on the slopes. Even if you don't intend to tackle any serious challenges, be aware that Greece's footpath network is not well marked; often the only directional signs are blobs of red paint dabbed onto rocks.

The southern Pindos Mountains are covered elsewhere in this chapter, as they are full of prime visitor attractions such as the Zagorian villages, the Vikos Gorge, Ioanina, Dodoni, and Metsovon. The northern sector of the mountains are more remote and less developed for tourism, and will satisfy anyone looking for a more rugged and arguably more Greek mountain experience. The accommodations in some towns may be much simpler than you will find elsewhere, but the hospitality will more than compensate—and it is unlikely you will ever be short of something to eat or somewhere to sleep.

The small town of **Konitsa,** just a few miles from the Albanian border, is a popular center for walkers There are a handful of hotels and eating places here, and a chance to hire local guides if you want to explore this remote corner

Bears & wolves

I n the mountains of northern Greece, some magnificent wild creatures survive—despite the Greek fondness for hunting and the farmers who kill anything that might threaten their often meager livelihood. The most splendid—and rarest—of these wild animals are the European brown bear *(Ursus arctos)* and the European silver wolf *(Canis lupus)*.

Sadly, you are unlikely to see either species as they are seriously endangered, but it is to be hoped that increased ecological awareness in Greece has come in time to save them. There are thought to be less than a hundred bears, and perhaps a few hundred wolves, mostly concentrated in the national parks in northern Greece: Vikos-Aoös, Pindos, and Prespa. ∎

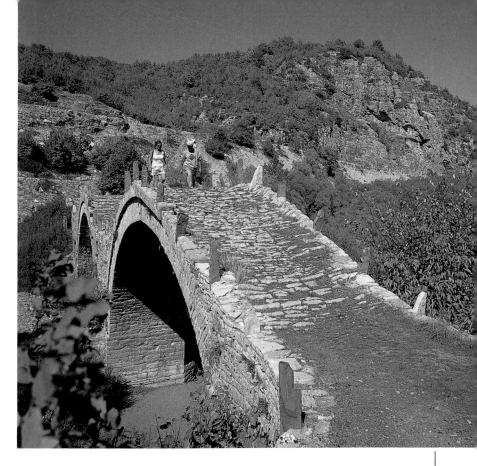

of the country. Konitsa has a beautiful setting, overlooked by Mount Trapezitsa and in turn overlooking the River Aoös. The waters are spanned by a huge and imposing bridge built in 1870, and river-kayaking, a fairly new sport in Greece, is becoming popular here.

Konitsa was badly damaged by an earthquake in 1996, and some of its older buildings were destroyed. The old bazaar area survived, however, as did the small Turkish quarter, and both add spice to the lively but remote town.

From Konitsa it is possible to walk south to climb **Mount Gamila** (8,134 feet/2,497 m). This requires a night's stay at the mountain hut at Astraka, and you can take in a visit to the mountain lake of Drakolimni. Alternatively, heading east takes you to Mount Smolikas via the mountain hut at Naneh and another mountain lake, Drakolimni (Dragon's Lake).

The road running northwest from Konitsa heads toward the Albanian border, which until a few years ago would have been out of bounds to travelers. It is still a sensitive area due to the recent Balkan conflicts, and you may be required to show your passport before being allowed to proceed. The reward for your adventure will be a visit to the village of **Molivdoskepastos,** right by the border and providing unrivaled views into Albania and back toward the Pindos peaks of Smolikas and Gamila. Venture here and you have truly reached one of the most remote corners of Greece. ■

A packhorse bridge with three spans marks the old trail near the village of Kipi.

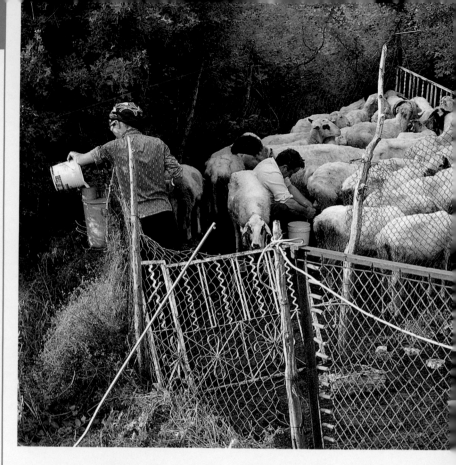

Greece's nomads

Few visitors realize, when lying on an Aegean beach or enjoying a meal in a five-star hotel in Athens, that Greece is still home to small groups of nomads whose cultural roots go back thousands of years. There are not many left these days—it is a way of life that is dying out everywhere—but they are still to be found in the more remote parts of Epiros, around the mountain town of Metsovon, and in the depths of the Pindos Mountains.

The largest group is the Vlachs, whose name is linked to the Romanian region of Wallachia. They were shepherds who led a nomadic existence, wandering throughout Central and Eastern Europe and down into the Balkans, traveling to wherever they could find the best grazing for their sheep.

The Vlach "capital" has always been Metsovon (see p. 154), close to the highest road pass in Greece, on the road between Meteora on the Thessaly plains, and Ioanina, the main town in Epiros. Many Vlachs live in Metsovon today, but they have settled into houses and no longer live as shepherds. Although their way of life is dying out, it is still possible to catch a last glimpse of a proud and independent people.

Some maintain their traditional way of life, taking their flocks of sheep down to warmer climes and better grazing in winter, and back up again into the cooler Pindos Mountains in summer. Although nomads, these shepherds live in houses, simply migrating from one base to another over the year, unlike the Sarakatsani (see below) who carry their tents with them. In older times, a wealthy

Left: The long-legged mountain sheep are valued for their milk yield as well as for their meat and fleece. You'll hear the "tonk" of sheep bells all over the Greek countryside.
Above: Older people such as this Vlach shepherd remember a nomadic way of life.

Vlach shepherd might have had as many as 10,000 sheep, though today the handful of flocks that remain and are moved between winter and summer pastures number only a few hundred.

No one knows for sure where the Vlachs came from. One theory suggests that they were descendants of Roman legionaries, who were stationed or settled in Central Europe. Another theory is that the Greek Vlachs are native to the area, and the origins of their nomadic lifestyle go back to the Roman occupation, when the local mountain people would have been put to work as shepherds or as guards on the Via Egnatia. This road connected Rome with the more distant parts of its empire, going through the Pindos Mountains, through Meteora, on to the important Balkan port of Thessaloniki, and beyond that all the way to Constantinople (Istanbul). When the Romans eventually left, the nomadic way of life would have continued.

The Romans left behind aspects of their language. The Vlach people have their own tongue, with many linguistic connections still to Latin and Italian. In fact, Vlachs were often employed as interpreters when Italy occupied these mountains during World War II.

The other main nomadic group—rivals to the Vlachs—is the Sarakatsani, who were also traditionally shepherds. They occupied the area of Macedonia and Thrace in eastern Greece, and even fewer survive. The Sarakatsani are native Greeks and speak Greek. Some still move their flocks between the plains of Thrace in winter and the Pindos Mountains in summer.

To learn more about the Sarakatsani, and to see examples of their traditional costumes and the tents they lived in, visit the Folklife and Ethnological Museum in Thessaloniki (see p. 184) and the Museum of Greek Folk Art in Athens (see p. 65). ∎

Zagorian villages & the Vikos Gorge

NORTH OF IOANINA, AS YOU HEAD TOWARD THE Albanian border, you come to Zagoria, one of the most intriguing regions of northern Greece. Forty-six Zagorian villages, with their own distinctive architecture and culture, are linked together by a network of paths that make ideal walking through the superb scenery of the lower Pindos Mountains.

One of the great natural features of the area is the **Vikos Gorge,** which runs for 7 miles (12 km) and is only 2 miles (3 km) shorter than the Samaria Gorge in Crete (see pp. 300–301). In places its walls rise 3,117 feet (950 m) sheer from the ground, while elsewhere it opens out to flower-filled meadows, with the opportunity to swim in the Voidhomatis River at the right times of year. If you are reasonably fit and have arranged transport and accommodations, it is possible to walk the gorge in one day.

Extra care must be taken for the gorge is relatively free of other walkers. Traveling at the best times—in early and late summer—you may see only a handful of other people, so a twisted ankle or dehydration could become a serious problem. In winter the gorge may not be passable, and the same applies in April and May, when the mountain snows melt and turn the trickling rivers into thundering torrents. Always take local advice on conditions, and let people know where you are planning to walk.

It would take at least a week just to begin to explore this region. The **Zagorian villages** are fascinating, and the history and the landscape are richly intertwined. The cultural wealth is a result of the region's past poverty. The harsh landscape made it hard for people to scrape out a living here, and many were forced to seek work abroad, but sent money to their families left behind. The Turks, who ruled from Ioanina 31 miles (50 km) to the south, granted Zagoria autonomy, so that the steadily growing wealth from abroad was largely retained, and was used in the 18th and 19th centuries to build houses known as *archontika*. These are modest in size, but grand in comparison to the average mountain home. Some are derelict and romantically crumbling, others are lived in, while some have been restored for use as museums or guesthouses. This corner of the Pindos is not thickly wooded, so the mansions are mostly built from the local limestone, with slate roofs. Often there is space for the animals on the ground floor and a walled yard. They give the small Zagorian villages a very distinctive look.

Some of the villages are now deserted or have just a handful of families supporting themselves by agriculture, but others prosper from the increasing tourism in the area. They are popular with mountaineers, walkers, and more adventurous visitors. The best bases for exploring are the main villages of **Monodendri, Tsepelovo,** and **Megalo** and **Mikro Papingo.** They have guesthouses, restaurants, and stores, and walking guides are usually available. If you don't have a car, you can reach these villages by the regular bus from Ioanina. ■

Vikos Gorge
🄰 138 B4

A waymarked track runs through the bottom of the gorge, which is part of the Vikos-Aoös National Park.

Ioanina

Ioanina
⚑ 138 B4
**Visitor
information**
✉ Epiros Region H.Q.,
Dodonis 39
☎ 0651 41868

**Byzantine
Museum/Silverwork
Hall**
✉ Inside citadel
☎ 0651 25989 or
39580
🕓 Closed Mon.
💲 $

**Beaten silverware
for sale in Ioanina
shows Turkish
influences.**

THE SLIM MINARETS OF ALI PASHA'S CITADEL POKING
above the lakeside trees are a distinctive feature of this beautiful
regional capital. Idyllically situated on the shores of Lake Pamvotis,
with the Pindos Mountains on the far side beyond the delightful
central island of Nissi, it is a lovely place to spend a few days.

It is wise not to make too many
complimentary remarks around
here about Ali Pasha, the
murderous tyrant who dominated
the city from 1788 until his death
on Nissi in 1822, for local feeling
still runs high. Ioanina was under
the Turkish yoke for almost 500
years, the longest and blackest spell
in Greek history, and Turkish
influence has survived here more
strongly than elsewhere. Yet the
name of Ali Pasha is inextricably
entwined in the town's history,
whether the present citizens like
it or not.

Under the Ottomans Ioanina
flourished as a center for arts and
crafts, notably for silversmiths.

Even today, silver from Ioanina is
considered to be among the finest
in Greece, and you might still find a
few craftsmen working in cramped
workshops in the back streets.
Samples of their best work can be
seen in an annex to the **Byzantine
Museum,** which is inside the
citadel and contains excellent and
well-explained collections of
Byzantine art. The nearby
Silverwork Hall includes some
exquisite pieces and a reconstructed
silversmith's workshop.

Next to the Byzantine Museum
is the **Fethiye Tzami,** or Victory
Mosque *(not open to the public)*. In
front stands the unmarked and
untended grave of Ali Pasha.

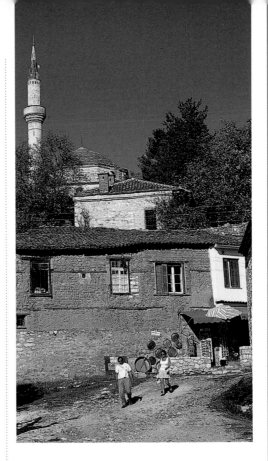

Also within the citadel, and inside the Aslan Pasha Tzami mosque, is the **Popular Art Museum.** This is worth visiting if only to see inside the mosque, which was first built in 1619, but it also has a good collection of folk costumes, jewelry, and other arts and crafts from the town.

Outside the citadel, the town's **Archaeological Museum** is an essential visit if you plan to go to Dodoni (see pp. 166–67), as many of the finds from that historic site are displayed here.

The other essential visit in Ioanina is to **Nissi,** the island in the lake, reached by a regular ferry service from in front of the citadel walls. The name Nissi is Greek for "island." There is one small, straggling village on the island, where the inhabitants make a living from fishing or tourism. Visitors and local people like to sail across for lunch or dinner on the island, for it has several excellent fish tavernas. However, contrary to what the owners may tell you, most of the fish served on Nissi comes from fish farms in the mountains, not from the lake. A unique ingredient is found on the menus of Nissi: frogs' legs. These are so abundant in the area and so tasty that they are even exported to France. Now is the time to give them a try!

A trail goes all the way around the island, which makes for a lovely short walk. Because Nissi is not spoiled it is still good for wildlife, and you might see or hear nightingales, as well as reed buntings, kestrels, woodpeckers, and a variety of waterfowl. Look for signs to the island's only cultural attraction, the **Ali Pasha Museum** (Closed Oct–April, $), in the Monastery of Panteleimon. This was built in the 16th century but the present building is a modern reconstruction, the original having been demolished by a falling tree. It was here that Ali Pasha was assassinated, not by the local Greeks but by Turks from Istanbul. Ali's own rulers had become concerned at the power and wealth he had accumulated, and knew he had declared his ambition to create an independent state. Ali was besieged in his citadel but managed to escape to the island in the lake, taking refuge in the monastery. Unsympathetic locals gave away his hiding place, and the Turks shot him through the floorboards from a downstairs room; the bullet holes can still be seen. Ali was beheaded and his head sent to the Sultan in Istanbul to prove that the mission had been accomplished. It is a violent past, at odds with the peaceful nature of the lake today. ■

Elegant minarets are a prime feature of this intriguing town.

Popular Art Museum
- ✉ Inside citadel
- ☎ 0651 20515
- 🕐 Closed Sat.–Sun.
- 💲 $

Archaeological Museum
- ✉ Plateia 25 Martiou
- ☎ 0651 33357
- 🕐 Closed Mon.
- 💲 $

Walking in Ali Pasha's Ioanina

You may be forgiven for thinking in some parts of Ioanina that you have wandered into a Middle Eastern city, or at any rate a Turkish one: 500 years of Turkish rule have left a significant legacy. No one had more impact on the town than the evil ruler Ali Pasha, and this walk takes in some of the sites associated with him, beginning with the citadel from which he ruled with an iron hand.

A small ferryboat links Nissi to the mainland.

The walk begins at the main entrance to the **citadel ❶**, which is the second entrance through the thick fortress walls on your right as you walk down Karamanli from Plateia Neomart Yioryiou. A small shrine is in the wall beside the entrance. Go through the entrance and turn immediately left along Ioustinianou. You will pass on the right the **Old Synagogue** (*not open to the public*), which was built in 1790. Ioanina had a big Jewish community that dated back to the 13th century, but only a few dozen Jewish people survived World War II.

Follow the street past the synagogue until the end, when it bends to the right and leads you toward the Aslan Pasha Tzami mosque. This contains the **Popular Art Museum ❷** (see p. 163). The other rooms around the courtyard are not open to the public, and it was in these that one of the worst episodes of Ali's tyrannical rule took place. He raped the mistress of his eldest son, then threw her and 17 other women into the lake in weighted sacks so that they could not reveal his dreadful crime.

On leaving the mosque by the way you came in, turn left to resume the walk. Keep to the left, just inside the citadel walls, and ignore

- ⓜ See area map p. 138
- ► Main entrance to citadel
- ⟷ 1.25 miles (2 km)
- ⏱ 2 hours
- ► Nissi

NOT TO BE MISSED
- Popular Art Museum
- Byzantine Museum
- Silverwork Hall
- Island of Nissi
- Ali Pasha Museum

the sign that points you down "To the Lake" through a gateway. Instead carry on ahead and through the entrance gates into the inner citadel. On the left is a café, and the modern building ahead of you is the **Byzantine Museum ❸** (see p. 162), with the **Fethiye Mosque** *(not open to the public)* to its left, in front of which is the probable tomb of Ali Pasha. The museum's **Silverwork Hall ❹** annex is over to your right, in what was once Ali Pasha's Treasury building.

Return to the gate that gives access to the lake, and take the steps down to the lakeside, turning left until you reach the departure point for the **ferries to Nissi ❺** (see p. 163). The little ferryboats leave every 30 minutes in summer, and every hour in winter, from 8 a.m. to 11 p.m. Take the ferry across to the island. No doubt you'll be in the company of a few other visitors, but for the most part with islanders returning from their errands.

On reaching the island turn left to walk through a small network of streets, following the signs that direct you to the **Ali Pasha Museum ❻** (see p. 163). This has an interesting collection of Ali Pasha artifacts, and you can see the holes left by the bullets that killed him. From the museum you can

Ali Pasha's house was reconstructed after being damaged by a falling tree.

safely continue on around the rest of the island, which is surrounded by reed beds. There are lovely views across to the Pindos Mountains, and back across the lake to Ioanina, although in places you will be unaware of the busy town's existence.

Carry on along the path, where you may see fishermen mending their nets, until you return to the ferry quay for the boats back to Ioanina. ■

Limni Ioaninon

Popular Art Museum

Ferries to Nissi

❺

Nissi Island

KARAMANLI

Old Synagogue

Silverwork Hall ❹

Fethiye Mosque

Ali Pasha Museum ❻

START ❶ Citadel Main Entrance

❸ Byzantine Museum

PLATEIA NEOMART YEORYIOU

0   300 meters
0   300 yards

More places to visit in Central Greece

DODONI

Although the oracle at Delphi is the world-famous one, Dodoni too had its oracle. The Oracle of Zeus is much older, and second in importance only to Delphi. Religious ceremonies took place here at least as early as 2000 B.C. The site is beautifully set in a high valley (2,065 feet/630 m) below a range of hills, some 14 miles (22 km) southwest of Ioanina.

Either before or after visiting the site, you should visit the **Archaeological Museum** in Ioanina (see p. 163), where finds from Dodoni are on display. The most interesting of these are tablets on which some of the questions put to the oracle were inscribed. They include such timeless dilemmas as "Am I the father of her children?"

The most impressive feature at Dodoni is its **theater,** which is one of the largest in Greece and dates back to the third century B.C. It was reconstructed in the late 19th century, and again in the 1960s, and is still used in the

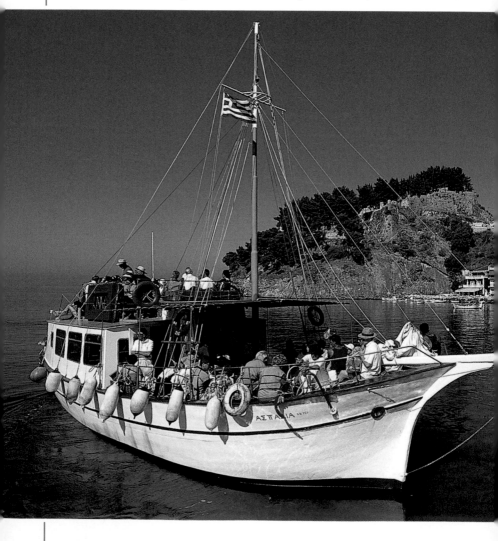

summer for occasional performances. Its thick walls tower over the visitor. Note the drainage channels around the sides, built by the Romans when the theater was used to stage animal fights and gladiatorial contests. You can still see the pens on either side of the stage where bulls, lions, tigers, and other fierce creatures would have been kept before their release into the arena in front of 17,000 yelling spectators.

It was right next to the theater that the Sanctuary of Zeus was located, and the oracle. A good deal is known about the process of consulting the oracle here. A sacred oak tree was completely surrounded by cauldrons on tripods, each one touching the next. The seeker's question was written down on a lead tablet and passed to a priest, who read the question to the oracle. The answer was the priest's interpretation of the noise made by the leaves on the oak tree and the sounds emanating from the cauldrons.

138 B4 ☎ 0651 82287 $

PARGA

The beach resort of Parga is one of the most attractive and popular along the Ionian coast. There are several good beaches both in and near the town, a choice of excellent fish restaurants, and easy access to Dodoni, Ioanina, and even the Zagorian villages and the Vikos Gorge (see p. 160). You need your own transportation to get to all of these, and Parga makes a good base from which to explore. It is possible to get ferries to the island of Paxi, which in turn gives access to Corfu. It is also not too far from airports at Preveza, for international charter flights, and at Ioanina, for internal flights. Everything considered, it is not surprising that Parga is popular—and finding a room in the height of summer is not easy unless you make a reservation.

For all its appearance as a simple resort town, Parga has had a fascinating history. At one end of the harbor, lined by restaurants and souvenir shops, is an imposing **Venetian fortress** built in 1624, as a date over one of the gates indicates. You can see the symbol of Venice, the Lion of St. Mark, carved into one of the walls in the keep. The town was conquered by the Turks but then taken by the Venetians at a time when the Turkish Empire dominated most of modern Greece. The British then captured it from the Venetians, and in 1819 sold it back to the Turks, where it came under the control of Ali Pasha at Ioanina. Under his despotic rule many of the natives went into exile in Corfu, the families only returning when Parga became Greek again in 1913.

A cruise boat plies the clear waters off Parga, a resort town with a richly checkered history.

Beyond the headland is one of the town's best beaches, a long sandy stretch, and there are several more to the north and south of the center. Look for dazzling whitewashed houses in the town, with vivid dabs of color from bougainvillea, hibiscus, and morning glory plants that cascade down from walls and balconies. Here too are the small hotels, restaurants, and more souvenir shops that mark it out as a tourist resort. Outside the high season (June–Aug.) these back streets are pretty enough to retain their Greek picture-postcard charm.

🅰 138 A3   **Visitor information**
✉ Alexandrou Paga 18   ☎ 0684 32107

EFYRA

Some 14 miles (22 km) southeast of Parga, on the edge of the village of Mesopotamo, is one of the smallest yet most unusual and haunting ancient sites in Greece. A few apparently insignificant buildings stand on top of a small mound which was once an island, when the level of the Ionian Sea was much higher. This is the **Necromanteion** of Efyra. The spot was believed to be the source of the mythical River Styx and the entrance to Hades (Hell). It was, logically, also the site for the Oracle of the Dead, where people would try to make contact with those who had died, by asking questions of the oracle through the priests here. Hallucinogenic drugs were given to the questioners, who were then led through the small maze of passages that can still be seen, into the center of the underground sanctuary to consult the oracle.

🅰 138 A3   💲 $

KASSOPI

A further 17 miles (27 km) southeast of Efyra, on a hillside above the village of Kamarina, is the site of Ancient Kassopi. A walk along a path through pine woods leads to what was once a city-state. Very little remains of the city, which was abandoned when its citizens moved to Nicopolis, a few miles south, in 31 B.C. But with a little imagination and help from the map at the entrance, it is possible to piece together the basic shape of the settlement. The main attraction is the location, well worth going out of your way to see.

🅰 138 B3

NICOPOLIS

The ancient city of Nicopolis is 4 miles (7 km) north of Preveza. Little is immediately visible on the ground today, but an exploration of the overgrown site starts to reveal something of the shape of what was once a very significant city.

The name means "Victory City," for it was built on the site where the Roman army of Octavian camped before the Battle of Actium in 31 B.C., when they defeated the combined forces of Antony and Cleopatra. It was a victory which was to lead to Octavian becoming the first Emperor of Rome under his adopted name of Augustus and to the founding here of his Victory City.

Some of the walls that remain give an indication of the huge scale of the place; there is also a theater, some remains of baths, and a small museum. The site may have been a good army camping ground but it did not make for the foundation of a successful city, being geographically isolated and with no convenient freshwater supply, as well as subject to subsidence. Nevertheless Nicopolis survived for about a thousand years before being abandoned in 1040.

🅰 138 B3   🕐 Closed Mon.   💲 $

PERAMA CAVES (PERAMA SPILAIA)

One of the best cave systems open to the public is situated on the outskirts of Ioanina. It was only discovered during World War II when a shepherd was looking for a shelter from bombing raids. The explored part of the caves extends for some miles, with more yet to be discovered in what is believed to be the largest cave network in Greece. Parts of these are open to visitors, but only on a guided tour.

The guides illuminate and pick out some of the more striking stalactites and stalag-mites, including natural rock formations said to resemble such objects as the Statue of Liberty, the Leaning Tower of Pisa, and the Sphinx. In all there are around 5,600 feet (1700 m) of passages open to the public, with the caves extending for several miles under the hillside.

🅰 138 B4   ☎ 0651 81650   💲 $$
🚌 Bus 8   ■

Stretching from the Pindos Mountains to the Turkish border, the huge area of northern and eastern Greece comprising Macedonia and Thrace is an area of fascinating geographical, historical, and political diversity.

Macedonia & Thrace

Mosaic floor, Dion

Macedonia & Thrace

MACEDONIA (MAKEDONIA) IS THE COUNTRY'S LARGEST ADMINISTRATIVE district, or prefecture, and it has much to offer the visitor including Greece's second largest city, Thessaloniki. This lively waterfront city has a wealth of history only rivaled by Athens. East of Macedonia is the long, thin prefecture of Thrace (Thraki), where the Turkish influences are more notable the closer you get to the border.

The west of Macedonia is a remote and rugged region bordered by the Pindos Mountains, where wolves and bears still roam the forests. Here, too, are the beautiful Prespa lakes, surrounded by magnificent snowcapped mountains. Mount Olympus, the home of the gods, provides challenging walking and an opportunity to climb to the highest point in the country.

Historic highlights include sites such as ancient Pella, which has some outstanding mosaics. Vergina, where the Macedonian kings had their royal palace, has produced some of the finest archaeological discoveries in Greece.

Hardly seeming to belong to the 21st century, Mount Athos is known as the Monks' Republic and remains devoted to the contemplative life as it has been for the last thousand years. There could be no greater

contrast than the busy beaches and modern nightlife on the neighboring peninsulas of Chalkidiki, which jut into the Aegean Sea.

Although relations with Turkey have improved in recent years, the border is still a sensitive area so take care not to wander too far off the beaten track. And there are plenty of beaten tracks to wander off, as Thrace is not only outstandingly beautiful but also contains some of the most unspoiled and unvisited parts of Greece.

In northern Thrace the Rhodope Mountains separate Greece from its Balkan neighbor, Bulgaria. In the extreme east of the region are the Evros Delta and the Dadia Forest, where wildlife flourishes. There may be no wolves and bears at the eastern extremity of this region, but eagles soar in the sky, and you can feel you are on the very edge of the country. ■

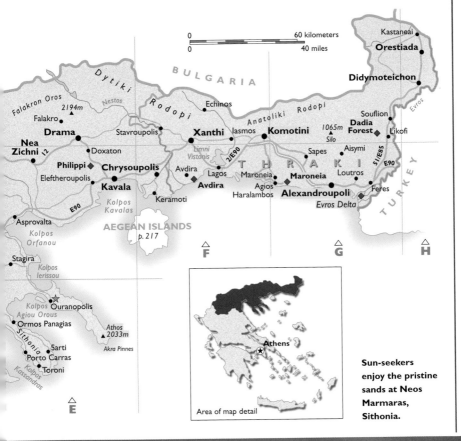

| 0 | 60 kilometers |
| 0 | 40 miles |

BULGARIA

Dytiki
Falakron Oros 2194m ▲
Falakro •
Drama •
Nestos
Rodopi
Echinos •
Anatoliki Rodopi
Kastaneai •
Orestiada •
Didymoteichon
Souflion •
Dadia Forest ★
1065m ▲
Silo
Likofi •
Evros
Stavroupolis •
Xanthi Iasmos •
Komotini
Nea Zichni
12 • Doxaton
Philippi ◆
Chrysoupolis
Limni Vistonis
Avdira •
2/E90
T H R A K I
Sapes •
Aisymi •
Chrysoupolis
Eleftheroupolis •
Kavala
Lagos •
Maroneia •
Avdira ◆
Maroneia •
Loutros •
S1/E85
E90
Alexandroupoli
Feres •
Kolpos Kavalas
Keramoti •
Agios Haralambos •
Evros Delta
TURKEY
Asprovalta •
Kolpos Orfanou
E90
AEGEAN ISLANDS
p. 217
Stagira •
Kolpos Ierissou
Kolpos Agiou Orous **Ouranopolis** ★
• **Ormos Panagias**
Athos ▲ 2033m
Akra Pinnes
Sithonia
• Sarti
Porto Carras
Kolpos Kassandras
• Toroni

△ **E**   △ **F**   △ **G**   △ **H**

Athens ★
Area of map detail

Sun-seekers enjoy the pristine sands at Neos Marmaras, Sithonia.

Mount Olympus & Dion

THE HIGHEST MOUNTAIN IN GREECE IS ALL THE MORE
dramatic because the short range that it belongs to rises sharply from
a flat plain and juts straight up into the sky. It is less than 12 miles
(20 km) from the top of Mount Olympus (Olympos) to the shore of
the Aegean Sea. The main Athens–Thessaloniki highway runs
through the plain that stands between mountain and sea, giving
motorists the chance to stop and admire the spectacular mountains.
As you gaze at the peaks you are looking across Mount Olympus
National Park, home to deer, boar, badgers, and European wildcats, as
well as birds of prey and some 1,700 different plant species. There
are oak and beech forests, and stretches of Macedonian fir, as well as
a centuries-old rare yew grove near the Monastery of Dionysos.

The entire Olympus range is only
12 miles (20 km) from end to end.
The highest point is referred to as
either Mount Olympus or Mount
Mitikas, but there's no doubt about
its height, which is 9,571 feet
(2,917 m). It was not scaled by
mortal man until 1913.

The Greek gods, of course, got
there first. Greeks believed this to
be the site of the Battle of the
Titans, when the 12 Greek gods led

by Zeus defeated the Titans; thus
the wild natural forces, represented
by the Titans, were tamed by the
gods, who introduced some kind of
civilization to the world.

Today, anyone who is reasonably
in shape and does some advance
planning can get to the top, but the
six-hour trek means you must
spend at least one night on the
mountain, either camping out or by
making a reservation at one of the

two mountain refuges. On no account should the trek be attempted by anyone inexperienced, unless accompanied by a local guide.

The base for approaching the mountain and the surrounding park is the busy village of **Litochoron,** which has several hotels and restaurants and is a convenient place for an overnight stop. Here you can stock up on maps, guides, and any equipment you may need.

DION

A 9-mile (14 km) drive from Litochoron brings you to the village of Dion, whose name derives from the word *dios,* meaning "of Zeus." At its center is an excellent small **Archaeological Museum** that displays finds from the site of **Ancient Dion,** found on the edge of the village. Visiting the museum first will help you understand the site; videos show details of the site's excavation and explain its significance. The guidebook is top of the line, and the superb

teaching room on the bottom floor is a must.

Some of the best finds are statues that were beautifully preserved when the ancient city was covered in mud after an earthquake. It was a considerable city, home to about 15,000 people in the fourth century B.C. when it was regarded as a sacred city by the Macedonians. The remains that can be seen today are mostly from the later Roman era and include a fine example of a Roman bathhouse. There are also the remains of a theater and a stadium. The site is well laid out and well marked. Elsewhere there are the remnants of houses both humble and grand, including a splendid mosaic remaining in what was once a banqueting hall.

Don't miss the sanctuary to the Egyptian goddess, Isis, located across the road from the main area. Copies of original statues from the site stand white against the lush greenery around a small pond. It is a gorgeous spot, with a magical setting between mountains and sea. ∎

The home of the gods became Greece's first national park in 1937.

Dion
🅰 170 C1

Archaeological Museum
☎ 0351 53206
💲 $

Greek gods

The highest mountain in Greece, Mount Olympus looms spectacularly from a plain close to the Aegean Sea. Sometimes shrouded in mystical mist, it is easy to understand how ancient Greece regarded Olympus as the home of the gods. To tell the full story of the gods would take an entire book, but a few pointers may help to unravel the stories.

Zeus, fifth century B.C.

The stories were originally oral, passed on in the same way as the Homeric legends of the *Iliad* and the *Odyssey,* by a skilled storyteller to a rapt audience. They were not written down until about the sixth century B.C., and subsequently we have been able to compare similarities in these tales with stories of gods from other countries. In Greece the gods are no longer part of the nation's modern religious beliefs, which are 99 percent Christian, but they are dramatically bound up in the folktales and legends of its prehistory.

Where the stories came from is uncertain, but it is likely that many different strands were involved. One such was Hesiod, an eighth-century B.C. Greek poet who, around the time that Homer was relating his own two epic poems, was responsible for *Theogeny,* a poetic work that tells of "the origin of the gods." This would have been influenced by tales from other cultures of the Near East, as well as by myths and legends handed down by the Mycenean civilization dominant in Greece in the second millennium B.C.

The Father of the Gods was Zeus, who ruled over all the gods from Mount Olympus. Zeus was the youngest son of two of the Titans, children themselves of the Heaven and the Earth. Zeus seized control of the universe and became the god of the sky, the rain god, and father of all later gods and mortals.

Poseidon, a brother of Zeus, became the god of the sea and was the father of the winged horse, Pegasus. Susceptible to the charms of the water nymphs, Poseidon fathered many children. Another brother, Hades, became the god of the Underworld. Zeus' son Apollo, the god of music, agriculture, healing, and prophecy, epitomized civilization. Zeus' favorite child, however, was his daughter, Athena, the goddess of industry, the arts, and wisdom, who gave her name to the city of Athens.

Aphrodite, goddess of love, rose from the waves and became the mother of Cupid. Lesser gods and goddesses were heroes and formed the links between gods and humans, exhibiting some of the qualities of both. ■

Above right: Athena accepting tributes. The gods expected offerings from mortals and responded with anger if offended.
Right: Mount Olympus, throne of Zeus

Kastoria

VISITORS TO THE GREEK ISLANDS AND THE MAINLAND resorts may feel that they are seeing the most beautiful parts of the country. But more adventurous travelers who find themselves in towns such as Kastoria will have a different opinion. Unassuming Kastoria has a magnificent location around a headland that juts into Lake Kastoria (also called Lake Orestias). Just keep in mind, as you wander around, that it's easy to become disoriented, thanks to Kastoria's maze of cobbled streets and hidden alleyways and the fact that water nearly surrounds the entire town perimeter.

Kastoria

170 B2

Visitor information

✉ Plateia Dimarchiou

☎ 0467 26777

Byzantine Museum

✉ Plateia Dexamenis

☎ 0467 26781

🕐 Closed Mon.

However, getting lost here is no bad thing, as some of the town's best features are hidden away, like its numerous **Byzantine churches.** There are 54 of these, some of them over 1,000 years old, including the ninth-century church of Taxiarkhes tis Mitropoleos. It has some superb frescoes, added over the centuries. The tenth-century church of Agios Stefanos has an unusual women's gallery. Most of the churches are usually locked—to see inside you will either have to be lucky and arrive when there is a service or when the church is being cleaned. Or you can track down

the keys, normally held at the Byzantine Museum.

Although small, the **Byzantine Museum** is worth seeing for the beautifully detailed and colorful examples of icons from Kastoria's churches. The museum is situated at the top of the town just off the main Plateia Dexamenis. If you ask the way, remember that many local people refer to it as the Archaeological Museum.

The very name of the town comes from the Greek word for beavers, *kastoria*. This animal's fine pelt placed the town at the center of the Greek fur trade from the 17th century onward. Although the local beavers had been hunted to extinction by the 19th century, the furriers continued to import fur, and still do so today. It is turned into coats, gloves, hats, and other items that you will see for sale in some of the stores, although many items are produced for export.

The town also has a **Folklore Museum** that merits a longer visit, not least for the building that houses it, the Alvazi Mansion. This 17th-century mansion was lived in until 1972, when it was converted into an excellent museum with household items, costumes, agricultural implements, and a restored kitchen and wine cellar. There are also some very good displays on the fur trade.

The wealth that was created by the fur trade over the centuries led to the building of some more very handsome **mansions.** While the Alvzi Mansion is the only one you can explore inside, there are other impressive examples around the town that can be viewed from outside, several in the streets within the vicinity of the museum. Look

for the Skoutari, Natzi, Basara, and Immanouil Mansions. Typically built of stone on the first floor, they have more elaborate upper floors with wooden balconies, sgraffito plasterwork, and occasionally stained glass in the windows. The living quarters are on these upper floors, while the first floor provides storage, as you will see in the Folklore Museum.

Stroll along the lakeshore—a very pleasant walk especially in the spring or autumn when the many trees are at their best—and look for the unusually shaped local boats tied up at the water's edge. The lake's waters are somewhat polluted, but still harbor some wildlife, such as frogs and turtles (known in Europe as terrapins).

A walk all the way around the headland takes you past another of the town's attractions, the **Monastery of Panagia Mavriotissa.** It is no longer a working monastery, and all that remains are two churches. These date back to the 11th and 14th centuries, and have particularly well-preserved frescoes. ∎

With its projecting upper floor and large windows, the Immanouil mansion is one of the finest in Kastoria.

Folklore Museum

✉ Kapetan Lazou

☎ 0467 28603

🕐 Closed daily 12–3 p.m.

💲 $

Prespa lakes

**Prespa Lakes
Information
Center**

🅰 170 B2

✉ Agios Germanos

☎ 0385 51452

THE BORDERS OF ALBANIA, GREECE, AND THE FORMER
Yugoslav Republic of Macedonia meet in the waters of the larger of
the two Prespa lakes, Megali Prespa. Mikri Prespa is divided between
Greece and Albania. This frontier land, perched in the remote northwest corner of Greece, feels untouched by the modern world. The
lakes' inaccessibility has made them a haven for wildlife.

**Passing the time
with a game of
dominoes under
the trees in Agios
Germanos**

In the 1970s, no visitor was allowed
near this area as the border with
Albania was a very sensitive
political region. To visit it required
advance permission, and you had
to be accompanied by a soldier at
all times. For this reason the region
is much less known than other
parts of Greece, although the world
is gradually discovering that it is a
unique, idyllic, and incredibly
beautiful place.

Tourists may have been
restricted, but that restriction has
never applied to the wildlife, and
Prespa National Park is a vital
European breeding ground for
many species. Visitors must be
sensitive to this at all times, and
a thorough exploration of the
Information Center in the tiny
village of Agios Germanos is the
best way to start any trip here. It
gives a great deal of information
about the area in several languages,
provides leaflets and walking maps,
and sells local produce and crafts.
Guided tours of the park can be
arranged in advance from here.

It is possible to make a one-day
visit to the lakes from somewhere
like Kastoria, but if you wish to
stay overnight you should make
reservations ahead at busy times of
the year (Easter and August), as
accommodations are limited.
There are a few guest houses in
Agios Germanos, which also has
the area's only post office. More
accommodations are available in
the lakeside village of Psarades.
Wherever you choose to stay, the
accommodations will be simple
but pleasurable.

Rare Dalmatian pelicans, of
which there are only about 1,000
pairs left in the world, live here.
Up to 150 pairs will normally
nest around the Prespa lakes,
although they may fly farther
south to the island of Corfu if
winter in the mountains here is
particularly hard and long. Many
other bird species live here,
including herons, cormorants,
egrets, geese, grebes, and the only
population in Greece of the
goosander. In the skies look for a
variety of birds of prey, including
the golden eagle, short-toed eagle,
booted eagle, and both lanner and
peregrine falcons.

Amphibians that live here
include several species of frog,

toads, newts, and the fire salamander, while there are also 20 species of reptile—including snakes, so be careful when walking—and over 1,300 different plant species. It is a vibrant, rich landscape for wildlife.

The area is also rich in religious culture. In the village of **Agios Germanos,** be sure to see the 11th-century church of the same name, which is adorned with frescoes, some of them original. The church of **Agios Athanasios** in the same village is also worth a visit. To see one of the area's more unusual churches, however, you must take a boat ride out onto Mikri Prespa, which can be arranged at the village of Psarades.

The ruined Byzantine church of **Agios Akhillios** is on the small islet of the same name, where you will also be shown the ruins of a monastery and may meet some of the few families who still live here, eking out a living from fishing and farming.

You can also take a boat trip on the larger lake, Megali Prespa, where the main attraction is the 15th-century church of **Panagia Eleousas,** surprisingly built into the rock near the lake's shore. Other sights seen only from the water include an icon of the Virgin Mary painted on a rock. The boat trip is in itself a wonderful experience, taking you out into the middle of a large and peaceful lake, surrounded by hills and with those invisible borders stretching across the waters. You feel privileged to be there. ■

Reed beds along the margins of the Prespa lakes provide an important habitat for wildlife.

Vergina

ONE OF THE MOST EXCITING ARCHAEOLOGICAL FINDS IN Greece in the last century took place in 1977, with the excavation of the royal tombs at Vergina, 8 miles (13 km) from the town of Veria. They placed Vergina as the ancient Macedonian capital of Agai, later abandoned for Pella (see p. 181).

Vergina

⚠ 170 C2
☎ 0331 92397
🕐 Closed Mon.
$ $$

The discovery was made by Professor Manolis Andronikos (1919–1992), who uncovered an entrance to a tomb. Unlike the over-confident Schliemann, he did not claim to know in advance what lay inside the tomb. It is believed that what he had found was the burial place of the fourth-century B.C. King Philip II of Macedonia, the father of Alexander the Great. The skeleton of this ancient ruler was complete and preserved inside a golden funeral casket emblazoned with the emblem of the 16-point Macedonian star.

Two further royal tombs were discovered close by, complete with carved friezes and funerary artifacts. The first of the two main tombs found by Andronikos had been looted long before, but the second contained those priceless treasures. The find effectively meant a rewriting of the history books, as it had long been thought that the Macedonian kings had been buried at Edessa (see p. 204). These amazing finds are now among the highlights of the Archaeological Museum in Thessaloniki (see p. 183), but the tombs are well worth seeing, even without them.

The discovery of the tombs led to a flurry of activity, and a great deal of archaeological work is still going on, adding to the excitement of a visit. A first-class museum was built at Vergina, and you can view the tombs, which are displayed behind protective glass.

In addition to the royal tombs (and other minor ones nearby), this is the site of the **Palace of Palatitsia,** which postdates Philip II and Alexander and was probably built in the third century B.C. as a summer palace for the then king, Antigonus Gonatus. The extent of the site is spectacular. The nearby theater, which is much older, is thought to be where Philip II was assassinated in 336 B.C., possibly at the instigation of his son, Alexander (see p. 29). ∎

Whose bones are they anyway?

Ever since a study in 1984, it has been accepted that the skeleton found in the royal tomb at Vergina was that of King Philip II, father of Alexander the Great. The evidence included an apparent head wound above the right eye socket, consistent with the way in which the king is known to have died. However, in 2000 Greek historian Dr. Antonis Bartsiokas claimed that the bones were in fact those of Alexander's half-brother, King Philip III Arrhidaeus, who took up the throne on Alexander's death. Dr. Bartsiokas claims that there is no evidence of an eye injury, and that some artifacts found in the tomb dated from after Philip II's death. For the moment though the Archaeological Museum sticks by the original assessment. ∎

Pella

THE UNASSUMING-LOOKING SITE OF PELLA IS ABOUT 27 miles (44 km) west of Thessaloniki, and straddles the main road that runs from northwest Greece. As you approach, it is hard to believe how important this place once was, but it could be regarded as the first capital of a state that approximated to modern Greece. Pella was the capital under King Philip II of what was then called Macedonia. When Philip defeated the Greek armies in 338 B.C. (see p. 29), he united under his banner for the first time the various city-states that until then had been almost constantly at war with each other. This created a union that covered much of what is now Greece.

The original pebble mosaic of "The Lion Hunt" is preserved in the site museum.

Pella was established in the late fifth century B.C. by King Archelaos (*R.* 413–399 B.C.), and both Philip II and Alexander the Great were born here. The town was destroyed by the Romans in the second century B.C., and today the overriding reason for visiting Pella is to see the magnificent **mosaics** that have survived there. Some are still in situ, and they date for the most part from about 300 B.C., not long after the death of Alexander the Great. The mosaics are exquisite works of art. Several depict hunting scenes, including naked hunters attacking a lion with clubs and swords, a deer being attacked by a griffin, the hunting of a stag, and an outstanding depiction of the god Dionysos riding a panther.

Many of the mosaics are in the **House of the Lion Hunt,** thought to have been an official building of some kind. It had a dozen rooms ranged around three open courtyards, and was 300 feet (90 m) long and 165 feet (50 m) across. Across the main road is the terrific site **museum,** which has more mosaics as well as statues, ceramics, and other artifacts. ∎

Pella
- 170 C2
- 0382 31160
- Closed Mon.
- $

Thessaloniki

Modern high-rise condominiums contrast with the ancient White Tower on the waterfront.

THE CAPITAL OF MACEDONIA, THESSALONIKI IS A VIBRANT metropolis located right on the Aegean, full of history yet very much a modern city too. It has a large student population, and a walk along the seafront in the evening takes you past rows of bars and cafés, all filled with animated young Greeks.

At one end of the waterfront stands an imposing statue of Alexander the Great, whose half-sister gave her name to the city. She was married to King Kassandros, who founded the city in 315 B.C. by amalgamating 25 towns with the town of Therme, which was already here. After the Romans conquered Greece, they made it the capital of the region of Macedonia prima in 146 B.C.

Thessaloniki lay on the Via Egnatia, the mighty road that linked Rome with its eastern outpost at Constantinople. Its main street today is still called Egnatia. Just off this road, at the eastern end of the city center, you will find the **Arch of Galerius,** erected by the Emperor Galerius (died A.D. 313) in A.D. 303 to commemorate his victory over the Persians six years previously. It is covered in detailed carvings of Galerius's exploits. Almost next door is the **Rotonda,** believed to have

Thessaloniki
▲ 170 D2 & 184)
Visitor information
✉ Mitropoleos 34
☎ 031 222935 or
031 271888

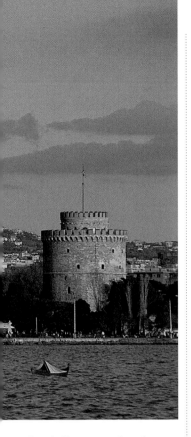

The **Archaeological Museum,** one of the city's essential visitor attractions, is a short walk from here. Some of the finds here date back to the neolithic and Iron Age periods, showing that Macedonia was one of the first parts of Greece to be settled.

In a specially built annex, at the end of a long, dramatic corridor, there is the skeleton of King Philip II of Macedonia. Here, too, is the golden casket in which his body was buried, and many other splendid finds from the royal tombs at Vergina (see p. 180). These include ivory models of the royal family, a golden wreath, and armor that was buried with King Philip.

In the same room are finds from a significant site just north of the city at Derveni; the best objects are on display here—a visit to the site

Byzantine Museum

✉ White Tower, waterfront

☎ 031 267832

🕐 Closed Mon.

Archaeological Museum

✉ Manoli Andronikos/ Leoforos Stratou

☎ 031 830538

💲 $$

A heroic pose for Alexander the Great

been built as a mausoleum for Galerius, although it was never used as such. It has been used as both a church and a mosque in its time, and today houses occasional art exhibitions.

Close by is the city's most famous landmark, the **White Tower,** which you will see on many posters and postcards. It was previously known as the Bloody Tower because it had served as a prison and a place of execution. Today it houses a fascinatingly eclectic **Byzantine Museum,** which extends over five floors and brings together many Byzantine objects, including mosaics and jewelry as well as icons. Be sure to walk up to the roof for a good view of the city's extensive waterfront.

Railway Station

LAGKADA

MONASTIRIOU

AGIOU

Dodeka Apostoli

Agia Aikaterini

OLYMPIADOS

Osios David

EPTAPYRGIOU

Voltadon Monastery

Chain Tower

26 OKTOVRIOU

DODEKANISOU

PLATEIA DIMOKRATIAS

DIMITRIOU

DIMITRIOU

DRAGOUMI

Profitis Ilias

Agios Dimitrios

AGIOU

OLYMPIADOS

Agios Nikolaos

Church of Panagia Chalkeon

DIMITRIOU

Old Market

TSIMISKI

IONOS

LEOFOROS

ARISTOTELOUS

OTE

Agia Paraskevi

EGNATIA

FILIPPOU

AGIOU

PLATEIA ARISTOTELOUS

MITROPOLEOS

Agia Sofia

Rotonda

Arch of Galerius

DIMITRIOU

NIKIS

K o l p o s

T h e s s a l o n i k i s

Museum of the Macedonian Struggle

TSIMISKI

ANGELAKI

EGNATIA

White Tower

Theater

Folklife and Ethnological Museum

Archaeological Museum

0   500 meters
0   500 yards

is not as rewarding. Highlights include the burned remains of a roll of papyrus from the fourth century B.C., and the huge three-foot (1 m) high Derveni Krater, an ornately decorated bronze vase used for mixing wine.

The museum also has some delicate mosaics found mainly in Roman houses within the city boundaries. These are together in a room that has been presented as if it were a Roman courtyard, with floor and wall mosaics all around. Look for the lifelike mosaic of three horses.

Several smaller museums are also worth visiting. The **Folklife and Ethnological Museum** is housed in a 19th-century mansion east of downtown. It has a good collection of traditional costumes and a large photographic archive, among many other fascinating

items. One block back from the waterfront in the center of Thessaloniki is the **Museum of the Macedonian Struggle.** The claim to the name of Macedonia by the Former Yugoslav Republic of Macedonia naturally caused great concern throughout Greece, and especially here in what they have always regarded as the true Macedonia. A visit to this gripping museum explains the Greek case, with dramatic displays on the struggle for Greek control of the region, including weapons used by freedom fighters and vivid dioramas.

CHURCHES

Thessaloniki has many fine churches. **Agia Sofia** is a downtown landmark, built in the eighth century. It is easily distinguished as it resembles Agia Sofia in Istanbul, and this building, too, was used as a

Folklife & Ethnological Museum

- ⊠ Vasilissis Olggas 68
- ☎ 031 83059
- ⊕ Closed Thurs.
- 💲 $

Museum of the Macedonian Struggle

- ⊠ Proxenou Koromila 6
- ☎ 031 229778
- ⊕ Closed Sat.

mosque from 1585 to 1912. Note the base of a minaret that remains in one corner of the church, and see also the frescoes and mosaics that have, remarkably, survived from the ninth and tenth centuries.

Thessaloniki can also proudly boast the largest church in all of Greece, which is dedicated to the city's patron saint, **Agios Dimitrios.** A comparatively modern building, having been rebuilt in 1917 after a horrific fire that devastated the city, it stands on the site where St. Dimitrios was murdered by the Romans in A.D. 305 for refusing to denounce his faith. The crypt where this happened still exists, a haunting place beneath the main altar. The feast day of St. Dimitrios is October 26, when there are processions and festivities in the city.

For a contrast to the largest church in Greece, visit the tiny fifth-century chapel of **Osios David** in the back streets of the Upper Town. Its claim to fame is behind its altar. There you find the finest mosaic in Thessaloniki, "The Vision of Ezekiel." Even those with no interest in churches or mosaics will appreciate the incomparable beauty of this work, the way it has retained its colors, and the fact that, unusually, it depicts a beardless Christ. Although the church is kept locked because of the mosaic, there is usually a caretaker on site to open the doors for you.

CHAIN TOWER

While in the Upper Town check out the Chain Tower for great views over the city. It formed part of the (incomplete) Byzantine city walls visible in various places in this district, one area of which is known as Eptapyrgiou—"Seven Towers."

The intricate detailing on the Dervani Krater depicts scenes of Dionysos.

Walk straight down toward the seafront from here to pass close by the house where the first president of the modern Turkish state, Mustafa Kemal Ataturk (1881–1938), was born. Inside is a small museum dedicated to the life of this extraordinary man, and the rest of the house is kept as it was when Ataturk's family lived there. If you wish to see inside, go first to the adjacent Turkish consulate to obtain permission. With the fragile state of relations in the past between Greece and Turkey, and the fact that the Greeks hold Ataturk responsible for the exchange of populations that shamed Greece in 1923, Turkish officials have to be careful who they admit to the house, as it has been threatened on many occasions. Have your passport on you as proof of identification. ■

Chalkidiki

MOST PEOPLE THINK OF CHALKIDIKI AS THE THREE peninsulas that dangle like fingers in the Aegean Sea, but there is a fourth part of the area, northern Chalkidiki. This hilly, wooded region is a world away from the bustling beach resorts on the two westernmost peninsulas, and much less visited. The easternmost peninsula is the serene Mount Athos, known throughout the world as the place where no female—human or animal (except the Virgin Mary)—is allowed to set foot (see pp. 188–89).

Chalkidiki
🅰 170 D2

Petralona Cave
🅰 170 D1
✉ 34 miles (55 km) southeast of Thessaloniki
💲 $

However, the western peninsula, **Kassandra,** is where you'll find packed beaches and plenty of females. This is the place to head for if you want a lazy day in the sun followed by a lively time at night. In the northwest of the area the beach towns run into each other and eventually merge into the suburbs of Thessaloniki.

Situated at the narrow top of the peninsula, the town of **Nea Moudaniais** is the gateway to Kassandra, and most people head on through without stopping. The town is less attractive than resorts farther south, but it has all the facilities you might want. It is a departure point for boats to the Sporades islands and the Pilion peninsula. You can drive around Kassandra in a very short time to get a feel of the place. There are resorts on both the east and west sides of the peninsula, all fairly similar, although those on the east coast have good views across to the next peninsula, Sithonia.

Sithonia is quieter and more attractive, with more of the green hills that are also typical of northern Chalkidiki. The resorts are comparatively low-key and spread out, and again the east coast has the advantage of views—across to Mount Athos. For a boat trip to see the monasteries of Mount Athos (see pp. 190–91), go to Ouranopolis at the top of the Athos peninsula, or pick one up from

Ormos Panagias, the main town on the east coast of Sithonia.

The better beaches are toward the southern tip of Sithonia, at small resorts such as Toroni and Aretes. If you want all the comforts of a planned vacation complex, head for **Porto Carras,** the largest such complex in Greece, spreading out behind a 6-mile (10 km) stretch of beach.

Northern Chalkidiki has plenty to see, including beautiful wooded hills and hill villages hardly touched by tourism. A major attraction is the cave near Petralona, sometimes called the **Petralona Cave** but more correctly known as the Kokkines Petres, or Red Stones Cave. It was here that Greece's oldest archaeological find was discovered in 1960, a Neanderthal skull thought to be around 700,000 years old. The historical interest of the cave is illustrated by reconstructed prehistoric scenes, which are very effective in their natural setting.

A charming road winds through some of the best scenery in northern Chalkidiki. It passes through the large village of **Arnaia,** worth a stop to admire some of its attractive old houses and inspect the distinctive local carpets and crafts that are for sale. Farther on is **Stagira,** the birthplace of the philosopher Aristotle (384–322 B.C.), commemorated with a marble statue on the edge of the village. ■

A fisherman in the harbor of Nea Skioni, Kassandra, sorts his nets.

Mount Athos

MOUNT ATHOS (AGION OROS) MEANS HOLY MOUNTAIN.
A visit to this special area requires a permit and some advance
planning, but anyone can take a boat trip around the peninsula
to take a look at the monasteries that dot the landscape (see
pp. 190–91). Some of these are in spectacular cliff-top settings, which
make you wonder how they were ever built. Toward the southern
end of the peninsula is the imposing sight of Mount Athos itself,
which at 6,668 feet (2,033 m) is the highest point in Chalkidiki.

St. Athanasius founded the first
monastery, the Great Lavra
Monastery, on Athos in A.D. 963.
At that time the place was already
regarded as a holy site and had been
attracting hermits who sought a
contemplative life. That first
monastery was set on a rocky outcrop at the very southeastern end of

the peninsula, about as far away
from civilization as possible. It was
followed by the building of other
monasteries in the 10th and 11th
centuries, until at one time there
were 40 active monasteries with as
many as 1,000 monks in each one.

The population today is nothing
like that, with fewer than 2,000

Just a few pilgrims are permitted to join the monks of Mount Athos in their austere lifestyle.

still a part of the Greek state. There have been suggestions that this should change, but at the moment Athos still goes its own way.

If you are male and wish to set foot on Athos, rather than merely observe it from a boat, there is a strict procedure to follow. You must first obtain a letter of recommendation from the Greek Consul in your own country. You must show that you have a good educational, religious, or cultural reason for wanting to visit. You must then send or take your letter to the Ministry of Foreign Affairs in Athens, or to the Ministry of Macedonia and Thrace in Thessaloniki, which is responsible for issuing the permits. No boat will take you to the island without such a permit.

If your reason for visiting is approved, you then join the waiting list of applicants, as each ministry issues only ten permits per day in order to control the numbers and give the monks the peace they desire. When a permit is issued it will be for a specific day and allow a stay of up to four nights, although when you are on Athos you can apply for permission to stay an extra two nights. You must use your permit on the day for which it is issued, so anyone wanting to see Athos must be dedicated and also flexible with their travel plans.

If you do get to Athos, you will see the strict regime under which the monks live. Services begin in the early hours of the morning, about 3 or 4 a.m. The monks are called to prayer by the banging of a piece of wood known as a *simandro,* which is suspended near the entrance to the church. Only two meals a day are allowed, and there are many fast days when only one limited meal is served. When not praying, the monks spend their day at work in the fields or maintaining the monasteries. ■

monks living in the 20 monasteries that are still inhabited. However, there has been an increase in numbers in recent years as younger people have turned to the monastic life, influenced by the arrival of the new millennium and also as a reaction against increased hedonism.

Famously, no woman is allowed to set foot on the peninsula. This has been the case since 1060, when Emperor Constantine Monomachus of Byzantium (modern Istanbul) issued an edict banning all women from visiting Athos, which was reserved for the Virgin Mary alone. Even female animals are banned. The unique status of Athos was confirmed by a government decree in 1926 that created a Theocratic Republic on Athos, making it independent and self-governing, but

The shoreline at Ouranopolis is overshadowed by the Byzantine Phosphori Tower.

A boat trip around Mount Athos

Few people get the chance to set foot on Mount Athos (Agion Oros). Most have to
content themselves with a boat trip along the coast, taking in the sight of the magnificent
monasteries in their clifftop settings, against the backdrop of Mount Athos itself.

Some trips take visitors around the whole
peninsula, to see the monasteries on the
eastern side as well, but the majority of boats
leave from **Ouranopolis** ❶ on the northwest of the peninsula and limit themselves to
the more spectacular western side of Mount
Athos. Ouranopolis itself is not an especially
attractive place to be based—most visitors stay
in Chalkidiki or Thessaloniki—but you may
wish to spend one night there in order to take
one of the earlier boat trips.

Boats are not permitted to venture closer
than 550 yards (500 m) to the shore, so take a
pair of binoculars and, if you want to get
close-up photographs, a telephoto lens for
your camera. If you only have a pocket
camera, don't leave it behind: You may get
some wonderful photos of the dolphins that
sometimes swim alongside the boats and leap
teasingly out of the water. The boat trips take
at least four hours, and although some food
and drink is sold on board, the choice is

limited so you may wish to take your own
picnic lunch. The boats provide a commentary
in Greek, English, and German, but the
public-address systems on some boats are
poor. The accompanying map will help you
identify the main monasteries.

The first monasteries you pass are inland:
Zografou is the most northerly and, shortly

🅰 See area map p. 171
▶ Ouranopolis
🔄 about 50 miles (80 km)
🕓 4–6 hours
▶ Ouranopolis

NOT TO BE MISSED
- Dochiariou
- Agiou Pandeleimonos
- Simonopetra
- Agiou Dionisiou

afterward, Kastamonitou. The former was founded in the tenth century but, like many monasteries, was rebuilt in the 18th and 19th centuries. Today it is home to a small community of Bulgarian monks. **Kastamonitou** is 11th century and is also still inhabited.

The first monasteries of which you get good views are down on the coast. **Dochiariou** ❷ comes into sight first, a cluster of attractive buildings on a hill behind a jetty. This working monastery was founded in the tenth century, and, in addition to some original frescoes in its churches, claims to have a piece of the True Cross. Farther along the coast is **Xenofondos** ❸, founded in the tenth century by St. Xenofondos, and also very much a working monastery—it even has a sawmill. Like many monasteries, however, it has been damaged over the years by fires and now reflects a mixture of periods and styles.

The next coastal monastery is the hugely impressive **Agiou Pandeleimonos** ❹,

dating back to the 12th century, with additions built by Russian monks in the 19th century. Inside you can glimpse the onion domes of churches standing above the red-roofed buildings. Farther on is the port of **Dafni** ❺, where pilgrims come ashore and where a small population exists to service the practical needs of the monks and their visitors. Inland from here is the monastery of **Xeropotamou,** another one which has suffered fire damage and been rebuilt in various styles.

One of the most impressive sights is **Simonopetra** ❻, on top of a rocky ridge, which was founded in the 14th century. So too was **Grigoriou,** also on a clifftop if not quite as spectacular, and then **Agiou Dionisiou** with its pink and white balconies is perched 260 feet (80 m) above the sea. **Agiou Pavlou** ❼ is even higher, nestling below Mount Athos itself. At this point most boats turn around and head back for Ouranopolis, leaving the monks to their contemplative existence, shared by just a select few pilgrims. ■

Clifftop monastery of Grigoriou

**The lush green
Nestos Valley**

Nestos Valley

THE NESTOS RIVER STARTS ITS JOURNEY HIGH IN THE
Rhodope Mountains (shared with Bulgaria), then runs for 80 miles
(130 km) through Greece before dividing and flowing into the
Aegean Sea. Its main course marks the administrative boundary
between Macedonia and Thrace, and the area is influenced by a
variety of cultures. To the west is modern Greece, to the east lies
Turkey, and to the north, Central Europe, with its flamboyant tales
of gypsies and vampires. The Nestos River delta is a vital wetland
site for the north of Greece, teeming with plants, reptiles, and
amphibians, and around 250 species of birds.

Nestos Valley
171 E3

Stavroupolis
171 F3

Head inland for a wonderful drive
through the valley, following the
course of the river between Xanthi
(in Thrace) and Drama (in Macedonia). This is a remarkable part
of Greece, influenced by nearby
Turkey and Bulgaria. Very few
visitors explore this region, but
those who do venture here are
assured of a warm welcome and a
very special experience. Be careful
if you are driving in winter as the
road can be cut off in severe
weather: Warning signs are posted
at either end of the valley if this
is the case. Make sure you have

a full tank, too, as there are few
gas stations.

The road winds through thick
beech forests and below the
mountain tops, which are covered
in snow for several months of the
year. There are several small, idyllic
villages, where you should stop and
walk around, to get a glimpse of
mountain life in this remote part of
Greece, light-years from Athens. At
Stavroupolis you can fill up both
yourself and your car, but there are
no accommodations. **Xanthi** (see
pp. 196–97) is by far the best base if
you plan to spend time here. ■

Philippi

THE IMPRESSIVE REMAINS OF THE ONCE THRIVING TOWN of Philippi, 9 miles (15 km) northwest of Kavala, straddle the main Kavala–Drama road. The site was named after King Philip II of Macedonia, the father of Alexander the Great (see pp. 29–30), after he captured it from the Thracians in 356 B.C. However, the remains you now see date mostly from the Roman period.

The most famous part of the site is the remnants of the **prison.** St. Paul was reputedly held here when he arrived on his first visit to Europe in A.D. 49.

In ancient times the town was most notable for the Battle of Philippi, fought in 42 B.C. Brutus and Cassius, the murderers of Julius Caesar, killed themselves here when confronted with certain defeat by the pursuing forces of Mark Antony and Octavian.

There is a sizable **theater** on the site, dating from the time of Philip II. It was rebuilt during the Roman era for use as an amphitheater. On this side of the road—part of the Via Egnatia that links Rome with Istanbul—is also the site **museum,** although if time is limited it can be skipped as the main attractions are actually still in place.

On the opposite side of the road are the bulk of the town's remains, including two contrasting features. One is the impressive foundation of a huge church known as **Basilica B,** and the other is the remains of the **public latrine,** equally impressive for the state of preservation of its 50 marble seats! Nearby are the ruins of the Roman baths, built in A.D. 250 but destroyed soon after in a fire. ∎

Philippi
- 171 E2
- 051 516470
- Closed Mon.
- $

Basilica B was built in the sixth century A.D. but collapsed under the weight of its domed roof.

From Kavala to Alexandroupoli

THE PORT OF KAVALA IS RECOGNIZABLY GREEK AND, WITH its harbor, fortress, and seafront restaurants, could be in almost any part of the country. East of here, however, the mood changes, and in towns such as Xanthi and Komotini you realize you are nearing the frontier. By the time you reach Alexandroupoli, you know without being told that this is the last major town before the Turkish border.

Kavala
🗺 171 E2
**Visitor
information**
✉ Plateia Eleftherias
☎ 051 222425

KAVALA

This very lively port is a gateway to the islands of the northern Aegean and northern Dodecanese. A popular resort with good beaches either side of the center, it has interesting museums illustrating the historical and cultural interest of the town and surrounding area.

Your first impression may not be favorable, as Kavala is big and busy, but it is well worth spending a few days exploring.

Kavala has been a port since ancient times, and was founded as long ago as the sixth century B.C. by emigrants from the island of Paros. St. Paul first set foot on

European soil here in A.D. 49 before traveling to Philippi (see p. 193). The town has been fought over throughout history. At different times it was occupied by the Franks, Turks, Venetians, Normans, and others, including the Bulgarians during both World War I and World War II.

The Turkish occupation, from 1371 to 1912, had the biggest impact. Among Turkish legacies is the town's **aqueduct,** which dates not from the Romans as you might expect, but from the 16th century. A **citadel** dominates the eastern end of the harbor. Its imposing walls, built in the 10th and 16th centuries, make an impressive sight when floodlit at night. Inside the walls is the area of town known as Panagia. This is a terrific place in

which to get lost, with its meandering streets and its 18th- and 19th-century houses. Among these is the **birthplace of Mehmet Ali** (1769–1849), who became the Pasha of Egypt. The house can be identified by the nearby bronze statue of Ali on horseback. You can visit the house, although the door is not always open. Simply knock and wait for the custodian to show you around the garden and rather grand rooms, including a harem.

The most notable building, known as the **Imaret,** overlooks the harbor on the right-hand side of one of the main streets as you enter the citadel area. This is the largest Islamic building in Europe, and was founded by Mehmet Ali. It originally housed theological

Archaeological Museum

⊠ Erythrou Stavrou 17

☎ 051 222335

🕒 Closed Mon.

💲 $

Folk and Modern Art Museum

⊠ Filippou 4

☎ 051 222706

🕒 Closed Sun.

students and provided them with inexpensive meals. After standing derelict for many years, it has been refurbished as a restaurant, where the meals cost more than they used to but the setting overlooking the harbor is still superb. If you merely want to take a look around the interior, there is also a simpler bar set around the courtyard.

The **harbor** at Kavala is a busy place, with hints of the Eastern bazaar in the market area just behind it. You can be sure of good fresh fish in the many restaurants that line the front, although if you want somewhere more unusual and Turkish-influenced, head into the Panagia area at night.

At the far side of the harbor, the excellent **Archaeological Museum** has finds from several classical sites nearby, including Philippi (see p. 193). Some of the best exhibits are from Avdira (see pp. 197–98), including an exquisite dolphin mosaic and a huge sarcophagus, unusual in that its paint has survived. The site of Amphipolis, west of the town, is also represented, notably by some fine laurel wreaths made of pure gold in the third century B.C., looking far too delicate to have survived for over 2,000 years. There are also extensive collections of ceramics, jewelry, coins, statues, and many other items.

The **Folk and Modern Art Museum,** also known as the Municipal Museum, is a superior example of its kind, not dealing just with the past but also finding space for displays of more modern Greek art. Among the highlights are several sculptures by an artist from the island of Thassos, Polygnotos Vagis (1894–1965). In other rooms there are the usual displays of traditional folk costumes, as well as household and agricultural items, but the collection is very eclectic

and well worth an hour or two of browsing time.

XANTHI

Xanthi has an undeniable fascination that will make you want to stay for longer than the usual quick look around. You may even decide to use it as a base. It has a distinctly Eastern feel to it, which combines with youthful energy provided by the large numbers of students at the local University of Thrace. Xanthi is a town of bars, bistros, and galleries. The liveliest spot is the main square, which is attractive and modern, with fountains in the middle and restaurants and cafés surrounding it.

Xanthi is home to one of the best **markets** in the region, and if you are here on a Saturday

Xanthi

🅰 171 F3

Folk Museum

⊠ Antika 7

☎ 0541 25421

🕒 Open daily 11 a.m.–1 p.m., & Mon., Wed., Fri.–Sat. 7 p.m.–9 p.m.

💲 $

Students enjoying
the fun at the
Xanthi carnival

morning you will see the town invaded by a colorful mix of Greeks, Turks, gypsies, and Pomaks, all here for the bazaar. The Pomaks are a highly localized indigenous group—Muslims with Slav rather than Greek origins. There are about 40,000 of them, most living to the north of Xanthi, and their language is a mix of Bulgarian, Greek, and Turkish. The Greeks do not treat the Pomaks favorably. They are required to have travel permits, and visitors need a permit (not easily obtained) to go to one of their villages. The Pomak language is also under threat as the Greeks discourage the people from using it, for instance putting sizable obstacles in the way of the Pomaks who would like to have their own language newspaper.

Xanthi became rich on the proceeds of the large tobacco plantations you will see as you travel through Thrace. Tobacco merchants' mansions, most of them built in the 19th century, are concentrated in the old town, a jumble of narrow streets and alleys. One such mansion now houses the town's **Folk Museum,** with displays on the tobacco industry as well as local costumes and jewelry. It is also a chance to see inside one of the mansions, restored to its former glory.

AVDIRA
Modern Avdira is a small farming village several miles from the coast. It also lends its name to the nearest beach, which attracts many Greek vacationers in the summer,

Avdira
🅰 171 F2

Komotini

⚏ 171 F3

Tourist information

✉ Ap Souzou 14

☎ 0531 70996

Archaeological Museum

✉ Symeonidi 4

☎ 0531 22411

🕐 Closed Mon.

Museum of Folk Life and History

✉ Agios Yeoryios 13

🕐 Closed Sun.–Mon.

but few foreign visitors as it is somewhat out of the way. Nearby is Lake Vistonis; the marshlands around it are an important area for wildlife, especially wading birds and rare birds of prey, such as the sea eagle. Observation towers help interested bird-watchers get the best views.

Near the beach of Avdira is the site of **Ancient Avdira,** from which many of the best finds have been taken for display in the Archaeological Museums in Komotini and Kavala. The site is pretty overgrown and requires dedication to get the best from it. It stands on a small headland, surrounded by the remains of the acropolis walls. There are the few remnants of a theater and it is also possible to identify a Roman bathhouse. The foundations of some Roman houses are close by, and the entrance gate to the city is also identifiable, flanked by two towers.

The city was founded in about 656 B.C. by refugees from Klazomenae in Asia Minor, and refounded in about 500 B.C. by more refugees from Persia. It grew into an important member of the Delian League (a fifth-century B.C. confederation of Greek states against the Persian threat), and was known to be a fair-size city until at least the ninth century A.D. At that time it was still the site of a bishopric. Excavations, which did not begin until 1950, unearthed some valuable items, including in one place 2,000 small votive vases.

While the site is not especially attractive or spectacular, for that very reason it does not get crowded and you may well be able to wander over the extensive remains by yourself—an evocative experience, and somehow just as rewarding as exploring more significant sites

in the company of hundreds of other visitors.

KOMOTINI

Komotini, like Xanthi (see pp. 196–97), reveals a fascinating mix of influences, and is even more Turkish than its near neighbor. It lies only about 60 miles (100 km) from the Turkish border to the east, and even closer—14 miles (22 km) —to Bulgaria to the north. Both those countries add their color to the Greek melting pot that is eastern Thrace.

The Turkish influence is most immediately seen in the minarets and domed roofs of mosques around the town—14 of them still in use today. Komotini was part of Turkey until as recently as 1920, when the borders were changed. It had been in the Ottoman Empire since 1363. Little wonder that it feels as much Turkish as Greek, although it would not be tactful to express that view to the local people until you know where their affinities lie. Greek-Turkish relations are a touchy subject for discussion, and about half the population are of Turkish origin, with a number of Pomaks living here too (see p. 197).

Komotini was founded in the fourth century A.D., and its early history is well told in the **Archaeological Museum.** This also has some of the best finds from the nearby sites at Avdira (see above) and Maroneia (see p. 204). There is some beautiful gold jewelry recovered from graves, as well as examples of painted sarcophagi, gravestones, statues, and ceramics, and an extensive coin collection.

The town's other museum of note is the delightfully old-fashioned and jumbled **Museum of Folk Life and History,** which spreads through the rooms of an 18th-century mansion.

Foraging around the museum provides many rewards, and it has a good selection of traditional folk costumes, domestic items, and especially embroidery, for which the area is noted.

In keeping with the Turkish influence Komotini has a lively **bazaar,** with the Eastern tradition of similar shops being clustered together, so that you will find, for example, a row of shoe stores all in line. You can find everything here from valuable antiques to the day's fish catch, as well as the region's best tobacco leaves.

ALEXANDROUPOLI

Although dismissed by some as mainly a military base, Alexandroupoli, at the eastern end of the coast of Thrace, is actually a very pleasant coastal resort, with a long promenade and a long stretch of sandy beach. It is very much a family resort town, and the beach has lots of facilities for children, as well as waterskiing, parasailing, and other water sports for adults. Beyond the promenade is the old part of the town, a warren of narrow streets with a delightful mix of workshops, junk shops, food stores, souvenir shops, bars, and several good restaurants and cafés.

In the evening the promenade fills with Greek families doing their evening *volta,* the customary parade up and down prior to eating and drinking. It's a pleasing sight: Grandparents walk hand-in-hand with their little grandchildren, and groups of teenagers take the chance to eye each other.

The town's most notable sight is also on the promenade. The lighthouse was built in 1880, and its illumination at night adds to the atmosphere. Alexandroupoli is a port as well, with ferries to the northeast Aegean islands and as far south as Rhodes and Kos in the

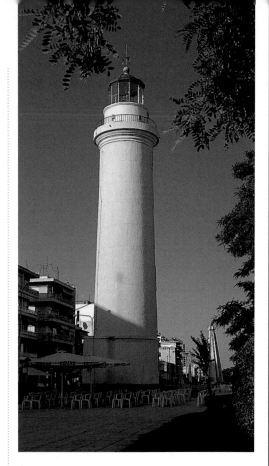

Dodecanese. It is also the region's closest town to the Turkish border (hence the military presence), and has railroad links with Istanbul in Turkey, Sofia in Bulgaria, and Athens via Thessaloniki.

Despite these links the town is not as multicultural as Komotini or Xanthi. It expanded only in 1878 during the Russo-Turkish war, when the Russians turned what had been an insignificant fishing village into a purpose-built modern city. It was known then by its 15th-century Turkish name of Dedeagac. It acquired its modern name in 1919 for the then Greek king, Alexandros. While Alexandroupoli is still a military base, and you will certainly see soldiers in the streets, it is much more attractive than that designation implies. ■

The building of the lighthouse in 1880 marked a general rise in Alexandroupoli's fortunes.

Alexandroupoli
🅰 171 G2
Visitor information
✉ Tourist Police
☎ 0551 37411

Birds of Greece

Like the vacationing visitors, birds flock to Greece. It's the ideal stopover for migrants crossing the Eastern Mediterranean, particularly those flying on their way from Central and Eastern Europe to the warmer climes of North Africa.

Crete, ideally placed between Greece and North Africa, attracts many such migrants, and has particularly good opportunities for bird-watching in spring and fall. A microcosm of the best of the mainland, it offers a variety of habitats for avian visitors, including marshy wetlands in the south that appeal to stilts and other waders, saltpans to the east favored by avocets, and open plateau that is attractive to birds such as the colorful hoopoe.

Several places in Greece are vital breeding places for birds, including some seriously endangered species. For example, the Prespa lakes near the Albanian border are one of the few remaining breeding grounds in Europe for the Dalmatian pelican, a bird regarded as vulnerable by the International Council for Bird Preservation. There are fewer than 1,000 pairs worldwide, and around one fifth of these nest in the Prespa lakes area. This is the only breeding place in Greece for the more common white pelican. Other important species breeding there include the pygmy cormorant (also vulnerable), the goosander, and magnificent birds of prey such as the golden eagle, short-toed eagle, and booted eagle.

The politically sensitive area of the Evros River delta, east of Alexandroupoli and close to the Turkish border, is a haven for thousands of wintering ducks and geese. Over 75 percent of Greece's 408 bird species have been seen in the Evros Delta. These include pygmy cormorants, common cormorants, white pelicans, herons, egrets, storks, and any number of waders. You can also find sea eagles here.

The best place to see birds of prey is north of the Evros Delta, in the Dadia Forest. An incredible 36 of Europe's 39 species of raptors have been spotted here, and 26 of those species are known to live and nest in the pine forests on the slopes of the Evros Mountains. They include the griffon vulture, Egyptian vulture, golden eagle, and Levant sparrowhawk, as well as sea eagles, and one of the rarest in Europe, the black vulture.

On the western coast of mainland Greece, the wetlands around Messolonghi are among the most important ecological sites in Greece. Rivers such as the Acheloös and Evinos, flowing down from the mountains, have created between them a vast series of lagoons, mudflats, marshes, and reed beds. Almost 300 species of bird have been observed here, and in winter there are vast numbers of coots (an estimated 30,000) and ducks (over 20,000). Messolonghi is a vital stopping-off point for the slender-billed curlew, which is endangered in Russia where it nests. It pauses here on its migratory journey to and from its winter home in North Africa.

The islands of the eastern Aegean are especially interesting to bird-watchers. Species more usually found in Asia occur here. For example, Kruper's nuthatch, familiar in Turkey, has made its way to the island of Lesvos (see pp. 236–37) and is not uncommon in the woods around the mountain village of Ayiassos. Also on Lesvos, the Gulf of Kalloni is a well-known haven for migrants, notably water birds such as ducks, stilts, and avocets. The rare Eleanora's falcon is a common visitor to these islands; the sight of them is unforgettable. ∎

Left: The huge untidy nests of storks are seen on roofs and chimneys of north and eastern Greece.
Above: The redshank, identified by its bright legs and bill, feeds in shallow waters.
Above right: Griffin vultures are just one of 15 species of Old World vulture, recorded here long before the discovery of the Americas.
Right: The goshawk is one of Greece's most common and widespread birds of prey.

**Dadia Forest
Reserve
Information
Center**

⚛ 171 G3
☎ 0554 32209

Evros Delta &
Dadia Forest Reserve

THE EASTERN EXTREMITY OF GREECE INCLUDES TWO
regions that are among the best wildlife sites in the country: the Evros
Delta and the Dadia Forest. The Evros River rises in Bulgaria, and for
much of its length marks the border between Greece and Turkey.
For this reason the delta is politically sensitive as well as ecologically
sensitive, and the Greek authorities take an interest in anyone visiting
the area. Don't be surprised if, when wandering around with
binoculars and notebooks, you are approached and asked to
produce identity papers. Until the late 1990s a permit was needed to
visit certain parts, but this no longer applies.

The town of **Loutros Traiano-
polis,** on the edge of the delta, has
a choice of simple accommodations
if you wish to explore the area. From
here you can go on foot, as there
are numerous paths that lead into
the delta area, but be careful with
directions as it is easy to get lost.

The region has some poisonous
snakes and, while you are unlikely
to be bitten (snakes usually make
themselves scarce when they
hear approaching footsteps), it

is sensible to exercise caution.
Species found here include the
nose-horned viper, sand boa, cat
snake, grass snake, dice snake, and
leopard snake. There are plenty of
other reptiles, including several
species of tortoise, turtles, and
lizards. Amphibians are abundant
too, such as the warty newt,
yellow-bellied toad, marsh frog,
and fire salamander.

The rarest mammal to look for
is the (now misnamed) common

otter. Wolves, jackals, and polecats also inhabit the area, indicating that the delta is not all marshland.

There are some magnificent sights to enjoy, and if you are lucky you might be treated to the spectacle of a sea eagle or an osprey hunting—diving to pluck fish out of the water. During the winter, when the weather in Greece can remain surprisingly clement, vast numbers of wildfowl can be seen here.

Head northeast from the delta and you will reach the small town of **Feres,** which makes a good base for exploring the area to the north of here, the 80,300-acre (32,500 ha) **Dadia Forest Reserve.** Set in the Evros Valley and overshadowed by the Evros Mountains, this is another scenically splendid area of Greece, visited chiefly by those with an interest in its wide-ranging wildlife.

The **forest information center** is reached from the village of Likofos, and has good information about the flora and fauna of the reserve, which is especially noted for its rare birds of prey (see p. 201). You can also get advice here on exploring the reserve, which can be done on foot or with an organized tour that goes into the areas where other vehicles are banned.

The two main paths are well marked. One leads to the highest point in the reserve, at 2,034 feet (620 m), and the other to a hide that looks out over the Mavrorema Canyon. This is a great place to watch for birds of prey, as they soar on the thermals that rise up from the canyon.

In addition to eagles and vultures, species to look for include the lanner falcon, black kite, goshawk, Levant sparrowhawk, and honey buzzard. You may be lucky enough to see a black stork, but these are increasingly rare, and only a few remain in the forest.

You can stay in the reserve at the very pleasant low-key hostel next to the information center, but reserve a place ahead at migration times in spring and fall. There is a café nearby, and more eating options and stores in the village of **Dadia,** about half a mile (1 km) away. ∎

Few visitors discover Greece's tranquil yet vital wetlands.

More places to visit in Macedonia & Thrace

EDESSA

The waterfalls at Edessa are one of the major attractions for Greek vacationers in the hills of western Macedonia. In the biggest fall, the water plunges 82 feet (25 m) over a precipice and down toward the Macedonian plain. A walkway allows you to go behind one of the falls and into a small cave.

But the appeal is more in the overall setting rather than the sight of the falls themselves. The area around them has been turned into a pleasant public park, with plenty of trees and brightly colored flowers, cafés, and a restaurant. Edessa itself is a popular summer resort town on the edge of an escarpment, overlooking the broad Macedonian plain.

⛰ 170 C2   🚆 Train from Thessaloniki

FLORINA

The mountain town of Florina is 25 miles (40 km) east of the Prespa lakes. It makes an acceptable base for a few nights' stay if you want to explore these northern Pindos Mountains and some of the smaller lakes nearby, although the town of Kastoria (see pp. 176–77) is much more attractive and better situated.

Florina is very close to the border with the Former Yugoslav Republic of Macedonia, giving something of a frontier feel. One of its main attractions is the old part of the town, which is filled with picturesque Turkish houses and neoclassic mansions. There is also a good small **Archaeological Museum** *(Closed Sat.–Mon., $)*, and a range of hotels and restaurants.

⛰ 170 B2   🚆 Train from Thessaloniki

MARONEIA

Ancient Maroneia is another of those delightfully remote Greek historical sites that are worth visiting for the journey there and the setting as much as for the remains themselves. The road goes through the cotton and tobacco fields of Thrace, past farms and woodland, and through modern Maroneia, a tiny rural community where your journey is likely to be delayed by tractors on the road, or animals, or both. It

is well worth breaking the journey here, as the village's more prosperous history is hinted at by some grand old mansions whose attractive balconies look down over the narrow streets.

Beyond Maroneia a sign to Agios Haralambos directs you down a rough track along the coast, where you soon find the overgrown ruins of **Ancient Maroneia.** The star attraction is a small theater, like a toy version of the great theaters at Epidavros and Athens (see p. 104 and p. 56), which has been renovated and is used for modern performances and concerts. There are also the remains of what was a sanctuary probably dedicated to Dionysos, the party-going god of wine, inebriation, and jollity known to the Romans as Bacchus. Dionysos was the father of Maron, the founder of the city of Maroneia.

The ancient city was vastly different from the ruins that you see today. It flourished from the eighth century B.C. right up to about A.D. 1400. Its walls were 6 miles (10 km) in overall length, which gives an idea of the scale of the city, by far the most important in this area.

Continue on to **Agios Haralambos** to find an appealing little harbor with a hotel, a few tavernas, and a scattering of houses, with small-scale tourist development. It is a great place for those who like to get away from it all.

⛰ 171 G2

SAITISTA

Like Kastoria, 44 miles (70 km) to the north, Saitista was also once an important fur trading center. The business is now only a fraction of what it once was, but you will still see furs for sale in some of the town's stores.

Here too are the 18th-century mansions of the wealthy, with their ornate interiors, some of which can be visited. Most are well maintained and still lived in by families, while a few have fallen into ruin.

The main town church of **Agia Paraskevi** has frescoes dating from the 17th-century that are well worth seeing.

⛰ 170 B1 ∎

Evia is Greece's second largest island after Crete, separated from the mainland by just a narrow channel. Its size makes for great diversity, from the busy capital of Halkida to remote mountain villages.

Evia

Gorgon head from Eretria

Evia

THE GREEKS KNOW ALL ABOUT EVIA'S BEAUTY, BUT RELATIVELY FEW visitors get to appreciate it. This is partly because guidebooks often overlook it. Although Evia is an island, it is connected to the mainland by a bridge. Books about the Greek islands, therefore, frequently treat it as part of the mainland, and books about the mainland leave it out because it's an island. This is a great advantage if you want to spend time in a part of Greece that is not overrun by visitors—and Evia's large size means that the people who do go there tend to be well dispersed.

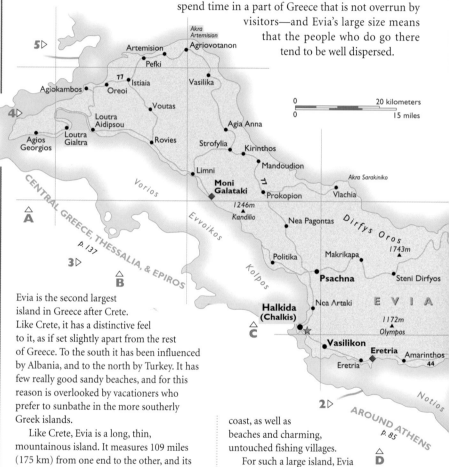

Evia is the second largest island in Greece after Crete. Like Crete, it has a distinctive feel to it, as if set slightly apart from the rest of Greece. To the south it has been influenced by Albania, and to the north by Turkey. It has few really good sandy beaches, and for this reason is overlooked by vacationers who prefer to sunbathe in the more southerly Greek islands.

Like Crete, Evia is a long, thin, mountainous island. It measures 109 miles (175 km) from one end to the other, and its highest point, Mount Dirfys, is 5,737 feet (1,749 m) above sea level. It is extremely fertile, filled with woods, orchards, olive groves, and vineyards. The best retsina in Greece comes from here, they say. There is good grazing land too, and in fact the original Greek name of the island (still frequently used) is Euboea, which translates as "rich in cattle." There are rugged cliffs around the

coast, as well as beaches and charming, untouched fishing villages.

For such a large island, Evia is not rich in classical sites. However, one that is widely known and should be on everyone's itinerary is ancient Eretria (see p. 212). Despite the lack of important sites, there are vast numbers of minor ones, including many Frankish and Byzantine fortresses.

According to mythology, Evia became an island when the god Poseidon created the

The silvery gray-green of olive groves covers Greece's second largest island.

channel separating it from the mainland with a blow from his trident. It then became his favorite island, and he lived in an underwater palace there. A list of later residents has almost everyone who ever invaded Greece, including Macedonians, Romans, Franks, Byzantines, Venetians, and, of course, Turks, who handed the island back to Greece in 1830.

All these varied historical cultures have left some kind of mark on Evia, but today the impact of foreign visitors is much less than on most of the other Greek islands. If you plan to spend some time here, make sure you have a Greek phrase book with you, especially if you're hoping to visit the lovely villages of the interior—other languages are not widely spoken here. ■

Area of map detail

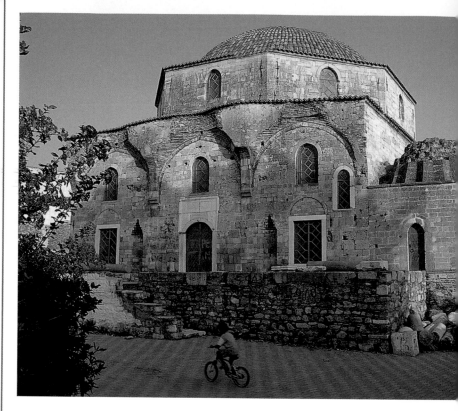

Halkida

⚑ 206 C3

Visitor information

✉ Tourist Police

☎ 0221 77777

Folk Museum

✉ Skalkota 4

☎ 0221 21817

⏰ Closed Mon.–Tues., Thurs., & Sat.

Halkida

THE INDUSTRIAL PORT OF HALKIDA (OR CHALKIS) IS THE capital of Evia, and your first sight of the island if you have driven across from the mainland. The Evvoikos Channel is at its narrowest here—a mere 130 feet (40 m) across. The channel is renowned for its inexplicable currents: It is still not understood how they can sometimes change direction more than a dozen times a day, and on other days change only once. According to legend, the philosopher Aristotle was so frustrated at his inability to understand the phenomenon that he threw himself into the waters and died. Aristotle did die in Halkida in 322 B.C., but whether in this fashion is another matter.

Halkida is very much a working island capital, with lots of industry, including a cement works, and a large population. Its attractions include a lively Turkish quarter, but the town should not be taken as a reflection of the island as a whole.

The Evvoikos Channel has been bridged since 411 B.C. (the present bridge dates only from the 1960s), and the town was one of the independent Greek city-states until it was conquered by Athens in 506 B.C. Like the rest of the island,

Halkida was later ruled by a range of peoples: Macedonians, Turks, Franks, and Venetians.

The name Halkida is thought to derive from the Greek word for copper, *halkos,* as this mineral was one of the island's major early sources of wealth. The town once controlled and gave its name to the Chalkidiki peninsula (also spelled Halkidiki in Greek, see p. 186), and it had several Italian colonies too.

For many years, Halkida vied with Eretria for ultimate control of Evia—especially the fertile Lelantine Plain, which feeds much of the island. It was not until the seventh century B.C. that Halkida finally proved its superiority and developed as Evia's capital.

Today, although at first glance not immediately appealing, Halkida is still worth a day or two of your time for its museums, old town, and waterfront areas. The main **waterfront** is to the left as you cross the bridge; here you will find restaurants, cafés, ouzeries, and hotels. It makes a good place to sit over a coffee or a full meal, gazing over the channel to the mainland. The fish restaurants are rated so highly that it is said Athenians will drive out for the evening to eat here, a distance of 55 miles (88 km). Here, too, is the market, where island produce is brought in by the farmers to be sold. It is busy most days, especially Saturday. It is worth noting that Saturday morning is, therefore, the worst time of the week to drive through Halkida or across the bridge connecting the capital with the mainland.

Head for the quarter known as **Kastro,** turning inland and to the right away from the bridge, to find much quieter streets. Many of the old houses here testify to the Turkish and Venetian legacies of the town. A community of Muslims from Thrace, much farther east, brings an unusual touch of the Orient to this part of town, augmented by an imposing 15th-century mosque, a Turkish aqueduct, and the remains of a 17th-century fortress. The aqueduct used to bring water to Halkida from springs on Mount Dirfys some 16 miles (25 km) to the northeast.

Christianity is represented by the somewhat bizarre and dominating church of **Agia Paraskevi** (not far from the bridge), originally constructed in the 13th century. In the 14th century the Crusaders converted the exterior of this vast building into a Gothic cathedral, complete with rose window, but the interior remains a mixture of all of the island's historical influences. Take note of the ornate wooden pulpit and the wooden ceiling.

Halkida's **Folk Museum,** just by Agia Paraskevi, has the usual collection of folk costumes and rural artifacts.

The town's **Archaeological Museum** is better. In the modern part of Halkida, it has excellent sculptures from the Temple of Apollo at Ancient Eretria, as well as items from some of the island's lesser-known sites, such as Karystos. The building that houses the collection is almost one hundred years old and has some very ancient artifacts to show. Ceramic items and figurines dating from the third century B.C. were found in the cemetery and historic town of Manika, just north of Halkida. There is little to see at the site itself, but excavations continue and may yet yield up further treasures. Other historic sites on the island represented in the museum include Agios Stephanos and Tries Kamares. ■

The venerable mosque at the entrance to the Kastro quarter shows signs of wear and tear over the centuries.

Archaeological Museum
✉ Venizelou 13
☎ 0221 76131
🕐 Closed Mon.
💲 $

Drive: Exploring northern Evia

This drive takes you from the busy town and port of Halkida, out along the coast road, and up into the mountains for a glimpse of life in the rugged and beautiful north of the island.

Assuming that you enter **Halkida** ❶ (see p. 208) from the mainland across the bridge, stay on the main road through the town center, turning left onto Route 44 and then right onto route 77, marked for Mandoudion. Outside the main town most road signs are written only in Greek, so you need to have a copy of the Greek alphabet with you to help you make sense of the Greek place-names. You will also need patience.

The road north out of Halkida takes you through some salt marshes and along the coast, with great views across to the mainland. After about 7.5 miles (12 km) look for the right fork on a local road marked for Psachna, which you reach in just over a mile (2 km). **Psachna** ❷ is an attractive market town, worth a brief stop to admire the 13th-century frescoes in the main church.

From Psachna, follow the signs for Prokopion, which takes you back to route 77. Prokopion is 19 miles (30 km) farther. The road to it is a marvelous drive, passing through olive groves, and then into pine forests as the landscape becomes more mountainous.

There are now even more spectacular views back to the mainland, as well as vistas over Evia itself, showing how green this island is—especially in the spring and early summer. For a time the road runs alongside a river, through the deep, narrow, and lushly wooded ravine of the **Kleisoura Valley,** with walnut, plane, and poplar trees. Continue along this road to Prokopion.

Prokopion ❸ (see p. 215) is an essential stop along the route. It is a settlement that grew up after the arrival of Greek refugees forced out of Turkey during the population exchanges in 1923. Its church of **Agios Ioannis o Rosos** (St. John the Russian) contains the mummified body of that saint, brought from Turkey. Prokopion is also the home of the **Kandili Center,** a base for specialist arts vacations. This is set

around the once-feudal estate of Englishman Edward Noel, a relative of Lord Byron, and takes its name from the mountain to the south. It is worth visiting just to see the handsome old mansion and the beautiful grounds.

From Prokopion continue on route 77 for 5 miles (8 km), following the signs for Limni and Mandoudion. **Mandoudion** ❹ is a beautiful village of whitewashed houses, about half a mile (1 km) off to the right of the main road. Don't hesitate to make the slight detour to stop off here for a while and relax in the pretty main square.

Go back to route 77 and turn right, following the signs for Strofylia and Limni. The road takes you through more agricultural land, past rows of vines bent under the weight of the grapes in the fall. In Strofylia the road forks. Follow the left fork, which passes through a few more hill villages, before dropping down toward the pretty coastal village of **Limni** ❺ (see p. 215). A good seafood lunch or supper awaits you here. Make time, if you can, for the walk to the spectacular **Moni Galataki** (see p. 215). There are no formal opening hours, but anyone arriving in the morning or early afternoon will be welcome to look around, if he or she is respectably dressed. ■

▲ See area map p. 206
▶ Halkida
🔁 50 miles (80 km)
🕐 2 hours
▶ Limni

NOT TO BE MISSED

- Halkida
- Psachna
- Prokopion
- Mandoudion
- Limni

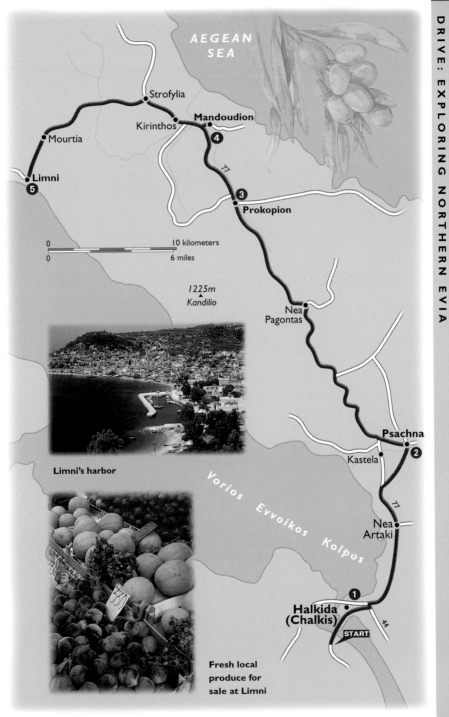

AEGEAN
SEA

Strofylia

Mandoudion
Kirinthos
4

Mourtia

Limni
5

3

Prokopion

0   10 kilometers
0   6 miles

1225m
Kandilio

Nea
Pagontas

Limni's harbor

Psachna
2

Kastela

Vorios Evvoikos Kolpos

Nea
Artaki

Fresh local
produce for
sale at Limni

**Halkida
(Chalkis)**
1

START

44

Cut off from the rest of Evia by mountains, Karystos sits on a curving bay.

Around Evia

BEYOND THE MAIN TOWN, THE LARGE AND BEGUILING island of Evia awaits the curious traveler. From ancient sites to modern beach resorts, from lowlands to mountains, this is an island with something for everyone.

Eretria
🅰 206 D2

Archaeological Museum
✉ Eretria
☎ 0229 62206
🕐 Closed Mon.
💲 $

ERETRIA

Ancient Eretria is the most important historical site on Evia. At one time the city rivaled Halkida for dominance of the island, before Halkida took power in the seventh century B.C. Eretria itself was finally destroyed in 87 B.C.

Unfortunately for the archaeologists, modern Eretria has grown up on top of the ruins of the ancient city, instead of on a nearby site as often happened. There is still much to enjoy here, both ancient

and modern, though the best artifacts from the site are in the archaeological museum in Halkida (see p. 209).

Displays in Eretria's own **Archaeological Museum** include a fearsome Gorgon's head, retrieved from a villa of the fourth century B.C. Nearby is the **House of Mosaics,** a restoration of a fourth-century house with well-preserved floor mosaics; the key is held at the museum. A cluster of other remains in this northwest corner of the town includes the **theater,** which is particularly interesting for a passageway under the stage. This led to the place from where the *deus ex machina* (providential interruption) could pop up. An unexpected event brought about by the sudden appearance of the gods, who control human fate, was a favorite theatrical device often used to resolve a Greek drama. There are also the remains of a gymnasium and a palace.

Above the theater a short walk leads to the acropolis, with some remnants of its walls and towers, and good views northwest over the Lelantine Plain, the fertile ground that was desired by both Eretria and Halkida in ancient times.

In the center of town, look for the foundations of the **Temple of Apollo** and the site of the agora. The modern town of Eretria now sprawls along the coast as one of the island's main resorts but is not the most interesting place to stay on Evia. Far nicer resorts beckon the traveler.

KARYSTOS

Almost at the southern tip of Evia, Karystos is an attractive town of mainly modern origin, having been built up only after the War of Independence (1821-1829). Otto, the first king of modern Greece, liked the site so much that he modestly renamed the town after himself, Othonoupolis. He made it the new capital of Greece, inviting a Bavarian architect to create a grand town plan of long, wide streets lined with mansions. But

Karystos
🗺 207 F1

Built by Venetians, Castello Rosso overlooks Karystos's waterfront.

not long after this first stage was completed, Otto was gone. Karystos reclaimed its name and kept the streets. Today it is one of the destination points for the ferries from Rafina (see p. 91) on the mainland, making it busy—especially during the summer—but in a lively, appealing way.

Dominating the town, the **Castello Rosso** is a massive medieval fortress that looks over modern Karystos from the site of the ancient acropolis. Nothing much remains inside the fortress, which gets its name from its ruddy-colored walls, but it gives good views back down over the town and farther inland to Mount Ochi.

KYMI

Kymi lies halfway along Evia's northern coast, a town set among vineyards and orchards. The **Folk Museum** is outstanding, with a fascinating collection of old photographs showing life in the last century in this quiet, rural place. The town's sleepy nature and remote location belie its rich past, evident from the fine 19th-century

mansions that line the streets. These houses were built on wealth from a combination of local silk production and international maritime trade.

Kymi also has an interesting church dedicated to the **Panagia Koimisis** that contains a rare seventh-century icon of the Madonna and Child. North of the town is the dramatically situated clifftop monastery of **Moni Sotira,** built in the 17th century and still inhabited today by a small number of nuns. Men are not admitted.

STENI DIRFYOS

Thanks to its location at the foot of Evia's highest point, **Mount Dirfys,** the mountain village of Steni Dirfyos has developed into a thriving tourist town. The peak gives wonderful views over the island, out to the Aegean, and back toward the Greek mainland. It is relatively accessible, provided you are in reasonably good shape and are used to hiking. Take the four-hour walk to the summit for a good day out and enjoy a picnic lunch at the top.

Kymi
🗺 207 E3

Folk Museum,
☎ 0222 22011
🕐 Closed Mon.–Tues., Thurs.–Fri.
💲 $

Steni Dirfyos
🗺 206 D3

You will need a map. The walk begins at the end of the main road that runs through Steni Dirfyos, which peters out into a parking lot after about 2 miles (3 km). Follow the trail and look for the turning to the left that is clearly marked "Fountain of Liri Refuge." From the refuge another trail, marked with dabs of red paint on rocks, leads straight up to the summit.

PROKOPION

Prokopion is another mountain village, overlooked by the highest point in the north of the island, Mount Kandilio (4,087 feet/ 1,246 m). The drive on pages 210–11 passes through Prokopion, where it is well worth taking a break. Many pilgrims stop here to visit the church of **Agios Ioannis o Rosos,** which contains the remains of St. John the Russian. A Ukrainian, he served in the tsar's army, was captured and enslaved by the Turks, and then killed by the Turks in the town of Prokopion in central Turkey. With the exchange of populations in 1923, his devoted followers brought his bones to Greece. They named their new settlement Prokopion and built a church to house the relics. You may see Russian Orthodox visitors here, too; in 1962 St. John was also canonized by the Russian Orthodox faith.

LOUTRA GIALTRA & LOUTRA AIDIPSOU

There is a pleasant surprise at the remote northwestern end of Evia, where you find a beautiful wide bay surrounded by wooded slopes. Spa resorts sit on either side of the curve. The smaller spa, Loutra Gialtra, is a pretty harbor town with an old windmill and a decent beach, and with access to even better beaches toward the extreme northwestern tip of the island.

Across the bay, Loutra Aidipsou is the largest spa town in Greece and renowned for its sulfur springs—a reputation that brings visitors flocking here every summer at the prospect of being made young and beautiful. It is not the best time of year to turn up without making reservations. However, the influx of summer visitors means that the town has ample accommodations (many hotels have their own hot springs) at other times of year. Then you can enjoy the town's excellent beach and the picturesque charm of a working fishing harbor, with the prospect of day trips to the Sporades (see pp. 226–31).

LIMNI

By contrast, Limni, 28 miles (45 km) down the coast from Loutra Aidipsou, is a peaceful fishing village. It is just starting to wake up to the tourist trade. It lacks the good beaches of Loutra Gialtra, Loutra Aidipsou, and some other Evia resorts, and so for the moment remains a low-key traditional village of whitewashed, red-tiled houses, with boats bobbing in the harbor, some grand 19th-century houses, and a relaxing waterfront with cafés and tavernas. See it while you can.

More energetic visitors make the 5-mile (8 km) walk to the Byzantine monastery of **Moni Galataki.** This is the oldest monastery on Evia, with remains going back to the 13th century, although most buildings date from the 16th. Frescoes in the church, also from the 16th century, have survived in vivid detail, including a Last Judgment guaranteed to frighten anyone onto the path of righteousness. The monastery was deserted for many years but reinstated as a convent in the 1940s. It is still inhabited by nuns today and can be visited. ■

Prokopion
🅜 206 C4

Loutra Gialtra
🅜 206 B4

Loutra Aidipsou
🅜 206 B4

Limni
🅜 206 C4

Goats set their own speed restrictions in the hills around Styra.

More places to visit on Evia

AKRA ARTEMISION

On the northern coast of Evia is the attractive headland of Artemision. Several sandy beaches nearby are very popular with local people in summer. Above the curving bay sits the pretty village of **Agriovotanon.** It was off the cape here in 1928 that local fishermen found a statue of Poseidon, now one of the star exhibits in the National Archaeological Museum in Athens (see pp. 78–81). Poseidon, the god of the sea, is said to have lived on Evia.

206 C5   Bus from Halkida

MOUNT OCHI

At 4,587 feet (1,398 m), Mount Ochi is the highest point in the south of Evia. It is surrounded by quaint little villages, both inland on its slopes and on the surrounding coasts. The hill village of **Mili** overlooks Karystos near the Castello Rosso (see p. 214) and is the starting point for those wishing to climb the mountain. However, this is a serious four-hour hike, and you will need to be healthy and have a good map or guide.

The exceptional views from the top include one of Evia's so-called **dragon houses**—so named because it was thought that only dragons could have transported the massive stones to the high locations where the buildings are found. (In reality, it is likely that slaves were used to shift the huge rocks.) No one knows their purpose for sure, but it

is thought they may have been miniature temples for the worship of Poseidon in the sixth century B.C.

207 F1

OCHTHONIA

The hill village of Ochthonia is a bewitching place, with a more prosperous past indicated by neoclassic mansions and ruined towers, and by the remains of the Frankish castle above the village. Down on the coast below, three long stretches of white sandy beach are too remote to attract big crowds, so they are good places to aim for if you like to sunbathe in seclusion.

207 E3   Bus from Halkida

STYRA

On Evia's west coast, the busy port of Nea Styra (New Styra) is linked by ferry to Rafina on the mainland. It has developed into a small summer resort especially popular with Athenians, who can reach it very easily. It has a wonderful long sandy beach, which is packed in midsummer. At other times of the year Nea Styra makes a convenient base for a few days.

Climb inland for 3 miles (5 km) and you reach the hill village of Styra itself, a quiet place noted for its mysterious **"dragon houses"** (see Mount Ochi, left), just outside the town.

207 E1   Bus from Halkida ∎

T he diverse Aegean islands
range from uninhabited
specks of land to mass-market
tourist destinations with miles
of sunbathing bodies. Between
these extremes lie numerous
places that seduce the curious
traveler.

Aegean islands

Embroidery from Skiros

Aegean islands

THE RICH DIVERSITY OF THE AEGEAN ISLANDS DRAWS MANY TRAVELERS back year after year. No matter how many islands you explore, another one always awaits just over the horizon. Other visitors prefer to return to the same island again and again, the islanders welcoming them back like the return of migrating swallows.

If your time is limited, plan carefully to select the island or islands that best suit you. If your preference is for a relaxing stay and an authentic Greek island experience, avoid the tourist traps of larger islands such as Rhodes and Kos, or disco-centered party islands such as Mikonos and Ios. On the other hand, if you like a choice of eating places and want to meet other travelers, don't go to a small island out of season. It can be almost dead, with the hotels and restaurants all closed, their owners having returned to Athens for the winter.

If you have time to explore, go to one of the groups of islands, such as the Cyclades or the Dodecanese. Travel around, experiencing their tremendous variety before settling on the island that fulfills your needs—and every island is unique. It is usually easy to travel between islands from spring to fall; the exception is the northeastern Aegean islands, which are more widely scattered.

The Saronic Gulf islands make for safe and easy traveling, conveniently close to Athens. However, in summer and on weekends they are busy with fun-seeking Athenians, and they have all been discovered by overseas tour groups and cruise ships. This means most of the islands are bursting at the seams with visitors.

The Sporades, farther north, are greener and more cosmopolitan. Skiathos has crowds and beaches, Alonissos is quieter, and Skopelos is somewhere in between—as it is geographically. In the northern and eastern Aegean, larger islands such as Lesvos and Hios are big enough to encompass both vacation resorts and unspoiled villages, while Samothraki is harder to get to and remains one of the least developed islands. The Dodecanese and the Cyclades, with their whitewashed houses gleaming in the sunshine, offer the best-known images of the Greek islands. Somewhere within those large groups is likely to be everyone's island dream. ∎

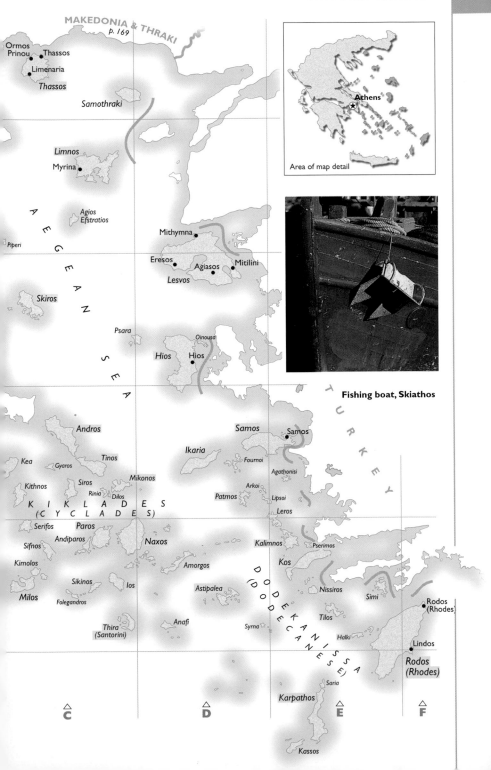

MAKEDONIA & THRAKI
p. 169

Ormos
Prinou
Thassos
Limenaria
Thassos

Samothraki

Area of map detail

Athens

Limnos
Myrina

A E G E A N

*Agios
Efstratios*

Piperi

Mithymna

Eresos
Agiasos   Mitilini
Lesvos

Skiros

S E A

Psara
Oinousa

Hios   Hios

Fishing boat, Skiathos

T U R K E Y

Andros

Samos   Samos

Ikaria
Fournoi

Kea   Gyaros
Tinos
Agathonisi

Kithnos
Siros
Mikonos
Rinia   Dilos
Arkoi
Patmos   Lipsoi

K I K L A D E S
(C Y C L A D E S)
Leros

Serifos   Paros
Sifnos
Andiparos
Naxos
Kalimnos   Pserimos

Kimolos
Kos
D
Sikinos
Ios
Amorgos
O

Milos
Folegandros
Astipalea
D
Nissiros
Simi
E
K
Anafi
Tilos
Rodos
(Rhodes)
*Thira
(Santorini)*
Syrna
A
N
Halki
Lindos
I

S
*Rodos
(Rhodes)*
S

A
Saria

Karpathos

Kassos

△   △   △   △
C   D   E   F

Argo-Saronic islands

Lying in the Saronic Gulf just off the coast of Argolid, this archipelago is easily accessible to Athens—and, therefore, inundated with locals wishing to escape the summer heat. Nevertheless, each island retains its individual identity—from stylish and charming to rustic and green. Good ferry connections make it possible to visit all of them in the course of a few days.

Egina, the biggest of the Saronic islands, has residents who commute to Athens. The reverse happens on weekends, when hordes of Athenians descend here for a break. It has some great mansions and one of the best temples in Greece. Like all of these islands it is best seen in spring or fall, without the summer crowd. Egina and the other islands in this group are a regular stop for cruise ships on their way to and from Athens. Combined with weekend visitors, the summer tourists make it a hive of social activity.

Poros, farther south, appeals to walkers with its gently rolling terrain. Nightlife is lively in the summertime. The proximity of the adjacent Peloponnese mainland is a bonus, allowing easy access for exploration of the Argolid (a car ferry crosses the connecting strait every 20 minutes in summer).

Idra was discovered in the 1950s by bohemian artists and became a very fashionable hangout, which it has remained to this day. Idra is too rugged to be spoiled, and it retains a chic charm around the harbor area, which contrasts with the rocky interior and the remote monasteries scattered around the coastline.

A donkey waits patiently by a *caïque* for its next load at Idra's harbor.

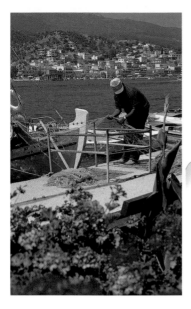

Untangling the nets in Poros

The farthest island from Athens, Spetses, has some grand architecture. Its pine groves, even having suffered from fires, make it the greenest island in the group. It attracts mainly wealthy Athenians and more upscale travelers.

These islands are an hour or two away from Athens by Flying Dolphin (hydrofoil) and can be used as a place to stay while commuting to Athens to see the sites, if you don't want to stay in the city itself. In fact, the Argo-Saronic islands are the ideal group for the newcomer to Greece to try some island-hopping. They are close enough to get from one to another quite easily, and yet all are distinctively different.

Island-hopping is great for those who don't like a fixed itinerary and prefer the freedom to travel from one island to the next as the mood takes them, staying longer in the places that really appeal.

Provided you are not traveling in August or at Easter, finding accommodations is not usually a problem. ∎

Egina

🅰 221 C3

Visitor information

✉ Leonardou Lada,
Egina town

☎ 0297 27777

Temple of Aphea

☎ 0297 32398

💲 $

Egina

EGINA MEANS "PIGEON ISLAND," A NAME GIVEN IT BY early Phoenician settlers. Today Egina is an elegant spot, even when busy with vacationing Athenians out for the weekend. Behind the crowds are fine 19th-century mansions testifying to a prosperous past as a trading port. During Greece's classical period Egina town was a major rival to Athens. It was also the first town in Europe to issue its own silver coins, minting a currency that was later adopted throughout Greece. In 1828 the town was briefly the capital of Greece—hard to believe if you compare it with Athens today. Nowadays the island's economy is based on pistachio nuts and tourism.

Egina town has a wealth of churches and other historical buildings to explore. The remnants of the ancient town scatter across the acropolis on a low hill near the beach. The distinguishing feature of the acropolis is a still-standing column from the Temple of Apollo.

The island is famous, however, for the magnificent **Temple of Aphea,** standing about 7.5 miles (12 km) east of Egina town. It is easily accessed by bus or car and close enough to walk to from the beach resort of Agia Marina. The temple is an excellent example of Doric architecture, built on a hill known to have been a place of religious worship since at least the 13th century B.C. The remaining temple was built around 490 B.C., making it 60 years older than the Parthenon. Like the Parthenon, its pediment sculptures are no longer in place. Even without them, the temple is well worth seeing. ■

A statue of the goddess Aphea was housed in the inner chamber, or *cella,* where offerings were made.

Sculptures on the east pediment showed Athena.

Limestone was covered in stucco and brightly painted.

Entrance ramp

TEMPLE OF APHEA

Poros

POROS IS ALMOST A PART OF THE PELOPONNESE, separated from the mainland by a narrow channel, just 380 yards (350 m) wide at its narrowest point. The channel gives the island its name (*poros* means "passage"), and small boats chug back and forth all day taking people between Poros and the mainland town of Galatas, from where you can catch buses to Epidavros and Nafplio.

Poros offers two islands for the price of one. **Sferia,** on which Poros town stands, is separated from the much larger Kalavria by a small road. **Poros town** is a popular destination for cruise ships, weekending Athenians, and Europeans, despite a lack of good beaches. The town itself is very attractive, with its picturesque mix of white and pastel-colored houses on the hillside above the harbor. The waterfront is filled with bars and restaurants and is certainly the place to be for an entertaining night out.

For a quieter time, walk or cycle along the single main road that loops around the main island, **Kalavria.** This leads past the abandoned little 18th-century monastery, **Moni Zoödochou Pigis,** right by the sea. Higher up on this wooded, hilly island are the scant remains of the **Temple of Poseidon,** dating from the sixth century B.C. It is free and open to anyone who makes the small effort to get there.

When you have fully explored Poros, take the short and inexpensive boat ride to tiny **Galatas.** Turn left from the quiet harbor and walk until you reach the wonderful lemon groves of Limonodassos. There are tens of thousands of lemon trees here, and it's really wonderful to stroll up the gentle hills, through the groves, taking in the scent of citrus on the breeze. ■

Poros
🅜 221 C2
Visitor information
✉ Tourist Police, waterfront
☎ 0298 22256

Idra

Idra

🅐   221 B1

Visitor information

✉   Tourist Police, Odos
Votsi

☎   0298 52205

IDRA (OR HYDRA) IS SMALL, VERY ROCKY, AND QUITE barren, but is nonetheless a fascinating island. The main town clusters around the harbor, and while it is attractive, its popularity can mean severe overcrowding and shortage of accommodations in July and August. It is also expensive, by island standards. The waterfront, lined with chic boutiques and art galleries, shows a much more sophisticated face than most other Greek islands.

Idra became fashionable in a bohemian way in the 1950s and early 1960s, when painters and poets—including Canadian songwriter Leonard Cohen—made their homes here.

Like other Saronic islands, Idra has some fine 18th- and 19th-century mansions, funded by the wealth created by the island's astonishing fleet of merchant ships. Looking at the tiny harbor today, it is hard to believe that the island owned some 150 ships that traded across the Atlantic with North America. It is also hard to believe that there was once a population of 40,000 people here, when today there are barely 3,000.

Idra is not an island for sun worshippers, as there is only one sandy beach and that is attached to the Miramare Hotel, just over a mile (2 km) from Idra town. There are a number of pebble beaches scattered around the island, which is big enough to enable you to escape the crowded harbor during the day by walking along the coastal paths or taking the roads inland. ■

A jumble of little boats shelter around the jetty in Idra's harbor.

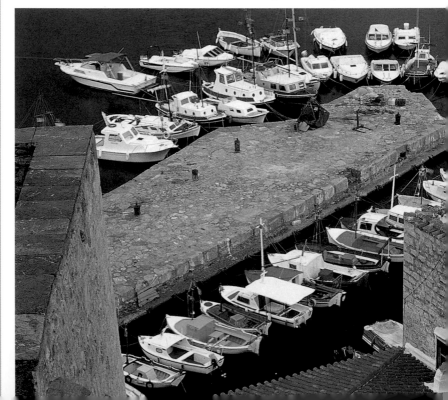

Spetses

SPETSES, LIKE IDRA, BECAME VERY RICH THROUGH SHIP-building and maritime trade in the 18th and 19th centuries. The grand houses that date from this prosperous period can still be seen around Spetses town. Many of these are now the weekend retreats and vacation homes of well-to-do Athenians. Spetses has become fashionable, and while it is more sophisticated than boisterous little Poros, it lacks the artistic chic of Idra.

Spetses
🅰 221 A1

The islanders are proud of their maritime heritage and in particular of their most famous daughter, Laskarina Bouboulina (1771–1825), whose statue graces the harbor. Bouboulina became an admiral in the navy and was prominent in fighting the Turks during the War of Independence in the 1820s. Her coffin and bones are displayed in the **Chatzi-Giannis Mexis Museum** (*Spetses town, tel 0298 72994, closed Mon.*), which takes its name from the former owners of the late 18th-century mansion and has displays on local history, especially the War of Independence. Close to the harbor is **Bouboulina's House** (*near Plateia Ntapia, tel 0298 72416, closed Oct.–April*), which is also now a museum in her memory. The house is still owned by descendants of Bouboulina. Admission is by way of a guided tour every half-hour in season, in both Greek and English.

A more recent resident was British novelist John Fowles (born 1926), whose 1966 novel *The Magus*, later filmed, became a cult classic among young people in the late 1960s. Fowles turned Spetses into the fictional island of Phraxos. Fowles taught at Anaryiros College, on the edge of Spetses town, and used this as a location. The Hotel Possidonion also featured.

There are no major historical remains around the island, but there are a number of good beaches, like the one at Agii Anargiri, and quiet villages, making Spetses a rewarding island to explore. Its original name, Pityoussa, referred to its pine forests, and these still scent the air in the heat of summer.

You can get around on foot or by renting a bike or motorbike. For a long time cars were banned from here. Now local residents are allowed to bring cars onto Spetses, although cars are still prohibited downtown. This makes Spetses town one of the more pleasant capitals in the Greek islands. ∎

Despite her naval command, Bouboulina never abandoned her traditional Spetses costume, complete with bodice and wimple; she is depicted this way in Spetses' harbor.

Sporades

This small group of four main islands gets its name from the Greek for "scattered." They have all been opened up to tourism in varying degrees, in roughly inverse proportion to their size. The smallest, Skiathos, is by far the busiest and has the best beaches, while the largest, Skiros, retains much more of its traditional Greek ambience.

The islands were once extensions of the Pilion peninsula (see pp. 150–51), and like that part of the mainland they are green with thick pine woods. The lushness means that mosquitoes can be more of a problem here than in the drier islands farther south in the Aegean, so come prepared.

Mere mosquitoes can't keep the crowds from rushing to Skiathos in the height of summer, so visit in the spring or fall if you want its superb beaches to yourself. Another option is to take the ferry to the neighboring island of Skopelos to the east, which is scenically much more dramatic, making it a good base for walkers. Its beautiful beaches are almost as good as those on Skiathos.

Alonissos, the next Sporadic isle to the east, is unusually long and thin, and has few roads. It was left behind in the tourist boom, although many foreigners, notably from Germany, bought property here either to live in cheaply or to start up tiny businesses. Alonissos has many small islets around it, home to Europe's rarest mammal, the Mediterranean monk seal. In 1992 the Greek government created the country's first national marine park here to protect the seals and bring ecotourism to Alonissos.

On Skiros, old customs and costumes survive, helped by the fact that it is remote from the other islands and harder to reach from the mainland. ■

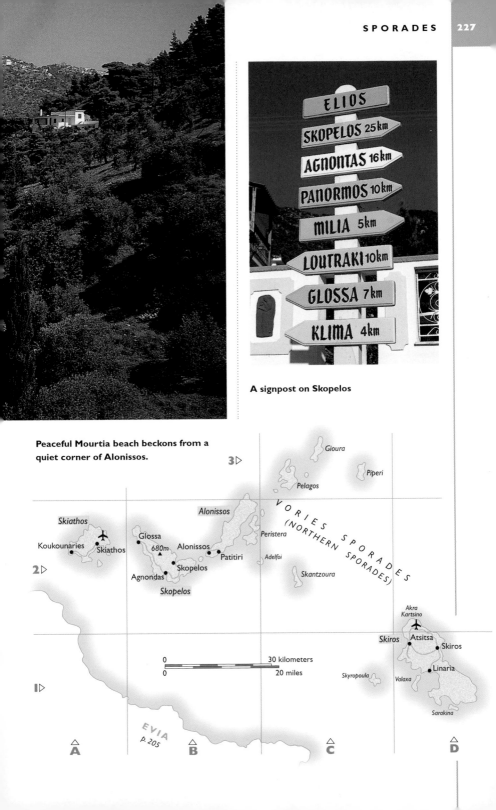

A signpost on Skopelos

Peaceful Mourtia beach beckons from a
quiet corner of Alonissos.

3▷

Gioura

Piperi

Pelagos

Alonissos

V O R I E S   S P O R A D E S
(N O R T H E R N   S P O R A D E S)

Skiathos

Peristera

Koukounáries

Glossa

Skiathos

680m ▲

Alonissos

Patitiri

Adelfoi

2▷

Skopelos

Agnondas

Skopelos

Skantzoura

Akra
Kartsino

Skiros   Atsitsa

Skiros

Linaria

Skyropoula   Valaxa

I▷

Sarakina

EVIA
p. 205

| 0 | | 30 kilometers |
| 0 | | 20 miles |

△
A

△
B

△
C

△
D

Skiathos

IF YOU WANT TO SEE RAMPANT TOURIST DEVELOPMENT AT its best, or worst (depending on your tastes), then visit Skiathos in the height of summer when its wonderful beaches become a veritable mecca for sun worshippers. The south and east coasts are filled with endless lines of villas, hotels, souvenir shops, bars, and restaurants, so that one area merges into the next, depriving them of individuality.

Skiathos

▲ 227 A2

Visitor information

✉ Tourist Police

☎ 0427 23172

As with many popular destinations, only a narrow strip of land near the beach is affected. The interior of Skiathos is beautifully wooded and rugged, with wonderful opportunities for walking.

Monasteries carry on their peaceful existence here as they have done for centuries. The 18th-century monastery of the Evangelistria is just an hour's walk north of Skiathos town. Take the airport road and look for the left turn that directs you to this magnificently located and peaceful set of buildings. For other walks, check the local bookstores for the recommended-walks booklets.

Most of the island's population lives in **Skiathos town,** with

its twin harbors and twin existence. One harbor is for pleasure boats, the other for the fishermen. Enter the back streets and you could be in any Greek town, but get into the shopping areas or down onto the waterfront and you could be in a tourist town almost anywhere in the world. Even the medieval fortress known as the **Bourtzi,** which separates the two harbors, is now occupied by a restaurant.

The town looks best from the sea, and more discerning travelers make sure they are quickly out there, heading for one of the other islands. There are daily outings from the harbor to Skopelos and Alonissos. ∎

Skiros

SOME DISTANCE FROM THE OTHER ISLANDS IN THIS group, Skiros has maintained its Greek individuality and character. A notable example of this is the Skiros Goat Dance, a tradition descended from pagan festivities, which still takes place during the island's pre-Lenten carnival. Masked revelers roam the streets of Skiros town, and the principal figure is the rather alarming *geros*, or old man, wearing a goatskin mask and with numerous goat bells strapped to his back.

Another unique sight on Skiros is its tiny wild horses, some of which have been tamed. During the festivities of August 15, local children race the horses near Magazia beach, just outside Skiros town.

Skiros town would look more at home in the Dodecanese or the Cyclades, with its jumble of white houses at the foot of the slopes topped by a Venetian fortress. Little remains of the fortress, which was built on the site of the original acropolis and is accessed via a tunnel. The fort offers great views down over the town.

Different aspects of the island's history are told in the town's museums: the **Archaeological Museum** and **Municipal Museum,** *(Megalou Stratou, tel 0222 91256, closed Nov.–March)* and the **Faltauïts Museum** *(Palaiopyrgos, tel 0222 91232, closed Nov.–March),* a folk-art museum housed in a grand mansion.

Near Treis Mpoukes, the deep-water harbor at the southern end of Skiros, is the simple grave of British war poet Rupert Brooke (1887–1915). He died of septicemia on a hospital ship that was bound for Gallipoli during World War I. He is best remembered for his prophetic and patriotic lines: "If I should die, think only this of me: that there's some corner of a foreign field that is forever England." ∎

Skiros
🅰 227 D1
Visitor information
✉ Tourist Police
☎ 0222 91274

Archaeological Museum
✉ Plateia Brooke
☎ 0222 91206
🕐 Closed Mon.
💲 $

Tradition is important in Skiros; older men may still be seen wearing the old-style baggy pants.

Alonissos

227 B2

Alonissos

A HILLY WOODED ISLAND, ALONISSOS IS NOT THE MOST attractive of the Sporades groups—the upside being less tourist development. The island suffered extensive earthquake damage to its main town, Patitiri, in 1965. Before that, in 1950, a disease destroyed the island's vineyards and grapefruit orchards.

The creation of an offshore **national marine park** in 1992 has contributed to an upturn in the island's fortunes. It was established to protect the rare and endangered Mediterranean monk seal. Fewer than 800 of these creatures survive worldwide, and about 30 of them breed on the tiny islands that surround Alonissos. Fishing is banned in certain areas, as local fishermen used to regard the seals as rivals for the diminishing fish stocks. If anyone offers to take you to see the seals, refuse—monk seals are very shy creatures and easily disturbed. Other wildlife takes advantage of the marine park, from migrant birds to dolphins.

The park has created new tourism for Alonissos through the attention it has brought to the island and surrounding waters. Yachts visit in much larger numbers than before, as many of the islands outside the protected area offer good harbors, isolated beaches, and excellent swimming.

Alonissos itself consists mainly of the little port of **Patitiri,** the attractive restored old town of **Palaia Alonissos** high above it, and a few other traditional villages scattered around. None of these is very developed, and all make simple, ideal getaways for travelers who want to avoid the trappings of tourism. ■

Picturesque wooden *caïques* share the harbor at Patitiri with modern hydrofoils.

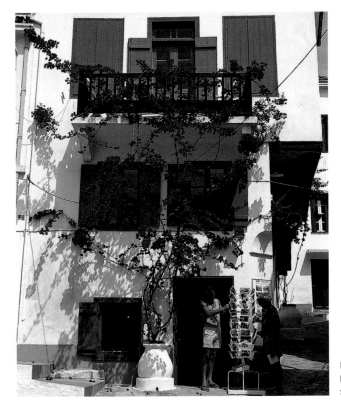

Dazzling bougainvillea, Skopelos town

Skopelos

POSSESSING ONE OF THE MOST BEAUTIFUL PORTS IN Greece at Skopelos town, Skopelos is densely vegetated, with pine forests sweeping down to secluded coves. Fruit and nut orchards fill its interior—the source of the island's famous plums and almonds.

Before moving on from Skopelos town, take a look at some of its 123 churches, including that of **Agios Athanasios,** built in the ninth century and boasting 16th-century frescoes. This church lies within the sturdy walls of the **Venetian fortress,** which stands above the harbor on the site of a temple to Athena.

Outside Skopelos town there is only one main road, but many paths lead to other resorts and villages. A good walk climbs up through olive groves to the island's highest point, **Mount Delphi** (2,230 feet/680 m).

In the hills east of the town are five monasteries and convents, three of them open to visitors. The nuns at **Evangelistria** sell their own handicrafts in a small gift shop, while the monastery of **Metamorphosis,** closed in 1980, has reopened after restoration by the monks. The convent of **Prodromos** looks across the Aegean to Alonissos. ∎

Skopelos
🅰 227 B2
Visitor information
✉ Waterfront
☎ 0424 23220

A sandy bay on Thassos epitomizes the beauty of the Greek islands.

Northeastern Aegean islands

The several islands, large and small, in this corner of the Aegean form no particular group, geographically or politically, so they are invariably lumped together. Because they are widely scattered and, in some cases, difficult to get to, they are among the least visited.

That is not to say that they are all untouched by tourism—parts of Thassos, Samos, and Lesvos are as busy as anywhere else in the Mediterranean in high summer—but if you go to tiny Samothraki or to Limnos, for example, you are likely to be welcomed as that rare creature, a foreign visitor.

Lesvos is Greece's third largest island and offers variety and plenty to explore, even though you can drive across it in a leisurely few hours. Hios and Samos are also sizable islands, if you want a place to stay for several days. All three are linked by ferries to Turkey. Samothraki, connected to the mainland (Alexandroupoli) by summer hydrofoil, is notoriously difficult to visit, as it has no natural harbor and the regular ferries cannot always come in to dock during stormy weather. That's something to bear in mind if you have to catch a flight from Athens!

There are several even smaller islands in this area, such as Ikaria near Samos, named after the legendary youth Icarus, who flew too close to the sun. Oinousa and Psara, off Hios, both have just one village and plenty of empty beaches if you want a real get-away-from-it-all island.

The islands share a proximity to Turkey, so there is a noticeable defensive military presence, and it is not unusual to hear the roar of jets overhead as they patrol the edge of Greek airspace. Despite this closeness, there are fewer signs here of Turkish domination than elsewhere. This is because Turkey's western coast was home to many Greek settlers, before the exchange of populations in 1923. ■

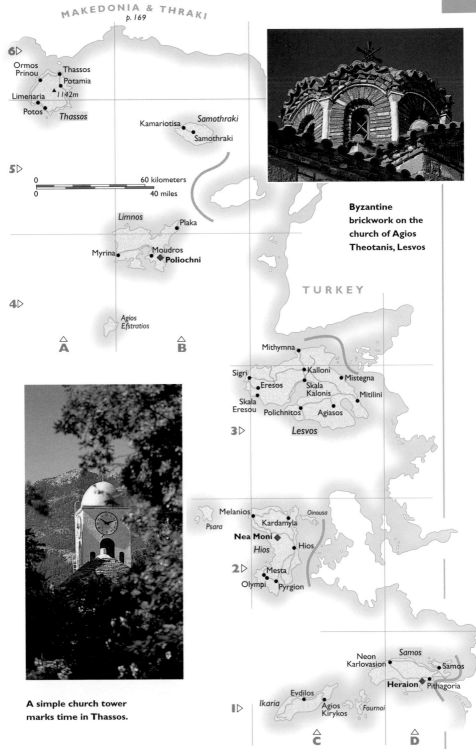

MAKEDONIA & THRAKI
p.169

6▷

Ormos Prinou
Thassos
Potamia
Limenaria ▲1142m
Potos
Thassos

Kamariotisa
Samothraki
Samothraki

5▷

0 — 60 kilometers
0 — 40 miles

Limnos
Plaka
Myrina
Moudros
◆**Poliochni**

TURKEY

4▷

Agios Efstratios

△ A   △ B

Mithymna

Sigri
Kalloni
Eresos
Skala Kalonis
Mistegna
Mitilini
Skala Eresou
Polichnitos
Agiasos

3▷ *Lesvos*

Byzantine
brickwork on the
church of Agios
Theotanis, Lesvos

Melanios
Oinousa
Kardamyla
Psara
Nea Moni ◆
Hios
Hios

2▷
Mesta
Olympi
Pyrgion

A simple church tower
marks time in Thassos.

Neon Karlovasion
Samos
Samos
Heraion ◆ Pithagoria

Evdilos
Ikaria
Agios Kirykos
Fournoi

▮▷

△ C   △ D

Thassos

Thassos

🅰 233 A5

Visitor information

✉ Tourist Police,
waterfront

☎ 0593 23111

**Archaeological
Museum**

✉ Next to Roman
agora, Thassos town

☎ 0593 22180

🕐 Closed Mon.

💲 $

ATTRACTED BY THASSOS' PINE-COVERED MOUNTAINS,
beaches, and ancient remains, Greek vacationers have flocked to the
island for years. Hikers love the remote north coast. In more recent
times, overseas travelers have discovered its charms, thanks to the
convenience of the Thessaloniki airport. Most visitors stay in and
around Thassos town, the island's modern capital, and make day-
trips from there.

Confusingly, **Thassos town** is
also known as Limin, Limenas, or
just Thassos, something you need
to know if traveling by bus or ferry.
To add to the confusion, the island's
second town, on the southern side
of Thassos, is called Limenaria.
Regular ferries link Thassos with
the Macedonian port at Kavala—
though most ferries actually dock at
the port of Ormos Prinou, 7 miles
(11 km) west of Thassos town.

Out of high season Thassos
town is a pleasant place to stay, with
added interest provided by the
Roman remains scattered about.
Because it is close to the mainland

(only 7.5 miles/12 km), Thassos
was inhabited as long ago as the
Stone Age. As a known source of
gold, silver, and other minerals
including white marble, it was
fought over in ancient times. It was
an important and wealthy port during the Roman occupation.

The most extensive area of
surviving Roman buildings is the
agora. It is fenced off and not
officially open, but if the gate is
unlocked no one minds if you
wander through and take a look.
With a little imagination and a
good map, available locally, you can
make out the remains of shops and

**Situated close to
the mainland,
Thassos is a
popular getaway.**

the foundations of temples and other public buildings. The ruins of a temple to Athena Poliouchou (meaning "patroness of the city") from the early part of the fifth century B.C. are located just below the site of the **acropolis,** and on the far side of this is one of the gates in the original city wall, the **Gate of Parmenon.** This still has its immense lintel and takes its name from that of the mason who made the gate (his name is carved on a nearby wall). It is worth taking a walk up to the remains of the **theater,** not so much for the ruined building itself but for its breathtaking views over the Aegean.

The other main sight is the **fortress,** dating mainly from the 13th–15th centuries but incorporating stonework from a Temple of Apollo that stood on the site. The best of the finds are on display in a newly revamped **Archaeological Museum** in Thassos town.

AROUND THASSOS

Thassos has a hilly interior. Unfortunately, many of its pine forests were wiped out in extensive forest fires a few years ago. A coastal road goes all the way around this almost circular island, and you can do the whole journey easily in one day, whether with your own transportation or on the local bus service. This makes it easy to sample different resorts over the course of a few days. Several roads branch inland from the coastal road, going into the hills to the remoter villages and monasteries of the interior.

Limenaria, on the south coast, is an appealing town that manages to combine vacation resort and business center. It has some attractive old mansions but no good beach. However, the best beaches are on the south coast, and one of them is at **Potos,** 2 miles (3 km) east of Limenaria. It is the

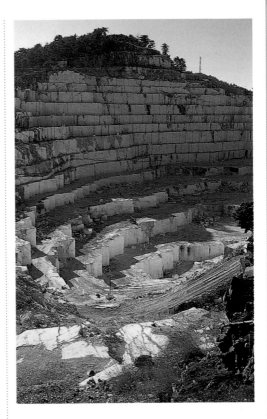

island's second busiest resort.

If it is peace you seek, then head for the interior of Thassos. Many of the coastal resorts have a village inland, where the inhabitants used to find refuge from pirate raids. Most of these villages have simple rooms to rent and a handful of tavernas to eat in. **Potamia** is one of the biggest villages, and you can begin the climb to the island's highest point, **Mount Ipsarion,** at 3,746 feet (1,142 m). This is a tough hike of three and a half hours, and a guide or a good map is essential. Maps can be purchased locally.

Inland from Potos is the pleasing old village of **Theologos—** founded in the 16th century by refugees from Constantinople (modern Istanbul)—which was the island's capital for a time. ■

Marble was first quarried for export from the island in the seventh century B.C.

Lesvos

Lesvos

🅰 233 C3
Visitor information
✉ Aristarchou 6,
  811 00 Mitilini
☎ 0251 42511 or
  0251 42513

BY FAR THE LARGEST OF THE ISLANDS IN THE NORTHEAST Aegean, Lesvos is better known to English speakers as Lesbos, from which we get the word *lesbian.* The seventh-century B.C. poet Sappho (see p. 238) was born here, in Eresos, making her a Lesbian—that is, simply, a native of Lesbos. The island is more familiar to Greek people as a popular vacation destination and as the source of some of the best ouzo in the country.

The sheer size of the island makes for plenty of variety, from the busy port and capital of Mitilini to quiet mountain villages, and from bustling beach resorts to good bird-watching sites around Skala Kalonis. Lesvos has been a vacation paradise since at least Roman times, as people have always been attracted by its magnificent beaches, thick forests, and majestic mountains. It has two high points: Mount Olimpos at 3,173 feet (967 m) in the south part of the island, and Mount Lepetimnos at exactly the same height in the north. Naturally there is rivalry between the local communities, each one maintaining that its mountain is actually higher.

Labyrinthine streets wind up from Mithymna's harbor to its castle-crowned hill.

Theophilos Museum

✉ Mikras Asias, Varia

☎ 0251 41644

🕐 Closed Mon.

💲 $

The name of the main town, **Mitilini,** is also sometimes used for the island itself, a common Greek practice that can confuse visitors when boarding or disembarking from ferries. It is a big and busy port of mostly modern buildings, but worth a day's exploration before moving on to more appealing towns and villages around the island.

Mitilini has its **fortress** (*Kastro, Ermou 201, tel 0251 27970, closed Mon., $*), almost mandatory for harbors in these parts. The sprawling ruins here date mainly from the 14th century although the original castle on the site was founded in the sixth century by Emperor Justinian (527–565). It's a good place to wander, to see the views, and to escape the noise of town for a while.

Other escapes include three museums. The **Byzantine Museum** (*Agios Therapon, tel 0251 28916, closed Sun. and Oct.–May, $*) has a good collection of icons ranging from the 13th to the 18th centuries, but is probably mostly of interest to the specialist.

The **Archaeological Museum** (*Argyris Eftaliotis, tel 0251 28032, closed Mon., $*) is housed in one of the town's many Belle Époque mansions. It has some stunning Roman and Greek mosaics, as well as a wealth of prehistoric finds from the site of Thermi, just to the north of the town.

The most interesting museum of all is about 2 miles (3 km) south of the center of town, in Varia. This was the home of the primitive Greek artist Theophilos Hadzimichalis (1873–1934), who was born in Mitilini. His vivid paintings, full of life and the Greek spirit (see p. 40), are displayed in the **Theophilos Museum,** a former schoolhouse.

AROUND LESVOS

Of the rest of the island, the main attraction in the south is the pretty hill town of **Agiasos,** with ancient houses, cobbled streets, and the 12th-century Church of the Panagia Vrefokratoussa, a place of pilgrimage for an icon reputedly painted by St. Luke.

In the western part of Lesvos, **Eresos** is a place of pilgrimage for lovers of the poetry—or just the reputation—of Sappho, and the glorious beach at Skala Eresos is one of the best on the island. Farther west still is the charming fishing port of **Sigri,** which remains unaffected by the comparatively small number of visitors who venture there each year.

Skala Kalonis, on the Gulf of Kalonis in the center of the island, is a busy resort at the height of summer. But each spring sees the arrival of other visitors: Thousands of migrating birds, attracted to the surrounding salt flats and pursued by hundreds of bird-watchers. Storks and waders are particularly prominent, while sardines and anchovies feature both in the diet of the birds and on local menus.

No one should visit Lesvos without seeing the town of **Mithymna,** (also known widely as Molyvos) on the north coast. Its red-roofed houses cluster around a Genoese castle, and its cobbled streets are in many places completely shaded with vines, while below is a picturesque harbor. South of Mithymna is the expanding coastal village of **Petra,** noted for its flaming sunsets.

The harbor just along the coast at **Skala Sikaminias** is even prettier. Featuring a lovely chapel perched on some rocks at the end of a jetty and dedicated to the Virgin Gorgona (a mermaid), it seems designed with the picture postcard in mind. ■

Great Greek poets

For such a small nation, Greece has produced an astonishing number of exceptional poets, including in modern times two winners of the Nobel Prize for Literature. Names known in most countries around the world include those of Homer, Sappho, and C.P. Cavafy.

Homer (see pp. 330–31) can justifiably be regarded as the Father of Poetry. Nevertheless, he is far from being the only Greek figure of importance in the world of verse.

Consider the female poet Sappho (circa 610–580 B.C.), whose very name has entered the language in the term *sapphic* to describe lesbian love. The word *lesbian* itself comes from the fact that Sappho was born on the island of Lesvos in the northern Aegean. In fact there is no concrete evidence that Sappho was herself a lesbian, and much to indicate the opposite. She is said to have been a lover of the male poet Alcaeus (circa 620–580 B.C.), to have married and had a child by another man, and to have committed suicide by throwing herself off a clifftop on the island of Lefkada because of unrequited love for a boatman. The belief in her lesbianism came from another poet, Anacreon (circa 582–485 B.C.), who claimed that Sappho was sexually attracted to the women to whom she taught poetry.

Of the poetry itself only fragments survive from the nine books that Sappho wrote, but she was highly regarded long after her death. The philosopher Plato (circa 428–347 B.C.) described her as the tenth Muse.

Of modern Greek poets, one of the greatest is Constantine Cavafy (1863–1933). Although he was born and spent most of his life in Alexandria, Egypt, Cavafy was a Greek and incorporated many Greek myths and historical incidents in his work. This included such poems as "Ithaca," "Returning from Greece," and "In Sparta," but he published comparatively little during his lifetime.

Poet and diplomat George Seferis (1900–1971) was an admirer of Cavafy. In 1963 he became the first Greek poet to win the Nobel Prize for Literature. Although no Greek writer can ignore the country's long and rich history, Seferis wrote more about what it was to be a modern Greek and about the question of alienation. He himself was born in Smyrna (now Turkish Izmyr) when it belonged to Greece. He studied in Athens and at the Sorbonne in Paris, and in addition to his own work undertook the challenging task of translating T.S. Eliot's *The Waste Land* into Greek.

In 1979 Odysseus Elytis (1911–1996) became the second Greek poet to be awarded the Nobel Prize. Elytis was born in Crete and, like Seferis before him, was educated in Athens and Paris. He fought against the Italians when they invaded Greece during World War II and wrote powerfully and poignantly about the experience, continuing the tradition of war poetry that goes back to the unknown Greek poets who originally told the tale of the Trojan Wars. Elytis began writing poetry in 1929, at which time he was still a regular visitor to the Greek islands, where he would return every summer. His poems from the 1930s celebrate the islands but make references to the long shadow of the war to come. Fifty years later, when well into his seventies, he was still as prolific as ever. His popularity in Greece increased when some of his poems were set to music by composer Mikis Theodorakis. ∎

Far left: Homer, believed to have been blind, told his epic tales in verse.
Next left: Sappho is commemorated on her native island, Lesvos.
Below left: George Seferis combined poetry with his career as a diplomat.
Below: Odysseus Elytis was the pseudonym adopted by Odysseus Alepoudelis.

Tomatoes strung up like rosary beads dry in the sunshine on Hios.

Hios

DESPITE THE OBVIOUS ATTRACTIONS OF ITS GREEN, FERTILE valleys and the hilly north of the island—Mount Pellinaion Oros is 4,255 feet tall (1,297 m)—Hios is surprisingly free of visitors. This makes it an ideal island for those who want a more adventurous trip, where they can see authentic Greek life and where they will be welcomed with true Greek hospitality. The latter can come as a surprise, for Greek people like to look after their guests in a generous manner.

Hios
🅰 233 C2
Visitor information
✉ Kanari 18, Hios town
☎ 0271 22581

Justiniana Museum
✉ Plateia Frourio, Hios town
☎ 0271 22819
🕐 Closed Mon.
💲 $

The sizable island of Hios, 29 miles (47 km) from north to south, is known as the Mastic Island because it owes much of its prosperity to the resin produced from the native mastic trees. This versatile sticky substance was once much in demand as a base for paints, varnish, cosmetics, and medicine, and is still used today, in a more limited way, for chewing gum and even as a liqueur. Hios has a wealth of lemon and orange groves and once had a flourishing sea trade, so it is not surprising that there are some splendid mansions in Hios town, although sadly most were lost in a devastating earthquake in 1881.

One of the island's major attractions is a cluster of **"mastic villages"** in the south, about 20 villages that were the focus of the mastic trade. They are unique in Greece, with houses compacted into tiny spaces, surrounded by an outer circle of houses that also acted as a defensive wall in case of attack by pirates. When the Genoese ruled it in the Middle Ages, Hios was considered to be the most prosperous island in the whole Mediterranean, making it a natural target for pirates. **Pyrgion** is known for its patterned houses in black and white, **Olympi** retains its original central defensive tower, and **Mesta,** the best of the villages, still has the outer defensive

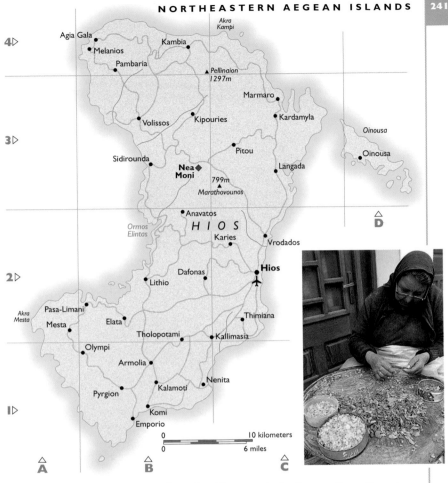

Separating out the mastic is a painstaking chore.

towers that existed at the corners of each village.

In contrast to these little villages, **Hios town** has 25,000 inhabitants and is the kind of bustling port typical of a Greek island capital. Its dominant feature is the **fortress,** with parts dating back to the Byzantine era, but extensively renovated and expanded when the Genoese took Hios in 1261. Within the castle walls are a Turkish mosque and cemetery, the remains of a bathhouse, and centuries-old houses. At the castle entrance is the **Justiniana Museum,** with a wide collection of religious art including icons, frescoes, mosaics, and wood carvings. Hios town also has the **Byzantine Museum,** which is just as much an archaeological museum, and the **Philip Argenti Museum** *(Odos Korai 2, closed Sun., $),* a folk arts and crafts museum, which also has portraits of members of the prominent local Argenti family.

The island's prime attraction, one that should not be missed, is the 11th-century **monastery of Nea Moni,** beautifully located in a rural retreat 9 miles (15 km) west of the capital. It is noted throughout Greece for its outstanding original 11th-century mosaics, which rival those at Osiou Louka near Delphi (see pp. 142–43). ■

Byzantine Museum
- ✉ Plateia Vounakiou
- ☎ 0271 26866
- ⏱ Closed Mon.

Monastery of Nea Moni
- 🅰 241 B3
- ☎ 0271 79370

Smaller northeastern Aegean islands

LIMNOS

Limnos produces top quality retsina, as well as other wines. The vineyards are in the western, more volcanic half of the island. Limnos is almost cut in two by the deep gouge of Moudros Bay, one of the biggest and most beautifully situated natural harbors in the Aegean. For this reason, and because of the island's closeness to Turkey, there are several military bases, and unfortunately the sound of jet fighters is not uncommon.

In complete contrast to the rocky west, the east is mostly low-lying and agricultural, apart from some areas of marshland. There are good beaches scattered around the coast, but few visitor facilities. The main town is **Myrina,** on the west coast, the ferry port that links Limnos with other islands and the mainland.

Myrina is pleasantly situated, with an attractive waterfront, a couple of nice beaches close by, and a picturesque fishing port. The ruins of its **Byzantine castle,** on the site where the original acropolis stood, offer awesome views over the town and the entire west coast. The old part of town has cobbled streets and grand Ottoman houses; the **Archaeological Museum** (*Romaikos Gialos, Myrina, tel 0254 22087, closed Mon., $),* in a 19th-century mansion, does its best with limited displays. Several ancient sites dot the island, including the fortified town of Poliochni (dating from 3000 B.C.), the once-important city of Ifaistia, and the sanctuary site of Kabireio. A great deal

of work remains to be done on these sites.
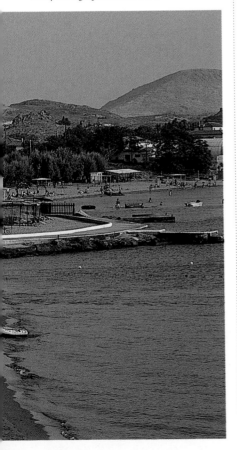 233 B5 **Visitor information** ✉ Town
Hall, 814 00 ☎ 0254 22996

SAMOS

One of the most sublime islands in the
Aegean, Samos is fertile and green, with
rolling hills covered in pine forests and with
valleys of vineyards and olive groves—all this,
and fantastic beaches too. Little wonder that it
has been admired through the centuries—
even Antony and Cleopatra are known to have
relaxed together on Samos—and it is a very
popular vacation destination today.

A visit in high summer will mean that
many hotel rooms are reserved by travel
companies. However, when the spring flowers
bloom, and again in the fall when the vines are
heavy with grapes, Samos is a dream island

destination. Its vines provide a dessert wine as
sweet as honey, which is exported around the
world. Look for a Samos Grand Cru or Samos
Anthemis from the Samos Co-op vineyards.

Samos town, also known as Vathi, is the
capital, and its gleaming white houses spread
out between a swath of green hills and a
beautiful horseshoe-shaped harbor. In the
upper town, the maze of narrow, shaded, cobbled lanes is a world away from the bustle of
the port below (the area where you will want
to be at nighttime).

Samos has a long and fascinating history,
having been inhabited since about 3000 B.C.
Much of the story is told in the world-class
Archaeological Museum (*Kapetan
Gymnasiarchou Katevani, tel 0273 27469, closed
Mon., $*). This has one of the best
collections of votive offerings in Greece,
thanks to the popularity of the Heraion
Sanctuary, where the goddess Hera was
worshiped. The museum's other star feature is
a 16-foot (5 m) *kouros* (archaic marble statue
of a youth) from the sixth century B.C.

Heraion (*tel 0273 95259, closed Mon., $*)
is 14 miles (22 km) to the southwest of Vathi.
The first temple on the site, built in the eighth
century B.C., was replaced by another in the
sixth century B.C., but this was soon destroyed
in an earthquake. Work began on a replacement, which, though never completed, was
nevertheless much used. The site is confusing,
even after extensive archaeological work, but it
fills in part of the picture of ancient Samos.

Nearby **Pithagoria,** the original capital
built in the sixth century B.C., is now a
fashionable tourist town. Its attractions
include the remains of some Roman baths
and the startling Efpalinion Tunnel, an
aqueduct almost two-thirds of a mile (1 km)
long, dating from 539–524 B.C. Pithagoria was
named after the philosopher and mathematician Pythagoras, born here in about 580 B.C.
Little is known for certain about his life, but
his advanced ideas, not only about mathemat-
ics but also about music and the harmony of
the universe, live on.
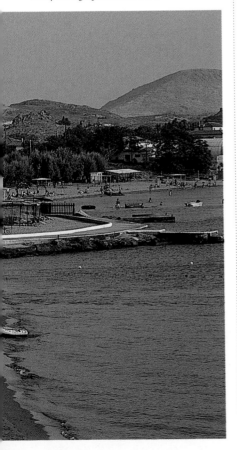 233 D1 **Visitor information** ✉ Martiou
25, Samos town ☎ 0273 28582 ■

**Limnos's craggy interior gives way to a
sandy beach at Aktamarina.**

Cyclades

If you see a photograph illustrating the Greek islands, there is a strong chance it was taken on one of the Cyclades (Kiklades). It will show an ink-blue sky, a jumble of dazzlingly white houses set higgledy-piggledy against a hillside, and, somewhere, a blue-domed church. In many people's minds, this is the archetypal picture of a Greek island. On these particular islands, you'll also find red poppies growing from bare white rock, the aroma of wild herbs filling the air, and idyllic beaches gleaming in the sun. To top it off, lively nightlife, bountiful shops, fine restaurants, and bustling bars fill picturesque town streets, making the Cyclades the epitome of summer fun.

The name Cyclades comes from *kyklos*, a circle, and a glance at the map indicates that the islands circle the sacred isle of Dilos (see p. 251). In historic terms, the Cyclades are probably the most significant group of all the Greek islands. Over the period 3000–1000 B.C. the so-called Cycladic civilization flourished here, producing extraordinary works of art that have had a lasting impact on the world. Incidentally, it is the only Greek civilization to have a museum entirely dedicated to it: the Museum of Cycladic Art in Athens (see p. 74).

The administrative capital of the Cyclades is Siros, and this is less affected by tourism than you might expect, given its status.

Naxos, the largest island, along with its neighbor Paros, is more precisely in the geographical center of the group than is Dilos. Despite being at the hub of the transportation network in the Cyclades, neither Naxos nor Paros has been spoiled by tourism. Unfortunately, the same cannot be said of nearby Ios and Mikonos, which almost sink under the weight of incoming fun seekers in summer. But it is easy to get away from noise and people if you wish, as there are 24 inhabited islands in the Cyclades, some with very small populations, and island-hopping is relatively straightforward.

Most travelers visiting only one island in the group choose to stop off at the extraordinary Santorini, whose rugged volcanic crater and black sand beaches give a contrasting but equally potent picture of the Cyclades. ■

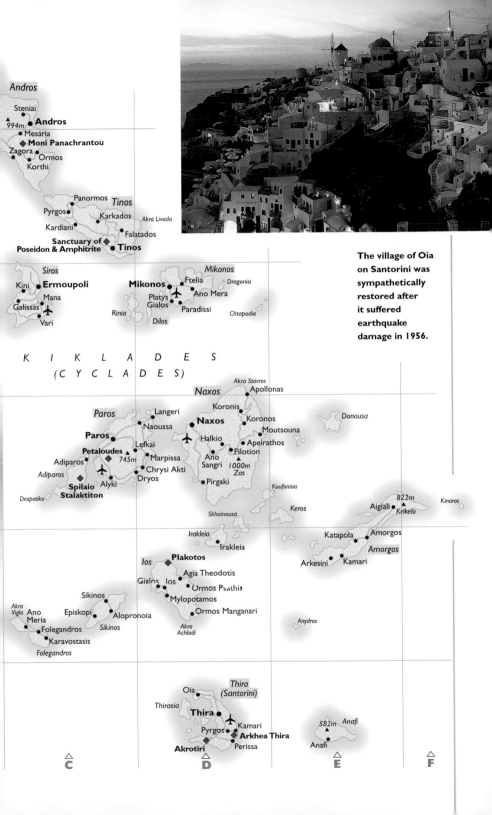

Andros

Steniai
994m ▲ **Andros**
Mesaria
◆ **Moni Panachrantou**
Zagora
Ormos
Korthi

Panormos *Tinos*
Pyrgos
Karkados
Akra Livada
Kardiani
Falatados
Sanctuary of
Poseidon & Amphitrite ◆ **Tinos**

Siros
Kini ● **Ermoupoli**
Mana
Galissas
Vari

Mikonos
Mikonos ● Ftelia
Dragonisi
Platys Ano Mera
Gialos
Rinia Paradissi *Chtapodia*
Dilos

The village of Oia
on Santorini was
sympathetically
restored after
it suffered
earthquake
damage in 1956.

K I K L A D E S
(C Y C L A D E S)

Akra Stavros
Naxos Apollonas

Koronis
Langeri
Naxos
Naoussa Koronos
Paros Moutsouna
Paros
Lefkai Halkio Apeirathos
Petaloudes ▲ Filotion
Adiparos 745m Marpissa Ano ▲
Sangri 1000m
Adiparos Chrysi Akti Zas
▲ Dryos
Spilaio Alyki Pirgaki *Koufonisia*
Despotiko **Stalaktiton**
Skhoinousa *Keros*

Irakleia
Irakleia

Ios
● **Plakotos**
Agia Theodotis
Gialos Ios
Ormos Psathis
Mylopotamos
Sikinos Ormos Manganari
Akra
Vigla Ano Meria
Episkopi *Akra*
Alopronoia *Achladi*
Sikinos
Folegandros
Karavostasis
Folegandros

Aigiali 822m
Krikelo *Kinaros*

Katapola
Amorgos
Arkesini Kamari *Amorgos*

Anydros

Thira
Oia (Santorini)
Thirasia
Thira
Pyrgos Kamari
Perissa **Arkhea Thira**
Akrotiri

582m ▲ *Anafi*
Anafi

△ △ △ △
C D E F

Andros

ANDROS IS THE MOST NORTHERLY OF THE CYCLADES AND
second largest of the group. Its ease of access from Rafina on the
mainland has made it popular with Athenians seeking a second home
and with other Greeks as a vacation getaway. Tourism is
likely to increase dramatically with the opening of the new Athens
airport (see Travelwise, p. 339), which will turn Rafina into the
closest port for foreign visitors to the Cyclades.

Andros
🗺 245 C6
**Visitor
information**
✉ Gavrion
☎ 0282 22300

**Archaeological
Museum**
✉ Plateia Kairi
☎ 0282 23664
🕐 Closed Mon.
💲 $

**Museum of
Modern Art**
✉ Plateia Kairi
☎ 0282 22444
🕐 Closed Mon.–Tues.
💲 $$

Extending more than 21 miles
(34 km) from one end to the other,
the island is large enough to absorb
plenty of visitors. Andros is
mountainous: **Mount Petalo**
(3,261 feet/994 m) in the center
divides the island into two distinct
halves—the north rugged and
barren, the south fertile and green.
The Ionians settled here in about
1000 B.C., and Andros has seen
Romans, Venetians, and Turks
come and go over the centuries.

Andros town (or Chora),
with its many elegant neoclassic
mansions, shows the influence of
the wealthy Athenians who have
lived here over the past 200 years.
The town has a prosperous air, its
main street pedestrianized with

marble slabs. Andros has been
particularly rich in archaeological
finds, many of which are displayed
in the fine **Archaeological
Museum.** The best exhibit is a
second-century B.C. marble copy of
an original bronze statue, the
Hermes of Andros. The excellent
Museum of Modern Art, a
rarity in these islands, is housed in
two buildings and features work by
Picasso and Braque on permanent
display, with changing exhibitions
of contemporary art and a
delightful sculpture garden.

Don't miss the monastery of
Moni Panachrantou in the
mountains south of Andros town.
It was founded in A.D. 961 and is
still immaculately maintained. ∎

Tinos

ONLY A TINY STRETCH OF WATER SEPARATES ANDROS FROM Tinos, a miniature version of its neighbor—roughly the same shape and with a mountainous spine down the middle. Like Andros, Tinos was settled by the Ionians, then inhabited by Romans, Venetians, and Turks; its landscape is dotted with the same type of Venetian dovecotes you see on Andros.

Tinos town lacks the wealth of Andros town and is more typical of a Cycladic island capital, with a busy little port and narrow streets zigzagging among blindingly white-washed buildings. Its **Archaeological Museum** is surprisingly interesting. The island's principal site is the remains of the fourth-century B.C. **Sanctuary of Poseidon and Amphitrite,** 2.5 miles (4 km) northwest of town.

To all Greeks, Tinos is known for just one thing: the **Church of the Panagia Evangelistria** (the Annunciation). On August 15—the Feast of the Assumption of the Virgin, a national holiday in Greece—Tinos is packed with pilgrims who come to pray to a miraculous icon. Many of them crawl up the main street that leads to the church to prostrate them-selves before the Virgin; the street is lined with stalls and stores selling candles, icons, and votive offerings. The icon is carried through the streets in a solemn procession, an event repeated on March 25, when the Feast of the Annunciation and Independence Day are celebrated.

The pilgrimage dates from 1822, when a nun at the convent of Moni Kechrovouniou, in the hills above Tinos town, had visions of the Virgin Mary. The Virgin told her where an icon lay buried. When the nun's directions were later followed, an icon depicting the Annunciation of the Archangel Gabriel was found, having lain buried for 850 years. The icon was still in good condition. It is believed to have healing powers, so Tinos has become a Greek Orthodox equiva-lent of the holy shrine at Lourdes, in France. If you want to be on Tinos on either March 25 or August 15, plan well in advance, as ferries and accommodations are always reserved well ahead. ■

Tinos
 245 C5
Visitor information
✉ Tourist Police, Plateia L. Sochou 5
☎ 0283 23670

Archaeological Museum
✉ Megalochori, Tinos town
☎ 0283 22670
🕒 Closed Mon.

On her knees, a pilgrim approach-es the Church of the Panagia Evan-gelistriaon.

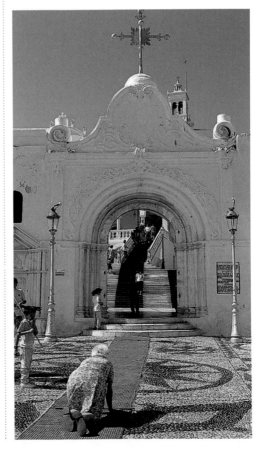

Siros

DESPITE BEING A FAIRLY BARREN AND ROCKY PLACE, Siros is the administrative center of the Cyclades. It owes its status to a good natural harbor at Ermoupoli, once the main port for all of Greece. As recently as the 19th century it was still the most powerful port in the eastern Aegean, and as a result there are many fine mansions here. Ermoupoli is the best-preserved neoclassic town in the country by some accounts and, with a population of 13,000, is the largest settlement in the Cyclades.

The blue-tiled dome of Agios Nikolaos overlooks the commercial harbor.

Siros

245 C4

Visitor information

✉ Cyclades Islands H.Q., Dodekanissou 10, 841 00

☎ 0281 22375 or 0281 86725

Although important, Siros is not overwhelmed by tourism. Its role as the administrative and cultural center for the Cyclades means that, unlike some of the smaller islands, it prospers without needing to cultivate visitors. Nevertheless, tourists do come in increasing numbers, drawn by the island's small resorts, little fishing villages, and enough good beaches to keep everyone happy. Some of these, such as the ones at Armeos and Delfini, are secluded enough to have become nudist beaches.

Siros, probably first inhabited by the Phoenicians, is known to have been an important center for the Cycladic civilization by the year 2800 B.C. Later the island became part of the Roman Empire like the rest of Greece. When the Romans left, the island was abandoned until the 13th century, when it was taken by the Venetians. They founded the town of **Ano Siros,** on one of the two hilltops that now join up as Ermoupoli (the other is Vrondado). Because of its Venetian pedigree, Ano Siros was unusual in Greece in being a Roman Catholic town long before Vrondado was established as a Greek Orthodox community.

Below and between Ano Siros and Vrondado is the lower town, with a grand marble-floored main square, **Plateia Miaouli,** as its central focus. The whole area around here has been designated a National Historical Landmark, and so has protected status. Fine mansions and shaded cafés line the square, which has an amazing marble bandstand in the center. At one end of the square, the grand town hall of 1876 was designed by the German architect Ernst Ziller, who designed several of Athens's fine neoclassical buildings, including the Presidential Palace.

Alongside the town hall is Siros's small **Archaeological Museum,** worth a quick visit. Nearby is the **Apollo Theater,** built in 1864 as the first opera house in Greece. A copy of La Scala in Milan, it was restored in the 1990s to something of its former glory. Close by the 19th-century church of **Agios Nikolaos** has a stunningly grand marble iconostasis (a screen with doors and tiers of icons, found in Eastern churches); outside is the world's first monument to an unknown soldier, erected in the late 19th century. There are many other churches worth seeking out in Ermoupoli, notably the Byzantine church of the Anastasi at the top of the Vrondado hill, and the baroque Cathedral of St. George crowning Ano Siros.

Most of the island's population lives in villages in the southern half of Siros, easily reached by car or by local bus. On the west coast are the two most popular resorts, Kini and Galissas. Located on a scenic bay **Kini** is still very much a fishing village alongside its development as a resort. Its main advantage for the sun-seeking vacationer is that it is just a short walk from here to the best and biggest beach on Siros, Delfini. The sandy beach is popular with nude sunbathers.

A couple of miles south, **Galissas** is at the head of a long bay and has a good beach nearby, at

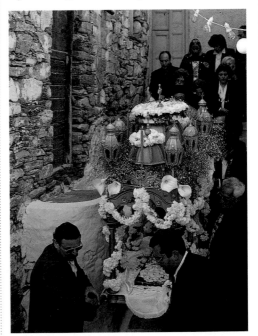

Armeos. It also has the only two campgrounds on the island, which in the summer attract crowds of youngsters who can turn Galissas into the liveliest spot on Siros.

In the northern part of the island the roads peter out into dirt roads leading to villages such as Chalandriani and Syringa, where few visitors are seen—which should result in a warm welcome for the more adventurous travelers who explore this area. ■

An effigy of Christ is carried through Ano Siros on Good Friday.

Archaeological Museum

✉ Plateia Miaouli, Ermoupoli

☎ 0281 88487

🕐 Closed Mon.

💲 $

Mikonos

🗺 245 D4

Visitor information

✉ Waterfront

☎ 0289 22990

Folk Museum

✉ Waterfront

☎ 0289 22591

🕐 Closed Oct.–April

The back streets of Mikonos are the prettiest of the Cyclades.

Mikonos

MIKONOS WAS RENOWNED IN THE 1980s AND 1990s AS THE gay center of the Aegean. Although this aspect of its reputation is much less evident now, it retains its place as one of the partygoer's islands of choice at the height of summer. Visitors in spring and fall can enjoy the island without the all-night revelries.

The interior of the island is small and barren, and won't occupy you for long. Mikonos owes much of its popularity to its plentiful golden sandy beaches. The main beach is at Platys Gialos. The resorts have become the focus for the tourist trade, with plenty of lively, noisy discos and bars.

Mikonos town is one of the most attractive capitals in the Cyclades. It is easy to get lost in the maze of winding back streets between the brilliant white houses that lead you sometimes to quiet churches with their distinctive blue domes, sometimes simply to dead ends. If you are exploring the island from a cruise-ship base, allow plenty of time to get back to the boat. You might like to buy a town map from one of the many stores and kiosks.

The town has other attractions, which mean that it warrants at least a day's visit even if you don't want to linger for the nightlife. The **Folk Museum** is one of the best of its kind in the whole of Greece: Mikonos has always been a cultured and independent island, and its local arts and crafts have flourished. The **Archaeological Museum** *(Waterfront, tel 0289 22325, closed Mon.)* has a good range of interesting finds, including many from the nearby sacred island of Dilos (which is reached from Mikonos, see p. 251).

In addition the town has a **Maritime Museum** *(Enoplon Dynameon, tel 0289 22700, closed Oct.–April)* and a good **Municipal Art Gallery** *(Matogianni, tel 0289 22615, closed Oct.–April).* The **fortress** dates from the 15th to 17th centuries. Below this is the area known as **Little Venice,** the artists' quarter, named because of its many tall buildings with their elegant iron balconies. ∎

Dilos

THIS PARCHED, UNINHABITED HOLY ISLAND CAN ONLY BE visited by day. It lies about a mile and a half (2 km) southwest of Mikonos, and no one is allowed to stay overnight there. This is to protect one of the most priceless archaeological sites in Greece. Ionians arrived here about 1000 B.C., although it was probably first inhabited more than a thousand years earlier by migrants from Asia Minor.

The Ionians made Dilos their religious capital and dedicated it to the god Apollo. They began an annual festival of arts and sports in honor of Apollo, and by 700 B.C. Dilos was a major pilgrimage center. It became a successful port but fell into decline after the Romans left, a hideaway for pirates but otherwise cut off from the world.

Dilos's precious ruins spread over a large area. Its most famous sight is the **Lion Terrace,** overlooking and protecting the **Sacred Lake** that was said to have witnessed the birth of Apollo. Originally there were nine lions, made of marble from nearby Naxos in the seventh century B.C., but only five have

survived. The originals are in the site's museum, leaving replicas to guard the now dry lake.

Other highlights include a **theater** from 300 B.C., beautiful **mosaics** in houses such as the House of the Dolphins and the House of Dionysos, and the **Sanctuary of Apollo,** with the remains of three temples alongside one another.

It is a site that merits as much time as you can give it. Boats for Dilos leave Mikonos in the early morning and return in the early afternoon. The site closes at 3 p.m. There is a small café on the island with limited choices, so take supplies with you—especially water. ■

The House of Masks and the House of Dolphins (center) dominate the lower site of Dilos.

Dilos
- 245 D4
- 0289 22259
- Closed Mon.
- $$

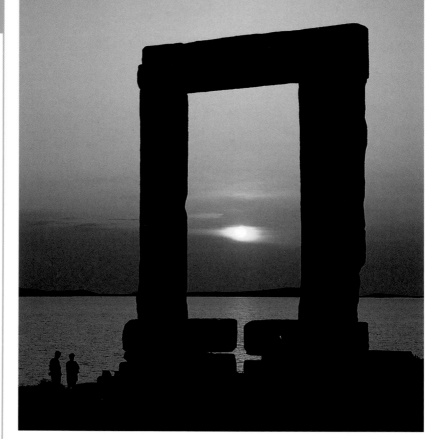

The Portara Gateway frames a perfect sunset

Naxos

THE LUSH ISLAND OF NAXOS, ITS GREEN VALLEYS FILLED with endless olive groves and orchards, is the largest and one of the most fertile of the Cyclades. It is mountainous—Mount Zas in the south rises to 3,280 feet (1,001 m)—and has excellent beaches, many of them deserted. Despite these attractions, the island has not been overrun with tourist development, although the recent opening of an airport may change that.

Naxos
🗺 245 D3
Visitor information
✉ Waterfront, Naxos town
☎ 0285 24799

Naxos became one of the main centers of the Cycladic civilization when it started to flourish around 2800 B.C. and was one of the first islands to use marble for sculpture and architecture. Naxian marble was used for some of the finest *kouros* statues, including several in the National Archaeological Museum in Athens (see pp. 78-79), and for the Lion Terrace on Dilos (see p. 251). In more recent times, Naxos was conquered by the Venetians and later the Turks, both of whom left their cultural and architectural mark on the island.

Naxos town is a bustling port and a lively town, with bars and busy restaurants around the harbor, and in the area leading up to the high-walled **Venetian *kastro*** (fortress). In the district below, known as Bourgos, is the impressive 18th-century **Cathedral of Zoödochou Pigis,** built using stone from older churches and an even older temple.

One of the oldest and most impressive sights in Naxos town is the **Portara Gateway,** on the islet of Palatia in the harbor, which is connected to the land by a road. This huge gateway was intended to be the entrance to a Temple of Apollo, begun in 530 B.C. but never completed. Today it is frequently used as a symbol for the town and the island, and gives visitors arriving by ferry a dramatic greeting.

The fascinating **Archaeological museum** houses an extensive collection of local artifacts, which naturally includes a good number of the graceful carvings made during the Cycladic civilization. The museum is also of interest for the building that houses it, a palace built in 1627 that later became the French School. One of its pupils was Cretan novelist Nikos Kazantzakis (see p. 283).

Naxos is large enough to reward a long stay, allowing time to explore its natural charms. These include the **Livadi Valley,** where the best Naxian marble was mined, and the **Melanes Valley,** which has some of the distinctive Venetian watchtowers. The **Tragaia Valley,** with wonderful mountain villages and excellent walking country, is at its best in spring when the flowers and blossoms are out, and again in the early fall when the fruit trees offer their bounty. **Halkio** is one of the most appealing villages, with attractive old churches. But if you want to stay and use it as a base

for walking, there are no accommodations and so you will have to take pot luck in getting a room in somebody's house—which can be a wonderful way to experience Greek hospitality.

Of the resorts, **Apollonas** in the northeast is one of the most popular, not least for its choice of excellent fish restaurants. In the ancient marble quarries on a hillside outside the village is an unfinished statue, thought to represent the god Apollo, which has been lying there since being abandoned about 600 B.C. It is over 30 feet (10 m) long and an imposing sight.

Archaeological Museum

- ✉ Palace of Sanoudo
- ☎ 0285 22725
- 🕐 Closed Mon.
- 💲 $

For good beaches head for **Ormos Avraam** on the north coast or **Moutsouna** in the east. Don't forget to pick up some local woven goods, embroideries, honey, and cheese before you move on. ∎

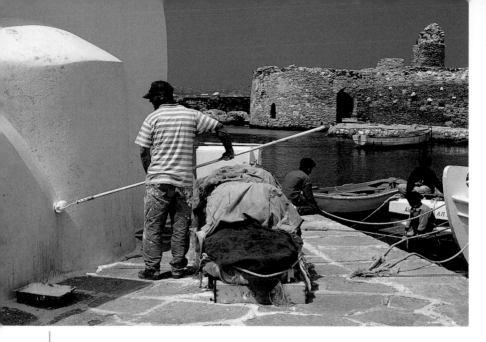

Buildings opposite the old Venetian fortress on Paros receive their annual freshening up.

Paros

PAROS, THE THIRD LARGEST OF THE CYCLADES ISLANDS, IS even more famous for its marble than Naxos. As the raw material desired by all the finest sculptors and architects, it was transported throughout Greece in classical times. The second-century B.C. Venus de Milo (see p. 255) is made from Parian marble, as is the celebrated Winged Victory of Samothraki (circa 200 B.C.), both prime exhibits in the Louvre, in Paris.

Paros

🅰 245 C3

Visitor information

✉ Tourist Police, Plateia Mando Mavroyenous, Paroikia

☎ 0284 21673

Archaeological Museum

✉ Paroikia

☎ 0284 21231

🕐 Closed Mon.

💲 $

As a result of this natural bounty, and the island's abundant fertility, Paros has always been prosperous and has had no need to court tourism to the extent of some of its neighbors. It has retained its Greek customs and culture much more than, say, Mikonos or Ios.

This is not to say that the island does not get busy, especially at the height of the summer when the strong winds that blow across it attract windsurfers from all over the world. The best beaches are in the north, around Langeri.

Paros town, or Paroikia, in a sheltered harbor on the west coast, is a focal point for ferry services around the Cyclades. It has all the activity, bars, and restaurants you might expect. Away from the waterfront it is a town of typical Cycladic streets and houses, with seductive flower-hung courtyards.

The Byzantine **Cathedral of the Panagia Ekatondapiliani,** dating from the tenth century, is a splendid example of a building made from the local marble. Next to it is the **Archaeological Museum,** with displays of further work in Parian marble, and a unique fragment from the *Parian Chronicle.* It sounds like a daily newspaper, and it is, in fact, a record, carved on marble, of the history of Greece from the 16th century B.C. ■

Milos

MARBLE FROM PAROS WAS USED TO CARVE ONE OF THE most famous figures in the world, the beautiful Venus de Milo—a statue of Venus found on the island of Milos. It came to light on April 8, 1820, when a local farmer uncovered a cave in one of his fields. Inside was half of the statue. The other half was soon found, and the whole statue was purchased as a gift for Louis XVIII of France (R. 1795–1824), subsequently finding its way to the Louvre.

A plaque marks the spot where the first half of the statue was found, close to the **Christian Catacombs,** in Trypiti. The catacombs are the only example of their kind in Greece, believed to contain up to 8,000 bodies in the 291 tombs that have been discovered.

Trypiti is almost a suburb of the main town, Plaka, although to talk of suburbs is misleading; the entire island has a population of less than 5,000. This figure is boosted in summer by visitors, although not yet in great numbers. **Plaka** stands on what is thought to be the original acropolis, dating back to 1100–800 B.C. The **Folklore Museum** tells the island's

more recent history, with fascinating old photographs alongside the local folk costumes and crafts.

There is an **Archaeological Museum,** too, where a copy of the famous Venus greets visitors in the entrance hall. Displays include remains from the island's most significant site, that of ancient Fylakopi. This is toward the north of the island, but much has been lost to the sea. Two of the most exquisite finds from the site are in the National Archaeological Museum in Athens (see pp. 78-79): the famous fourth-century B.C. statue of Poseidon and a *kouros*— a statue of a young man—from the sixth century B.C. ■

Like Santorini, the island is the shell of an old volcanic crater.

Milos
◮ 244 B2
Visitor information
✉ Waterfront, Adamas
☎ 0287 22445

Christian Catacombs
✉ Trypiti
☎ 0287 21625
🕓 Closed Mon.

Folklore Museum
✉ Plaka
☎ 0287 21292
🕓 Closed Mon.
💲 $

Archaeological Museum
✉ Main square, Plaka
☎ 0287 21620
🕓 Closed Mon.
💲 $

Ios

IF ONE OF THE CYCLADES CAN BE DESCRIBED AS AN ISLAND of contrasts, it is tiny Ios. The permanent population of fewer than 2,000 is outnumbered many times over in the summer by young visitors attracted by its nightlife and golden beaches.

Ios

⚑ 245 D2

Visitor information

✉ Ano Chora, Ios town

☎ 0281 90128

If you stay in Ios town in August there won't be time for a peaceful night's sleep, as the bars and discos thump away into the early hours. However, that is not your first impression of this achingly beautiful little Cycladic town with immaculate whitewashed houses, blue-domed churches, and, above the town, 12 windmills. There used to be several more windmills, and not all are in pristine condition, but they still look pretty even if they no longer function. Here too at the top of the town is what remains of the Venetian fortress built in 1400.

Ios is said to be the last resting place of Homer (see pp. 330–31). Some say that Homer's mother was from Ios and that the great poet came back here to die. Others say that he simply happened to pass away on board a ship while

traveling to Athens. His grave is at **Plakotos,** a small town in the hilly north of the island (only the rock on which the tomb was supposedly built remains). Every year on May 15—a much better time to visit than midsummer—the Homer Festival takes place. This includes a procession in which the people of Ios carry a flame from the port where Homer died to the place where he is buried, a pilgrimage of 6 miles (10 km).

The island is said to have some 400 chapels, along with its many superb sandy beaches—some deserted and some packed with young bodies recovering from their nights on the town. For a quieter time head for the beaches at Psathi or Kalamos, or walk on the quiet roads inland to visit the monasteries of Kalamos or Mount Pyrgos. ■

Amorgos

THE RUGGED MOUNTAIN SCENERY OF AMORGOS SETS IT apart from most of the other islands in the Cyclades, and the lack of accessible beaches means that it has not succumbed to mass tourism. Instead it attracts visitors who want to enjoy the Greek way of life, finding that a better mode of relaxing than simply lying in the sun.

Amorgos
🏛 245 E2
Visitor information
✉ Quay, Katapola
☎ 0285 71246

Amorgos is a long, thin island, and the mountains are such a dominant feature of the landscape that it was not until the 1990s that a decent road was built, making for easier connections between the northeast and the southwest. Until then, it was just as quick, and often more comfortable, to make the journey by boat.

Amorgos's challenging scenery has been no barrier to cultural development. The island was settled as long ago as 3300 B.C. and was one of the most influential centers of the Cycladic civilization, with three important cities: Minoa, Arkesini, and Egiali. The Romans used it later as a place of exile before it fell, like nearby islands, under the Venetians and then the Turks. During the regime of the Colonels (see pp. 36–37) it was again used as an island of exile for political prisoners, but it received a boost to its image and its tourism figures when it featured in the 1988 movie *The Big Blue,* by French director Luc Besson (born 1959).

The main town is **Amorgos town,** or Chora, a wonderful example of a Cycladic town, with whitewashed houses gathered below a 13th-century Venetian castle, several windmills, and more than 40 churches and chapels. Don't miss **Agios Fanourios,** the smallest chapel in Greece, with room for just three people inside.

Katapola is the main port and is a typically lively Greek town, although made up in effect of three separate small villages. You'll find plenty of fine hotels and restaurants, and all the facilities you might need. If you are looking for good beaches there are better elsewhere, such as at **Ormos Aigialis** in the north, which has the island's only real sandy beach but remains small and unspoiled. ■

The remarkable monastery of Panagia Hozoviotissa, founded in 1088, is built into the cliffs below Amorgos town.

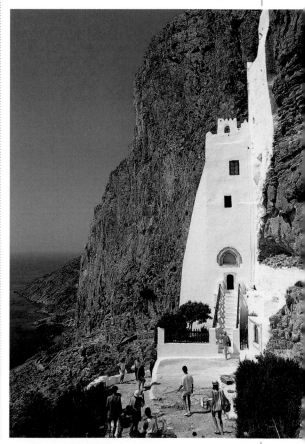

Santorini

SANTORINI (THIRA) IS DRAMATIC AND UNIQUE, FORMED from the remains of a volcanic crater. Ferries sail into the flooded crater to reach the port of Skala Thiras. High above perches the town of Thira. It's a very steep hike up the zigzag path from the port to the town, but there are always plenty of donkeys for rent to help you on your way, and now there's a cable car too.

A famous Akrotiri fresco becomes an icon (right) appropriated for a restaurant sign in Nauplie.

Opposite: The stark white and blue of a church mellow in the setting sun.

Santorini

△ 245 D1

Visitor information

✉ Tourist Police, Martiou 25, Thira

☎ 0286 22649

Akrotiri

△ 245 D1

🕐 Closed Mon.

💲 $$

Archaeological Museum

✉ Thira town

☎ 0286 22217

🕐 Closed Mon.

💲 $

Ancient Thira

△ 245 D1

🕐 Closed Mon.

💲 $$

The name by which the island is more commonly known in Greece, **Thira** is also the capital. Devastated by an earthquake in 1956, it was rebuilt and now welcomes vast numbers of tourists. The season lasts longer here than elsewhere, as cruise boats and ferries bring visitors on one-day trips from spring through fall, when other islands are much quieter.

There are some quiet spots on Santorini, too, such as the village of **Oia,** dramatically perched on the rim of the caldera at the northern end of the island. At the other extremity is **Akrotiri,** the remarkably well-preserved remains of a Minoan city devastated in the massive volcanic eruption of 1625 B.C. that also destroyed the old island, creating the present one. The

cataclysm may also have unleashed a tidal wave, the possible cause of the destruction of the Minoan civilization on Crete. The **Archaeological Museum** in Thira has finds from Akrotiri, and a new museum is being built opposite the bus station to house the island's famous frescoes, until recently held in the National Archaeological Museum, Athens. On the east coast, the remains of **Arkhea Thira** (Ancient Thira) overlook the sea.

Santorini produces surprisingly good wine. At first glance you might think it was too windy, too hot, and too dry, but the *assurtiko* grape flourishes here. The oldest vines are thought to be almost 200 years old, and they are deliberately cultivated to grow low to the ground, as protection from the wind. Fields of what look like basket trees are actually vines covered by cane baskets. The white wines made on Santorini range from dry to sweet and are stronger in alcohol than the average table wine.

Tucked in and around Santorini's caldera are several tiny islands, accessible by boat trip from Thira. The largest, **Thirasia,** was part of the main island until an earthquake in 236 B.C. caused it to split away. Like Santorini, it has a fertile volcanic soil. **Manolas** is the island's harbor, with eating places and some rooms to rent. The second largest island, **Nea Kameni,** only appeared in 1720 and is uninhabited as it still erupts, most recently in 1950. ∎

Dodecanese

6▷ Kambos
Skala
Holy Cave of the Apocalypse
Patmos
Patmo

Dodecanese (Dodekanissa) means "twelve islands," although, given the Greek genius for improvisation, there are actually 14 major islands, three minor ones that are inhabited, and dozens more that are uninhabited. As they are the most southerly group of islands, they are very popular with visitors because of their hot summer climate. Of course, spring is the best time to visit if you want to see greenery and wildflowers. During the long hot summers there can be water shortages. By fall the islands can appear quite barren.

Levitha
Kinaros
5▷

For the most part the islands hug the Turkish coastline, with Kastellorizo lying less than 2 miles (3 km) off Turkey. Kastellorizo has a population of fewer than 300. By contrast, the biggest island, Rhodes, is home to a permanent population of 100,000, and many more in summer as it is also the most developed for tourism. The much smaller island of Kos is close behind.

In between there are islands like Tilos and Halki, where tourism has arrived but on a modest, manageable level, and where visitors are still met with friendliness. The group also includes Patmos, where St. John is said to have had the vision described in the Book of Revelation, and little Nissiros, a volcanic island whose sulfurous crater today bubbles quietly. Two hours by ferry from Rhodes, Simi is one of the gems of the Aegean, with a port almost too perfect to be true—as anyone will know who has ever sailed into it at dusk with the harbor lights twinkling.

4▷ Vathi
Analipsi
Ofidousa
Livadia Astipalea
Astipalea

Despite their proximity to Turkey, the Dodecanese show no more Turkish influence than other island groups. They have an Italian ambience: Occupied by the Italians during World War II, they were returned to Greece by a treaty signed only in 1948. Since then, the Dodecanese have welcomed tourists, needing the boost to their economies once provided by shipbuilding, fishing, and sponge fishing. ■

3▷

Sofrana
△
A

Working windmills on Karpathos grind flour that is then baked in stone ovens under the hillside.

Arkoi

Agathonisi

Lipsoi

Farmakonision

Agia Marina

Leros

Xirokambo

Emborio

Kalimnos

Telendos

Mirties

Vathi

Pothia

Pserimos

Kos

Marmari

Asclepio

Mastichari

Kos

Asfendiou

Pylion

Kardamaina

Kefalos

Akra Krikellos

Giali

Mandrakion

Pali

Nissiros

Nikia

Megalo Horio

Tilos

Livadia

Syrna

Trianisia

TURKEY

Nimos

Emporeio

Simi

Simi

Panormitis

Seskli

Moni Taxiarchis
Michail Panormitis

Rodos
(Rhodes)

Kremasti

Paradeision

Ialyssos

Faliraki

Ancient
Camirus

Petaloudes

Afandou

Alimia

Salakos

Kritinia

Ebonas

Archangelos

Halki

1215m

Halki

Akropoli

Monolithos

Lardos

Lindos

Kastello

Apolakkia

Gennadion

Kattavia

Rodos
(Rhodes)

Akra Prasonisi

DODEKANISSA
(DODECANESE)

2▷

Astakida

Saria

Diafani

Olimpos

Karpathos

Spoa

Lefkos

Aperi

1215m

Karpathos

Arkasa

Menetai

1▷

Armathia

Fri

Akra Kastellos

Kassos

B△

C△

D△

E△

0   30 kilometers

0   20 miles

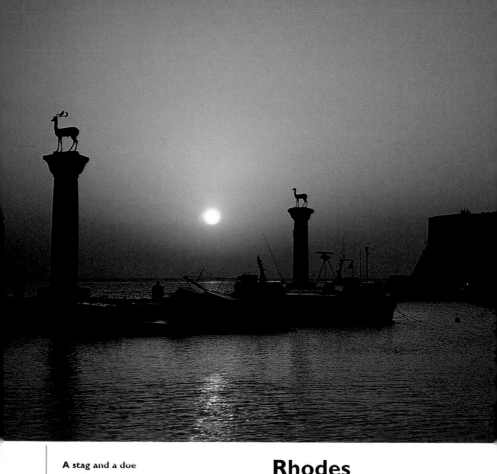

A stag and a doe stand sentry over Mandraki harbor, Rhodes town.

Rhodes

RHODES (RODOS) IS THE LARGEST OF THE DODECANESE and also their capital. Much of the coast on the northern end of the island is given over solidly to tourism, as one town has merged into the next resulting in one long stretch of hotels, tavernas, and souvenir shops. This part of the island has great beaches, so it's the perfect place to be if you simply want to lie in the sun all day and then have a good time at night in the bars and discos. But the island is big enough to provide alternative attractions.

Rhodes

🗺 261 D2 & D3

Visitor information

✉ Dodecanese Islands H.Q., Papagon 0241 23255

✉ Makariou, Rhodes town

☎ 0241 23655

Rhodes town is a mixture of the very old and the very new. The medieval walled Old Town is one of the jewels of the Aegean and was designated a World Heritage site in 1988. Many cruise ships use the harbor, giving their passengers a few hours ashore to explore the Old Town—and to experience the high quality shopping in the New Town.

The Old Town, as it is today, dates back to the arrival of the Knights of St. John in 1306, although a town has existed on the spot since 408 B.C. and the island has been historically significant since at least the fifth century B.C.

you see authentic life still going on as it does in any close-knit Greek community.

Near the main entrance to the Old Town is the **Archaeological Museum,** a place of historical interest in itself as it is within the former hospital of the Grand Knights, built between 1440 and 1481. Rhodes is rich in archaeological discoveries, and there are examples here from its main sites, including Kamiros, Ialyssos, and Lindos. Its star exhibit is the Aphrodite of Rhodes, a sensuous first-century B.C. carving in marble.

Other museums of note within the Old Town's thick walls include the **Byzantine Museum,** set in a 13th-century church that became the Mosque of Enderum during the Turkish occupation. The **Decorative Arts Museum** has a fine collection of works that are unique to the island, with decorative tiles from Lindos, and a reconstructed house showing traditional raised sleeping platforms and the local style of courtyard patterned with black and white pebbles.

In the center of the New Town, the **Nea Agora** market building is of interest, just across the main street from the harbor. It is small but invariably lively, with simple but good cafés and restaurants.

LINDOS

South of Rhodes town, on the eastern side of the island, the resorts at first merge one into another. Eventually the towns regain their distinct identities, and no town is more distinctive than Lindos. It is a popular spot with an excellent beach, yet the back streets of whitewashed houses manage to retain their beauty. Above the town and the beach, the impressive acropolis stands on a huge outcrop of rock.

Lindos has been inhabited since

However, it was the medieval Knights of St. John who stamped their lasting identity on the place by building the Old Town, which they ruled until 1519. The imposing fortress at the top of the hill known as the **Palace of the Grand Masters** and the cobbled **Street of the Knights (Odos Ippoton)** are unrivaled in the Dodecanese for their splendor and beauty. Heavily restored over the centuries, the latter is lined with Inns of the Order of the Knights of St. John. The inns were meeting places for different nationalities—hence the Inn of Italy, the Inn of England, and so on. That the Old Town has also turned into a tourist bazaar is inevitable, but only the few main streets have been affected. If you venture into the back streets

Palace of the Grand Masters
- ✉ Ippoton (Street of the Knights)
- ☎ 0241 23359
- 💲 $$

Archaeological Museum
- ✉ Plateia Mouselou
- ☎ 0241 27657
- 🕐 Closed Mon.
- 💲 $$

Byzantine Museum
- ✉ Apellou
- ☎ 0241 27674
- 🕐 Closed Mon.
- 💲 $

Decorative Arts Museum
- ✉ Plateia Argyrokastrou
- ☎ 0241 21954
- 🕐 Closed Mon.
- 💲 $

Lindos
- 🗺 265 C2

Acropolis
- ☎ 0244 31258
- 🕐 Closed Mon.
- 💲 $$

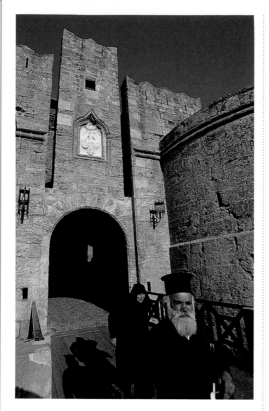

Impressive gateways pierce the ancient walls of Rhodes town, built about 1330.

Petaloudes
265 C3

Ancient Camirus
265 B3
0246 40037
Closed Mon.

are unable to get around the majority of these narrow, winding lanes. Inevitably there are souvenir shops and sometimes far too many people, but at other times you can explore the quiet alleys and admire the mansions. Most of these were built by sea captains who became incredibly wealthy between the 15th and the 18th centuries, thanks at first to the Knights, who helped make Rhodes such a powerful base.

On the far side of the acropolis from Lindos's own beach is **St. Paul's Bay,** where the Apostle Paul arrived in A.D. 43 to bring Christianity to the island. A small white chapel is dedicated to St. Paul. In sharp contrast nearby, there is a beach much favored by nudists.

AROUND RHODES

The most popular destination on the western side of Rhodes lies at the end of a side road off the main coastal road, just past the airport. The side road leads to **Petaloudes,** which has been renamed Butterfly Valley—a misnomer, but Moth Valley just doesn't have the same ring. Between June and September millions of Jersey tiger moths live here, attracted by the unusual storax trees. Their resin smells like vanilla and is used in the manufacture of frankincense. Unfortunately, the tour guides who lead bus loads of tourists up here daily in summer encourage visitors to clap their hands to make the moths fly into the air. This thoughtless practice has led to a serious decline in moth numbers over the last few years.

Farther south is the fascinating site of **Ancient Camirus.** It is one of the best-preserved examples of a classical Greek city and has been compared to Pompeii in its significance. Many of the remains go back to the sixth century B.C.,

about 3000 B.C., and the remains on the acropolis, which towers 380 feet (116 m) high, date back to the fourth century B.C. with the **Temple of Lindian Athena.** This was one of the most sacred temples in ancient Greece, and even Alexander the Great made a pilgrimage here. Just a few of its columns remain, but it is still a fabulous sight. The 13th-century church of Agios Ioannis also stands on the acropolis site. The battlements surrounding the acropolis rock were added in the 13th century by the Knights of Rhodes.

The village of **Akra Lindos** looks almost impossibly beautiful as you approach, and its charm is maintained by the banning of traffic from the streets—a ban that is not difficult to enforce as vehicles including a cistern that supplied water for 400 families and the Temple of Athena. Camirus was destroyed in an earthquake in 142 B.C. and lay undiscovered until 1859. Local farmers reported finding a few graves, after which excavations took place in earnest and revealed the remains of an entire city.

Monolithos is the main village in the southwest corner of Rhodes, and it is easy to see how it acquired its name. The area is dominated by a huge monolith of rock that towers 774 feet (236 m) above the surrounding woods and drops almost sheer to the sea. At the top of the rock is a 15th-century castle built by Grand Master d'Aubusson, and within its walls are two 15th-century chapels, both with original frescoes. It is a demanding and precarious walk to the top, but this does not deter large numbers of people from going, particularly to watch the sunset over the sea. ∎

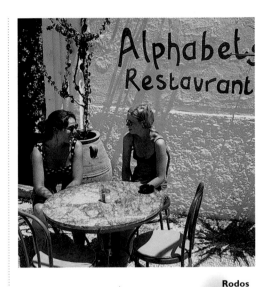

Waiting for refreshment at a Lindos hot-spot

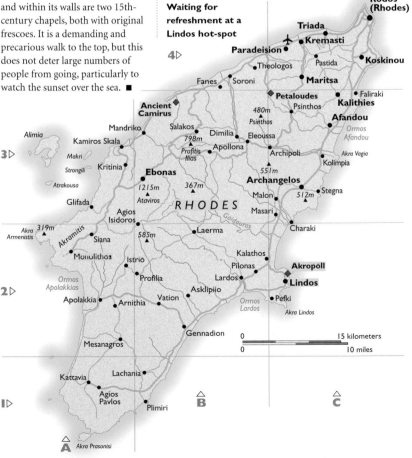

A walk through Rhodes Old Town

The Old Town of Rhodes may be a World Heritage site, but many visitors see only the few main streets lined with souvenir shops that are no different from anywhere else in Greece. Yet there are many fine monuments and quiet back streets, not to mention the stunning fortifications of the Old Town. The following short walk leads you to them.

Begin at either side of the entrance to **Mandraki harbor** ❶, the narrow channel where it is said that one of the seven wonders of the ancient world, the the great Colossus of Rhodes statue, once stood, a leg on each side.

Walk along the harbor front with the town on your right and the walls of the Old Town ahead of you. Cross the busy street at the first traffic lights and carry on walking in the same direction, under trees and past kiosks, to reach the **Eleftherias Gate** ❷. The name means

Visitors throng the streets around the 1523 Mosque of Suleiman.

"Liberty" to commemorate the Greek independence from Turkish rule. Pass through the imposing walls, which date back to 1330 and in places are 40 feet (12 m) thick.

Walk straight ahead along Apellou, passing on your left the remains of the Temple of Aphrodite and on your right the **Decorative Arts Museum** and, opposite it, the **Byzantine Museum** (see p 263). Immediately after the Decorative Arts Museum turn right onto Ippoton, otherwise known as the **Street of the Knights** ❸. Built in the 14th century, the cobble-paved street is lined on either side with the Inns of the Knights of St. John, once used as eating clubs and temporary residences for visiting dignitaries. Architectural details on each facade reflect its respective country. On your right as you walk up the street are the Inns of Italy and France, and on the left is the Inn of Spain. The inns today house offices and foreign embassies.

At the top of the street on your right is the entrance to the **Palace of the Grand Masters** ❹, from where the 19 Grand Masters of the Order of the Knights of St. John ran the affairs of the order. The original 14th-century palace was destroyed in an accidental explosion in 1856. What you see now is a faithful reconstruction carried out

- ▲ See area map p. 265
- ► Mandraki Harbor
- ↔ 1.2 miles (2 km)
- ⏱ 1 hour
- ► Plateia Ippokratous

NOT TO BE MISSED
- Eleftherias Gate
- Street of the Knights
- Palace of the Grand Masters
- Town walls

by the Italian rulers of Rhodes in the 1930s as a summer home for dictator Benito Mussolini (1883–1945), who never actually stayed there. It is well worth visiting for the wonderful central courtyard and the fine mosaic floors.

Carry on past the palace to the very end of Ippoton and turn left along Orfeos, past the souvenir shops, cafés, and restaurants. Where the road swings around to the left look for the 1523 Mosque of Suleiman, opposite the Turkish Library. Turn right after the library, down Ippodamou. At the far end of Ippodamou follow the road left, and at the first intersection turn right. This takes you outside the **town walls.** Go through the **Agiou Athanasiou Gate 5**, turn left along the main road, and take the next left back into the Old Town through the Koskinou, or **Gate of St. John 6.** Turn left at the first T-junction and follow Pithagora, which takes you to **Plateia Ippokratous,** where there are several excellent cafés. ■

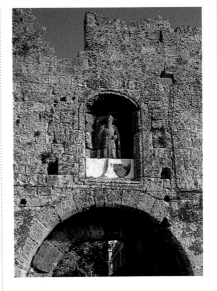

The Amboise Gate lies on the eastern side of the town.

Patmos

Patmos
🗺 260 A6

Visitor information
✉ Dimou, Skala,
   Patmos town
☎ 0247 31666

Posing in Patmos town: Cats are a familiar sight in Greece.

Patmos

ST. JOHN THE DIVINE ARRIVED ON PATMOS IN A.D. 95, AND it was here that he had the vision described in the Book of Revelation, which he then dictated to a disciple. The vision took place in the Holy Cave of the Apocalypse, which can be visited inside the church of Agia Anna, founded in 1090, two years after the founding of the Monastery of the Apocalypse. It is the presence of the monastery and the Holy Cave that has kept Patmos a place of religious significance, one of the most important in the Greek Orthodox Church. As a result the island, while welcoming tourists, has retained much of its original charm and spiritual peace.

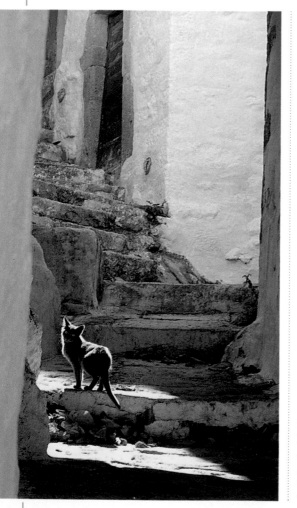

Patmos is a beautiful island, with excellent beaches, a scattering of hill villages, and great mountain scenery to attract avid walkers. The highest point, at the southern end of the island, is Mount Prasino, which is 2,543 feet (775 m) above sea level, plunging steeply to the Aegean Sea. To its west, at **Psili Ammos,** is the best beach on Patmos, a fine stretch of sand backed by dunes, with the mountains as a backdrop.

Patmos town is divided into two parts. Below is the harbor, or **Skala,** with an attractive waterfront that is much more chic than many such places. It is a steep but spectacular walk up to the high part of town, the **Chora,** which has lots of impressive old mansions as well as about 40 churches, chapels, and monasteries. The **Monastery of St. John** *(tel 0247 31234)* is the most famous of these. Built in 1088 with fortified walls to resist attack by pirates, it is still a working monastery—only certain parts are open to visitors.

The **Monastery of the Apocalypse** *(tel 0247 31234)* lies between Skala and Chora. Here you can see frescoes and icons, as well as the Holy Cave, and the fissure in the rock from where it is believed that God's voice spoke to St. John. ∎

Sponge fishing

Ancient vase paintings show that the Greeks have been sponge fishermen for several thousand years. The islands of Kalimnos and Simi are the two best-known centers. On either you may still see men with twisted legs—divers who ascended too quickly.

Local sponge fields no longer provide the rich harvests they once did, having been badly affected by a disease. The introduction of synthetic sponges, inferior to the real thing but much cheaper, has continued the demise of the industry. If you buy sponges, remember the best quality sponges have the greatest concentration of holes; those with fewer holes tend to fall apart. ■

Trimming the sponges

Kalimnos

KNOWN THROUGHOUT GREECE AS THE ISLAND OF THE sponge fishermen, Kalimnos has struggled to survive. Blight destroyed the best sponge fields, others were overfished, and some (such as Libya's) went off-limits for political reasons. Kalimnos diversified into shipping and tourism, but a few of the old sponge-fishing fleets still set sail for a few months in late spring and early summer.

Kalimnos
🅰 261 B5
Visitor information
✉ Plateia Charalampous, Pothia
☎ 0243 29301

Astor Sponge Workshop
✉ Off Plateia Eleftherias

Archaeological Museum
✉ Near Plateia Kyprou, Pothia
☎ 0243 61500
🕐 Closed Mon.
💲 $

There is no doubt when you are in **Pothia**—also known as Kalimnos town—that you are in a sponge-fishing center. Souvenir shops have sponges by the hundred, and retailers will offer to show you how to tell the best sponges, which they naturally all sell. At **Astor Sponge Workshop** they will demonstrate the entire process, showing how sponges are turned from black, odorous objects into clean and pleasant ones that you are happy to share your bathtub with.

Away from the busy harbor, the back streets of Pothia remain authentically Greek, and life goes on pretty much as it has for centuries. Seek out the 19th-century cathedral of **Agios Christos,** with its distinctive silver dome, and visit the **Archaeological Museum,** which is actually more of a general island museum.

The main vacation spots are on the northwest coast, at **Mirties** and **Masouri,** which have nice beaches. You can also catch boats from there to the island of **Telendos,** where there are quieter beaches and a few places to eat and to stay. East of Pothia, **Vathi** is and often called the Fjord of Kalimnos. A deep inlet of the Aegean, which leads into a lush valley with several beautiful traditional villages, it is one of the island's most attractive spots. ■

Kos

AFTER RHODES, KOS IS THE SECOND LARGEST ISLAND OF the Dodecanese; it is also the second busiest when it comes to mass market tourism. Because of its size—almost 28 miles (45 km) from end to end—Kos still has places to escape the crowds. At the height of the summer season you need to be careful in choosing where to go.

Wayside shrine in the model of a church, Kos

Kos

🅰 261 B5

Visitor information

✉ Akti Miaouli 2, Kos town

☎ 0242 29200

Castle of the Knights

✉ Plateia Platanou, Kos town

☎ 0242 28326

🕐 Closed Mon.

💲 $

The island is one of the more fertile in the Dodecanese, with bountiful orchards, olive groves, and vineyards. It is not particularly mountainous, although Mount Dikaios in the southeast does reach 2,779 feet (847 m) in height. Kos has some excellent beaches, part of the reason for its popularity. **Kos town** is an enjoyable mix of ancient culture and modern hedonism.

Hippocrates (460–357 B.C.), the Father of Modern Medicine, was born on Kos. A plane tree that he is said to have planted and to have taught under stands in Plateia Platanou in Kos town. In fact the tree is almost 2,000 years too young for that to be true. Close by is the town's dominant feature, the **Castle of the Knights,** which dates back to the days when the

medieval Knights of St. John ruled the island. It was built over several centuries, mostly from the 14th to the 16th, and incorporates marble taken from the island's principal archaeological site, the Asclepio (see below).

Kos is rich in both Greek and Roman remains, and the town's **Archaeological Museum** has a good collection of the best of them, including a marble statue of Hippocrates that has been dated to the fourth century B.C., when he may still have been alive. Kos town also has the splendid remains of the **Casa Romana** *(Grigoriou, Kos town),* a grand Roman villa restored in the 1930s that has wonderful mosaics, painted walls, and, within the site, part of a Roman road. The **Roman Agora** survives nearby as part of the Ancient Agora site with several layers of history, including the Temple of Herakles from the third century B.C.

Two and a half miles (4 km) north of Kos town, in a seductive hillside setting, is the **Asclepio,** built in the fourth century B.C. It is the ancient Greek equivalent of a health club and dedicated to Asklepios, the god of healing. Gymnasia such as this were scattered throughout Greece, and the fine remains here include baths and several temples.

Kos's biggest resort is at **Kardamaina,** along the south coast, a one-time fishing village that has been transformed beyond

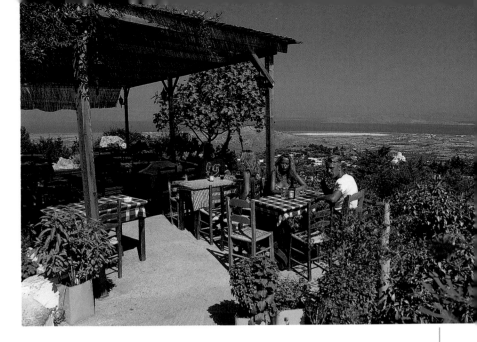

recognition into a cosmopolitan rendezvous for young people drawn here by bars, discos, and long stretches of beautiful sandy beach. The island's best beaches lie farther west and include the white-sand Paradise Beach. Many of these beaches are somewhat remote from the resorts, but that doesn't prevent them from getting busy as large numbers arrive by boat. For a more peaceful experience, visit the villages on the slopes of Mount Dikaios, known as

the **Asfendiou Villages,** although even here the peace may be shattered by the arrival of regular tour buses. Take a walk in the woods until the tourists have disappeared, then experience the villages as they really are. ∎

A hillside taverna on Zia offers fabulous views.

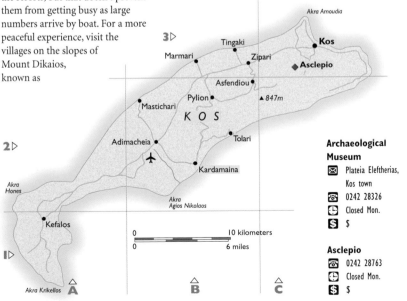

Archaeological Museum

✉ Plateia Eleftherias, Kos town
☎ 0242 28326
🕐 Closed Mon.
💲 $

Asclepio

☎ 0242 28763
🕐 Closed Mon.
💲 $

Astipalea

SHAPED LIKE A BUTTERFLY, THE LOVELY ISLAND OF Astipalea is the most westerly of the Dodecanese. With a tumble of whitewashed houses on the slopes below its Venetian castle, and with a string of windmills silhouetted against the sky, it could just as easily be one of the Cycladic islands. Astipalea is hilly and has lots of good beaches, its peculiar shape giving it much more coastline than other islands of similar size. The main town is busy in summer, but there are still numerous quiet retreats to be found.

Astipalea
🅰 260 A4

The original town of Astipalea was built on top of the hill, where the castle now stands on the site of the former acropolis. The castle followed in the 13th century and is remarkably preserved, with two 14th-century churches incorporated into the walls, houses also built into the walls for protection, an art collection, and stunning sea views.

The ruins of a Byzantine castle stand on the west coast at **Agios Ioannis,** which has an excellent beach and—a rarity in the Greek islands—a waterfall. Also on this western "wing" is the main resort, **Livadia.** Even this has far fewer visitors than comparable resorts on more popular islands. It is easily reached on foot from Chora, and if you wish to cast your clothes to the wind, carry on a little farther to Tzanaki, where there is an unofficial nudist beach.

Heading east from Astipalea, the road crosses the narrow neck that links the two halves of the island, with the sea visible on both sides. Just beyond is this region's main resort, **Analipsi** (or Maltezana). Relatively quiet, it is increasing in size and popularity. At the very northern tip of the eastern "wing" are the caves of **Drakospilia,** accessible only by boat and not yet a recognized tourist attraction. ■

Simi

IF YOU COME TO SIMI ON THE FERRY FROM RHODES, AS most people do, it is hard to imagine that this tiny place, with just one main town and a few scattered villages, once had a population greater than that of Rhodes. In its prime, from the 17th to the 19th centuries when the island prospered thanks to sponge fishing and ship-building, there were as many as 30,000 people living here, often in conditions of some splendor. Today the population is less than one-tenth that figure, but it is boosted by the arrival of summer visitors.

Looking down on the beautiful old harbor of Gialos from the upper town

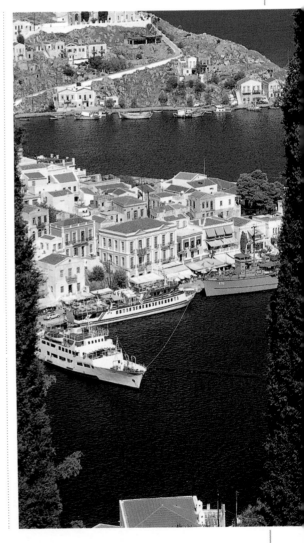

There is very little sponge fishing now, but plenty of sponges are for sale along the harbor in **Simi town.** The last remnants of the shipbuilding trade are seen around the corner from the main harbor, on the road that leads to the tiny, rocky town beach. For a glimpse of how wealthy the island must have been, take the steep walk from the harbor part of the town, known as **Gialos,** to the upper town, or **Chora.** On either side of the street, with its 375 steps, are exam-ples of the neoclassic mansions that graced the town. Many are now decayed beyond repair, but others are being restored thanks to the prosperity that tourism has brought to Simi.

Villages and beaches are scattered around the island. The monastery of **Moni Taxiarchis Michail Panormitis** *(opens to greet ferries and other organized visits)* is in Panormitis Bay, in the far south. Most sight-seeing boats from Rhodes bring visitors to the monastery first, and some ferry services stop at the cluster of houses here. It is not a particularly old monastery, dating back only to the 18th century, with many later addi-tions. There is a small museum and a church, and most notably an icon of the Archangel Michael, the patron saint of Simi and of mariners. Many a Greek sailor has made a pilgrimage here, to thank St. Michael for a safe passage at sea. ■

Karpathos

THE THIRD LARGEST OF THE DODECANESE ISLANDS, Karpathos remains one of the most traditional despite recent increases in tourism following the opening of its own (domestic) airport. Before that, visitors faced a long ferry ride from Rhodes, but what greeted them was a dramatic and rugged island with a high mountain range running down its spine. The highest point is the 3,674-foot (1,120 m) Mount Kalimni, almost dead center on this long, thin island.

A girl in traditional dress for Easter celebrations, Olimpos

Opposite: The village of Olimpos, isolated for so long, retains many of its old ways.

The capital, **Karpathos town** (also known as Pigadia), is in the south at one end of a long, sheltered bay with a 2-mile (3 km) sweep of sand. It has a delightfully old-fashioned fishing harbor, where the fishermen still mend their nets, not yet having surrendered their places to fashionable yachts. This is naturally the best place to go for the freshest fish, straight from the sea.

The essential trip on Karpathos is to one of the unspoiled mountain villages, the best example being

Olimpos in the far north of the island. The village was founded in 1420 and for most of its existence remained virtually cut off from the rest of the island. The only way to get there was to sail to the nearest landing at the coastal village of Diafani, then make a long, steep haul up to Olimpos at some 2,000 feet (600 m), its houses clustered along a mountain ridge. Because the village was so remote, its traditions remained untouched by the modern age. Even today you will see many women, and some men, still wearing traditional costumes. You can visit Olimpos on a day trip from Karpathos town.

There are more mountain villages closer to the town, each with its own attractions. **Menetes** is also high in the mountains, if not quite as high as Olimpos at only 1,150 feet (350 m) above sea level. Several of its streets are covered with vines, making it a wonderful place to visit in the fall when the grapes are heavy and ready for picking.

Aperi, in the hills north of Karpathos town, is also well worth a visit. It was the island capital until 1896 and is said to be the wealthiest village in Greece per capita. Many villagers have made their fortune in the United States and then returned. One family who stayed was that of TV and movie star Telly Savalas (1924–1994). ■

More islands to visit in the Dodecanese

HALKI

Not far from Rhodes, little Halki has seen a renaissance in its fortunes recently, thanks to sensitive tourism development. The island badly needed some kind of boost to its fortunes. It had relied on sponge fishing until the early 20th century, when the industry collapsed as disease swept through the sponge fields. The island's population slowly dwindled but is now reviving with the restoration of some of the elegant houses. You will find plenty of English-speaking tourists here, with restaurants catering for local people and tourists alike. In summer, make reservations in advance if you want to be sure of a room in one of the island's many hotels.

🄰 261 C3

KASTELLORIZO

Kastellorizo is a delightful anomaly, as its official name is Megisti. This means "the biggest," but it is actually the smallest of the Dodecanese. Its name derives from the fact that it is the biggest of the handful of islands that cluster here in a small group. The other curious point to note is that Kastellorizo is 75 miles (118 km) from its closest Greek neighbor, Rhodes, yet it is tucked just 1.5 miles (2.5 km) off the coastline of Turkey.

The island remained a remote little outpost, largely forgotten by the Greeks and undiscovered by foreign vacationers until 1987, when its new airport brought it more into contact with the outside world. Even so, its present population of just 300 does not compare with the 15,000 or so who lived here a century earlier. In those times the closest Turkish towns were still Greek, and Kastellorizo had a flourishing shipping trade. Its prowess was due in no small part to the magnificent harbor of the capital, Kastellorizo town, said to be the finest natural harbor in the eastern Mediterranean.

Today the island is still a peaceful backwater, and even at the height of summer you'll see few visitors around. There are no beaches, accommodations are basic, and restaurants are pricier than you might expect.

🄰 Near Kos, off coast of Turkey

NISSIROS

This volcanic island is the one to choose if you want to get away from it all. It makes a popular one-day visit from Kos, although it does have a few hotels of its own. The volcanic crater is the island's particular attraction, with its bubbling sulfurous vents and its heat captured by the surrounding rim—intensified in summer by the sun's rays. More conventional delights are to be found in the small port of **Mandraki,** with a few rooms to rent and a maze of narrow whitewashed streets.

🄰 261 C4

PSERIMOS

Little more than a speck in the sea, with one small town and fewer than 100 permanent inhabitants, Pserimos is swamped by visitors in midsummer, who come across on daily visits from the nearby islands of Kos and Kalimnos. After the tourists depart, the village and its pretty beach return to normal, with just a handful of visitors left to enjoy its peaceful charm and simple accommodations and friendly tavernas.

🄰 261 B5

TILOS

Tilos is the perfect escape, if you like your pleasures simple and want a taste of a Greek island with just a small amount of tourist development. The island's remoteness—even by fast hydrofoil it is a two-hour journey from the nearest port at Rhodes—has discouraged large-scale development. Once there, however, you are made very welcome, and local people will soon be greeting you in the street.

The port and main town is **Livadia,** with some accommodations and several very good eating places, but not much more to it than that. There is a small pebble beach, and plenty of paths lead to coves along the coast. A bus links Livadia with the island's other village, **Megalo Horio** (Big Town!), which is set below the ruins of a Venetian castle and is, despite its ambitious name, even sleepier than Livadia.

🄰 261 C4 ∎

C rete is more a country than an island, and its patriotic citizens will proudly announce that they are Cretans first, Greeks second. It is awesome in its beauty, with high mountain ranges and a character of fierce independence.

Crete

Worry beads

Crete

CRETE (KRITI) IS THE LARGEST ISLAND IN GREECE AND THE FIFTH LARGEST
in the Mediterranean (after Sicily, Sardinia, Cyprus, and Corsica). It is a long, thin island,
155 miles (250 km) from one end to the other, yet at its narrowest only 7.5 miles (12 km)
wide. Within its shores are high mountain ranges, the longest gorge in Europe, hundreds
of excellent beaches, and one of Greece's most significant ancient sites: Knossos.

Knossos is only one of countless historical
sites on Crete, although the island will satisfy
the sun worshipper just as much as the
historian, the archaeologist, the plant lover,
and the photographer. Long stretches of the
north coast have been developed for tourism
in a way that makes them indistinguishable
from other beach meccas all over the world,
but the rugged southern coast limits access
and therefore further development. In the
interior, the mountain villages remain much
as they have been for the last few centuries,
and it is here that you will encounter the most
generous hospitality. Crete is, after all, the
island of Zorba the Greek and his creator,
novelist Nikos Kazantzakis. Zorba brilliantly
sums up the proud, fiery, life-loving side of the
Cretan character.

Crete is fiery in its climate, too. The little
offshore island of Gavdos is the most southerly
point in Europe, and Crete is actually farther
south than some places in North Africa,
including Tunis and Algiers. Temperatures in
midsummer can reach over 100°F (38°C),
making the spring and fall better times to visit
if you don't like the heat. However, if a
summer visit is unavoidable, there are always
the cooler mountains to escape to, and you
can follow the Greek custom of having an
afternoon siesta, thus staying out of the sun
in the hottest part of the day. Crete has very
little rainfall from late May through mid-
September, but it's wetter in the winter, when
temperatures remain pleasantly warm.

Crete leaves an indelible impression, no
matter what time of year. Some resorts, such

as Agios Nikolaos, combine rampant commercialism with great beauty. Hania is one of the most charming towns anywhere in the Aegean. First impressions of the capital, Iraklio—a big and noisy city by Greek island standards—are seldom favorable, but even here the Cretan charm can work its magic as you get beneath the skin of the city. Travel elsewhere and you will still find that it is Crete that gets to you. ■

Dusted with snow, the White Mountains form a spectacular backdrop to the ruined monastery at Aptera.

Area of map detail

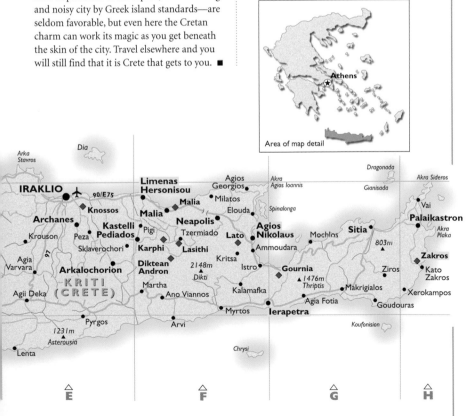

Iraklio

Iraklio

⚑ 279 E2

Visitor information

✉   Crete Island H.Q.

☎   081 228225

✉   Zanthoudidou 1

☎   081 228203

GREECE'S FIFTH LARGEST CITY HAS PLENTY TO OFFER. AS with Athens, you have to take time to get acquainted with it. Iraklio suffered very badly from bomb damage during World War II and now has many unappealing modern concrete buildings. But it also has great character and a treasure house of an archaeological museum containing some of the world's most renowned antiquities.

Iraklio has been settled since Neolithic times, and it flourished as the harbor for the Minoan center at Knossos (see pp. 284–87), 3 miles (5 km) to the south. The Venetians conquered it in the 13th century and made it their capital for the Aegean, building a fort to protect the harbor. The **fort** that stands there today was built in the 16th century after the first was destroyed in an earthquake, and it played an important role in the city's history. It was the focal point when the Turks beset the city in 1648, a siege that lasted until 1669, when the Venetians surrendered the island

Opposite: Iraklio's squat Rocco al Mare fortress is also known as the Koules.

to the Turks. Thirty thousand Cretan and Venetian residents of the city lost their lives, as did 118,000 Turks, which gives an idea of the ferocity with which the city was defended.

On the southern side of the harbor is another Venetian structure, the **Arsenal,** constructed in the 16th century as the place where the shipping fleet for the Aegean was both built and repaired. Iraklio's magnificent **city walls** are from the same period. They run for 2 miles (3 km) around the old part of the town and can be followed for their whole length,

Archaeological Museum
- ✉ Plateia Eleftherias
- ☎ 081 226092
- ⏱ Closed Mon. a.m.
- 💲 $$

Historical Museum
- ✉ Lysimachou Kalokairinou 7
- ☎ 081 288708
- ⏱ Closed Sun.
- 💲 $

passing several impressive gates such as the Porta Kornarou, where the walls are 60 feet (18 m) high and 130 feet (40 m) thick. By the Martinengo Bastion at the southernmost corner of the walls lies the grave of Nikos Kazantzakis (see box), who asked to be buried here.

ARCHAEOLOGICAL MUSEUM

The Archaeological Museum is one of Iraklio's undoubted highlights. Rich finds have been made all over this large and historically important island, and most of them have ended up on display here. The result is an immense, outstanding collection that warrants plenty of your time, maybe even two short visits instead of one longer one. It can get crowded with tour groups combining the museum with a visit to Knossos. If your schedule is flexible, visit in the middle of the day when tour groups are likely to be eating lunch.

The rooms are arranged in roughly chronological order, and good guides and maps are on sale at the entrance. If you have limited time be sure not to miss the Town Mosaic on display in Room II, which goes back to the Old Palace period (2000–1700 B.C.), and the breathtaking Hall of Frescoes, upstairs in Rooms XIV–XVI. Most of these heavily restored Minoan works come from Knossos and date from 1600-1400 B.C. Don't miss the elegant priest-king, or Lily Prince, or the graceful dolphins from the queen's apartment. Perhaps the most famous of the collection is "La Parisienne," so dubbed for her red lips and fancy dress; she was likely a priestess or goddess.

The museum is close to **Plateia Eleftherias** (Liberty Square), very much the heart of Iraklio. A busy traffic hub day or night, it is pedestrianized and tree-shaded in the center. The square comes alive in the evenings, when the bars and restaurants open and half the city seems to congregate here for the evening *volta* (communal stroll).

It is only a short walk from Plateia Eleftherias to the city's other main square, **Plateia Venizelos,** also known unofficially as Fountain Square. The fountain in question was originally built in the 17th century by the Venetian governor, Francesco Morosini, and has recently been restored to its full glory.

There's a Turkish fountain on nearby Plateia Kallergon, where you'll also find the 17th-century **Loggia.** Originally a meeting place for the Cretan nobility, this building has been lovingly restored and now serves as the city hall. If you need a respite from the traffic-filled streets, just off this square is **El Greco Park,** which also offers some shade in the heat of the day.

Behind the Loggia is the church of **Agios Titos.** Built in the tenth century and dedicated to the island's patron saint, St. Titos, who brought Christianity to Crete, it was reconstructed in 1878. It contains the saint's relics and is therefore a holy place to Cretans, to be treated with respect.

HISTORICAL MUSEUM

From Plateia Venizelos, Chandakos leads toward the waterfront and, just to the right, the Historical Museum of Crete. Smaller than the Archaeological Museum, it nevertheless gives a good picture of Cretan life through the ages. There are examples of art from the Venetian period, as well as an interesting collection of Byzantine art. The highlight is the only painting by El Greco (1541– 1614) displayed on the island where he was born. The "Monastery of St. Catherine on Mount Sinai" (also referred to as "The Landscape of the Gods-trodden Mount Sinai" and "View of Mount Sinai and the Monastery of St. Catherine") warrants its own room and a reverential display; it is a powerful work painted about 1570.

No museum on the history of Crete could ignore the events of World War II, and in particular the bloody Battle of Crete (see p. 305). The Historical Museum tells the full story of the suffering on the island in sometimes shocking detail, illustrated with photos from the period. Another glimpse of Cretan life is given in a reconstructed study of Nikos Kazantzakis, indicating the esteem in which he is held on his native island.

Iraklio has other museums worth seeing if time allows. The **Museum of Religious Art** is appropriately situated next to the city's 19th-century cathedral of Agios Minas and contains an extensive collection of Byzantine icons and frescoes and fine examples of religious manuscripts. The building itself is a 16th-century church built by the Venetians in honor of St. Catherine and was originally a monastery and center for art and learning. El Greco studied here. The **Museum of Natural History** has displays on the flora and fauna not only of Crete—which is incredibly well blessed in this respect—but of the whole Aegean. ■

Museum of Religious Art
- ✉ Plateia Agias Aikaterinis
- ☎ 081 28825
- 🕐 Closed Sun.
- 💲 $

Museum of Natural History
- ✉ Neoria
- ☎ 081 324366
- 💲 $

Nikos Kazantzakis (1883–1957)

If there is one fictional figure who typifies most people's idea of the exuberant, emotional Greek character it is Zorba, portrayed by Anthony Quinn in the 1964 movie *Zorba the Greek*. The character was created in the novel of the same name by Nikos Kazantzakis, the greatest modern Greek novelist. Born in Iraklio, he traveled widely in Europe, Africa, and Asia before starting to write. Best known for novels such as *Christ Recrucified* and *The Greek Passion* (both 1948), he also wrote essays, poetry, and plays. Martin Scorsese's 1988 movie of his novel *The Last Temptation of Christ* proved controversial in its attempt to depict the human nature of Jesus Christ. ■

The 1964 film of Zorba brought Kazantzakis's work to world attention.

Knossos

Knossos

▲ 279 E2

✉ 3 miles (5 km) south of Iraklio

☎ 0812 31940

$ $$

🚌 Bus: 2 from Iraklio

THE REMAINS OF THE VAST ROYAL MINOAN PALACE AT Knossos, 3 miles (5 km) south of Iraklio, are the major tourist attraction on Crete. You should plan to spend at least two hours here if you hope to see much of the palace and surrounding town. If you are visiting in summer, take a bottle of water as it can be very hot and dry. Summer is a very busy time here, so you are advised to arrive at the very start of the day or in the early evening (in summer the site remains open until sunset). It is well worth purchasing the guidebook. Consider being shown around by an official guide—the fee will depend on the length of the tour and the number of people on it.

The splendidly reconstructed Lustral Bath was for bathing in company—many individual clay baths were discovered on the site.

The remains you see today at Knossos are far from being the earliest on the site, which was first settled in Neolithic times, about 6000 B.C. The first palace here has been dated to 2000 B.C. This was destroyed in an earthquake in about 1700 B.C. The most recent palace was built after that earthquake and survived until 1380 B.C., when it too was destroyed, this time by fire. This palace was built on a vast scale, with some 1,300 rooms, and in its heyday, at the height of the Minoan civilization, it is estimated that there would have been 12,000 people living here, with four times as many in the immediate surroundings. The site is extensive, covering 185 acres (75 hectares) in all, but only a part of it is open to the public.

One of the best-known legends of Ancient Greece originated here, that of the Labyrinth and its monstrous guardian, the Minotaur. After the wife of King Minos of Knossos gave birth to a beast that had the head of a bull on the body of a man, the king imprisoned the Minotaur (the name means "Bull of Minos") in a labyrinth beneath his palace and fed it with human sacrifices. The Attic hero, Theseus, with the help of Minos's daughter, Ariadne, tracked down and slew the formidable Minotaur and, in so doing, liberated Athens from an oppressive bondage.

For a long time it was thought that King Minos was just a legend, too, until British archaeologist Sir Arthur Evans (see pp. 288–89) found the Minoan Palace at Knossos. In fact the word *labyrinth* derives from *labrys,* which is a double-headed ax, a Minoan symbol seen throughout the palace. Bulls and bull symbols figure largely, too.

Buildings scattered over the site today are reconstructions by Evans. His reconstruction and restoration work using modern materials is still the subject of controversy, but it is fascinating to see some of the palace rooms brought to life. When you enter the site you pass a **bust** of Evans, and behind this are three large pits, probably used for storing grain. As you progress you will see on the right one of the famous symbols of Knossos, the **Horns of Consecration.** It has been restored and represents the horns of the sacred bull that would originally have stood at the very top of the palace. Left of the main path, almost opposite the Horns, are steps leading to the **piano nobile,** the upper floor, which has the remains of some shrines and good views over much of the site.

Stylized frescoes, including that of the Water-carriers, have been copied on the site and re-stored, showing bold use of color, pattern, and design.

In this area, look for the **Throne Room.** When Evans discovered it, the room was in a state of turmoil, leading him to speculate that some significant final event had occurred here, such as an earthquake, coinciding with the destruction of the palace. In one room is a copy of the original throne, maybe the oldest in the world, and all around it is a wonderful restored fresco showing griffins, sacred Minoan symbols.

There are many more frescoes around the site, replicas of originals that have been removed for safekeeping or display in the Archaeological Museum in Iraklio (see p. 282). The Priest-King Fresco, which is just beyond the Horns of Consecration, is a highlight. Also known as the Lily Prince, it is a delicate depiction of a figure in a crown made of lilies and feathers.

Bull-leapers fresco

Throne Room

The paved Royal Road once ran right across the island.

The Theatral Arena seated about 500 people.

South Propylon, originally the main entrance to the palace

West Court

Corridor of the Procession, lined with frescoes

The delightful Bull-leapers fresco indicates the purpose of the palace's large central courtyard.

In the center of the site is a large, open central courtyard, where the sport of bull leaping took place. Sportsmen would face charging bulls head-on and leap over them by grasping their horns and performing a somersault. Beyond this area are the main parts of the palace, including the royal apartments. The Queen's Hall is decorated with a replica of the famous, vivid dolphin fresco. ■

Central courtyard

King's Apartments

Evans's much-criticized restorations help bring the palace to life.

Hall of Double Axes, named for the Minoa symbol carved into the stones

Queen's Apartments, with Dolphins fresco

Grand staircase

Huge clay storage jars, or *pithoi,* held honey, grain, and other vital foodstuffs.

Priest King fresco

Steps lead to the piano nobile, or upper floor.

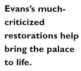

Arthur Evans

The British archaeologist Sir Arthur John Evans (1851–1941) is the man who brought Knossos to the attention of the world. He was born in Hertfordshire, England, then educated at the famous public school Harrow before going to Brasenose College at Oxford University. He later attended the University of Göttingen, in Germany, and became the curator of the Ashmolean Museum in Oxford, a position he was offered at the age of 33 and held for 24 years.

It was while he was working at the Ashmolean Museum that Evans developed an interest in the coins and seals of ancient Greece, and in particular the strange, indecipherable script that appeared on those of Crete. He first visited the island in 1894 in order to learn more about and devoted much of the rest of his life to unearthing its secrets.

By 1899 Evans had begun excavations at Knossos, where he quickly unearthed a Bronze Age city and a royal palace that he named Minos after the legendary Cretan king and son of the god Zeus—the plan of the palace appeared to him to be something of a labyrinth. The civilization he dubbed Minoan. Although he completed the bulk of the important excavations in the first few years of the 20th century, Evans continued work on the site until 1935, by which time he was 84 years old.

The most controversial aspect of his work is the reconstruction and painting of the royal palace, which he undertook in order to give some idea of its appearance some 3,500 years ago. To some scholars this was sacrilege, while to others it was a bold attempt to bring the palace back to life, conveying some of its grandeur to the general public. Anyone who has seen the Stoa of Attalos at the Ancient Agora in Athens, splendidly reconstructed by the American School of Archaeology (see p. 59), will have some sympathy with this view.

Another important discovery made by Evans at the site was 3,000 clay tablets covered with two distinct types of indecipherable writing. One of these was referred to as Linear A, which is regarded as the language of the Minoans and has still not been fully deciphered to this day. The other was called Linear B, and this was also a mystery until 1952, when it was shown to be an early form of Greek dating back to about 1500–1400 B.C. This was an important step in understanding the development of the Ancient Greeks, as it showed they had a written script much earlier than had previously been thought.

It is thought that one reason Evans found so much material on the site still intact was because the grounds of the palace were taboo to such an extent that looters would not go near them. One theory suggests that the famous bull-leaping scenes were not a macho demonstration of skill but rather a prelude to some brutal sacrificial rites that involved young children and virgins of both sexes. This theory proposes that the palace was then destroyed, not by natural forces such as a tidal wave, but by its own guards, repelled by the debauchery of their rulers. Subsequently, the sense of evil here kept people away for ever.

Such theories did not meet with Evans's approval. He felt very possessive about Crete and invariably dismissed any theories put forward that did not coincide with his own. Evans himself worked on books in which he attempted to decipher the two scripts, but he is mostly remembered as the man who discovered the Minoan Palace of Knossos.

Not as well known is the fact that he was a war correspondent in the Balkans in his early days, and that in the 1880s he researched and wrote a book that would sadly be just as relevant a century later: It was about the plight of the Slavs and Albanians in the regions of Bosnia and Herzegovina, at that time struggling for their independence from Turkey.

Arthur Evans was created a Knight of the British Empire in 1911 and died in 1941 at the age of 90. ∎

Portrait of Evans at Knossos, by Sir William Blake Richmond (1842–1921), with the Water-carriers fresco behind

Kastelli Pediados

KASTELLI PEDIADOS—NOT TO BE CONFUSED WITH KASTELLI Kissamos in western Crete—is the principal village in an area known as Pediada, to the southeast of Iraklio. There are basic accommodations and tavernas, and you will be warmly greeted if you do stray here, but most visitors pass through on their way to the area's main attractions, the Lasithi Plateau and Diktean Andron (see p. 291).

Kastelli Pediados
A 279 F2

There are some beautiful unspoiled villages in the region, where people make their living from the soil, as they have for thousands of years. The landscape is dotted with ancient churches, such as the one dedicated to Isodia Theotokon near Sklaverochori, which dates from the 15th century and has some original murals inside. **Agios Pandeleimon,** near the village of Pigi, is mainly 13th century but contains fragments from a 10th-century basilica in the structure.

East of Kastelli the road climbs toward **Mount Dikti,** 7,045 feet (2,148 m) high, taking you first to the villages and windmills of the **Lasithi Plateau.** This fertile and much-photographed place, hemmed around by mountains, contains a reputed 10,000 windmills. These simple, elegant, white-sailed structures were once used to pump water to the fields, but most are now electrified or purely for decoration.

The plateau has several other sites worth visiting, including the **Cave of Trapeza.** Take a flashlight to explore the oldest inhabited site yet discovered on Crete, with tombs dated from 7000 B.C. Nearby is the small site of **Karphi,** where Minoan culture and religion were still alive in 1000 B.C., hundreds of years after the civilization had vanished elsewhere. Most visitors then go on to visit the area's biggest attraction, Diktean Andron. ∎

Diktean Andron

THE ORIGINS OF DIKTEAN ANDRON (DIKTEAN CAVE), IN legend at least, go back even further than the Neolithic remains found at the nearby Cave of Trapeza. It was here that the goddess Rhea gave birth to Zeus. His father, Kronos, had been told that he would one day lose his throne to a son and was so fearful of the prophecy that he ate all his children the moment they were born. Tired of seeing her children devoured, Rhea concealed Zeus in Diktean Andron and tricked Kronos into eating a stone instead.

Diktean Andron

⚑ 279 F2

✉ Psychro

$ $

Zeus did indeed go on to take control of the Universe and become father to all the other gods (see pp. 174–75). However, there is a suggestion that the Zeus born here was not the same Zeus who later resided on Mount Olympus but was rather a Cretan Zeus, worshiped as a fertility god who died and was reborn each year.

If you have never visited a cave before, you will be amazed by the enormity of this one and by the extraordinary shapes of the stalactites and stalagmites. Even if this is not your first cave, you will not be disappointed. Take a flashlight and wear rubber-soled shoes or boots. A guide is available, but it is easy enough to go it alone.

To reach the cave you must stop in the village of Psychro and follow the sign up a pleasant track that weaves through oak woods; it takes about 15 minutes on foot to reach the cave entrance. Donkeys are always available to rent for those who find the going difficult. Be very careful on entering the cave itself, as the steps down are awkward and can be slippery—your flashlight is for these as much as for viewing the rock formations. As with many sites in Greece, viewing is best done early or late to avoid the crowds. Long lines can form during the day in summer.

The **main chamber** is 230 feet (70 m) deep, and impressive; several smaller chambers lead off it. At the bottom is a small pool, and it is in the chamber off to the left of this that Zeus—whichever Zeus it was—is said to have been born. ∎

The cave became a shrine during the Minoan period, and many small offerings have been recovered from that time.

Malia

MALIA IS A VERY LIVELY RESORT—A GREAT PLACE FOR THE young at heart! At the same time it has one of Crete's most evocative and least visited Minoan sites, with the remains of a palace. It is also one of the best coastal spots on Crete for seeing migrating birds in the spring and fall.

Malia
 279 F2

Minoan Palace
✉ 2 miles (3 km)
   east of Malia
☎ 0897 31597
🕒 Closed Mon.
💲 $

The summer wildlife is found in the center of town, where you can enjoy music in the bars and discos until the early hours of the morning. During the day, the glorious long, sandy beach is the ideal place for sun worshippers, but it does get very crowded. While you may have to search for a spot on the main beach, there is another excellent beach near the **Minoan site** that is often empty because so few people make the short 2-mile (3 km) journey to visit it.

French archaeologists have been working on the site for some time, and the slow, painstaking work continues, but visitors can wander over much of the site. Information boards have been placed to help you make sense of it all. There is also a burial site known

as Chrysolakkos. Treasures found in the tombs are held in the Archaeological Museum in Iraklio.

The main area to see is the former **palace,** which was built in 1900 B.C., destroyed in 1700 B.C., rebuilt, and then destroyed again in about 1450 B.C. in the cataclysmic annihilation of the Minoan civilization on Crete. The central courtyard is a focal point from which to try to understand the sumptuous buildings that would have surrounded you. A prior visit to Knossos will give you some idea of what Malia might have looked like. The remains of storage areas and pits, as well as a huge administration block, indicate that the palace was as well populated and well stocked with provisions as any large modern town. ■

Elouda

LIKE MALIA, ELOUDA IS A MIX OF ANCIENT AND MODERN. It has a long and rich history, but today it is mainly known as a popular beach resort. There are several good hotels in Elouda and a pretty little fishing harbor. It has some surprises waiting for you—but you must look into the sea to find them.

The most popular tavernas in Elouda cluster around the harbor.

Elouda is on the site of the ancient Greco-Roman town of **Olous.** If you look from the bridge joining Elouda and the Spinalonga peninsula, you can make out the remains just beneath the surface of the water. Olous had one of the most important harbors in eastern Crete, and there are at least two remaining temples. It is thought that the city was destroyed in the second century B.C., when immense land movements caused several areas of eastern Crete to sink below the waves, while parts of western Crete rose.

On either side of the bridge are the remnants of Venetian salt pans. It was the Venetians who developed Elouda as a port in 1579. On the sheltering peninsula, which is a good place to escape the crowds, there is a church that was once part of Ancient Olous and still has some of its original frescoes. From here, if the light is right, you can make out parts of the old harbor beneath the waves.

Spinalonga island, offshore, helps protect the bay and is where the Venetians built their defensive fortress. This was such an effective stronghold that it was the last place on Crete to surrender to the Turks, in 1715, some 40 years later than most of the rest of Crete. From 1903 to 1957 the island was renowned throughout Greece as a leper colony, where a thriving town built up. The ruins can still be seen. It is a haunting spot, filled with the ghosts of those who lived out their lives in enforced isolation on the island. ∎

Elouda
🅼 279 F2

Agios Nikolaos

THE PORT OF AGIOS NIKOLAOS IS ONE OF THE PRETTIEST—and most popular—places on Crete. Beautifully situated on the Gulf of Mirabello, it retains some of its old mansions and has not one but two harbors: A lovely fishing harbor and, right in the town, an inner harbor that is really a lake. All these attractions, and many more in and around the town, turn it into one of the busiest places on Crete in the middle of summer. Despite all this it manages to retain its character and has not been swamped by the anonymous tourist development that blights much of the island's north coast.

Agios Nikolaos was a thriving place in ancient times, serving as the port for the city-state of Lato, inland from here. It remained a port under the Venetians, who called it Agios Nikolaos after a church of the same name built in the 10th and 11th centuries. The Venetians also named the gulf Mirabello (Italian for "beautiful view"). The town declined under the Turks, who destroyed its Genoese fortress, but in the late 19th century it began to thrive again as a popular destination for travelers. Agios Nikolaos is still an important port, and you will

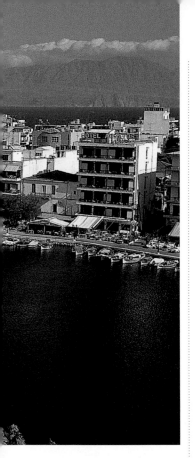

The pool that acts as the inner harbor, **Lake Voulismeni,** is known as the Bottomless Lake because of its very steeply sloping sides, and it is indeed deep for its size although it isn't bottomless. The depth has been measured at 210 feet (64 m). The lake is linked to the outer harbor by a channel built between 1867 and 1871. Overlooking the channel is the town's **Folk Museum,** well worth seeing for its Cretan costumes, and the distinctive crafts and folk art of the island.

Agios Nikolaos has an excellent and modern **Archaeological Museum,** slightly away from downtown to the northwest. The museum has a good display of artifacts from several Minoan sites. One notable exhibit is the "Goddess of Myrtos" vase in Room II, found at Mochlos just outside Gournia (see p. 296). This vessel is made of clay and dates from the early Minoan period. It was probably used for fertility purposes; the neck and head are clearly phallic, while the body of the vessel shows two breasts.

The most unusual—if unsettling—exhibit is a skull thought to be that of an athlete. It was found intact, complete with the golden laurel wreath tradition-ally given for victories in athletics, and a silver coin to pay the dead man's fare to the ferryman for the journey across the River Styx to the Underworld. The skull was found near the town and can be dated by the coin to the first century A.D. Its survival is remarkable.

The beaches around the town are not especially good, but this does not prevent them from getting overcrowded for much of the summer. You can find better beaches at Elouda (see p. 293) and at **Ammoudara** and **Almyros** on the road toward Sitia. ∎

Folk Museum
- ✉ Palaiologou 2
- ☎ 0841 25093
- 🕐 Closed Sat. & Oct.–April
- 💲 $

Archaeological Museum
- ✉ Palaiologou 68
- ☎ 0841 24943
- 🕐 Closed Tues.
- 💲 $

find fishermen drying their nets in the harbor, and ferry boats coming in regularly from the Dodecanese, the Cyclades, and Pireas.

The **harbor** is lined with bars, stores, cafés, and tavernas, which make full use of their setting by charging prices that are expensive by Greek standards. If you want better food and a more Cretan atmosphere, forgo the setting and follow your nose into the port's back streets.

On the south side of town is a small beach and a marina, home to some pricier restaurants. Near the bus station at the western end of the marina is the church of the **Panagia Vrefotrofou,** dating from the 12th century—another Cretan example of the ancient and modern standing side by side.

Gournia

Gournia
🅰 279 G2
🕐 Closed Mon.
💲 $

A MERE 12 MILES (19 KM) SOUTH AND EAST OF THE clamor of modern Agios Nikolaos is a magical place—one of the best-preserved of all the Minoan towns on Crete. Gournia is also a site that reminds us of what can happen to even the busiest of communities over long periods of time. Ancient Gournia, a flourishing town in Minoan times, was first inhabited about 5,000 years ago. It now stands deserted on a small hill overlooking the beautiful Gulf of Mirabello. Few visitors take the trouble to make the slight detour off the busy road between Agios Nikolaos and Sitia, but it is worth it.

The small Minoan town of Gournia was first excavated in 1904.

Gournia centers around the remains of a palace that, at only one-tenth its size, was significantly less important than Knossos. Yet it is that small scale, and the preservation of the ruins, that brings the town to life in the imagination. Here you see a maze of streets, lined with the foundations of simple one-roomed houses—very like the jumble of back streets you will find in the older Cretan towns today. The paving of the main street survives, so you are stepping on the very same place that the ancient Cretans walked around 1550 to 1450 B.C.

Most of the remains you see today date from that era. Like other Minoan sites on Crete, Gournia was destroyed in a fire caused by the cataclysmic event—probably an earthquake—that wiped out the Minoans around 1450 B.C. You can still see the steps that lead up to the palace entrance and alongside them a massive stone slab, pierced by a single hole, where animals were probably tethered prior to their sacrifice. Or it may simply have been a butcher's block.

It is known that Gournia was a busy commercial center, with evidence of pottery, carpentry, and metalworking as well as other activities such as fishing and weaving. Once again, the similarities with modern Cretan communities are evident. ■

Sitia & Ierapetra

Life in Sitia
centers around
the harbor, where
outdoor taverna
tables crowd
a seafront
promenade.

DESPITE BEING THE CAPITAL OF THE EASTERN PROVINCE of Crete, Sitia is off the main tourist trail and so makes a good base for anyone who wants to have a taste of the real Crete. Taste is the word, as the food here is far superior and more authentically hearty and Cretan than that provided in the tourist towns. Ierapetra is the main south-coast settlement in eastern Crete and boasts of being the most southerly city in Europe, although with a population of fewer than 8,000 it is more a large town than a city.

Sitia
🅰 279 G2
Visitor information
✉ Tourist Police
☎ 0843 24200

Folklore Museum
✉ Kapetan Sifi 33
☎ 0843 22861
💲 $

Archaeological Museum
✉ Piskokefalou 3
☎ 0843 23917
🕐 Closed Mon.
💲 $

Ierapetra
🅰 279 G2

SITIA

Here the principal crop is not tourists but raisins. Every year in August Sitia hosts the Raisin Festival. This is a lively occasion with music, traditional dancing, and all the Cretan wine you can drink: But be warned, some of it is powerful stuff. There is plenty to see and do in Sitia at other times, too, including visiting the remains of a 13th-century **Venetian fortress,** partly restored for use as an open-air theater. A typical small **Folklore Museum** has examples of regional crafts. In the excellent **Archaeological Museum** look for the Minoan *kouros* statue made of ivory; it shows the damage inflicted by the fire that wiped out Minoan settlements in 1450 B.C.

IERAPETRA

This was originally a Dorian settlement, its location making it a perfect gateway for trade with North Africa and the Middle East. Today the trade is in tourism. Outside the town are wonderful long stretches of beaches, now backed by equally long stretches of hotels, villas, and tavernas. Within the town are a small **Archaeological Museum** (*Adrianou Koustoula, tel 0842 28721, closed Mon., $*) and the remains of a 13th-century **fortress.** ∎

Phaestus

THE PALACE OF PHAESTUS IN SOUTH-CENTRAL CRETE WAS second only to Knossos in size and importance, but outshone—and still outshines—it in terms of location. Phaestus stands spectacularly on a plateau overlooking the wide and fertile Messara Plain. To the north you can see the slopes that rise to their peak in Mount Psiloreitis, more popularly known as Mount Ida, at 8,058 feet (2,456 m), the highest point on Crete. It is an incomparable setting.

The history of Phaestus is the history of many other Minoan sites. The first palace was built here in about 1900 B.C. but destroyed by the same earthquake that devastated the island and its cities in 1700 B.C. A second palace was quickly constructed, only to be wiped out along with the Minoans in 1450 B.C. At Phaestus, however, some remains of the first palace still survive. They were found by Italian archaeologist Frederico Halbherr, who undertook the first major exploration of Phaestus in 1900.

The layout of the site is similar to that of Knossos, but little attempt has been made at reconstruction. At Phaestus the remains have merely been uncovered and cleaned up, with small amounts of reconstruction here and there, for example where walls were known to have collapsed.

The hillside on which Phaestus was built has been incorporated into the construction as the **Grand Staircase** of the palace, 45 feet (13 m) wide and consisting of 12 steps that have been partly carved out of the ground. The steps use the common Greek architectural trick of being slightly curved, in this case marginally higher in the center than at either end, which makes them look straight and emphasizes their grandeur.

At the top of the Grand Staircase is the west entrance to the second palace, and over to the right is the equally grand **Central Courtyard,** a common feature of these great Minoan palaces. The colonnades that lined two sides of the courtyard have gone, but the view from the north side toward Mount Psiloreitis is as impressive today as it was 4,000 years ago. To the palace dwellers, the view was of particular significance because the Kamares cave, a sacred place to the Minoans, was visible high on the mountainside. Certain rooms in the palace also enjoyed a view of Kamares.

To the north of the courtyard is the entrance to the royal apartments, and you can still see the remains of the sentry boxes where the guards stood watch on either side. As you walk down the corridor note the drainage channel beneath your feet: This passageway was open to the elements. Beyond it are the **Royal Apartments,** which have been fenced off because they are among the most important areas of the site. They contain separate chambers for the king and queen, the remains of a swimming pool, and even the remnants of a lavatory. Beyond here and to your right is what was the **Archives Room,** which is where the Phaestus Disk was found (see below).

When visiting Phaestus, don't fail to make a small detour 2 miles (3 km) to the east to see the ruins of **Hagia Triada,** a villa or palace built about 1600 B.C., perhaps as a summer residence for the royal family or for a wealthy resident of Phaestus. It has some superb frescoes, and many important finds were made here that are now on display in the Archaeological Museum in Iraklio (see p. 282). Historians believe that the villa or palace originally stood much closer to the sea, which has retreated over the centuries. A sloping ramp in front of the villa may have led down to a small private harbor. ∎

A curve on the shallow steps of Phaestus enables rainwater to run off quickly—one example of the palace's extensive and sophisticated drainage system.

Phaestus Disk

I t was in 1903 that the Phaestus Disk was discovered. The code encrypted in this baked clay disk, 6 inches (16 cm) in diameter and dating from 1700–1600 B.C., has yet to be cracked. Both sides are inscribed with pictorial symbols, much like Egyptian hieroglyphics, including people, animals, ships, and flowers, all radiating from the center. The disk may have some religious significance, possibly containing the words to a prayer. See for yourself at Iraklio's Archaeological Museum. ∎

Samaria Gorge walk

One of the greatest experiences on Crete is to walk the Samaria Gorge (Farangi Samarias), the longest gorge in Europe. In fact, if visitor numbers are a guide, it is the island's second most popular attraction: Almost half a million people walk its length every year, a number exceeded only by visitors to Knossos.

Mount Gingilos rises at the head of the gorge.

You don't need to be a mathematician of the caliber of Pythagoras to work out that at the height of summer there are a few thousand people walking the gorge every day. If you can time your visit for the late spring or early fall, there is a greater chance that you will be able to appreciate the grandeur and solitude. But even if you have to walk in the company of many others, it is still well worth doing.

The walk is about 11 miles (17 km) in total, and most people do it in 5–7 hours. It is a demanding hike over some rough terrain, but as you are descending most of the way it is perfectly achievable by the reasonably fit, plodding walker. Wear hiking boots and take a plentiful supply of food and some water—although you can replenish your water at fountains along the route. The walk begins from a large, signed parking lot south

START
Omalos
1

2 Xyloskalon
(Wooden stairway)

2080m
▲
Gingilos
2116m
▲
Volakias

Agios
Nikolaos

3
Samaria

4
Sidiroportes
(Iron gates)

Agia
Roumeli   5

⛰ See area map p. 278
► Bus to Omalos
↔ 11 miles (17 km)
🕐 5–7 hours
► Agia Roumeli

NOT TO BE MISSED
• View from Omalos
• The *xyloskalon*
• Samaria
• Sidiroportes

0   3 kilometers
0   2 miles

of the village of **Omalos** , where accommodations are available if you make reservations in advance. In this way you can beat the crowds by making an early start. The gorge opens at 6 a.m. Keep your ticket, as it will be needed later.

From the parking lot head straight down the marked *xyloskalon* ❷, which means "wooden stairway." It is, in fact, a steep zigzag path cut out of the rock but with wooden rails for support and protection. This is one of the most spectacular parts of the walk, dropping by almost 2,300 feet (700 m) in just 2 miles (3 km). At the bottom is the tiny chapel of **Agios Nikolaos.** There are also benches if you want a rest after the challenging descent.

The path from here widens and levels out for a time and crosses back and forth over the stream that runs down the gorge. In winter and early spring, when the snows melt, this can turn into a torrent, which is why the gorge is closed until May. In summer the stream turns into a pleasant and cooling trickle of water. About 4 miles (6.5 km) into the gorge, to the left of the track, you pass the abandoned village of **Samaria** ❸, whose inhabitants left when the gorge was designated a national park in 1962.

Entering the most dramatic section of the walk, the gorge narrows until it is a mere 10 feet (3 m) wide at the so-called Iron Gates, **Sidiroportes** ❹, with the walls towering 1,000 feet (300 m) above. Then the walls widen out again, and you enter a broader valley with another abandoned village, Agia Roumeli, where safety procedures require you to hand in your ticket to show you have left the gorge.

Twenty minutes farther on is the modern village of **Agia Roumeli** ❺ and the sea—cool and welcoming for your tired feet. There are rooms here, or boats can take you to other coastal villages (principally Chora Sfakion, see p. 303) from where you can return to Rethimno or Hania by bus. Connecting buses run throughout the afternoon in summer but can get very crowded. ∎

Early in the season the wildflowers are at their best in the gorge. However, the river is still unpredictable, and the path may be closed at short notice, so check ahead.

Palaiochora & the south coast

CRETE'S SOUTH COAST IS A SERIES OF JAGGED INDENTS where mountains and gorges plunge dramatically to the sea. It would take a colossal feat of engineering to link the resorts by a coastal road, and as a result there is much less development here than in the north. However, in the height of summer the towns do get crowded.

The resort of **Agia Galini,** west of Phaestus, is a case in point. The archetypal Greek coastal settlement, it was once a small, quiet fishing village. Now it is a large, busy tourist town. An old part survives, in charming contrast to the rest of the town, and the area around the harbor has a row of lively tavernas.

A popular drive from here leads inland to the **Amari Valley,** in the shadow of Mount Psiloreitis (Mount Ida). This is the heart of Crete, where some men still wear the traditional costume of baggy black pants and high mountain boots. It's an area of rural villages, fertile valleys, and dramatic gorges.

West of here, the Kourtaliotiko Gorge leads down through splendid scenery to the coastal monastery of **Moni Piso Preveli.** It dates from the 17th–19th centuries. You can visit, but it is still a working monastery, so dress respectfully.

In the resort of **Plakias** farther along the coast, a 1.2-mile (2 km) strip of sandy beach attracts sunbathers galore, and more beaches are accessible along the coast. Plakias sits at the end of another scenic ravine, the Kotsyfou Gorge. The next major town west, Chora Sfakia, is close to the **Imbros Gorge,** almost as impressive as the Samaria Gorge and less visited.

Rising sternly from a rare stretch of coastal plain between Plakias and Sfakia are the remains of the Venetian fortress of **Frango-kastelo,** built in 1371, whose walls

survive in almost perfect condition. Little remains of the interior, but its atmospheric setting by the sea and the view from outside make a visit well worthwhile. It was built partly to protect this rugged coast from pirates, but also to keep the local population in order. The residents of the next town along the coast, Chora Sfakion, had a particular reputation for troublesome independence.

Chora Sfakion is the preferred base for those who want to enjoy some of Crete's finest scenery and see something of its traditional way of life. The town's location, hemmed in to the west by a steep mountain range—meant that for many years access was almost entirely by sea. Today the road across the island snakes down in a dramatic series of hairpin bends. Modern life has impinged less on the town than elsewhere. It is busy and popular with visitors, but local residents have held on to their

history and traditions much more strongly. Those traditions include tribal feuding, but also immense hospitality to the outside visitor. Here again, some of the older men still wear traditional costumes.

Tourism reached the westernmost resort of **Palaiochora** many years ago, and although it remained relatively quiet for a long time, in recent years it has boomed as a tourist resort. The town has two fine beaches on either side of a headland topped by the remains of a Venetian fortress and excellent conditions for windsurfing and other water sports. It is a good base for those who like to mix relaxation with exploration. ■

Chora Sfakion
🔼 278 C2

Palaiochora
🔼 278 B2

Rain and melted snow from the mountains feed the Preveli River, which cuts through the Kourtaliotiko Gorge.

West coast

THE WEST COAST IS A VERY SPECIAL PART OF CRETE THAT
has not yet been modernized. There are some busy resorts, of course,
but there are even more unspoiled villages where the men while
away their time in the cafés as they have done for centuries. The
beaches are wonderful and comparatively isolated.

Elafonisos
🗺 278 A2

**Kastelli
Kissamos**
🗺 278 B3

About 8 miles (13 km) northwest of
Palaiochora is the stunning beach
at **Elafonisos,** which has been
compared to the Caribbean with its
pink-white sand and deep-blue
water under an azure sky. Summer
temperatures remind you that this
part of Crete is only 190 miles
(306 km) from North Africa. The
sea is very shallow, and it's possible
to wade out to the nearest of the
little offshore islands, where
another idyllic beach awaits. While
the main beach gets very busy,
development at the moment is
limited. Access to the beach is
along a bumpy road, discouraging
car users.

Inland and overlooked by the
3,878-foot (1,182 m) peak of Agios
Dikaios is the main town of this
region, **Elos.** The area is known as

Kastanokhoria, or Chestnut
Villages, after the main local crop,
picked in the fall and celebrated
with a big Chestnut Festival in
late October.

The somewhat hair-raising coast
road takes you through fertile strips
of citrus orchards and olive groves,
with hills on one side and the
wine-dark Aegean Sea on the other.
The main town at the northern
end of the west coast is **Kastelli
Kissamos,** the perfect place for
those who want a few hotels and
eating places available. Kastelli, as it
is usually known, is a town that
goes about its own business, not
worrying too much about visitors
but welcoming them all the same.
Sit in the peaceful main square in
the evening, enjoy a coffee or an
ouzo, and people-watch. ∎

Maleme

THE BATTLE OF CRETE, WHICH RAGED FOR TEN DAYS IN May 1941, was a momentous event in Cretan history. To learn something of the grim truth of this disastrous episode and its aftermath, a visit to the main site of the battle at Maleme on the coast west of Hania, now the site of the German War Cemetery, is essential.

The Allied airfield at Maleme was the target of German paratroopers who invaded the island in 1941, after Greece had fallen to the German forces. The Allies, for whom Crete had been a vital naval base, retreated across the island and were mostly evacuated by sea from the south coast. It was an extraordinary operation that involved the help of many local people, who put their own lives in danger. Fierce fighting by the Cretan resistance continued until 1945.

The **German War Cemetery** is laid out on the crown of what was known as Hill 107. A small building near the entrance acts as the information center; with a map showing how the battle progressed. The hill is covered with rows of graves. The German losses were 6,580 men, many of them shot by snipers as they parachuted down. Today in the spring the lower slopes are strewn with wildflowers, bringing serenity to this turbulent spot.

From the top of the hill you can look down on the Maleme airstrip, the vital piece of land that was the focus for the attack and which had to be seized at all costs. The airstrip is still in military use.

For a fuller picture, go on to the smaller **Commonwealth War Cemetery,** at the end of the Akrotiri peninsula north of Hania. This is the burial place of 1,522 of the 2,000 Allies who died in the Battle of Crete—Britons, Australians, and New Zealanders who died alongside the Cretan men, women, and children who fought with them to defend their island. ∎

Graves in the German War Cemetery are tended with great care, despite long memories of the German occupation.

Maleme
🅰 278 B3

Hania

Hania

△ 278 B3

Visitor information

✉ Kriari 40, Megaro Pantheon

☎ 0821 92943

Archaeological Museum

✉ Chalidon 21

☎ 0821 90334

⊕ Closed Mon. Nov.–April

$ $

THE MAIN CITY IN WESTERN CRETE, HANIA IS ONE OF THE most appealing towns on the island (also written as Chania, Khania, or Kania). Its perfect setting, lively harbor, historical remains, busy market, interesting museums, and nearby beaches make it the ideal spot. It retains its unique charm and character no matter how many visitors pack into the streets. Big enough to have all the facilities of a city, Hania is nevertheless on a human scale, a place you quickly find your way around, where you soon start to feel at home.

The setting undoubtedly helps. To the north are the sparkling blue waters of the Sea of Crete, while to the south is the Lefka Ori range of mountains, the White Mountains, the backbone of this end of the island. If you choose your waterfront café carefully, you may be able to see snow-topped mountains and azure seas at the same time. There is no better place for a breakfast of Greek yogurt with local honey and fresh fruit—or for lunch, or maybe for a romantic dinner as the sun begins to set.

The narrow back streets of Hania offer refuge from the tourist crowds.

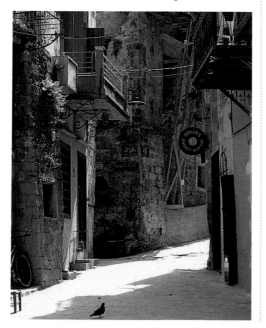

Parts of the **waterfront** are lined with tall mansions, creating an effect not unlike that of Venice. Of course the Venetians are just one of several groups of people who have made their impact on this beautiful place. It was an important Minoan city, but one that is relatively unknown, as the modern city has been added layer after layer on top of the Minoan remains. The site of **Kydonia** (as the Minoan city was called) is being excavated within the city boundaries, but it will be some time before it is open to the public.

The best finds from Kydonia are on display in Hania's **Archaeological Museum,** which is also rich in artifacts from other sites in western Crete. It has a fine pottery collection and several superb sculptures and mosaics. The building itself is of interest, although the outside belies the interior. It was once the Venetian Church of San Francesco and later converted into a mosque by the Turks. You can see the remnants of a minaret and a fountain in a pretty little courtyard.

Turkish influence is evident elsewhere, such as the **Mosque of the Janissaries,** right on the harbor. This dates from 1645 and is the oldest surviving Ottoman building on Crete. It was damaged in World War II, then restored, and for many years made an unmissable

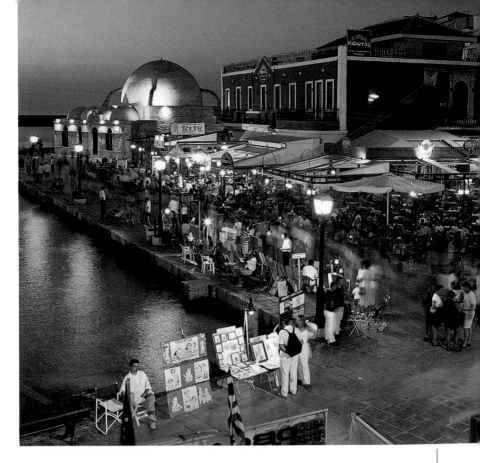

tourist information center; today it is undergoing further restoration.

The bulk of the harbor reflects Hania's Venetian era, especially in the restored **Firkas** fortress. It's an interesting place to wander around, with good views of the harbor. One of its towers contains the **Naval Museum,** with a collection of model ships and accounts of sea battles in the waters off the coast. Even if you are not a naval enthusiast, it is worth a visit to see an incredibly detailed scale model of Hania as it was in the 17th century, town as well as harbor, including the Venetian Arsenale, or boat-yards, which can still be seen on the harbor. The Naval Museum also contains one of the most vivid accounts of the Battle of Crete that you will see anywhere on the island.

Hania's Historical Museum, tucked away in the southeastern corner of the city, is well worth walking out to. You may want to stop on the way at the bustling **Central Market,** a huge hall offering souvenirs as well as the usual array of fresh fish, meat, vegetables, and delicious cheeses.

The **Historical Museum** is in what was obviously once an elegant town house, when this area was one of Hania's more fashionable districts in the late 19th and early 20th centuries. Among the memorabilia of local worthies are some gems, including excellent information on the Cretan resistance movement during World War II and the earlier struggle for independence from the Turks. ■

The deceptively space-age Mosque of the Janissaries stands out from Hania's busy waterfront.

Naval Museum
✉ Akti Kountourioti
☎ 0821 26437
💲 $

Historical Museum
✉ Sfakianaki 20
☎ 0821 42606
🕐 Closed Sat.–Sun.

Rethimno

Rethimno

⬛ 278 C2

Visitor information

✉ E. Venizelou, Paralia

☎ 0831 29148

Fortetsa

✉ Katechaki

☎ 0831 28101

🕐 Closed Oct.–May

💲 $

WITH A POPULATION OF SOME 25,000, RETHIMNO (SOME-times written Rethymnon or Rethimnon) is Crete's third largest city. It feels, however, more like a scaled-down, more touristy version of Hania, complete with a similar harbor, architecture with clear Venetian and Turkish influences, and a strong traditional culture.

The Greco-Roman town of Rithymna preceded modern Rethimno, and the site is known to have been occupied since Minoan times. There are no palatial remains but many from the Greco-Roman period, when Rethimno was already a busy trading center and port. During the 16th century the city boomed under Venetian rule,

acquiring a reputation for art and scholarship that it retains to this day.

The town's dominant feature is the **Fortetsa**, a Venetian fortress. It was built in the 1570s to defend against pirate attack as well as to keep one prescient eye on the Turks' increasing power. The strength of the fortress, however,

**Archaeological
Museum**
✉ Cheimaras
☎ 0831 54668
🕐 Closed Mon.
💲 $

Moni Arkadiou
🅰 278 D2
☎ 0831 71216
💲 $

**Above: Taking a
break from lace-
making outside a
Rethimno church**

**Left: Cafés and
fish restaurants
crowd around the
inner harbor.**

was short-lived: The Turks conquered it in 1645 after a siege that lasted 23 days.

The Fortetsa is said to be the biggest Venetian fortress ever built and is still in quite good condition. Inside are the remains of some administrative buildings, a barracks, cisterns, the church of St. Catherine, and the Sultan Ibrahim Mosque. It is even big enough to contain a small theater, used for performances in summer. The views from the huge ramparts over coast and town alone are worth the visit.

Opposite the entrance to the Fortetsa is the former prison, which now houses the **Archaeological Museum.** The conversion has been well done and the displays are arranged in rooms around a light, central atrium. Although the city itself is not rich in Minoan remains, the surrounding area certainly is, and the museum has an excellent collection of them, including a fascinating and large selection of painted burial chests known as *larnakes.* There is a good range of statuary, especially from the Greco-Roman period.

To the south of the Archaeological Museum lies the old part of the town, with numerous structures of historical interest that seem far removed from the jostle of foreign visitors in the harbor tavernas and on the town beaches. Life in the old town centers around the **Rimondi Fountain,** which stands at one end of a busy main street surrounded by cafés and stores. The fountain was built in 1629 by the Venetian governor (he was jealous of the Morosini Fountain in Iraklio, so they say), with waterspouts in the shape of the lions' heads that are emblematic of Venice. About 50 yards (46 m) to the south is an even older building, the 16th-century **loggia,** built

by the Venetians as a marketplace. The former home of the Archaeological Museum, it is currently being turned into a library.

Southeast of the loggia is the little **Venetian harbor,** able to take only smaller boats and the local fishing fleet; the bigger inter-island and Pireas ferries are forced to moor outside. It's here that the fishermen can be found mending their nets and in the mornings selling their catch from the night before. The 16th-century lighthouse here is another notable Venetian legacy. By night the scene is transformed, as all the world comes to the harbor to see and be seen, and to eat and drink the night away.

Some 14 miles (23 km) southeast of Rethimno, in a spectacular setting at the head of a gorge and surrounded by groves of fruit trees, stands the 16th-century monastery of **Moni Arkadiou,** a must on any itinerary. The audaciously ornate double-naved church is the most impressive feature, with its ornamental facade. ∎

More places to visit on Crete

ARCHANES

Another Minoan site lies at the twin villages of Kato and Archanes, south of Knossos, in a green region of olive groves and vineyards, the source of much of Crete's wine. On the site of the Temple of Anemospilia, in what was evidently a large town, the remains of four bodies were found in 1979. Their position has led to speculation that the Minoans were carrying out a human sacrifice when the temple was destroyed in an earthquake. Today the scene is much more peaceful.

🅰 279 E2

GAVDOS

The remote island of Gavdos, which can be reached by boat from Palaiochora or Chora Sfakia, has the distinction of being the most southerly point in Europe. It has few other distinctions, although the handful of people who still live here claim that this was the island of Calypso, described in Homer's *Odyssey*.

The capital, such as it is, is **Kastri,** and there are rooms and a taverna in the tiny resort of **Korfos,** with pretty beaches around the island. But if you're planning any kind of a visit, check ahead for both accommodations and return ferries. Out of season, even the two ferries per week are not kept up.

🅰 278 C1

LIMENAS HERSONISOU

One of Crete's major summer resorts, Limenas Hersonisou is the place to go for family fun. The streets are filled with bars and discos, and in summer there is little evidence of the original fishing village. A Roman fountain with delightful mosaic decoration, from the second or third century A.D., remains on the waterfront. But it's the culture of the **Aqua Splash Water Park** *(Open daily 10–4, $$$),* one of Crete's most popular attractions, that dominates the town.

🅰 279 F2 **Tourist Police** ☎ 0897 21000

THERISO GORGE

If your fitness does not allow you to walk the Samaria Gorge (see pp. 300–301), then take a drive through this gorge, south of Hania, for a glimpse of spectacular scenery. Vehicles on the snaking road are dwarfed by the sheer cliffs.

ZAKROS

The fourth largest Minoan palace on Crete is the Palace of Zakros, way out at the remote eastern end of the island, and usually free of visitors. It was an important trading port for the eastern Mediterranean and the Middle East, and while the palace itself has not survived so well, the surrounding houses and other buildings are well preserved.

🅰 279 H2 ∎

Crete's rugged southern coast, near Chora Sfakia

The green Ionian islands have experienced strong European influences and are the closest—culturally and physically—to Italy and the rest of Western Europe.

Corfu & the Ionian islands

Mellisani Caves, Cephallonia

Gaïos, on Paxi, has its own little tree-covered offshore island.

Corfu & the Ionian islands

LOCATED JUST A SHORT BOAT RIDE ACROSS THE IONIAN SEA FROM ITALY, Corfu (Kerkira) and the other Ionian islands have been popular vacation destinations since Roman times. Visitor numbers today are higher, especially in resorts such as Kavos and Benitses, which have opened the floodgates to mass tourism aimed at young people who want to party all night. This aspect of the islands is generally restricted to a handful of resorts, leaving the rest of the region in comparative peace.

There is plenty to enjoy. Anyone who has visited the dry, hot Aegean islands will be astonished at how green the Ionians are. They are extremely fertile, with vast stretches of olive groves, vineyards, and citrus orchards. This of course indicates that they receive more rain than the Aegean islands. Even in summer there can be brief showers, and fall storms are more common here than in the Aegean. But when winter departs, the spring here is glorious and recommended to anyone who loves walking amid carpets of wild-flowers and searching out the many species of orchid that grow here.

Be sure to sample some of the local food specialties. Among the most popular are *sofrito,* which is a flavorful veal dish, and *bourdetto,* a spicy fish dish. Kefalonia's golden honey is excellent, as are its quince preserves and almond pralines. The wines from Theo-taki and Liapaditiko come recommended as well.

The Ionian islands encompass enormous variety. Visit the largest town in the group, Corfu town, and you will find how much more cosmopolitan it is than other island capitals—more similar to other European Mediterranean cities due to the influence of the French, Venetians, and British who have all ruled here since the 11th century.

Yet an hour or so away from the southern tip of Corfu is the tiny island of Paxi, with just three small towns and a cluster of little inland communities. It's the smallest of the main Ionian islands, but some say the best olive oil in Greece is made here.

South again from Paxi is the even smaller island of Andipaxi, with just a handful of inhabitants, some rooms and villas to rent, and guaranteed tranquility. Ithaca is another tiny but famous island, the legendary home of Odysseus. The other main Ionian islands—Lefkada, Kefalonia, and Zakinthos—are all extensive, each one of them providing a mixture of mountains and beaches.

Because these islands are strung out in a long line, getting around them can be trickier than you might expect. To get from Corfu to Paxi is straightforward, for example, but reaching the next island, Lefkada, may require traveling via the mainland. There is a weekly ferry service from Corfu town to Kefalonia, from where you can hop back to Lefkada or move on to Zakinthos. Moving around between the southern islands is easier, but double-check sailing times in advance. Most islands have more than one port, so the ferry may not always take you to the main town. ■

Corfu

The architecture
of Corfu town has
been influenced
by Byzantine,
Venetian, French,
and British rulers.

THE MOST NORTHERLY OF THE IONIAN ISLANDS, CORFU
(Kerkira) is the closest to both Italy in the west and Albania in the
east, and it has been touched over the years by several other foreign
cultures. As a result it has acquired a certain sophistication and an
offbeat charm. It is the only place in Greece where the game of cricket
is played, a legacy from the days of British influence (1814–1908).

Kerkira

🏛 313 B5

**Visitor
information**

✉ Voulefton, Corfu
town

☎ 0661 37520 or
37639

The Greek name for the island is
Kerkira, which is something to
remember if you are heading there
by ferry or bus. (There are buses to
Corfu town from Athens and even
from as far as Thessaloniki in
Macedonia. The Greek bus network
doesn't let a little water stand in its
way—the bus goes onto the ferry
and continues its journey on the
other side.)

The name Kerkira derives from
Corcyra, who was the daughter
of the river god Asopos. The great
sea god Poseidon fell in love with
her and brought her to this island,
which he then named after her.
Their son Phaeax went on to
found the Phaeacian race (the
Phaeacians were kind hosts to

Odysseus on his ill-fated journey
home following the Greek victory
at Troy; see pp. 330–31). The
name Corfu is an Italian version
of the ancient Greek word *kory-
phai*, meaning "the hills," referring
not to the mountainous north of
the island, but rather to the two
elevated spots in Corfu town
where the Old and New Fortresses
were founded.

There is evidence of human
habitation 40,000 years ago in the
area of modern Corfu town, at a
time when the island was joined to
the mainland. The island's fertility,
size, and natural beauty all contributed to its development, and by
the time of the Persian Wars
(520–448 B.C.) it was so powerful

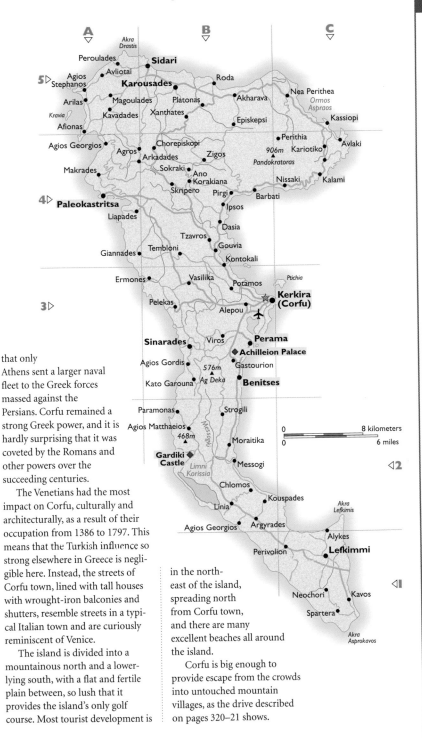

that only Athens sent a larger naval fleet to the Greek forces massed against the Persians. Corfu remained a strong Greek power, and it is hardly surprising that it was coveted by the Romans and other powers over the succeeding centuries.

The Venetians had the most impact on Corfu, culturally and architecturally, as a result of their occupation from 1386 to 1797. This means that the Turkish influence so strong elsewhere in Greece is negligible here. Instead, the streets of Corfu town, lined with tall houses with wrought-iron balconies and shutters, resemble streets in a typical Italian town and are curiously reminiscent of Venice.

The island is divided into a mountainous north and a lower-lying south, with a flat and fertile plain between, so lush that it provides the island's only golf course. Most tourist development is in the north-east of the island, spreading north from Corfu town, and there are many excellent beaches all around the island.

Corfu is big enough to provide escape from the crowds into untouched mountain villages, as the drive described on pages 320–21 shows.

CORFU TOWN

Nowhere is the pan-European background of the Ionian Islands more evident than in the beguiling **Corfu town.** It may have Greek tavernas in the back streets and may celebrate Easter even more exuberantly than the rest of Greece (try to catch the breaking of the crockery on the morning of Holy Sunday), but it also shows very strong influences from Britain, France, and Italy in its architecture. Residents of Corfu town proudly regard themselves as more sophisticated than people from other Greek island capitals.

This cosmopolitan mix is most evident in the very center of town, around the **Esplanade.** This combination of park and town square centers on a very English-looking cricket field, once a Venetian firing range. At the far end, on a promontory sticking out into the Ionian Sea, stands the Venetian **Palaio Frourio (Old Fortress),** completed in 1559 on a site believed to have been fortified since the seventh century A.D.

At the north end of the cricket field stands the **Palace of St. Michael and St. George,** constructed between 1819 and 1824 as the residence of the British High Commissioner. It was renovated in the 1950s and now contains administrative buildings, a library, the tourist office, and, in one wing, the **Museum of Asiatic Art** *(Tel 0661 30443, closed Mon.).* This collection, unique in Greece, was built up from 10,000 items amassed by Grigorios Manos (1850–1929), a Greek diplomat from Corfu who traveled extensively in the Orient.

At the western end is the **Liston,** a row of cafés and stores that could only be French. It was built by a Frenchman in 1807 at the request of Napoleon, who wanted its colonnades to echo the famous rue de Rivoli in Paris. The cafés along the Liston are where everyone comes to socialize. Your coffee will cost more here than anywhere else in Corfu, but it's *the* place to be.

At the southern side is a park with a magnificent fountain and, nearby, the **Enosis Monument (Unification Monument).** This celebrates the occasion in 1864 when the Ionian islands were at last united with the rest of Greece after their final period of British rule.

AROUND CORFU TOWN

There are numerous sites and museums around Corfu town that you should see. Stay for at least a few days if you can. The star attraction alone at the **Archaeological Museum** *(Odos Vraila 5, tel 0661 30680, closed Mon., $$)* is worth the visit: a fearsome Gorgon frieze made in the sixth century B.C. for the Temple of Artemis in the southern suburbs of Corfu town.

The enjoyable **Paper Money Museum** *(Ionian Bank, Plateia Iroon Kypriakou, tel 0661 41552, closed Sun.)* tells the fascinating story of how banknotes are made

and shows how Corfu's currency has reflected political changes. Exhibits include notes issued in German and Italian currency during World War II.

The **Byzantine Museum,** in the church of the Panagia Antivouniotissa *(tel 0661 38313, closed Mon.),* has a small and stylishly displayed collection of icons, some dating back to the 15th century. Look for examples of work by the so-called Cretan school, from the days when Cretan artists would visit Corfu on their way to study with the masters in Venice.

Don't miss the **church** dedicated to the island's patron saint, Agios Spyridon. His mummified body is contained in a silver casket inside, and four times a year this is carried through the streets to celebrate the occasions when the saint is believed to have come to the rescue of islanders during battles and plagues. Religious fervor combines with partying, and these are marvelous times to be in Corfu town: Palm Sunday, Easter Saturday, August 11, and the first Sunday in November.

Cricket and ginger beer are legacies of British rule on the island.

Palaio Frourio
✉ The Esplanade
💲 $

Opposite: With their balconies and arches, the narrow back streets of the town are reminiscent of Venice.

NORTHERN CORFU

The northern half of Corfu is by far the most dramatically diverse part of the island—although if you drive north out of Corfu town along the main coast road, the first few miles give no indication of the historical and geographical riches in store.

The first resorts you come to—Gouvia, Dasia, Ipsos, and Pirgi—offer wonderful beaches and plenty of water-sports facilities. Popular with families, they have lost any sense of individuality. It is not until the road approaches the lower slopes of Mount Pandokratoras, Corfu's highest point, that you start to see signs of true Greekness in villages like Nissaki and, later, Kalami.

Kalami, in particular, manages to stay much as it has always been, despite an increase in tourism, especially day visitors arriving from other resorts. One of its claims to fame is the White House (no presidents here, though), just behind the beach, where British novelist Lawrence Durrell (1912–1990) lived while writing his book about Corfu, *Prospero's Cell.* He was visited here by his friend, American writer Henry Miller (1891–1980). Miller's own book, *The Colossus of Maroussi,* includes his visit to Corfu and remains one of the most vivid books ever written about Greece.

Places such as Nissaki and Kalami are wonderfully enhanced by the backdrop of towering **Mount Pandokratoras,** which rises so steeply that its highest point, at 2,972 feet (906 m), is only 2 miles (3 km) from the coast. The mountain's bulk perfectly fits the translation of its name: the Almighty. Visible from almost everywhere, it dominates northern Corfu. You can drive all the way to the top of Mount Pandokratoras if you don't

mind some rough road toward the end, but the best approach is on foot from the village of Perithia. The mountain is crisscrossed with paths, and the flowers, especially in spring, are spectacular. At the top await a small monastery and an electricity pylon, and seemingly endless views over the island and across the sea to remote Albania.

The interior of northern Corfu has lots of mountain villages worth exploring, and the drive on pages 320–21 takes in some of the best. Apart from the occasional bus passing through on a scenic drive, the villagers live in a world hardly affected by the thousands of tourists on the nearby beaches.

The northern coastline has its own variety, and even within one of its busiest resorts—**Kassiopi,**

Kalami
■ 315 C4

Mount Pandokratoras
■ 315 C4

Kassiopi
■ 315 C5

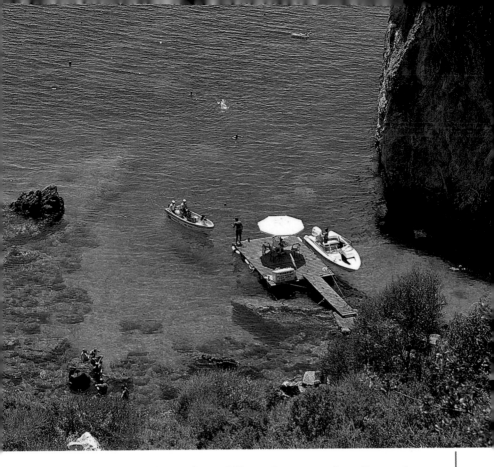

in the east—it combines bustle with friendliness, in a picturesque setting around a small harbor, with a wooded headland at either end. Fishermen and water-sports enthusiasts both enjoy the seas. Emperor Nero is said to have visited a temple of Jupiter here, but this no longer exists.

WEST COAST

The main resort in the west is **Sidari,** which is known to have had one of the first Neolithic settlements on Corfu, dating back to 7000 B.C. Today one of its main attractions—beaches aside—are the unusual rock formations. The sandstone has been weathered by wind and rain into surreal swirls, most famously in the gap between two rocks known romantically as the *Canal d'Amour.* One story says that any couple swimming through the channel will stay together forever.

Paleokastritsa is the second major west-coast resort. So strong was its appeal to one British High Commissioner, Sir Frederick Adam (commissioner 1824–1831), that he had the road built to make access easier for him from Corfu town.

It is easy to see the attraction. Green, wooded headlands stand over a deep blue sea, while a road zigzags down to a cluster of coves and sandy beaches, from where boats ride out to visit hidden grottoes. With the 17th-century monastery of Moni Theotokou and the ruins of a 13th-century Byzantine fortress both close at hand, it would be pretty hard to design a more perfect vacation spot.

Boats anchor in a rock-strewn cove near Paleokastritsa.

Sidari
▲ 315 B5

Paleokastritsa
▲ 315 A4

Drive: The two faces of Corfu

The marriage between traditional Greece and modern tourism affects every Greek island to some degree. Visitors who never stray from the beaches and the bars have no idea what life is like for the average Greek person. To drive through northern Corfu is to see both sides of the picture, from busy resorts to quiet mountain villages, as you take in some of the most breathtaking scenery on the island.

Leave **Corfu town ❶** (see pp. 316–17) on the main coastal road (No. 24) going north, following the signs for the first two resorts, Kontokali and Gouvia. (In Corfu, road signs are in both Roman and Greek alphabets.)

In Gouvia the road divides. Take the left fork marked for Paleokastritsa, which takes you around the lower slopes of Mount Pandokratoras and through a delightful wooded valley. Pass through the village of **Sgombou,** and just over a mile (about 2 km) beyond here the road divides again. Take the right turn, for Sidari.

The road now climbs to the **Troumbetas Pass ❷,** one of the prettiest spots on the island, with some of the most dramatic views. All of the fertile Ropa Plain in the center of the island spreads out below to the left. At the pass, take the right turn for Roda and Sidari. The road now winds and descends through the villages on the western side of Mount Pandokratoras, places where rural life goes on

as it has for centuries: Chorepiskopi, Valanio, Kiprianades, Xanthates, Platonas, and Sfakera. Stop in some of these places to walk around and get a feel for life in rural Corfu.

After Sfakera, continue toward the sea and the coastal road. When you reach it, turn left toward Karousades and Sidari. **Sidari ❸** (see p. 319) is the busiest resort on this part of the coast. You will find plenty of action on the waterfront, worth a stop to grab some lunch

---

▲ See area map p. 315
► Corfu town
⟷ 60 miles (100 km)
🕐 6–7 hours
► Corfu town

NOT TO BE MISSED
- Troumbetas Pass
- Sidari
- Avliotai
- Kavadades

Sandstone eroded by the waves at Sidari

or just to admire the unusual rock formations. Continue on the main coastal road, and stop at a lookout at **Avliotai ❹**, on the northwest corner of Corfu. There are three offshore islands here (Erikoussa, Othoni, and Mathraki), barely inhabited but with accommodations for a real get-away-from-it-all experience. Boats leave regularly from Sidari and other coastal towns.

Continue on through Arilas and, after about another mile (2 km), look for the left turn to Sidari. You are starting to complete a circle that will eventually return you to the Troumbetas Pass. At **Kavadades ❺**, leave the car and look for signs to the Viewpoint. This is a great view over the wooded mountains.

In Kavadades take the right turn toward Armenades. When you get there, turn right again through Dafni, then Agros, and back to the Troumbetas Pass. From here, return the way you first came, following the signs for Corfu town. ∎

Mount Pandokratoras

The red-capped belfry of Agios Spyridiou, Corfu town

SOUTHERN CORFU

The southern half of Corfu, from the capital down, is much less mountainous than the north but a lot more varied in its landscape.

For visitors interested in architecture, the first stopping-off point south of Corfu town is the **Achilleion Palace.** "A monstrous building," according to British writer Lawrence Durrell, who spent part of his youth on Corfu with his naturalist brother Gerald. It has to be said that this is not to everyone's taste with its mishmash of styles. But it cannot be denied that it is unique.

The Achilleion was built in 1890–91 for Empress Elizabeth of Austria (1837–1898), wife of Emperor Franz Joseph (1830–1916). Elizabeth used her new palace as a retreat from the difficulties she was experiencing at the Habsburg court, not least the unfaithfulness of her husband. Another woe had been the suicide at Mayerling of her second son, Archduke Rudolph.

Elizabeth commissioned a design from an Italian architect that reflected her admiration for Achilles, hero of the Trojan Wars. The palace is named after him, and he features prominently in statues and paintings throughout the house and gardens.

The gardens are absolutely beautiful, taking advantage of the climate to produce a riot of color, with terraces leading down to extensive breathtaking views along the coast. Some of the original furniture remains inside the house, although after the assassination of Elizabeth in 1898 the palace lay empty for nine years, until it was bought by Kaiser Wilhelm II (1859–1941). Today the Achilleion survives as a bustling tourist attraction, with a casino open in the summer.

Nothing could be further from the rarefied atmosphere of the Achilleion than the tourist resort of **Benitses,** a few miles down the coast. For those looking for a piece of the action, this is the place. In midsummer little remains of its origins as a fishing village, as it fills up with tourists. However, if you visit in the spring or fall you may get a glimpse of the way things used to be. There are some Roman remains here, including part of an old bathhouse, but it's hardly worth breaking a journey to find them.

Beyond Benitses the resorts are more spread out, and you can enjoy driving down the coastal road, with the Ionian Sea on your left and green hills dotted with villas on your right. The bustle builds up again as you approach the twin resorts of Moraitika and Messogi, now more or less merged into one.

Just south of here on the western coast is one of the most interesting areas in the south, the **Korissia Lagoon (Limni Korissia).** The lagoon stretches for about 3 miles (5 km), cut off from the Ionian Sea by equally long expanses of beaches and sand dunes. The beaches and dunes are far from undiscovered, but they are so big compared with the number of people who venture here that you are sure to find some quiet stretches to yourself if you are prepared to walk to them. The relative peace attracts wildlife, which also appreciates the abundance of fresh water (rare on Corfu) that the lagoon provides. Look for ibis and egrets, along with waders such as stilts, sandpipers, and avocets. Rare Jersey orchids flower here in the spring. Snakes and lizards inhabit the nearby dunes, while the ditches, creeks, and pools around the lagoon provide habitats for frogs and turtles.

To the north of the lagoon stands **Gardiki Castle,** built in the 13th century by Michail Angelos Komninos II, the Byzantine despot of Epiros. Komninos was also responsible for the Angelokastro, the ruined fortress near Paleokastritsa on the northwest coast. The walls and some of the towers of Gardiki still stand. The oldest human remains on Corfu were found near here, dated to 40,000 B.C. ■

Marble statuary adds feminine grace to the gardens of the Achilleion.

Limni Korissia
315 B2

Gardiki Castle
315 B2

Paxi & Andipaxi

PAXI, ALSO KNOWN AS PAXOS OR PAXOI, IS A CONTRAST TO its bigger and busier neighbor to the north. A speck of an island 7 miles (11 km) south of Corfu, Paxi has just three main villages and is small enough—only 5 miles (8 km) long and 2 miles (3 km) wide—to be walked across in a single day using the network of paths that traverse the numerous olive groves. Just as Paxi lies like a speck south of Corfu, Andipaxi is an even tinier dot south of Paxi.

PAXI

The visitors attracted to Paxi are those who like somewhere quieter, more laid-back, and more directly in touch with its own traditions than hectic Corfu. The symbol of Paxi is the trident, which is a nod toward one story of how it came into existence: The god of the sea, Poseidon, needing a place to hide

his lover Amphitrite, created Paxos by striking the sea with his trident.

Gods apart, Paxi is thought to have been uninhabited until settlers arrived from the mainland in the sixth century A.D. Even now there are fewer than 3,000 people here, spread among the three main harbor villages and a scattering of rural settlements inland.

The Venetians first exploited the potential for olive cultivation on Paxi.

Only limited accommodations are available, most reserved for the summer months by British and German tour companies—these two nations have taken to Paxi in a big way. The Paxiots have taken to them, too, as they welcome the prosperity that small-scale tourism has brought.

Paxi may be simple, but it is not inexpensive. Much of the produce has to be imported from Corfu, and the well-to-do on their visiting yachts have created a demand for more sophisticated food. This is one of the delights of visiting the island. Each of the three harbor towns, all delightfully pretty, can provide food of far better quality than you might expect.

The main settlement is **Gaïos,** a beautiful village huddled around a small harbor and a Venetian town square. Its charm is enhanced by two tiny islands in the bay. The remains of a Venetian fortress crown pine-covered Agios Nikolaos, while Panagia has a church of the same name. Boats from the harbor front will take you over to the islands for a closer look. There is only one hotel in Gaïos, but there are many apartments and villas to rent. Except in the height of the tourist season, finding somewhere to stay should not be hard.

North of Gaïos the island's solitary main road heads inland through quiet hill villages—well worth walking to if time allows—and then back down to the next main coastal settlement, **Longos** (or Loggos). This is equally charming, with a harbor that looks designed with picture postcards in mind, a small town beach, good walks in the vicinity (brochures are available in local stores), and several of the best restaurants on the island. There are more good walks either along the coast to quiet coves or by climbing the steep steps

Olives & olive oil

The Greeks consume more olive oil than anyone else in the world: about 48 pints (23 liters) per person per year. That amounts to an awful lot of olives—but then Greece produces an awful lot of the fruit. Its output is around 225,000 tons per annum, making it the world's third highest producer, after Spain and Italy.

Olive cultivation goes back at least 5,000 years on Corfu, where almost four million trees cover 30 percent of the island. The islanders harvest the fruits in an unusual manner for Greece, simply letting them fall to the ground when they are ready, rather than beating on the branches as is done elsewhere. Together with Kalamata in the Peloponnese, Paxi is said to produce the finest olive oil in all of Greece. ■

from the harbor to the white-washed hamlet of Dendiatika.

At the far north of the island is the delightful **Lakka,** with a large harbor surrounded by tree-covered hills, several stores and more fine restaurants, two town beaches, and more beaches along the coast offering sunbathing, swimming, and water sports.

ANDIPAXI

Only a handful of people live on the island, where there are no stores and only a few tavernas by the beaches. In the height of summer the island is inundated with day visitors from Corfu and Paxi, although the beaches are inferior. You can easily escape the crowds by going for a walk among the ubiquitous olive groves. ■

Lefkada

A 313 C3

Archaeological Museum

✉ Pfanerominis 20, Lefkada town

☎ 0645 23678

⏱ Closed Mon.

Folklore Museum

✉ Stefanitsi 2

☎ 0645 22473

⏱ Closed Sat.–Sun.

💲 $

Lefkada

LEFKADA (ALSO REFERRED TO AS LEFKAS) IS ONLY BARELY an island—it was joined to the mainland until the Corinthians created a 65-foot-wide (20 m) canal in the sixth century B.C. to ease the passage of ships down the western coast of Greece. The channel still exists, with an artery and a bridge that is raised on the hour to let boats through (this may hold up the traffic to and from the island).

Lefkada makes a good base if you plan to explore the mainland by car and visit other islands in the southern Ionian group. Regular ferries sail to Ithaca and Kefalonia, from where there are connections to Zakinthos. Boats leave from several places on the island, but the main point of entry is the capital, **Lefkada town,** which has developed around the point closest to the mainland.

It is an attractive setting, with a lagoon nearby and low-lying mountains almost immediately behind the town. The town was almost flattened in 1953 by a major earthquake, and hurried rebuilding has not produced a pretty result. The waterfront is pleasant, however. The busy main street, **Odos Dorpfeld,** is named after the German archaeologist Wilhelm Dorpfeld (1853–1940). Something has been learned of Lefkada's history through Dorpfeld's excavations, and he is regarded with great respect by the islanders. Settlers came here as long ago as 8000 B.C., and some Mycenean remains have also been discovered. Dorpfeld worked with Schliemann (see pp. 112–13) at Mycenae, and just as Schliemann was determined to prove that Agamemnon lived and was buried there, Dorpfeld believed that Lefkada rather than Ithaca was the home of Odysseus. He discovered no evidence, however.

Some of the artifacts found by Dorpfeld are on display in the small **Archaeological Museum** in Lefkada town. The little jumble of a **Folklore Museum** is more interesting, with scale models of some of the digs that Dorpfeld carried out, as well as photographs showing what the town looked like before the 1953 earthquake.

Dorpfeld is buried outside a church on a peaceful headland, at the far side of the lovely bay from the resort town of **Nidri.** This is the harbor for ferries to Meganisi, and to Ithaca and Kefalonia, but unless you like busy beaches and noisy nightlife, Nidri is a place to pass through. **Meganisi,** a small and tranquil island with rooms to rent and one pleasant hotel, can be visited on a one-day stop.

Vasiliki, in the south, is not as big as Nidri but still very commercial; it's popular with young travelers because of its excellent windsurfing.

The best beaches are on the west coast. **Porto Katsiki** is stunning, with unbelievably blue waters and lovely soft sand. Inevitably, it is also one of the busiest beaches, overcrowded in high summer. North of Katsiki, back toward Lefkada town, is one of the most attractive and un-spoiled resorts on the island, tiny **Agios Nikitas.** Its beach is not especially good, but it has some lovely old houses and is still very much a Greek village first and a vacation resort second. ∎

Opposite: Peaceful shrine in the old village of Agios Nikitas

Ithaki
🅜 313 C2

Archaeological Museum
✉ Kallinikou, Ithaca town
☎ 0674 32200
🕐 Closed Mon.

Folklore Museum
✉ Ithaca town
🕐 Closed Sat.–Sun.
$ $

Ithaca

LET THE *ODYSSEY* BE YOUR GUIDEBOOK, AND YOU WILL recognize Ithaca (Ithaki) from Homer's description: narrow and rocky, with a heavily indented coastline. The symbolic Ithaca—the notion of a homeland to which we all want to return—is recalled by a sign in the port reminding visitors that "Every traveler is a citizen of Ithaca." If you harbor such thoughts yourself, you'll find that arriving at Ithaca is like arriving at no other island.

On approach it looks forbidding and barren, with high rocky hills, hauntingly shrouded in mist at certain times of the year. Ferries arrive in several different places. Those on the Lefkada–Kefalonia route call at Frikes in the north, while those from Kefalonia or the mainland port of Astakos call either at Piso Aetos Bay in the shadow of Mount Etos or at the deeply indented bay with the main town, Ithaca.

To arrive at Ithaca town is itself something special, as the boat sails into the picturesque fjordlike harbor, past the remains of two French fortresses built in 1805 to guard the harbor entrance. There are mountains on either side, and the ferry passes the pretty little island of **Lazaretto,** covered in trees. Lazaretto was made into a quarantine station by the Venetians in 1668, used as a prison from 1864 onward, and today contains only a small chapel. At the far end of the horseshoe bay is the welcoming sight of the tiny main town.

Although ferries dock daily, each arrival is still an event, with people waiting to greet friends and family, or offering rooms to visitors. There are a handful of hotels, some pensions, and plenty of eating places, notably around the harbor.

Despite Ithaca's rich history in legend, few remains have been discovered to shed light on whether there was actually a palace here belonging to Odysseus. But the locals insist that this was the case, and they may well be right. The island certainly trades well on its Homeric connections, and several sites have been linked with episodes in the *Odyssey.* A local map is available that guides you to some of these, and they are pleasant places to visit in their own right, with or without a legendary link. Two miles (3 km) from Ithaca is the **Cave of the Nymphs,** where Odysseus is supposed to have concealed treasure, and it is about 7 miles (11 km) to the **Fountain of Arethusa.**

Exquisite ironwork adorns an otherwise ordinary house in Ithaca.

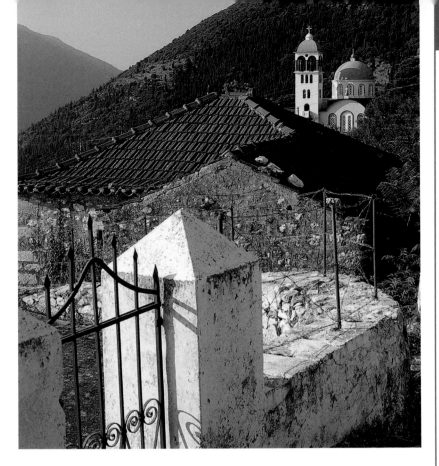

In Ithaca town (also called Vathi), a small **Archaeological Museum** has a few Mycenean finds. Next door is the **Library,** which collects editions of Homer, including a rare Japanese edition from 1600. There is also a charming little **Folklore Museum,** with displays on local life. The other place of note in the town is the **Church of the Taxiarchos,** containing an icon of the Crucifixion said to have been painted by the young El Greco.

On the south end of the island, the only other settlement of any size is the village of **Perahori,** which stands nearly 1,000 feet (300 m) above sea level on a fertile plain that contains most of the island's vineyards. From here a rough trail leads around the slopes of Mount Nerovouno (1,811 feet/552 m) to the handsomely set 17th-century **Monastery of the Taxiarchis.** Destroyed in the earthquake of 1953, its church was later rebuilt.

The second largest town on the island is in the north. **Stavros** is a lively market town in the hills, with a statue of Odysseus and, on the edge of the town, a small **Archaeological Museum** with local finds, including part of a terra-cotta mask on which the word *Odysseus* can be seen. It was found at nearby Pelikatas Hill, where there are the remains of a building, the closest anyone has come to establishing a possible location for the Palace of Odysseus. Down the hill from Stavros is the small resort and ferry port of **Frikes,** great for windsurfing. ∎

A blue-domed church gives a splash of color to the sun-baked hills of Ithaca.

Stavros

⬛ 313 C2

Archaeological Museum

☎ 0674 31309

🕐 Closed Mon.

Homer & the Odyssey

Little is known about the ancient Greek poet Homer, except that he may have been blind. We don't know where he was born, although Ithaca is one of several places that claim him as a son. Another is the island of Hios, where he is remembered in legend as a blind beggar poet. We don't even know when he lived, except that it was some time around the seventh century B.C.

Was Homer even the author of the two works with which he is credited, the *Iliad* and the *Odyssey*? As with the works of Shakespeare, it is sometimes hard to believe that one mind could have come up with such a rich and creative body of work. For some time it was thought that Homer might have been two different writers collaborating on the works, although the latest linguistic analyses suggest that both of them are indeed the work of one author.

The poems are based on a mix of history and myth, blended with the art of a supreme storyteller. In Homer's day, a poet was literally a teller of stories, for the great epics were related orally, not written down. The author had to be an actor, too—and possess a phenomenal memory.

The *Iliad* is set at the end of the Trojan Wars, which took place (if they happened at all) probably three centuries before Homer was born. There is no absolute proof of the existence of Troy, although it may have been established at Truva in Turkey, where archaeologist Heinrich Schliemann began excavating in 1870. He certainly believed that he had found the site of Troy, although Schliemann was always more noted for enthusiasm than accuracy. Research at Truva continues today.

The *Odyssey* is again an intriguing mix of legend, history, and heroism, leaving scholars guessing as to what is truth and what is fiction. The book follows the story of Odysseus, King of Ithaca, who after fighting in the Trojan Wars sets off on his voyage home, a journey so eventful as to make a Tom Cruise movie look tame.

Odysseus' journey from western Turkey to the Ionian islands takes ten years as a result of angering Poseidon, the sea god. An early encounter is with the Cyclops Polyphemus, a one-eyed giant who imprisons Odysseus and his men in a cave. To escape, Odysseus gets the Cyclops drunk and blinds him, but

Below: A full-size replica trireme, in dry-dock in Athens, shows how three sets of rowers would power these warships.
Right: Carved relief to the glory of Homer

unfortunately Polyphemus is the son of Poseidon, so….

Needless to say, when Odysseus does eventually make it home, after encounters with Sirens and whirlpools, shipwrecks and lotus-eaters, his adventures are still not over, for he must prove his identity to his faithful wife, Penelope (and confirm it with his old dog), and seize back power from those who have taken advantage of his absence and moved in. This he does after a tumultuous battle leads to a reunion in the best traditions of storytelling. ■

Kefalonia

ALTHOUGH CORFU IS THE BEST KNOWN OF THE IONIAN
islands, their administrative center, Kefalonia, is by far the largest at
301 square miles (781 sq km). The island encompasses a wide
variety of landscapes and features, from picture-perfect beaches
often used in Greek tourism advertising campaigns to mountains,
castles, and remote monasteries. This was the setting for Louis de
Bernière's novel *Corelli's Mandolin* (1994).

Kefalonia
🄰 313 C2
Visitor information
✉ Waterfront next to
Port Authority,
281 00 Argostoli
☎ 0671 22248

**Historical and
Folklore Museum**
✉ Ilia Zervou 12,
Argostoli
☎ 0671 28835
🕐 Closed Sun. &
Nov.–April
💲 $

Sadly, large parts of the island,
including the capital, Argostoli,
were badly affected by the devastating earthquake of 1953, and few old
houses remain. The one town that
did survive, in the far north of the
island, was **Fiskardon.** With its
18th-century mansions in bright
colors grouped around the
harbor, this shows how beautiful

the whole island was before the
natural disaster took its toll.
Fiskardon has been turned into a
fashionable resort, expensive by
local standards, but it is a memorable place to stay, with a lively
atmosphere and good restaurants.
    To find out what life was like
before the earthquake, and indeed
during it and the immediate

aftermath, visit the **Historical and Folklore Museum** in Argostoli. This is a superb museum by any standards, with emotional displays dealing with the quake, but also a large collection of furniture, costumes, historical documents, paintings, and re-created rooms. The capital also has an **Archaeological Museum** (*Rokku Vergoti, tel 0671 28300, closed Mon., $$*) with a room devoted to the Mycenean finds from the island.

Argostoli itself is a pleasant town with a busy port area and a good market nearby. Fishermen sell their catch from their boats by the waterside. There are waterfront tavernas and a lovely view across the bay to tree-filled slopes on the far side. The bay is crossed on the Drapanos Bridge, a flimsy-looking structure that nevertheless survived the earthquake. It was built in 1813 to provide easier access to the island's second town, Sami.

The road to the port of Sami on the east coast passes the **Drogarati Cave,** where steep steps lead down to one huge chamber, so big and acoustically perfect that concerts are held inside it in the summer. It is definitely one of the better caves open to tourists in Greece.

Another cave to the north of Sami is very different. The **Melissani Cave** is the site of an underground saltwater lake, wondrously illuminated by shafts of natural light where the roof of the cavern has fallen. The name translates as the Purple Cave, but it is usually a wonderful deep blue. Boats take visitors onto the water for a closer look at this haunting place, once a sanctuary to Pan.

A sanctuary to Aenios Zeus once crowned **Mount Ainos,** the highest point on the island at 5,340 feet (1,628 m). You can drive to the top, where the views are naturally impressive, but the latter part of the road is very rough. Many people leave their cars partway up and walk the rest of the way. The whole area is covered in the indigenous fir tree *Abies cephalonensis,* and the region is one of Greece's national parks, home also to wild horses.

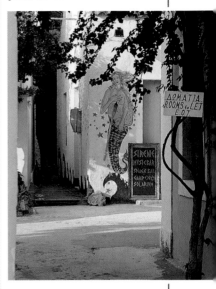

Northwest of the mountain is **Kastro,** the former capital of Kefalonia. Kastro normally means "castle," but in this case it is the name of the village that grew up around the mainly 16th-century Venetian **fortress of Agios Georgios,** whose walls afford excellent panoramic views. All of the huge overgrown interior is worth exploring.

The beach at **Mirtos,** on the west coast, is one of the most beautiful in the Ionians, if not the whole Mediterranean. There are many other gorgeous beaches, and while the tourism remains concentrated around **Lassi** and a few other south-coast resorts, the rest of this large island rewards those who are adventurous and look a bit farther. ■

Drogarati Cave
🕐 Closed winter
💲 $$

Melissani Cave
🕐 Closed winter
💲 $$

Agios Georgios Fortress
✉ Kastro village
🕐 Closed Mon.
💲 $

**Above right:
Rooms for rent in
a quiet corner**

Zakinthos

313 C1

Visitor information

✉ Tzoulati 1, Zakinthos town

☎ 0695 22518

Zakinthos

SOUTH OF KEFALONIA AND CONNECTED TO IT BY FERRY, Zakinthos (also known as Zante) is a popular island. Along with gorgeous sandy beaches and an interesting capital, the island posesses one unique asset: It is the principal nesting site in the Mediterranean of *Carreta carreta*, otherwise known as the green loggerhead turtle.

With dramatic cliffs and clear blue water, Wreck Beach is a popular stop on island tours.

The turtles have nested in **Laganas Bay** for thousands of years, but following the advent of tourism in the 1960s, they had competition for the lovely soft, golden sand in which they lay their eggs. Although the turtles came ashore at night to lay their eggs, during the day nests were being disturbed and eggs destroyed by the spikes on beach umbrellas. At nighttime the lights and music of increasing numbers of bars and discos disturbed and disoriented the animals. They also had the misfortune to nest on prime development land.

Thankfully, after pressure from environmental groups, the authorities took steps to protect the

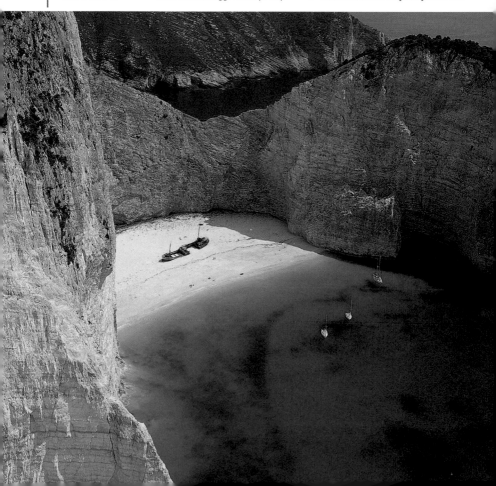

turtles to some extent, with stretches of the 8.5-mile (14 km) beach fenced off from visitors. Local people have also realized that the turtles themselves are a tourist attraction, even if hardly anyone ever sees them—buying the T-shirt is enough for most visitors. Laganas Bay is a gorgeous stretch of beach, but Laganas itself is a loud and tacky tourist town with few redeeming features.

The island's capital, **Zakinthos town,** was almost entirely wiped out in the earthquake of 1953 but has been tastefully rebuilt in a mostly successful attempt to re-create the original style. It has a very pretty waterfront, with lots of little fishing boats alongside the large inter-island ferries. Behind the waterfront are some attractive shopping streets, colonnaded to provide protection from sun in summer and rain in winter. They show the influence of the Venetians, who ruled here from 1484 until 1797 and who referred to the island as *fiore di Levante,* the flower of the East. They built a city here that was even finer than Corfu town, until the fateful earthquake razed it to the ground.

One building that did survive the earthquake (locals believe it was divine intervention) was the grand **cathedral** of 1925, dedicated to the island's patron saint, Agios Dionysios. Dionysios (1547–1622) is also the patron saint of fishermen. Interestingly, the church and chapel at the 16th-century monastery of **Moni tis Panagias tis Anafonitrias,** where St. Dionysios was the abbot for the last years of his life, also survived the earthquake. The monastery is on the northwest end of the island and is a popular inclusion in organized tours around Zakinthos.

The saint's bones are contained in a silver coffin in the cathedral in

National Anthem

The poet Dionysos Solomos was born on Zakinthos, and inside the museum to his memory is a piece of wood from a tree in the nearby hillside park of Strani. Solomos composed his poem "Ode to Freedom" beneath that tree in May 1823. Part of that poem, set to music, became the Greek National Anthem, "Hymn to Freedom."

Solomos was the first poet to compose in the vernacular rather than classical Greek. It was his belief that poetry should be available for everyone to read, not just the elite few. Now every Greek throughout the world knows at least one of his works. ■

Statue to Solomos in Zakinthos town

Zakinthos town, and his vestments are kept in the chapel of **Agios Nikolaos sto Molo,** at the far end of the harbor on Plateia Solomou. This fishermen's chapel was destroyed in the earthquake but lovingly rebuilt stone by stone, and given a new interior.

The square is named for the island's other famous son, the poet Dionysios Solomos (1798–1857), who like so many boys here was given the name of the local saint (see box). A **museum** to his memory stands next to his mausoleum. It has some of his personal effects, and there are displays on other prominent citizens, as well as photographs of the pre-earthquake town. The **Byzantine Museum** here is more interesting than many, for Zakinthos was one of the centers of the Ionian school of painting in the 17th and 18th centuries. The revolutionary, very realistic treatment of the saints by painters of the school is still striking today. ■

Solomos Museum
- ✉ Plateia Agiou Markou, Zakinthos town
- ☎ 0695 28982
- 🕐 Closed Mon.
- 💲 $

Byzantine Museum
- ✉ Plateia Solomou, Zakynthos town
- ☎ 0695 42714
- 🕐 Closed Mon.
- 💲 $

More places to visit in the Ionian islands

Some of the major Ionian islands have smaller offshore islands, where fewer visitors venture. Some offer accommodations, while others are accessible only by day. Whatever the options, you should see these smaller islands if time allows.

OFF CORFU

Corfu has a group of five small islands off its northwest coast, known as the Diapontia islands. Only three of these are inhabited, with very small populations, and while you might find basic rooms to rent if you wanted to escape the crowds for a few days, you could also take an organized boat trip to the islands from a resort such as Sidari or Agios Stefanos.

Ereikousa is the most popular destination, and this island has one good hotel and some excellent beaches. Many boat trips from Corfu just stop at Ereikousa, leaving people to enjoy themselves on the beach for a few hours and providing a tasty barbecue lunch.

Othonoi has some dramatic scenery inland and is the perfect choice if you want to spend your time walking. There are simple rooms to rent and a handful of tavernas.

Mathrakion, with only a few dozen inhabitants and a few rooms to rent, is the best of the three for both magnificent beaches and good walks. The beach is about 2 miles (3 km) long and occasionally busy with visitors from Corfu, but if you venture into the island's wooded and hilly center you will see no one, not even local people.
🄰 313 A5

OFF LEFKADA

Lefkada has several offshore islands, not all of which can be visited. The most famous is Skorpios, owned by the Onassis family. Aristotle Onassis (1906–1975) is buried here. Patrolled by armed guards, it is definitely off-limits to uninvited guests, as is Madhouri, another privately owned island.

You can visit **Meganisi,** the biggest island, easily reached by a short ferry ride from Nidri. Meganisi has a beautiful little harbor town, **Vathi,** where few visitors stay although some make the trip for a few days' visit over from Lefkada. It's a delightfully undeveloped place, little more than a village. A few minutes' walk up the winding, wooded road above Vathi brings you to **Katomeri.** This is the main village and the only one with a hotel, a pleasant and peaceful place to escape the crowds. You can easily explore Meganisi on foot. The deserted coves are little treasures.
🄰 313 C3 ∎

Local transportation in Meganisi

Travelwise

Getting about—in style

TRAVELWISE INFORMATION

PLANNING YOUR TRIP

WHEN TO GO

Greece is a year-round destination so if you can only travel in midsummer or midwinter, you'll still enjoy your visit. However, August is best avoided, not only because it is the peak vacation month, when space is short in hotel rooms and on beaches, but also because temperatures can soar to well over 100°F (38°C), and Athens in particular can be very uncomfortable. In midwinter there may be rain and temperatures below 50°F (10°C), but equally you may get clear blue skies and temperatures of 20°F (-6°C)— and no crowds outside the honeypots of Athens, Delphi, and Olympia.

The best time to visit is in the spring and the fall, when the weather is comfortably warm, there is little rain, and, since there are fewer vacationers, the naturally hospitable locals have time to talk to visitors. In the springtime wildflowers will be blooming and the landscape lush. If you wish to visit mountainous regions, late May onward is when the snow starts to melt and paths become passable again.

An especially good time to visit is during Easter week, when there are many celebrations: Easter is the most important festival in the Greek calendar. However, it only occasionally coincides with the dates of Western Christian Easter as it is determined by a different system, so check the dates.

WHAT TO TAKE

Greece is a casual country and in only a handful of more formal restaurants would men need a jacket and tie in the evening. If you're traveling in summer, casual dress such as shorts and T-shirts are all you will need during the day, plus a swimsuit as one is never far from a beach, and light cotton clothing for the evenings. It remains warm enough to eat outdoors until late at night during the summer, and even in spring and fall you would probably need to add only a sweater or light jacket. In summer it rarely rains in most of the Greek islands, and if it does it will be in the form of a short, sudden shower. Rain is more common in the Ionian islands and in the mountainous areas of northern Greece where a raincoat will be essential. In winter a warm coat or jacket and a sweater are advisable.

Mosquitoes occur in many places, especially in the greener Ionian and Sporades islands and on the mainland. They can be a minor nuisance almost anywhere and at any time of year, so carry plenty of repellent. This can be purchased locally, along with the effective plug-in mosquito-repellent devices that are now available.

Most medical supplies will be available unless you are traveling to a remote part of the country or an island where there is very little tourism. Pharmacies are usually well stocked and the staff knowledgeable, with good English. Make sure you have an ample supply of sunscreen— cooling breezes can be deceptive, and the Greek sun is fierce.

Take film for your camera with you. Color-print film is available everywhere, but it is expensive and may not be fresh. It could have been sitting in the sun for several weeks and have deteriorated in quality. Color-slide film is slightly more difficult to find; again it might not be fresh and will probably be more expensive than at home.

INSURANCE

You are advised to take out full travel and medical insurance for a visit to Greece. Public medical care is pretty basic, and while there is plenty of private medical treatment available, it is costly. Pharmacists or doctors' offices will deal adequately with minor injuries, but major ones could prove costly.

BOOKS ABOUT GREECE

There are numerous books about Greece, ancient and modern, which would enrich a visit here, depending on your interests.

Homer's *Odyssey* is a splendid adventure tale, while the *Histories of Herodotus* and the *Guide to Greece* by Pausanaias will add background to visits to many of the classical sites. *The Greek Myths*, by Robert Graves, will illuminate the often complex world of Greek mythology, and A.R. Burn's *History of Greece* is a good all-around introduction to the world of the ancient Greeks.

Modern Greece: A Short History, by C.M. Woodhouse, is a good way of bringing yourself up to date. The best of the 20th-century travelers' tales about Greece are those by Lawrence Durrell *(Prospero's Cell, Reflections on a Marine Venus)*, his brother Gerald Durrell *(My Family and Other Animals)*, Patrick Leigh Fermor *(Roumeli, Mani)*, and Henry Miller *(The Colossus of Maroussi)*.

For the Greek perspective read any of the novels by Nikos Kazantzakis, particularly his most famous *Zorba the Greek*. The poems of C.P. Cavafy, Odysseus Elytis, and Nobel-Prize winning George Seferis are also recommended. Other modern Greek novels available in translation include Eugenia Fakinou's *Astradeni*, the story of a teenage girl who moves to Athens, and Dido Sotiriou's best-seller, *Farewell Anatolia*.

HOW TO GET TO GREECE

BY AIR

Greece's main international airport is about 6 miles (10 km) east of downtown Athens, and it has two terminals, East and West. Greece's national airline, Olympic Airways (Tel 01966 6666), has scheduled flights to the West Terminal from major cities around the world. All other airlines use the East Terminal, a five-minute drive away. A new international airport, slightly farther from the city center, is scheduled to open in 2002, in readiness for the 2004 Olympic Games.

Direct flights to Greece from the U.S.A. include two a week from both New York and Boston on Olympic Airways, while Delta has a flight from New York to Athens. Other flights from major cities such as Chicago, Washington, D.C., Los Angeles, San Francisco, and Seattle are either through gateway cities in the U.S. or via European connections such as London (on British Airways, United, and others) or Amsterdam (on KLM).

From Athens there are numerous connecting flights to Greek airports on the mainland and throughout the islands. Olympic Airways has had a virtual monopoly of the internal services, but recently new carriers such as Cronos, Air Greece, and Kriti Air have provided competition.

BY SEA

There are several ferry services to Greece from Italy, notably from Bari, Brindisi, Ancona, Trieste, and Venice. Other services go from Croatia, including Dubrovnik. A journey between Italy and Greece costs from around $60 one-way for a foot passenger, up to around $250 for a car. Since agents in Greece normally only represent one ferry line, it is best not to consult them for general advice.

BY RAIL

Greek trains are cheaper than buses but also tend to be slower. If you are planning a long stay in Europe, it is worth considering crossing the continent by train. The route goes through France, Switzerland, or Italy and the journey takes about three days (You could stop off on the way). You can then cross by ferry from Italy to Patra in the Peloponnese and continue on to Athens.

ENTRY FORMALITIES

PASSPORTS & VISAS

A valid passport is required for all visitors to Greece, entitling them to stay for up to 90 days. Visas are required for a visit of over 90 days.

DRUGS & NARCOTICS

Customs inspections are usually fairly informal, but for anyone caught carrying drugs the penalties are severe. If you have prescription medicine, carry the prescription with you, both as a precaution at customs and in case you lose or use up your supplies. One anomaly is that codeine, which is widely available around the world as a painkiller, is illegal in Greece. You will not necessarily get into serious trouble for having it, but it may be confiscated.

PETS

Pets must have a valid health and rabies inoculation certificate issued between six days and six months before arrival for cats, and between six days and twelve months for other animals.

MONEY

There is no limit to the amount of foreign currency and traveler's checks that you can take into Greece, but if you are carrying more than $1,000 or its equivalent in cash then you should declare this on arrival.

Failure to do so may result in its confiscation. You cannot take out more money than you brought into the country, so there may be a problem if you cannot prove how much you brought in with you. Nonresidents can take into Greece up to 100,000 drachmas and take out again 20,000 drachmas.

GETTING AROUND

TRAVELING FROM ATHENS AIRPORT

BY PUBLIC TRANSPORTATION

You can get from the International Airport to Athens city center by public transportation. From 5:30 a.m. to 11:30 p.m. there are half-hourly express bus services from both East and West Terminals to central Athens. Most stop at Syntagma Square before going on to Omonoia Square, although some terminate at the bus station halfway between the two. During the night the service is hourly, on the half-hour. The cost is minimal, and journey time is about 40 minutes. Buy your ticket from the driver, and then stamp it in one of the machines on the bus. The return journey is usually easier by taxi.

BY TAXI

Do not take a taxi from solicitors inside the airport terminal building, but go outside and join the official line at the taxi rank. Check that the meter is switched on. If the meter is not working you should know that the fare from the present airport is no more than about 2,000 drachmas during the day for what should be a 15-minute journey, although the inevitable heavy traffic can slow that considerably. There is usually an additional charge for items of baggage. If you feel you are being overcharged then consult the reception desk at your hotel, where staff will know the correct fare. If all else fails, ask to call the Tourist Police (171 from any phone booth).

TRAVELING IN ATHENS

BY SUBWAY

Athens has three Metro (subway) lines, the main one (Line 1) running from Kifissia in the north to Pireas in the south, with useful central stops at Omonoia and Monastiraki. A new southeast–northwest line (Line 2) opened in 2000 and links Omonoia with Syntagma, and will eventually reach Glyfada on the coast. Line 3 will link Syntagma with Monastiraki and run out to Egaleo in the west, and eventually to the new airport at Spata in the east—in time for the Olympic Games in 2004 it is hoped.

The subway is divided into zones, and you pay according to how many zones you cross. Buy your ticket at the station and then time-stamp it in the machine as you enter the platforms. The service is very cheap and trains are frequent, but check destination boards as not all trains run the full length of each line. Lines 2 and 3 are wonderfully modern. While Line 1 shows its not inconsiderable age, its stations are slowly being renovated.

BY BUS

The Athens bus network is extensive and cheap. That said, buses are invariably very crowd-ed, hot in summer, and prone to cancellation. You will need geographical knowledge of the city and sometimes of the Greek alphabet to read the des-tinations if you plan to use buses. Within the center, walk-ing is usually the best option. If you do take a bus, note that tickets are bought in advance from kiosks near the major bus stops or from some stores. Stamp your ticket in a machine when you enter the bus.

BY TRAIN

The aboveground train network in central Athens is of little practical use to the visitor. The mainline stations serve the distant suburbs and the rest of Greece.

BY TAXI

Taxis are a convenient way of getting around and are very cheap, provided you have some idea of what the fares should be. The cars are yellow, and you simply wave them down in the street, although there are also several official taxi ranks. The bottom of Syntagma Square is a good place to pick up a taxi. They are not supposed to stop there other than to drop off passengers, but drivers usually take the opportunity to pick up a fare.

Athenian taxis are shared, and the driver is entitled to pick up other passengers to fill his vehicle; each person pays the fare on the meter. This arrange-ment counteracts a severe taxi shortage and boosts drivers' incomes without putting up individual fares. You will see Athenians standing in the street shouting their destination to passing taxis, in case they are headed in that direction.

TRAVELING AROUND THE COUNTRY

BY AIR

Greece has a good internal flight network, though most flights are to and from Athens, with a few connecting with Thessaloniki. It can frequently be more convenient to fly into Athens and out again, as a way of getting around the country. Fares are relatively inexpensive. Flights quickly get full during the summer months, so make advance reservations.

BY FERRY/BOAT

Greece has an excellent ferry service, as you might expect from one of the world's great maritime nations, although it can

be somewhat erratic. There are numerous rival ferry companies, and schedules change constantly (an up-to-date schedule can be obtained from the Greek National Tourist Organization). Boats may be canceled or delayed because of the weather conditions, so if you have a flight to catch allow an extra day in case of problems.

For travel between islands, or between the mainland and the islands, there are usually several choices. You will need to ask around to find out what these are, as travel agents often operate on behalf of one ferry line only. In addition to the slow and cheap regular ferries, there is a rapidly increasing network of hydrofoil services, which are much quicker but naturally much more expensive. If you get seasick, then you may feel the additional expense is worth it.

You will also find many small boats operating between neighboring islands or running excursion trips in the summer. Even if you don't want the full excursion these can sometimes be more convenient options than the larger commercial ferry services, and an individual running his own boat will be open to bargaining. Commercial fares are fixed, and tickets can be bought from a travel agent, sometimes from a table set up on the quayside or on the boat itself when it docks.

BY TRAIN

Because of its mountainous landscape and long tradition of traveling by sea, Greece has not developed an extensive railroad network. Trains are limited to the mainland, and whole areas of western Greece and the southeastern Peloponnese are not served at all. There are two mainline stations in Athens, one serving the Peloponnese, the other the more direct line to Thessaloniki and on through Macedonia and Thrace into Bulgaria and Turkey.

BY BUS

Greece has an excellent and extensive bus system, which is by far the most popular form of transportation for the Greeks themselves. There are few towns that do not have a busy bus station, and it can even be the simplest way of reaching some of the islands. For example, the Ionian islands have regular bus services to and from Athens, with the cost of the ferry included in the price.

Most rural areas are well served by buses, and the easiest way of traveling around many islands is by bus. On smaller islands buses will frequently meet an incoming ferry, to take passengers from the harbor to the main town. Rural bus journeys can be quite an experience, with passengers transporting all kinds of baggage and drivers carrying and delivering parcels for people and sometimes diverting from the route to do a favor for a friend. In addition to specific stops, most drivers will drop people off and pick them up anywhere that is convenient, so feel free to wave a bus down wherever you happen to be.

Tickets for the main intertown services (usually in reasonably comfortable air-conditioned buses) need to be bought in advance at the bus station; on local routes you may have to buy your ticket in a store near the main stop or on the bus itself. Schedules might be displayed on telegraph poles, placed in store windows, or pinned to walls, and may or may not be up-to-date and accurate. It is always best to check.

BY CAR

The general standard of driving in Greece is not good. Some drivers regard the middle of the road as their rightful place to be, which is disconcerting when coming around a blind bend. That said, provided you take care, driving in Greece can be enjoyable since it opens up areas of the mainland and the larger islands such as Rhodes, Crete, and Corfu, that are not easily accessible to tour groups.

Car rental

Renting a car in Greece is straightforward and a great pleasure, although expensive. All the major names such as Avis and Hertz have offices throughout the country, at airports, in major towns and cities, and on the larger islands. The established international names are usually more reliable. Some of the smaller firms run their fleets throughout the year, giving minimal attention to servicing, in order to keep costs down. However, if you travel at a quiet time of year, you are more likely to be able to negotiate a better deal with an independent company than with one of the international chains, whose prices are fixed.

An ordinary national driver's license is all you need, and car rental agreements automatically include third party insurance, which is a legal requirement. It would be wise to add personal accident insurance as accident rates here are among the highest in Europe. You must be at least 21 years of age, or 25 years for more powerful cars. There is a wide range of automobiles available. A credit card can be used as a deposit.

Roads & road signs

The standard of Greek roads is improving all the time, thanks to generous grants from the European Union. There are few roads of a standard comparable to expressways, but the average is a reasonable standard. Tolls apply on the expressways—but these are not expressways as you know them. Four lanes can become two without warning, and you may well encounter slow-moving farm vehicles. In rural areas a smooth-surfaced road can suddenly become a dirt track, with herds of animals a common hazard.

Road signs are not good and a decent map is essential. A knowledge of the Greek alphabet is also vital: main roads are usually marked in both Greek and Roman letters, but on side roads you may find signs in Greek only.

Regulations & rules of the road

In Greece driving is on the right, but in practice many drivers use the center of the road, especially when going around a corner, so be careful. Note that if a driver flashes his headlights at you, it is a warning that he is going ahead.

Speed limits are 31 mph (50 kph) in built-up areas, 49 mph (80 kph) outside built-up areas, and 62 mph (100 kph) on divided highways.

Seat belts must be worn where fitted, and drivers can be fined for not carrying a warning triangle, fire extinguisher, and first-aid kit.

Drunk driving (DWI) is a serious offense in Greece. One glass of wine or beer is probably enough to create a misdemeanor, and if you drink much more than that you will be committing a criminal offense leading to a possible prison sentence. Drivers should therefore observe complete abstinence.

Fuel

Unleaded gasoline is not available everywhere, although it is appearing much more widely. In remoter areas gas stations may be few and far between, so try to keep your tank full or check where there are gas stations. In smaller towns and villages stations will be family enterprises, so they may close on a Sunday, or you may find yourself being served by a small boy or girl who speaks no English. Many smaller stations don't accept credit cards, so be sure always to have some cash with you.

Parking

Parking in Greece is straight-forward, with only major cities having zones for which you need to buy a parking permit. Otherwise it is obvious that you either can or cannot park somewhere. If you do need a permit, there will be a notice in Greek and English on the street telling you where to obtain one (usually in a nearby store).

Accident & breakdown

In the event of an accident, for roadside assistance dial 104, the call-out number for ELPA (the main Greek recovery service, like the AAA). If you have a rented car you should have been given this or another emergency number to dial (see p. 346). It is an offense to drive away if you have been involved in an accident, which must be reported to the police. Do not sign any document that is written only in Greek.

Rental companies will tell you what to do in case of breakdown. They usually belong to one of the Greek equivalents of the AAA (ELPA, Hellas Service, or Express Service) and will give you the contact phone number in case of problems.

BY MOTORBIKE OR MOPED

Mopeds and motorbikes are usually available to rent in tourist centers and can be an excellent and economical way of getting around. Before taking to the road, be sure to check that the vehicle is in a safe condition. Although not mandatory, helmets are recommended. Rental rates can usually be talked down out of season.

HITCHHIKING

Hitching a short ride with a local is usually no problem as people are used to it. Hitching can be a good way to meet locals and try out your Greek. Longer rides might be less easy.

PRACTICAL ADVICE

COMMUNICATIONS

POST OFFICES

Post offices can be found practically everywhere in Greece. Even the smallest island has one, although it may also double as a bank or may be open only part-time. Major post offices, known as *tachydromeia*, are generally open Monday to Friday from 7:30 a.m. to 2 p.m., although some may stay open later on one night a week. Some also open on Saturdays until about noon. In larger post offices there will be separate lines for different services, so make sure you join the right one. Parcels have to be sealed in front of the post office clerk, which is why you will see people standing in line with scissors and scotch tape. If you only want postage stamps, look for the sign saying *grammatosima*.

Many post offices act as money exchanges, so look for an "Exchange" sign. The rates are often better than at travel agents or smaller exchange offices.

MAILBOXES

Mailboxes are yellow and usually small, so they are not always easy to spot at first. If you are visiting more isolated islands or remote places on the mainland, then you may well get home before your vacation postcards arrive. Otherwise, airmail letters to North America and elsewhere outside Europe take around 1–2 weeks (up to a week to European countries). Postcards can take even longer. Sometimes you will encounter separate boxes for domestic and international mail, and there are also red boxes, which are for express mail only.

TELEPHONES

There are numerous options for making phone calls in Greece, aside from in a hotel room where charges are excessive.

Local calls are cheap, but long-distance and international calls are very expensive.

You will see public pay phones all over the country, not just on the street but also at train and bus stations, by harbors, in hotel receptions, and at offices of OTE (the Greek national telephone company). Pay phones are increasingly taking phone cards, which are widely available, including from the little kiosks on every street corner. If you don't wish to buy a card, use the OTE office where the call will be metered and you can pay in cash or by credit card. Alternatively, do what many locals do, which is to use the phone that almost all street kiosks have, and pay in cash according to the meter. OTE offices can be found in most places, large or small, and are generally open from early in the morning until late in the evening, Monday to Saturday.

CONVERSIONS

Greece uses the metric system, so road signs are in kilometers, gas is sold in liters, and stores sell in grams and kilos.

1 mile = 1.61 kilometers
100 kilometers = about 62 miles
1 meter = 3.28 feet or 39.37 inches
1,000 meters = about 3,300 feet
1 liter = 0.264 U.S. gallons
10 liters = a little more than 2.5 gallons
1 kilogram = 2.20 pounds
2 kilograms = nearly 4.5 pounds

Weather reports are given in Celsius. The freezing point is 0°C. For an approximate conversion from Fahrenheit to Celsius, subtract 30 and divide by 2. To convert approximately from Celsius to Fahrenheit multiply by 2 and then add 30.

0°C = 32°F
10°C = 50°F
20°C = 68°F
30°C = 86°F
100°C = 212°F

Women's clothing

U.S.	6	8	10	12	14	16
Greece	36	38	40	42	44	46

Men's clothing

U.S.	36	38	40	42	44	46
Greece	46	48	50	52	54	56

Women's shoes

U.S.	6	6½	7	7½	8	8½
Greece	38	38	39	39	40	41

Men's shoes

U.S.	8	8½	9½	10½	11½	12
Greece	41	42	43	44	45	46

ELECTRICITY

The electricity supply is 220 volts/50 Hz AC. North American appliances will need a transformer. The Greek electrical socket is a simple one with two round pins and occasionally three where devices need to be earthed. If you forget to take an adapter with you, it should be possible to buy one in most vacation areas in supermarkets or electrical stores.

ETIQUETTE & LOCAL CUSTOMS

Greece is an informal country in many ways, yet good manners and courtesy are an essential part of everyday living. Most Greeks are very polite and exceptionally hospitable to strangers. They appreciate any attempts to speak their difficult language, and you should try to master at least the basic courtesy words. As in several languages, it is the custom when someone says *efharisto* (thank you) to reply with *parakalo* ("please," meaning "think nothing of it").

When Greeks meet they go through various formalities, such as asking about a person's family and health, and they take their time about this. Don't try to hurry them if you are waiting to be served. In Greece patience is not a virtue, it is a way of life. As with the French custom of always saying *bonjour*, you should first greet a Greek person politely with *kali mera* (good day) before starting the conversation.

Greece is a macho society, and you will seldom see Greek women sitting in male domains such as bars and cafés. Foreign women are allowed to break the rules and will never be made to feel uncomfortable. In return, they should dress modestly in public. In tourist areas it is increasingly common to see both men and women walking around in flimsy attire, but this is emphatically not approved of, simply tolerated. If you wish to respect your Greek hosts, you should dress discreetly. This applies particularly when visiting churches and monasteries, where you may not be admitted if you are wearing shorts and have bare arms, although some places are more open-minded about this than others. You will occasionally see Greek men and women wearing respectable shorts when visiting churches if there is no service taking place.

Topless sunbathing is quite widespread but not appreciated on busy beaches in town centers. Not many Greek women would go topless, but it is accepted that foreign women may wish to do so, with discretion. Nude sunbathing is officially restricted to a small number of designated nudist beaches, but provided you are sensible about it and do not offend anyone, you can usually find quiet coves and beaches where you can sunbathe naked if you wish.

INTERNET INFORMATION

www.greektravel.com/index.html
Excellent and comprehensive site with numerous links, from Greek enthusiast Matt Barrett

harpy.uccs.edu/greek/mycenae.html
Covers the art of the Aegean, Mycenae, and Tiryns

www.athensguide.com/athensmetro.html
For up-to-date information on the expanding Athens Metro

www.gogreece.com/
Guide to Greece and the islands

www.kypros.org/cgi-bin/lexicon/
Greek-English online dictionary

www.greekhotel.com/home.htm
Guide to Greek hotels and tour operators

www.hellasguide.gr/
General Greek guide

www.culture.gr/home/welcome.html
Hellenic Ministry of Culture

www.monopoli.gr/english.html
Now in Athens: listings magazine

odysseas.com/
General tourist guide to Greece

In addition, there are countless websites devoted to individual islands, districts, or towns, examples being:

www.psirri.gr/en
A guide to the newly fashionable Psirri district in Athens

www.symi-island.gr/
A guide to the island of Simi

LIQUOR LAWS

Greece has no restricting liquor laws. Alcohol is freely available in restaurants, bars, cafés, supermarkets, and other stores.

MEDIA

NEWSPAPERS

American newspapers are likely to be available in Athens the day after publication. Most major European newspapers are available on the evening of the day of publication. Try the kiosks around Syntagma Square. Foreign newspapers are also sold in major centers such as Thessaloniki and Rhodes town, and in summer in the main tourist destinations, but will probably appear a day or so late. In Athens there are several English-language publications to keep you abreast of world events from a Greek perspective. One of the longest standing is the *Athens News* (daily except Monday).

TELEVISION

Greece has two government-controlled television channels, ET 1 and ET 2. Both stations broadcast some foreign TV programs and movies with Greek subtitles. More recent movies tend to be dubbed into Greek. ET 1 has news summaries in English (check papers for timings), and most large hotels have cable or satellite TV picking up CNN and other English-language programs. There are numerous other channels, many of them regional and available by cable or satellite.

RADIO

Greek airwaves are full of stations—national, international, and local—and Greek music is never far away. The two state channels are known as ERT 1 and ERT 2; ERT 1 is divided into three programs on different frequencies. The BBC World Service can be picked up on short-wave frequencies and The First Program broadcasts a multilingual news service in English, French, German, and Arabic (728 KHz). English-only news bulletins are broadcast daily on ERT 2 (98 KHz).

The BBC World Service can be picked up on shortwave (MHz) frequencies with news broadcasts on the hour and a range of English-language programs. In Athens try 9.41, 12.09 or 15.07 MHz. In the Athens area the American Forces Radio Service also broadcasts, on 1484 and 1594 KHz, with news on the hour.

MONEY MATTERS

The Greek unit of currency is the drachma. There are coins for 10, 20, 50, 100, and 200 drachmas, with bills for 50, 100, 200, 500, 1,000, 5,000, and 10,000 drachmas. Change is normally given to the nearest five or ten drachmas, but you are often expected to produce the right amount for any transaction.

Traveler's checks can be changed at most banks, hotels, and post offices on production of a passport, and in some stores and restaurants in tourist areas, although at a less favorable rate of exchange. Post offices generally charge lower commission than banks or tourist exchanges. Look for the yellow English-language "Exchange" sign. Exchange rates are published in daily newspapers.

Credit cards are widely accepted in the more expensive hotels, stores, and restaurants in popular areas. Do not assume, however, that you need only travel with "plastic." In Greece it is normal to settle even large transactions in cash. "No checks" is a common sign, even in some mid-range Athens hotels.

NATIONAL HOLIDAYS

January 1 New Year's Day
January 6 Epiphany
March 25 Independence Day
February/March Shrove Monday (41 days pre-Easter)
March/April Good Friday, Easter Sunday, and the following Monday
May/June Whitmonday (50 days after Easter)
May 1 Labor Day
August 15 Assumption of the Virgin
October 28 Ochi Day
December 25/26 Christmas

On national holidays you will find almost everything closed, including sites, museums, banks, post offices, and some stores and restaurants. However, in

tourist areas and major cities, you will have no trouble finding somewhere to eat and to buy provisions. Traveling can be difficult, so check before setting off.

OPENING TIMES

Banks are generally open from 8 or 8:30 a.m. until 2 p.m. on weekdays only, and post offices from 7:30 a.m.–2. In larger towns some banks and post offices may open on Saturday mornings.

Stores open from 8 a.m. to 1 p.m., when they close for the afternoon. They generally reopen at about 5, until 8 p.m., but some supermarkets and stores catering for visitors stay open much later. Opening and closing times may vary by an hour or so, but all stores will close for those few afternoon hours. Stores are generally closed on Sundays, except in tourist areas.

It is difficult to be precise about opening hours for museums and ancient sites as the hours change from winter to summer, and at some sites according to the mood of the keeper. Most are almost invariably open all year-round, but are closed on Mondays and public holidays, except for major sites such as Delphi, Olympia, the Acropolis, and others in that league. Check locally for exact times.

PLACES OF WORSHIP

Greece is 97 percent Greek Orthodox, so only in major cities such as Athens and Thessaloniki will you find places of worship for other denominations or faiths. Contact the local visitor information center for details of locations and times of services. Elsewhere in Greece, you will not generally be able to attend services of your own religion. Visitors are always welcome to attend a Greek Orthodox Sunday morning service (you can stay for just as long or brief a time as you wish), and you should always dress respectfully.

REST ROOMS

Public lavatories in Greece are few and far between, and those that do exist are probably better avoided. Finding a friendly taverna or bar is the best bet, but standards still vary enormously. It's polite to ask if you can use the facilities, and most places will happily let you.

Greek plumbing is of a small nonstandard size, and pipes easily become blocked if toilet paper is flushed down them. Only in the latest hotels is this an exception, and even here you should check first. Bathrooms have a wastebasket for the disposal of toilet paper and sanitary napkins. It may seem unhygienic but it is better than a blocked pipe flooding the room.

PHOTOGRAPHY

The sun in Greece is strong, and slow film is ideal. Try to photograph ancient sites early in the morning before the crowds arrive and when the light is at its best. The deep blue seas and rustic villages make interesting subjects, and Greek people also like to be photographed, but it is polite to ask first. Never photograph near military bases, and ask permission first in museums and churches. Film is expensive, but major brands of film and camera batteries are widely available in tourist areas.

TIME DIFFERENCES

Greek time is seven hours ahead of U.S. and Canada Eastern Standard Time and ten hours ahead of Pacific Standard Time. It is two hours ahead of GMT (Greenwich Mean Time) and eight hours behind Australian New South Wales Time. Greek Summer Time begins on the last Sunday in March at 4 a.m. when clocks go forward an hour, and

ends at 4 a.m. on the last Sunday in September when they go back an hour. Take care if traveling at those times, especially spring, when ferries and flights could be missed. Dial 141 for a recorded time message in Greek.

TIPPING

In restaurants service is included, but it is normal to leave any small change left after paying the bill on the table. If you are very impressed with the service, a tip of a few hundred drachmas would not go amiss. A small bill also rewards the wine waiter or the person who clears the table.

In hotels you will seldom be pressured into tipping, but a small gratuity to the porter or barman of a 500 drachma bill will be gratefully accepted. For chambermaids, 500 drachmas per day, left at the end of the stay, would be generous. For taxi drivers, "keep the change" is the usual practice.

VISITORS WITH DISABILITIES

Visitors with disabilities may encounter difficulties in Greece. Hotels, transportation, and other facilities all lag behind the times. Although most Greeks are cheerfully helpful, you should assume nothing and check everything in advance. Things are slowly improving: For instance, most of the new Metro stations in Athens have disabled access. But be aware that visiting ancient sites and museums usually involves climbing steps and stairs and can be difficult if not impossible.

VISITOR INFORMATION

OFFICES ABROAD
The Greek National Tourist Organization (GNTO) has offices in:
Australia
51–57 Pitt Street, Sydney, NSW

2000, tel 612-9241 1663/5, fax 612-9235 2174
Canada
1300 Bay Street, Main Level, Toronto, Ontario M5R 3K8, tel (416) 968-2220, fax (416) 968-6533;
1223 Rue de la Montagne/Suite 101, Montreal, Quebec H3G 1Z2, tel (514) 871-1535, fax (514) 871-1498
United Kingdom
4 Conduit Street, London W1R 0DJ, tel (0207) 499 4976, fax (0207) 287 1369
United States
645 Fifth Avenue, New York, NY 10022, tel (212) 421-5777, fax (212) 826-6940;
168 North Michigan Avenue/Suite 600, Chicago IL 60601, tel (312) 782-1084, fax (312) 782-1091;
611 West 6th Street/Suite 2198, Los Angeles, CA 92668, tel (213) 626-6696, fax (213) 489-9744

MAINLAND GREECE
There are regional information offices in most large towns and cities on the mainland;
Head office of the GNTO in Athens PO Box 1017, Odos Amerikis 2, tel 01 331 0561, fax 01 323 0642.
There is a visitor information center at the same address, and information desks at the Athens airport East Terminal, tel 101 972 2395 and at Zea Marina in Pireas, tel 413 5716.
Thessaloníki Mitropoleos 34-54, tel 031 271888
Olympia Praxitelous Kondili, tel 0621 23100/23125

GREEK ISLANDS
Corfu Rizospaston Vouleuton & Iakovou Polyla, Corfu town, tel 0661 37520
Crete Marina Agiou Nikolaou, 72100 Agios Nikolaos, tel 081 228225
Rhodes Archiepiskopou Makariou and Papagou, 85 100 Rhodes town, tel 0241 23655
Samos 25th March 4, 83100 Samos, tel 0273 28582
Kos Akti Miaouli 2, 85300 Kos, tel 0531 70996

EMERGENCIES

CRIME & POLICE

Greece is one of the safest countries in the world, and you are unlikely to experience any problems with crime. Nevertheless, crime has increased in recent years—mostly petty theft—so keep your money and valuables in a money belt or leave them in the hotel safe. Athens is a city with very few no-go areas, and in tourist districts even late at night you should have no problems. Greeks are late-night people anyway, and the streets are often busy into the early hours of the morning.

Women traveling alone may be subject to the attentions of young Greek men known as *kamaki* (harpoonists). Most will stop if you are persistent in your refusals. If attention turns into harassment, ask the nearest Greek person for help: Most don't like to see this kind of behavior either. If you do need help, telephone the **Tourist Police** by dialing 171 from any pay phone in Athens. Note that outside Athens you will need to find the local number for the Tourist Police.

EMERGENCY TELEPHONE NUMBERS

Emergency calls are free from phone booths.
Medical emergency: In Athens dial **166**, or **171** for the Tourist Police. Elsewhere dial **166** for an ambulance *(asthenoforo)*, or **100**, which connects you to the branch of the police known as the *Ekato* (meaning "100"), who deal with fire and medical emergencies.
Fire *(fotyá):* **199**
Road assistance: 104 (call-out number for ELPA, the main Greek breakdown and recovery service, see p. 342). There are emergency telephones at regular intervals on highways.

EMBASSIES & CONSULATES

Canada G. Gennadiou 4, Athens, tel 01 725 4011

United Kingdom Ploutarchou 1, Athens, tel 01 723 6211

United States Vasilissis Sophias 91, Athens, tel 01 721 2951 e-mail: usembassy@pd.state.gov

There are also consulates in Thessaloniki for the United Kingdom (Venizelou 8, tel 031 278006) and United States (Nikis 59, tel 031 242905).

LOST PROPERTY

If you lose something there is a strong chance it will still be waiting for you if you can remember where you lost it, as the vast majority of Greeks are scrupulously honest. If you cannot recall where you lost your property, then report the loss to the hotel management or call the Tourist Police. You will in any case need a police report if you wish to make a claim.

HEALTH

There are no mandatory inoculations required for visiting Greece, but it is wise to be up-to-date with tetanus and polio injections.

Tap water is chlorinated and is considered safe to drink, but in the dry summer months drinking bottled water (which is inexpensive) may be safer.

MEDICAL TREATMENT

Greek pharmacists are highly trained and often multilingual. For minor ailments they can offer advice and a prescription. Look for the red cross sign or ask for the *farmakio*.

There are health centers in most towns, with signs in both Greek and English. Opening hours are usually 8 a.m.–noon only. If anything happens requiring

lengthy hospital treatment, you are advised to seek private treatment; it is superior to basic state care (which has to be paid for anyway). Medical insurance is therefore obviously essential. There are doctors in most large villages, and these are well trained and usually speak English. They are familiar with the common ailments that affect visitors and will do their best to help you.

Dental treatment is not available free of charge and should be covered by your private medical insurance. Check with the Tourist Police or at your hotel for the name of the nearest dentist. Have a check-up before leaving home.

HAZARDS

Sunburn is a common problem. Use sunscreen of as high a factor as your skin needs, and be particularly careful with children's skin. Wear a hat. To prevent dehydration, drink plenty of fluids (not alcoholic) and take salt with food.

When swimming beware of sea urchins and jellyfish. The former are common in rocky areas, so wear light shoes. If one of the black spines pierces your skin, it must be removed. Ask local people for help, or visit the farmakio. Jellyfish are less common and not all are poisonous, but if you are stung visit the farmakio for a remedy. Ammonia (urine) can be used in an emergency for both stings and urchin spines.

Mosquitoes can be a nuisance in many places, but they are not malarial. There are a few scorpions around, but they are very seldom seen, and the same goes for snakes. As long as you are careful when walking and don't turn over rocks or poke sticks into holes, you will probably never encounter either. Do not touch stray dogs, and if you are bitten seek medical help right away.

HOTELS & RESTAURANTS

The vast majority of accommodations in Greece are relatively inexpensive for the overseas visitor, with the exception of the top 5-star hotels. Standards vary enormously, and while there is a Greek accommodations rating system (see below) it is not a perfect guide. Don't automatically dismiss hotels in the lower categories, as many are spotlessly clean and beautifully located, but may lack some extras such as minibars or satellite television. If traveling in summer, especially in the popular tourist areas, it is vital to make advance reservations as a lot of accommodations are reserved by European travel companies. Outside these areas and outside the high season of July and August, finding somewhere acceptable to stay is rarely a problem.

Eating out is one of the great pleasures in Greece. For much of the year it is warm enough to eat outdoors, and there is a ready supply of fresh fish and meat, which, simply grilled and then eaten at a table right by the water's edge, is a delightful way to spend an evening. The Greeks are also natural hosts, and most restaurants and tavernas have a great atmosphere. As with hotels, appearances can be very deceptive. You are just as likely to find good food in a tiny back-street family taverna, where the husband waits on tables and his wife cooks in the kitchen, as in some seemingly classy restaurants that cater purely to the tourist trade and serve dishes adapted for it.

ACCOMMODATIONS

The official government rating system classifies all hotels and other accommodations from A to E, which very roughly corresponds to 5-star down to 1-star in other ratings systems. There is also a Deluxe category. The rating dictates the price, and accommodations are inspected and graded annually. The grading is taken seriously, and all establishments must display in each room an official notice that tells the grade of the hotel, the rate for that room at different periods of the year and for different numbers of occupants, and whether the price includes breakfast or not. If there is no such notice for you to check then the establishment is breaking the law, but early in

the year it is common to find the previous year's notice still displayed, until the new ones are available.

Checking in

If you are visiting a hotel without a reservation then it is the usual practice in Greece to ask to see the room first, before taking a room. When you check in, you must give them your passport for the hotel's records, and this will normally be returned to you within a day.

Breakfast is sometimes included in the price and sometimes an optional extra. In more expensive hotels, breakfast is normally a generous buffet including juices, fresh fruit, yogurt and honey, cereal, eggs, cheeses, cold meats, and a variety of breads. In more basic places, you may be offered just a few slices of cold toast and coffee. You may find more choice in nearby cafés.

Checking out

Most hotels will take major credit cards, but don't assume that you will always be able to pay by credit card in every establishment. Some smaller family-owned places will take only one type of card or none at all, requiring checks, or travelers' checks, or even preferring cash.

RESTAURANTS

There is no rating system for Greek restaurants, and ordinary-looking places can be wonderful, while classy-looking ones can be

dreadful. It is best to avoid any place that employs someone to stand outside and tempt you in, a ploy used only to inveigle overseas visitors who will probably never return, not Greek customers. So be cautious, although the rule is not infallible.

Many restaurants in tourist areas do not take reservations, so in some cases you will find no telephone number in the listings below. Most places are expandable; another table will be brought out unless they are absolutely at their maximum capacity, in which case you will be told how long you have to wait before a table is available. For this reason, the number of restaurant seats is not listed here, as for the vast majority of establishments it simply does not apply.

There are several types of eating establishment in Greece. Restaurants (estiatorio) are classier, and tavernas more casual. In a taverna you may well have a paper tablecloth, and in more out-of-the-way places the waiter may even use it to write the bill on at the end of the meal. There are also *psarotavernes*, which specialize in fish, and *psistaries*, which specialize in food cooked on a grill or spit roasted.

Eating times

Greeks tend to eat late, like other Mediterranean people. Lunch will not normally be before about 2 p.m., and dinner may begin as late as 9 or 10 p.m. Most restaurants catering to overseas customers open much earlier to suit their different dining habits.

Parking

Hardly any Greek restaurants have their own parking lots. In Athens and other major cities it would be madness to drive anyway, so take a taxi or walk. In smaller towns and on the islands, there is usually ample parking in streets nearby, and the Greeks take a relaxed attitude to parking. For these reasons, no indication is given in the restaurant listings as to parking availability.

Credit cards
Not all restaurants accept credit cards, so never assume that you can use one. Greeks prefer to pay in cash anyway, and as meals are generally inexpensive, paying in cash should not be a problem. Abbreviations used are AmEx (American Express), DC (Diners Club), MC (Mastercard), and V (Visa).

Facilities for visitors with disabilities
Few restaurants have customized facilities for customers with disabilities, as most are long established in old buildings. Despite this, the Greeks are wonderfully helpful, and staff will always lend a helping hand. Simply telephone first, and ask.

Summer or winter closing
A fair number of restaurants, especially in Athens, close for August and sometimes longer in the summer. This is often to escape the summer heat, at a time when many of their Athenian customers leave the city for a break on the islands. Some restaurateurs have island restaurants, which they open up for the summer months, before returning to Athens for the winter. Many island restaurants are therefore closed all winter! Set dates cannot be given here, as they vary year by year according to the whim of the owner, but where possible a rough indication of major closings is given in the listings.

In the following selection, under each location hotels are listed first, grouped according to price and in alphabetical order within each group, followed by restaurants similarly listed by price and alphabetical order.
L=lunch   D=dinner

ATHENS

As might be expected, there is a greater dining choice in Athens than anywhere else in Greece, with cuisines from all over the world as well as the best of Greek cooking. The Plaka is a popular eating area but has a number of poor places aimed purely at the passing foreign visitor trade, as well as some excellent and authentic Greek establishments. Nearby, the newly fashionable Psirri district (north of Monastiraki Square and to the west of Athinas) has a wide choice of truly Greek dining places, although you will certainly need your phrase book and menu reader.

SOMETHING SPECIAL

🏨 GRANDE BRETAGNE

Athens's landmark hotel right on Syntagma Square was built in 1864. It retains much of its old elegance but, inside are marbled interiors, a pool, modern business facilities, skyline city views, and a top restaurant. Illustrious guests have included Sir Winston Churchill, who stayed here in 1944 toward the end of World War II, and guests of King Otto, the first king of Greece, in the days when the nearby Parliament building was the Royal Palace. Top-floor front rooms are in demand, with their spectacular Acropolis views.

$$$$$
PLATEIA SYNTAGMATOS
TEL 01 333 0000
🛈 341   🚇 Syntagma   🅿
🛗 🚻   🐾 All major cards

🏨 HILTON
$$$$$
VASILISSIS SOFIAS 46
TEL 01 728 100
Typical Hilton high standards, and prices, but with an Athenian stamp on it. You'll enjoy its fine restaurants, and the lounges are a popular

PRICES

HOTELS
An indication of the cost of a double room without breakfast is given by $ signs.
$$$$$ Over $300
$$$$ $220–$300
$$$ $160–$220
$$ $80–$160
$ Under $80

RESTAURANTS
An indication of the cost of a three-course dinner without drinks is given by $ signs.
$$$$$ Over $80
$$$$ $50–$80
$$$ $35–$50
$$ $20–$35
$ Under $20

meeting place for coffee. Convenient for Syntagma, Benaki Museum, and National Gallery, but not the Plaka.
🛈 453   🚇 Evangelismos
🅿 🛗 🚻 📞 🐾 All major cards

🏨 ST. GEORGE LYKAVITTOS
$$$$$
KLEOMENOUS 2
TEL 01 729 0711
Very convenient and comfortable luxury hotel in the fashionable Kolonaki district. It has a highly recommended rooftop restaurant with good views of the city at night.
🛈 167   🚇 Syntagma   🅿
🛗 🚻 📞   🐾 All major cards

🏨 ANDROMEDA ATHENS
$$$$
TIMOLEONDOS VASSOU 22
TEL 01 641 5000
Luxury hotel in a quiet street aimed at the business traveler, with computers and fax machines available on request. **The White Elephant** is one of the best restaurants in town (see p. 352).
🛈 42   🚇 Evangelismos   🅿
🛗 📞   🐾 All major cards

HOTELS & RESTAURANTS

ATHENAEUM INTER-CONTINENTAL
$$$$
LEOFOROS SYNGROU
ANDREA 89–93
TEL 01 920 6000
Superb hotel from the Inter-Continental chain, adapted to Greek style with paintings and sculptures by modern Greek artists in the public areas. Range of stores, bars, and restaurants. A short walk into downtown.
[i] 520 🚕 Taxi P 🔁 🚭 🈁 🏋️ 💳 All major cards

DIVANI CARAVEL
$$$$
LEOFOROS VASILEOS
ALEXANDROU 2
TEL 01 720 7000
Very classy and modern hotel, much used by business travelers for its good facilities, and with a range of restaurants. Short walk or taxi ride to downtown.
[i] 470 🚇 Evangelismos; or taxi P 🔁 🚭 🈁 💳 All major cards

DIVANI PALACE ACROPOLIS
$$$$
PARTHENONAS 19–23
TEL 01 922 2945
One of the most chic modern hotels in the city, from the spacious, marbled reception area through to the deluxe rooms. It is also convenient to downtown and the Acropolis, with good eating places nearby.
[i] 253 🚕 Taxi P 🚭 🈁 💳 All major cards

DORIAN INN
$$$
PIREAS 15–17
TEL 01 523 9782
Very classy hotel near Omonoia Square, recently improved with the opening of the new subway lines. Centrally located and handy for the National Archaeological Museum. Beautiful

views of the Acropolis from the rooftop garden.
[i] 146 🚇 Omonoia P 🔁 🚭 🈁 💳 All major cards

ELEKTRA PALACE
$$$
NIKODIMOU 18
TEL 01 337 0000
Luxury option right in the Plaka, with rooftop pool and Acropolis views. All rooms have TV, telephone, and minibar. Extremely comfortable, and within walking distance of Syntagma and most of the main sights.
[i] 106 🚇 Syntagma P 🔁 🚭 🈁 💳 All major cards

HERODION
$$$
ROVERTOU GKALLI 4
TEL 01 923 6832
Classy hotel on south side of the Acropolis, away from the Plaka but with several highly recommended restaurants nearby. All rooms have TV and telephone. Rooftop terrace has magnificent views of the Parthenon.
[i] 90 🚕 Taxi 🔁 🚭 💳 All major cards

HOLIDAY INN
$$$
MICHALAKOPOULOU 50
TEL 01 727 8000
Located slightly away from downtown in the Ilisia district, this comfortable business hotel compensates by having all the facilities you might expect from a Holiday Inn, including a rooftop swimming pool and a choice of restaurants.
[i] 188 🚕 Taxi P 🔁 🚭 🈁 💳 All major cards

LEDRA MARRIOT
$$$
SINGROU 115
TEL 01 930 0000
One of the Marriot chain's superior hotels with light and spacious rooms plus all the facilities, close to downtown.

Don't miss its highly rated **Kona Kai** restaurant (see p. 352).
[i] 258 🚕 Taxi P 🔁 🚭 🈁 💳 All major cards

ROYAL OLYMPIC
$$$
ATHANASIOU DIAKOU 28-34
TEL 01 922 6411
Conveniently located near the Acropolis, and looking out over the ruins of the Temple of Olympian Zeus and Hadrian's Arch. The Olympic looks unimpressive from the outside, but its facilities are excellent and the rooms spacious.
[i] 304 🚇 Syntagma P 🔁 🚭 🈁 💳 All major cards

TITANIA
$$$
PANEPISTIMIOU 52
TEL 01 330 0111
Huge hotel with high standards, close to Omonoia and within walking distance from the Plaka and the National Archaeological Museum. Well-equipped rooms; roof bar with view of the Acropolis.
[i] 396 🚇 Omonoia P 🔁 🚭 💳 All major cards

ACHILLEAS
$$
LEKKA 21
TEL 01 323 3197
Newly renovated and reasonably priced hotel, very close to Syntagma. All rooms have bathrooms and are large, airy, and clean with balconies and phones. Don't let the mundane exterior put you off—there's a pleasant dining room on the first floor.
[i] 37 🚇 Syntagma 🔁 🚭 💳 All major cards

ACROPOLIS VIEW
$$
10 GKALLI AT WEBSTER ST.
TEL 01 921 7303
Good affordable upscale option on south side of the Acropolis, with wonderful

HOTELS & RESTAURANTS

views of the site. All rooms have telephones, and the hotel is in a quiet location near Philopappos Hill.
🛏 32   🚕 Taxi   🛗   ⊘
🐾 AmEx, Euro, MC, Visa

🏨 ATHENIAN INN
$$
HARITOS 22
TEL 01 723 8097
A quietly located and long-established hotel in the fashionable Kolonaki district, with views of Lykavittos from some rooms. Traditional furnishings in large rooms. This reasonably priced hotel is a favorite of authors and artists.
🛏 28   🚇 Syntagma   🛗
⊘   🐾 All major cards

🏨 ATHEAS ACROPOLE
$$
PIREAS 1
TEL 01 523 1111
This large, moderately priced hotel close to Omonoia has been renovated and has clean rooms, all with telephones. Bar, restaurant, and lounges.
🛏 167   🚇 Omonoia   🅿
🛗   ⊘   🐾 All major cards

🏨 LA MIRAGE
$$
KOTOPOULI 3
TEL 01 523 4755
On Omonoia Square but shielded from the noise, all of the rooms have telephone and minibar. Good example of a C-Class hotel, with restaurant, bar, and lounges. Reasonable rates for those who want to be where it's all happening.
🛏 208   🚇 Omonoia   🅿
🛗   ⊘   🐾 All major cards

🏨 NEFELI
$$
YPERIDOU 16
TEL 01 322 8044
This is a small, family-run hotel that has many regular visitors. It is inexpensive, friendly, modern, and spotlessly clean, although some of the rooms are small. It is

convenient to both the Plaka and downtown.
🛏 18   🚇 Syntagma   🛗
⊘   🐾 AmEx, V

🏨 PHILLIPOS
$$
MITSEON 3
TEL 01 922 3611
Good mid-range option for the Makriyanni district, south of the Acropolis and close to several excellent restaurants. All rooms have telephones and TVs.
🛏 48   🚕 Taxi   🛗   ⊘
🐾 All major cards

🏨 PLAKA
$$
KARNIKAREAS 7
TEL 01 322 2096
Slightly pricier Plaka option, but chic, clean, modern, and bright in both the public areas and the rooms. Extremely well located close to Mitropoleos. Some rooms have views of the Acropolis, as does the roof garden.
🛏 67   🚇 Monastiraki   🛗
⊘   🐾 All major cards

🏨 ACROPOLIS HOUSE
$
KODROU 6–8
TEL 01 322 2344
Inexpensive Plaka option in restored mid-19th-century mansion. Well maintained and family-run, it is a great place for those who prefer charm and character to modern conveniences (not all rooms have bathtubs).
🛏 19   🚇 Syntagma   🛗
⊘   🐾 V

🏨 ADONIS
$
KODROU 3
TEL 01 324 9737
Good standard, economical hotel in pedestrianized street right on the edge of the Plaka and not far from Syntagma. Helpful staff; breakfast room/bar with Acropolis views. Has many regular visitors.
🛏 20   🚇 Syntagma   🛗   ⊘

PRICES

HOTELS
An indication of the cost of a double room without breakfast is given by **$** signs.
$$$$$	Over $300
$$$$	$220–$300
$$$	$160–$220
$$	$80–$160
$	Under $80

RESTAURANTS
An indication of the cost of a three-course dinner without drinks is given by $ signs.
$$$$$	Over $80
$$$$	$50–$80
$$$	$35–$50
$$	$20–$35
$	Under $20

🏨 ATTALOS
$
ATHINAS 29
TEL 01 321 2801
Simple but clean and well-equipped C-class hotel with friendly service. Very convenient to the Plaka, flea market, and Monastiraki subway if you're heading for the ferries.
🛏 80   🚇 Monastiraki   🛗
⊘   🐾 All major cards

🏨 CAROLINA
$
KOLOKOTRONI 55
TEL 01 324 3551
A budget option that has seen better days but is perfectly acceptable if funds are limited. Some rooms are ensuite and most are small, but they are kept clean and it is a convenient central base.
🛏 31   🚇 Monastiraki   🛗
⊘   🐾 AmEx, Euro, MC, Visa

🏨 EXARCHION
$
THEMISTOKLEOUS 55
TEL 01 380 0731
Inexpensive option located close to the National Archaeological Museum in the lively student area of Exarchia. Many

rooms have a balcony, and there is also a rooftop dining area/bar.
(i) 49 🚇 Omonoia ⬍

🏨 IDEAL
$
NOTARA 142, PIREAS
TEL 01 429 4050
Hotels in Pireas can be expensive or seedy, but the Ideal is neither. Near the international ferry ports; the rooms are very clean. Worth making advance reservations if you need to spend a night in Pireas.
(i) 31 🚇 Pireas (long walk)/ Airport bus ⬍ 🌀
🌀 AmEx

🏨 KOUROS
$
KODROU 11
TEL 01 322 7431
Budget option in a street with several small hotels. In an ideal situation—quiet, but a few yards from the heart of the Plaka. No frills here, but rooms are clean and sizeable. The hotel was formerly a mansion.
(i) 10 🚇 Syntagma ⬍
🌀 🌀 No credit cards

🏨 LILIA
$
ZEAS 131, PIREAS
TEL 01 417 9108
Pleasant setting away from the noisy waterfront; clean, comfortable rooms. The closest harbor is Zea Marina, used by hydrofoils and catamarans to many destinations.
(i) 17 🚇 Pireas (taxi from here advisable)/Airport bus ⬍ 🌀 🌀 AmEx, V

🏨 MARBLE HOUSE PENSION
$
ZINNI 35A
TEL 01 923 4058
Friendly, inexpensive small hotel in quiet location, a short walk from the southern side of the Acropolis. Half the rooms are ensuite, some have vine-covered balconies.

Owners extremely helpful.
(i) 16 🚕 Taxi 🌀 🌀 No credit cards

🏨 MUSEUM HOTEL
$
BOUBOULINAS 16
TEL 01 360 5611
Behind the Archaeological Museum but overlooking its gardens. Quiet and well maintained, this is a good affordable option if you want to be in this area. All rooms have a telephone.
(i) 58 🚇 Omonoia 🅿️ ⬍ 🌀 🌀 AmEx, DC, V

🏨 ORION
$
EMMANUEL BENAKI 105
TEL 01 382 7362
Very cheap but perfectly acceptable if you're traveling on a strict budget and don't mind a long walk to the nearest subway station (Omonoia). In the lively Exarchia district, great for student nightlife and bars.
(i) 23 🚇 Omonoia ⬍ 🌀 🌀 No credit cards

🍴 L'ABREUVOIR
$$$
XENOKRATOUS 51
TEL 01 722 9106
Upscale French restaurant in Kolonaki, where Pavarotti and other celebrities have dined. Elegant decor and equally elegant food: steaks a specialty. Extensive and expensive wine list.
🌀 🚇 Syntagma 🌀 All major cards

🍴 BOSCHETTO
$$$
EVANGELISMOS PARK
TEL 01 721 0893
This delightful Italian restaurant, in Evangelismos Park on the edge of Kolonaki, serves fashionable food and fresh pasta, and uses ingredients popular in both Greece and Italy: squid, spinach, zucchini, cheese.

🕐 Closed Sun., L in winter, & 2 weeks in Aug. 🌀 🌀 All major cards

🍴 DOURAMBEIS
$$$
ATHENA DILAVERI 29, PIREAS
TEL 01 412 2092
A simple restaurant but with outstanding—and expensive—fresh fish dishes from the Aegean Islands, including a delicious crayfish soup. Established in 1932, this is one of the best in Pireas.
🚇 Pireas 🌀 🌀 All major cards

🍴 ERMOU & ASOMATON
$$$
ERMOU 137
TEL 01 324 6337
Stylish restaurant with extensive menu of sophisticated Greek and international dishes, including vegetarian and unusual options such as smoked eel or chicken in yogurt, mint, mustard, and lemon.
🚇 Theseion 🕐 Closed L Mon.–Fri. 🌀 🌀 All major cards

🍴 FAR EAST
$$$
STADIOU 7
TEL 01 323 4996
Excellent Chinese restaurant with a vast menu which incorporates Japanese and Korean dishes alongside Chinese favorites: hot and sour soup, sweet and sour pork, crispy duck.
🚇 Syntagma 🌀 🌀 All major cards

🍴 GB CORNER
$$$
GRANDE BRETAGNE HOTEL, PLATEIA SYNTAGMATOS
TEL 01 333 0000
Part of the **Grande Bretagne Hotel** (see p. 348), this restaurant with a piano bar serves a variety of good traditional Greek cuisine and continental cooking.
🚇 Syntagma 🌀 🌀 All major cards

🍴 GEROFINIKAS
$$$
PINDAROU 10
TEL 01 362 2719
Excellent food with a strong Middle Eastern influence. Chic and secluded.

🚇 Syntagma 🕐 Closed national holidays 🅱 🅰 All major cards

🍴 IDEAL
$$
PANEPESTIMIOU 46
TEL 01 330 3000
Chic restaurant, with attentive service and an extensive menu, including "drunkard's tidbits" (pork in a tomato sauce with olives, onions, mushrooms, and cheese) or shrimp with feta.

🚇 Omonoia 🕐 Closed Sun. 🅱 🅰 All major cards

🍴 KIKU
$$$
DIMOKRITOU 12
TEL 01 364 7033
One of the best, but most expensive, Japanese restaurants in Athens, with sushi and sashimi prepared by Japanese chefs. Located in the Kolonaki district, it caters more to business and diplomatic visitors than to tourists.

🚇 Syntagma 🕐 Closed Sun. L, & midsummer 🅱 🅰 All major cards

🍴 KONA KAI
$$$
SYNGROU 115
TEL 01 930 0000
This restaurant in the **Ledra Marriot Hotel** (see p. 349) specializes in Polynesian food (with decor as exotic as the dishes) but also has a Japanese menu. Very popular, so reservations are advisable.

🕐 Closed L Sun., & mid-Aug. 🅱 🅰 All major cards

🍴 PIL POUL
$$$
APOSTOLOU PAVLOU/ POULOPOULOU
TEL 01 342 3665

The Theseion and Psirri districts are the places to head for good modern Greek cooking, and this fashionable place also offers views of the Acropolis.

🚇 Theseion 🕐 Closed L daily & Sun. D 🅱 🅰 All major cards

🍴 SYMPOSIO
$$$
ERECHTHIOU 46
TEL 01 922 5321
Combines superior food with a relaxed atmosphere and a very popular late-night bar in an elegant house. Menu blends Greek and international dishes, such as pasta with cheese from Metsovon.

🕐 Closed L & Sun. D 🅱 🅰 All major cards

🍴 TA NISSIA
$$$
HILTON HOTEL, VASILISSIS SOFIAS 46
TEL 01 725 0201
The fresh fish dishes are particularly good. Try the Greek "Mezedakia Experience" for a starter— which may also finish you for the evening! An expensive treat.

🚇 Syntagma 🅱 🅰 All major cards

🍴 VARDIS
$$$
DELIGIANNI 66
TEL 01 623 0650
In the Pentelikon Hotel in Kifissia is this elegant French restaurant serving lobster, filet mignon, a range of other meat dishes, and salads. Pianist plays in the evening. Costly but good quality.

🚇 Kifisia 🅱 🅰 All major cards

🍴 VAROULKO
$$$
DELIYIORYI 14, PIREAS
TEL 01 411 2043
Modern Greek and Continental cuisine, with an unusual menu including such surprises as grape leaves

stuffed with fish. Monkfish is the chef's specialty. Reservations advised as there's often a line.

🚇 Pireas 🕐 Closed L, Sun., & Aug. 🅱 🅰 All major cards

🍴 WHITE ELEPHANT
$$$
TIMOLEONTOS VASSOU 22
TEL 01 643 7302
Based in the **Andromeda Hotel** (see p. 348), this is the place to come if your palate is in need of something from the Orient. Hot Szechuan and other Chinese dishes mix with Indian, Thai, and Polynesian specialties. Very pricey.

🕐 Closed L, Sun., & July–Aug. 🅱 🅰 All major cards

🍴 ALLI SKALA
$$
SERIFOU 57, PIREAS
TEL 01 482 7722
A distinguished restaurant with a wonderful courtyard, but not overpriced for Pireas. Has a wider menu than just seafish, including meats and excellent examples of good Greek homecooking.

🚇 Pireas 🕐 Closed L 🅱 🅰 All major cards

🍴 TO CAFENEIO
$$
LOUKIANOU 26
TEL 01 722 9056
Chic but relaxed restaurant in Kolonaki, serving excellent Greek specialties such as spinach pie, baked eggplant with cheese, chicken in lemon sauce, and other dishes to an international clientele.

🚇 Syntagma 🕐 Closed Sun. & all Aug. 🅱 🅰 All major cards

🍴 AL CONVENTO
$$
ANAPIRON POLIMOU 4-6
TEL 01 723 9163
One of the more affordable of Athens' several Italian restaurants, and claims to be the oldest. Very friendly place

serving spaghetti dishes and pizzas, and its house specialty: pasta and scallopine.

🚇 Syntagma 🕐 Closed L & Sun. ❄ 💳 All major cards

🍴 BOKARIS
$$
SOKRATOUS 17
TEL 01 801 2589
This renowned eating place in Athens's fashionable northern suburb of Kifissia has a pretty outdoor seating area, a good wine list, and excellent grilled meat and fish dishes.

🚇 Kifissia 🕐 Closed Mon.–Sat. L & Aug. ❄ 💳 All major cards

🍴 COSTOYANNIS
$$
ZAIMI 37
TEL 01 821 2496
Taverna of great character, appealing to everyone: students, businesspeople, tourists. Good reputation for appetizers and fish dishes, and a better-than-average house wine. Near the Archaeological Museum.

🚇 Omonoia 🕐 Closed L & Sun. ❄ 💳 All major cards

🍴 FAMAGUSTA
$$
ZAGORAS 8
TEL 01 778 5229
Many Greek restaurants you visit overseas are actually Cypriot, and this place near the Hilton Hotel shows why that island's food is popular, blending hearty Greek fare with Middle Eastern subtlety. Candlelit with music.

🚇 Syntagma 🕐 Closed L ❄ 💳 All major cards

🍴 KOLLIAS
$$
STRATIGOU PLASTIRA 3, PIREAS
TEL 01 462 9620
Renowned Pireas fish restaurant, which ranges superbly from the conventional (mackerel, mussels, lobster) to the unusual (shrimp and tomato

soup, scorpionfish). Friendly service, inspired cooking.

🚇 Pireas 🕐 Closed Sun., Aug., & L summer ❄ 💳 All major cards

🍴 PALIA TAVERNA
$$
MARKOU MOUSOUROU 35
TEL 01 701 7135
Established in the late 19th century, this taverna remains traditional in both its dishes and its atmosphere. There is often music, always good service, indoor and outdoor seating, and a reliable menu.

🕐 Closed L & Sun. ❄ 💳 All major cards

🍴 PANORAMA
$$
IRAKLIOU 18-20, PIREAS
TEL 01 413 3953
Near the Pireas acropolis and away from the bustle of the harbor, you can still get fresh fish (bream, mullet, swordfish) at reasonable prices with, as the name implies, panoramic views over Pireas.

🚇 Pireas ❄ 💳 All major cards

🍴 PICCOLINO
$$
SOTIROS 26/KYDATHINAION
TEL 01 324 6692
Similar to the other Plaka restaurants that surround it, but good service and food, such as a generous plate of taramosalata, tsatsiki, hummus, eggplant, and potato salads.

🚇 Syntagma ❄ 💳 All major cards

🍴 PRUNIER
$$
IPSILANTOU 63
TEL 01 722 7379
This French bistro near the Hilton Hotel offers a romantic setting with typical bistro dishes, such as coq au vin and escargots. Some more exotic choices too, like quail in oregano and lemon sauce.

🚇 Syntagma 🕐 Closed L daily, Sun., & Aug. ❄ 💳 All major cards

🍴 XINOS
$$
ANGELOU GERONTA 4
TEL 01 322 1065
In a Plaka back street that few tourists find, this is very popular with Athenians. Superior food, music late in the evening, and charming outdoor garden seating.

🚇 Syntagma 🕐 Closed L daily, Sat., Sun., & winter ❄ 💳 All major cards

🍴 BAKALARAKIA
$
KYDATHINAION 41
TEL 01 322 5084
Simple Greek food in what claims to be the oldest taverna in Athens, established in 1865. Salt cod in garlic is the specialty that gives this basement place its name.

🚇 Monastiraki 🕐 Closed L midsummer ❄ 💳 No credit cards

🍴 BARBA YANNIS
$
EMMANUEL BENAKI 94
TEL 01 330 0185
This great favorite frequently has lines outside the door. Brisk service, and a limited menu of good hearty Greek dishes. There is often impromptu music.

🚇 Omonoia 🕐 Closed Sun. D & Aug. ❄ 💳 No credit cards

SOMETHING SPECIAL

🍴 EDEN
This was the first purely vegetarian restaurant in Athens, and serves food so tasty that meat eaters will not notice its absence. The bread is delicious, baked daily, and your coffee cup will be endlessly refilled.
$
PLAKA 12
TEL 01 324 8858
🚇 Monastiraki 🕐 Closed Tues. ❄ ❄ 💳 All major cards

🍴 FIVE BROTHERS
$
EOLOU 3
TEL 01 325 0088
Indoor and outdoor seating near the Roman Agora with various fixed-price menu options, generous portions, and good grills and chops. A decent house wine and friendly waiters add to the appeal.
🚇 Monastiraki 🔄 💳 All major cards

🍴 HERMION
$$
PANDROSSOU 7–15
TEL 01 324 6725
Long-established restaurant just off the flea market, with both indoor seating and attractive courtyard dining area. Excellent service of good quality, moderately priced Greek favorites.
🚇 Monastiraki 🔄 💳 All major cards

🍴 KOUKLIS
$
TRIPODON 14
TEL 01 324 7605
Also known as To Yerani, this ouzerie is a well-established favorite, concentrating on hearty meze (snacks) such as *saganaki* (deep-fried cheese), taramosalata, fried fish, and sausages cooked in ouzo. Pleasant dining terrace too.
🚇 Monastiraki 🔄 💳 All major cards

🍴 NEON
$
MITROPOLEOS 3
TEL 01 322 8155
Neon is one of a chain of restaurants worth knowing about if you are in a hurry, or perhaps have children and want somewhere a bit less formal and more cafeteria-style. Inexpensive, clean, lots of seating and an international menu including pastas, steaks, chicken, and a range of simple Greek dishes.
🚇 Syntagma 💳 No credit cards

🍴 O PLATANOS
$
DIOGENOUS 4
TEL 01 322 0666
An Athenian favorite that offers few concessions to tourism. It has one of the best locations in the Plaka, with tables outside in the summer under the plane tree that gives it its name.
🚇 Monastiraki 🕐 Closed Sun. 🔄 💳 No credit cards

🍴 I SAITA
$
KYDATHINAION 21
Unpretentious basement taverna, wine from the barrel, murals on the walls, with a standard menu that occasionally offers some delicious surprises, such as pork in a cream of celery sauce.
🚇 Syntagma 🕐 Closed L 🔄 💳 No credit cards

SOMETHING SPECIAL

🍴 SIGALAS
For an authentic Athenian dining experience, Sigalas cannot be beaten. It is right on the busy Monastiraki Square, with the bustle extending into the warren of the restaurant itself. Waiters in red sweaters rush about, some looking as if they have been there since the restaurant opened at the end of the 19th century. It is a casual place, where arguments and laughter rage, old photos plaster every wall, and the food comprises good, inexpensive examples of standard Greek taverna fare. On weekends, arrive early.
$
PLATEIA MONASTIRAKI 2
TEL 01 321 3036
🚇 Monastiraki 🕐 Closed L 🔄 💳 No credit cards

🍴 SOCRATES PRISON
$
MITSEON 20
TEL 01 922 3434

<table>
<tr><td colspan="2" style="background:grey;text-align:center">**PRICES**</td></tr>
<tr><td colspan="2">**HOTELS**
An indication of the cost of a double room without breakfast is given by **$** signs.</td></tr>
<tr><td>**$$$$$**</td><td>Over $300</td></tr>
<tr><td>**$$$$**</td><td>$220– $300</td></tr>
<tr><td>**$$$**</td><td>$160–$220</td></tr>
<tr><td>**$$**</td><td>$80–$160</td></tr>
<tr><td>**$**</td><td>Under $80</td></tr>
<tr><td colspan="2">**RESTAURANTS**
An indication of the cost of a three-course dinner without drinks is given by $ signs.</td></tr>
<tr><td>**$$$$$**</td><td>Over $80</td></tr>
<tr><td>**$$$$**</td><td>$50–$80</td></tr>
<tr><td>**$$$**</td><td>$35–$50</td></tr>
<tr><td>**$$**</td><td>$20–$35</td></tr>
<tr><td>**$**</td><td>Under $20</td></tr>
</table>

Lively place justifiably popular for its unusual dishes such as pork stuffed with vegetables, an excellent house wine, and homemade desserts like walnut cake. Both outdoor and indoor seating.
🚇 Syntagma 🕐 Closed L & Aug. 🔄 💳 All major cards

🍴 STROFI
$
ROBERTO GKALLI 25
TEL 01 921 4130
With views of the Acropolis from the roof, this is an understandably popular place serving good Greek staples, especially roast lamb and a wide range of meze.
🚇 Syntagma 🕐 Closed L & Sun. 🔄 💳 All major cards

🍴 TAVERNA TOU PSYRRI
$
AISCHYLOU 12
TEL 01 321 4923
One of the eating places that has transformed the Psirri district. The taverna's owner is from Naxos and his menu reflects the fact, with an emphasis on good fish and meat, and fresh produce imported from the island.
🚇 Monastiraki 🕐 Closed D 🔄 💳 All major cards

VASILAINAS
$
ETOLIKOU 72, PIREAS
TEL 01 461 2457
There are inexpensive places in Pireas if you forget fresh fish, which is always pricey in Greece. This taverna has been here since the 1930s and is noted for its set menu of 16 different dishes, a rainbow of Greek flavors.
Pireas Closed L & Sun. All major cards

TO YPOGEIO TIS PLAKAS
$
KYDATHINAION 10
TEL 01 322 4304
Great basement restaurant in the Plaka, with old-fashioned murals by local artist George Savakis, good simple Greek food such as souvlaki and calamaris, with retsina straight from the barrel.
Syntagma Closed L No credit cards

ZONAR'S
$
PANEPISTIMIOU 9
TEL 01 322 6990
Snacks, coffee, delicious pastries, and light meals in a café that's been popular since the 1930s and manages to retain an atmosphere of that era.
Syntagma All major cards

AROUND ATHENS

AKRA SOUNION

EGEON
$$
AKRA SOUNION
TEL 0292 39200
Clean and spacious hotel right on the beach with good restaurant and moderate prices. Very well placed for enjoying Sounion's bay and, above, the famous temple.
45 All major cards

ILIAS
$$
AKRA SOUNION
TEL 0292 39114
An alternative to the eating places outside the Temple of Poseidon is this fish taverna on the beach below. Less impressive view but slightly cheaper. No surprises on the menu, but lots of good fresh fish.
No credit cards

MARATHON

GOLDEN COAST
$$$
MARATHON BEACH
TEL 0294 57100
Close to the Marathon sites and right on the beach, this huge hotel is a first-class option for anyone wanting to be near, but not in, Athens. Has four pools, nightclub, water-sports facilities, restaurants, and stores.
543 All major cards

VOULIAGMENI

ASTIR PALACE
$$$
VOULIAGMENI
TEL 01 890 2000
Luxury hotel complex that comprises three separate hotels, very convenient for the airport and right by the sea, with superb views over the Aegean. Superior facilities, with central Athens accessible by day.
571 All major cards

ARMONIA
$$
ARMONIAS 1
TEL 01 896 3304
This A-class hotel has spectacular views over the Saronic Gulf and caters for the business traveler, with numerous well-equipped conference rooms. Rooms all have telephone, TV, air conditioning, and piped music.

116 All major cards

PELOPONNESE

ANDRITSAINA

THEOXENIA HOTEL
$
ANDRITSAINA
TEL 0626 22219
The only hotel of any size in this mountain village. Facilities are basic but so are prices, and the rooms are clean and have telephones. Many also have splendid views of the surrounding mountains.
28 No credit cards

O YIORGIS
$
MAIN PLATEIA
TEL 0626 22004
The center of this mountain village is a perfect setting for this simple taverna. The food is staple hearty fare such as grilled chops and beef dishes, but the local produce is delicious. Go for either a freshly grilled souvlaki, or a succulent oven-baked dish such as youvetsi.
No credit cards

SIGOURI
$
SOPHOKLEOS
Hearty Greek dishes, made fresh each day in the kitchen of the owner. Specials might include moussaka or stuffed tomatoes, and there's wine from the barrel to drink.
No credit cards

CORINTH

EFIRA
$
ETHNIKIS ANTISTASSEOS 52
TEL 0741 22434
As in many of the mainland's most popular spots (Olympia, Delphi, Epidavros) there is a dearth of decent accommodations in Corinth, but

the Efira is an acceptable option. It has typical clean and simple Greek rooms and its own restaurant.
🛏 45 ⬍ 🅢 🚫No credit cards

KORONI

🏨 AUBERGE DE LA PLAGE
$
ZANGA BEACH
TEL 0725 22401
Given the superb views over Koroni's beautiful long bay of sandy beach and its castle, prices here are surprisingly reasonable. All rooms have balconies and sea views.
🛏 48 🅿 ⬍ 🅢 🚫No credit cards

🍴 OUZERIE KANGELARIOS
$$
WATERFRONT
TEL 0725 22648
The perfect place for an early or late ouzo, with a snack from the range of unusual meze on offer. Grilled fish are good, and other seafood includes shrimps, mussels, squid, octopus, and a rare chance to try sea urchins. (Eating them is far nicer than standing on them.)
🅢 🚫No credit cards

KITHERA

🍴 YDRAGOGEIO
$$
KAPSALI
TEL 0735 31065
This excellent restaurant on the edge of Kapsali has something for everyone. Enjoy a beautiful view, regular live music, friendly service, a convenient location, and, most important of all, excellent food. Vegetarian options include stuffed peppers, while the staples of fresh fish and grilled meats are enhanced by mouth-watering spinach-and-cheese pies and other homemade dishes.
🅢 🚫No credit cards

🍴 SOTIRIS
$$
AVLEMONAS
TEL 0735 33922
Sotiris sits right on the main square in Avlemonas but only opens on summer weekends. When open, though, there is no better place to sample the best of the day's catch from the local fishermen, such as tuna, mullet, and frequently obscure fish for which only the Greek name is known.
🕐 Closed Mon.–Fri.; winter
🅢 🚫No credit cards

MANI

🏨 EOT TRADITIONAL GUESTHOUSES
$$
EOT GUESTHOUSES, VATHIA
TEL 0733 55244
This government-run chain of hotels offers rooms in several converted Maniot tower houses, originally dating to the 18th and 19th centuries. They have small balconied rooms, with modern conveniences but in traditional style.
🛏 15 ⬍ 🅢 🚫No credit cards

🏨 KARDAMYLI BEACH HOTEL
$$
KARDAMYLI BEACH, KARDAMYLI
TEL 0721 73180
Excellent location in this popular beach resort, right by the beach, with many of the rooms having either sea views or views to the mountains of the Mani behind. The hotel stays open all year.
🛏 29 🅿 ⬍ 🅢 🏊 All major cards

🏨 LONDAS
$$
AREOPOLIS
TEL 0733 51360
The owners of this hotel are an artist and an architect, resulting in a sympathetic restoration from an old tower house into a comfortable

A-class hotel. There are only four rooms, so advance reservations are essential. The perfect base for exploring the Mani.
🛏 4 🅢 🚫No credit cards

🏨 PORTO VITILO HOTEL
$$
KAROVOSTASSI, NEAR NEO ITYLO
TEL 0733 59270
This B-class hotel shows that in Greece you don't need luxury ratings to provide stylish and comfortable rooms. All have canopied beds, and all have balconies with views of either the sea or the mountains. All are also air-conditioned, and there is a convenient on-site taverna as the hotel is a little way out of the village center.
🛏 24 🅢 Central heating
🚫No credit cards

🏨 AKTAION
$
VASILEOS PAVLOU 39, GITHIO
TEL 0733 23500
Right on the waterfront, this bright and pleasant hotel has been converted from one of the old port mansions. Front rooms have balconies with pretty harbor and sea views.
🛏 24 ⬍ 🅢 🚫No credit cards

🍴 KOZIA
$$
VASILEOS PAVLOU 13, GITHIO
TEL 0733 24086
Excellent seafood taverna with wide range of fresh fish along with meat dishes, vegetarian dishes, and salads as a cheaper option.
🅢 🚫All major cards

🍴 LELA'S
$
SEA FRONT, KARDAMYLI
TEL 0721 73541
Family-run taverna where mother cooks excellent home recipes. Friendly service and views out to sea.
🅢 🚫No credit cards

NISSI
$$
MARATHONISI
TEL 0733 22830
Take a boat out to the little island of Marathonisi, and dine with a view back to the town at this taverna whose name means simply "island." The menu is a reasonably safe list of Greek staples, such as moussaka and squid, but they are well done.
No credit cards

KLIMATERIA
$$
PLATEIA POLYTECHNIOU
TEL 0723 31544
One of the best restaurants in the Peloponnese, with lovingly prepared conventional Greek dishes, more imaginative gourmet options, a range of vegetarian meals, fresh fish and lobster, and fine wines. Choose whether you eat cheaply or more extravagantly.
Closed winter
All major cards

METHONI

ACHILLEAS HOTEL
$
METHONI
TEL 0723 31819
A small and simple B-class hotel in this popular resort, which exemplifies Greek value for money. If you are prepared to forgo TV and telephone in your room, and settle for the basic comforts, cleanliness, and a friendly and relaxed atmosphere, then this is a real bargain. The only facilities are a bar and a breakfast room, but it is convenient to town.
13 No credit cards

MONEMVASIA

MALVASIA
$$
KASTRO, MONEMVASIA
TEL 0732 61323
These converted old rooms are in the heart of the Monemvasia fortress, and

staying here at night gives the feeling of having closed the drawbridge on the world. Very tasteful rooms, some suites available.
16 All major cards

KANONI
$$
MAIN THROUGH ROAD OF OLD TOWN
TEL 0732 61387
Converted 17th-century mansion in the old town, where only the views can distract you from the food.
All major cards

MATOULA
$
KASTRO
TEL 0732 61660
Situated in the old part of Monemvasia, the Matoula has a terrace setting with tables looking out across the sea and along the Peloponnesian coast. The food does justice to the view, with hearty oven-baked dishes such as lamb casserole alongside grilled pork, chicken, and fish.
No credit cards

MYCENAE

BYZANTION
$
MYSTRAS
TEL 0731 83309
The best place for an early morning start to a visit to Mystras, which is visible from some of the upper rooms. Though only a B-class hotel it is clean and comfortable and has been recently renovated. It has its own restaurant, but there are a few other eating options nearby in this relaxed little village.
22 MC, V

OREA ELENI
$
15 HR. TSOUNTA
TEL 0751 76225
The long-established hotel in which archaeologist Heinrich Schliemann stayed while

excavating Mycenae, up the road. Simple but clean, with eight rooms, none ensuite. Terrific character makes up for basic amenities. The restaurant is also the best bet locally (see below).
5 Closed Nov.–April
All major cards

LA BELLE HELENE
$$
TEL 0751 76225
Eat in Schliemann's hotel (see above) for a sense of place. No surprises on the menu, but the restaurant is better than—if slightly pricier than—the tourist-trap tavernas that abound in the area.
All major cards

NAFPLIO

XENIA PALACE
$$$
KASTRO ACRONAFPLIAS
TEL 0752 28981
This luxury hotel in the government-owned Xenia chain occupies a prime position overlooking Nafplio's harbor, the sea, and across to the Peloponnese. It's an easy stroll down into the town, but a steep walk back up again, so take a car or a taxi. Rooms are pleasant, and there is little to complain about other than the slight lack of character.
96 All major cards

VYREON
$$
2 PLATONOS
TEL 0752 22351
It's impossible to miss this brightly painted, intimate hotel in a quiet back street, opposite the entrance to the Agios Spiridon church. Great personality, rooms with character.
17 All major cards

KING OTHON
$
KING OTTO/OTHEAN 4
TEL 0752 27585

This old favorite has 12 simple, cheap rooms, some overlooking the courtyard garden where breakfast is served. The Old World atmosphere compensates for the minimal amenities.
(i) 12 **⊕** Closed winter **⑤** **⊗** AmEx, MC, V

🍴 **KAKANARAKIS**
$
VASILISIS OLGAS 18
TEL 0752 25371
In a town where many tavernas are aimed purely at the tourist, this excellent place, two streets back from the waterfront, offers Greek specials even out of season: rabbit with feta or squid in a wine sauce are two examples.
⑤ **⊗** All major cards

🍴 **KANARI**
$
BOUBOULINAS 1
TEL 0752 27668
Seafront taverna that retains its Greekness. It's away from the more fashionable end of the waterfront, but food is good, basic, and inexpensive.
⊕ Closed L **⑤** **⊗** All major cards

🍴 **TA PHANARIA**
$
STAIKOPOULOU 13
TEL 0752 27141
A small shaded area by the side of this taverna gives a charming spot for a meal. Good vegetarian dishes alongside the Greek staples single this taverna out.
⑤ **⊗** No credit cards

🍴 **STATHMOS CAFÉ**
$
OLD RAILROAD STATION
Basic snacks, salads, and meze, but a good shady setting for a quick meal or a lingering coffee or beer.
⑤ **⊗** No credit cards

🍴 **ZORBA'S**
$
STAIKOPOULOU 30
TEL 0752 25319

Unpretentious taverna with friendly service and genuine homecooking. Zorba's offers moussaka light as a feather and other simple dishes cooked by the wife and served by the easygoing husband.
⑤ **⊗** No credit cards

OLYMPIA

🏨 **EUROPA BEST WESTERN**
$$
OLYMPIA
TEL 0624 22650
With a view from a hill overlooking Ancient Olympia, this A-class hotel combines the comfort of a well-established chain with the personal touches that come from being family run. Walking and horseback riding are available, and the hotel has its own tennis courts, too.
(i) 42 **⑤** **⊗** All major cards

🏨 **PRAXITELES**
$
SPILIOPOULOU 7
TEL 0624 22592
Small, affordable hotels like this are hard to find in the busy tourist town of Olympia. This is clean and extremely cheap, but don't expect frills. Do expect good food if you dine in the family restaurant (see below).
(i) 10 **⑤** **⊗** AmEx, V

🍴 **KLADEOS**
$
BEHIND RAILROAD STATION
TEL 0624 23322
Charming riverside setting for an old favorite serving seasonal specialties, from game to vegetarian and an excellent and substantial meze.
⊕ Closed L **⑤** **⊗** All major cards

🍴 **PRAXITELES**
$
SPILIOPOULOU 7
TEL 0624 23570

PRICES	
HOTELS	
An indication of the cost of a double room without breakfast is given by $ signs.	
$$$$$	Over $300
$$$$	$220– $300
$$$	$160–$220
$$	$80–$160
$	Under $80
RESTAURANTS	
An indication of the cost of a three-course dinner without drinks is given by $ signs.	
$$$$$	Over $80
$$$$	$50–$80
$$$	$35–$50
$$	$20–$35
$	Under $20

Justifiably popular eating place for locals and visitors alike, packed inside and out in season: salads, *stifado*, souvlaki, daily specials, huge meze.
⑤ **⊗** All major cards

PATRA

🏨 **RANNIA**
$
53 RIGA FEREOU
TEL 061 220114
Delightfully quiet hotel in the busy port of Patra, located on a pleasant square well away from the port and waterfront. Not all rooms are ensuite and amenities are basic, but the hotel is well taken care of.
(i) 30 **⊟** **⑤** **⊗** All major cards

🍴 **PHAROS**
$$
AMALIAS 48
TEL 061 336500
Every port has its seafood restaurant named Pharos, or Lighthouse, and the one in Patra is especially good. There are meat and regular Greek options, but the fish is so fresh it would be a shame not to sample something from the daily catch.
⑤ **⊗** All major cards

KEY   🏨 Hotel   🍴 Restaurant   **(i)** No. of bedrooms   🅿🅼 Metro   🅿 Parking   ⊕ Closed   ⊟ Elevator

🍴 EVANGELATOS
$

AGIOU NIKOLAOU 40

TEL 061 277772

On the main street running from the harbor to below the castle, this old-established and very traditional restaurant offers conventional Greek dishes, impeccably served.

🕐 Closed L 🈺 🈺 All major cards

PILOS

🍴 DIETHNES
$$

PARALIA

An ideal eating spot, right on the harbor, with fresh fish plucked from the sea that morning, perhaps mullet or swordfish, but with other Greek favorites too.

🈺   🈺 All major cards

🍴 O GRIGORIS
$

MAIN SQUARE

TEL 0723 22621

Attractive restaurant constructed of local stone, with a sheltered and shaded courtyard out back. It is noted for its grilled dishes, such as pork and chicken, as well as oven-baked stews such as stifado.

🈺   🈺 No credit cards

SPARTA

🏨 MANIATIS
$

PALEOLOGOU 72

TEL 0731 22665

The main choice in central Sparta, this is an acceptable if uninspiring hotel with 80 ensuite rooms. It has all the facilities, but this is a place to spend a night in order to see Mystras rather than spend a vacation.

ℹ️ 80 🈺 🈺 🈺 All major cards

🍴 DIETHNES
$

PALEOLOGOU 105

TEL 0731 28636

Tables in the shady garden are popular with locals and the few tourists who venture here. Prices are kept low and standards high by the demands of the locals, but apart from a few daily specials expect no surprise choices.

🈺   🈺 No credit cards

CENTRAL GREECE, THESSALY, & EPIROS

ARACHOVA

🏨 APOLLON
$

DELPHON 20

TEL 0267 31427

Superb example of a reasonably priced and excellently run little hotel that is ideal for exploring Delphi and Parnassos. Clean and pleasant rooms (although not ensuite) and friendly owners.

ℹ️ 10 🅿️ 🈺 🈺 🈺 All major cards

🍴 KARATHANASSI
$

DELPHON 56

TEL 0267 31360

You will dine much better in this long-established, family-run taverna (also known as Barba Yannis) than down the road in Delphi. Many hearty local specialties include excellent lamb, and there's an equally hearty range of local wines.

🕐 Closed L in summer 🈺 🈺 No credit cards

🍴 O SAKIS
$

DELPHON 51

TEL 0267 31511

Filling mountain food at this traditional old taverna on the main street. Strong on meat stews and grills, such as goat and lamb, and vast plates of tasty salads. Local wine from the barrel.

🕐 Closed midsummer 🈺 🈺 All major cards

DELPHI

🏨 OLYMPIC
$$

FREDERIKIS 57

TEL 0265 82780

Charming old-fashioned hotel with immaculate furnishings and stunning views. Has a central location, close to some of Delphi's better restaurants and the ancient site. Ideal for an early morning visit.

ℹ️ 20 🈺 🈺 🈺 All major cards

🏨 VARANOS
$

FREDERIKIS 27

TEL 0265 82345

Small, family-run hotel, ideal for the independent traveler on a budget. Extremely friendly owners, basic but clean rooms with balconies and superb views. A short stroll to the ancient site of Delphi.

ℹ️ 10 🈺 🈺 🈺 All major cards

🍴 INIOCHOS
$$

FREDERIKIS 19

TEL 0265 82710

Superb views over the valley and a very good and wide-ranging menu in a town where poor tourist fare is the norm: from mussels and fresh fish to lamb in pastry and several vegetarian dishes. Highly recommended.

🈺 🈺 No credit cards

🍴 TAVERNA ARACHOVA
$

FREDERIKIS 50

TEL 265 82452

Homegrown food (from the owners' farm) in a small, very Greek place. Limited range of dishes, mostly grills and salads, but well prepared and reasonably priced.

🕐 Closed L 🈺 🈺 No credit cards

HOTELS & RESTAURANTS

IOANINA

🏨 OLYMPIC
$$
MELANIDI 2
TEL 0651 25147
Very good standards in this long-established central hotel, convenient for all the town's attractions. The bright, clean rooms all have TVs, phones, and minibars.
🛏 51 🅿 ⇄ 🔊 🔊No credit cards

🍴 GASTRA
$$
1 MILE (1.5 KM) BEYOND AIRPORT
TEL 0651 61530
On the airport road, just before the turn for Igoumenitsa, this is one of the region's specialty restaurants where meat is cooked in an iron pot called a *gastra*. An iron lid is placed over the dish, which is covered in hot coals or wood. Slow cooking but mouthwatering when it arrives.
🕐 Closed Mon. 🔊 🔊All major cards

🍴 TO KOURMANIO
$
PLATEIA GIORGIOU 16
TEL 0651 38044
Wonderful, tiny Greek grill, always crammed with locals. Limited menu but everything's well prepared; generous helpings and service. Try the Florina peppers or souvlaki.
🔊 🔊No credit cards

🍴 TO MANTEIO
$
PLATEIA GIORGIOU 15
TEL 0651 25452
Non-touristy Greek taverna serving generous helpings, with local specialties such as fried peppers or eggplant, various *saganaki* dishes (including deep-fried Roquefort and feta), and *tsoutsoukakia* (slightly sweet, spicy sausages).
🔊 🔊All major cards

SOMETHING SPECIAL

🍴 PAMVOTIS

If staying in Ioanina there can be no finer place to dine in the evening than on the little island in the lake. There are several similar fish restaurants here, and all can safely be recommended, but Pamvotis is one of the oldest and best. Choose your fish fresh from one of the tanks, and have it grilled for a sublime meal in surroundings that are both simple and romantic. Fish include trout from mountain hatcheries, as fish stocks in the lake have dwindled.
$
NISSI ISLAND
TEL 0651 81081
🔊 🔊All major cards

METEORA

🏨 EDELWEISS
$$
VENIZELOU 3, KALABAKA
TEL 0432 23966
Pleasant hotel in Kalabaka, close to the Meteora monasteries: some rooms offer distant views of them. Prices are reasonable, and it has its own swimming pool.
🛏 56 🅿 ⇄ 🔊 🏊 🔊MC, V

🍴 METEORA
$
PLATIA DIMARCHIOU, KALABAKA
TEL 0432 22316
Simple but good, family-run taverna where the wife does the cooking and the husband and other relatives serve. Great moussaka, good choice of grilled meats.
🕐 Closed winter 🔊 🔊No credit cards

METSOVON

🏨 EGNATIA
$
TOSITSA 19
TEL 0656 41900

Moderately priced mountain hotel with traditional stone and woodwork decoration, right on the main street. Some rooms have mountain views, and the hotel has its own very good restaurant.
🛏 36 🅿 ⇄ 🔊 🔊All major cards

🏨 GALAXY
$
MAIN SQUARE
TEL 0656 41123
Good, clean, family-run hotel, furnished in mountain fashion and right in the heart of town. It has an adjoining restaurant, equally commendable and equally well run (see below).
🛏 10 🅿 ⇄ 🔊 🔊MC, V

🍴 GALAXY
$
MAIN SQUARE
TEL 0656 41123
Good mountain dishes, with local cheeses and wine, served in delightful traditional building in hotel of same name (see above) overlooking the main square. You will need a good appetite as portions are large.
🔊 🔊All major cards

🍴 METSOVITIKO SALONI
$
TOSITSA
TEL 0656 42142
Attractive restaurant with mountain decor and mountain dishes, especially game. Veranda overlooks main street.
🔊 🔊All major cards

NAFPAKTOS

🏨 NAFPAKTOS HOTEL
$$
KORYDALIOU 4
TEL 0634 29551
Spotless hotel, handy for the harbor. Some rooms have sea views, so be sure to ask for one. All the rooms have balconies.
🛏 50 🅿 ⇄ 🔊 🔊All major cards

PARGA

🏨 PARADISSOS
$
PLATEIA AGIOU NIKOLAOU
TEL 0684 31229
Friendly hotel in a renovated old building on one of Parga's most attractive squares. In the center of town but only a short walk away from the harbor with its restaurants, and the best town beach.
🛈 19 🅿 ➋ 🅢 🅢All major cards

🍴 FLISVOS
$
MAVROYENOUS 10
TEL 0684 31624
Located beyond the fortress away from the main waterfront tavernas. Has outstanding sunset views, good fish, good prices, good service.
🕐 Closed in winter 🅢 🅢All major cards

PILION

🏨 ARCHONTIKO MOUSLI
$$
MAKRINITSA
TEL 0428 99250 (MAIN OFFICE NUMBER, COVERING SEVERAL MANSIONS)
These restored Pilion mansions, with old furniture and decorated with embroidery and other wall hangings, make memorable but expensive places to stay. Advance reservations are recommended, as they are extremely popular.
🛈 8 🅢 🅢No credit cards

🏨 EFTIHIA
$$
AGIOS IOANNIS
TEL 0426 31150
Located on the way into the popular beach resort of Agios Ioannis, this Pilion-style hotel has sea views and its own restaurant. More peaceful than hotels on the waterfront.
🛈 15 🅿 🕐 Closed late Sept. to May ➋ 🅢

🍴 OSTRIA TAVERNA
$
AGIOS IOANNIS
TEL 0426 31331
Serves some of the best regional food in the Pilion, such as an established favorite—rabbit stew.
🕐 Closed Tues.–Thurs. L & winter 🅢 🅢All major cards

VOLOS

🏨 PHILIPPOS
$$
SOLONOS 9
TEL 0421 37607
Modern hotel with all facilities, by main square in the center of Volos, convenient for the ferry harbor and for exploring the Pilion. Some rooms have sea views.
🛈 39 ➋ 🅢 🅢No credit cards

ZAGORIA

🏨 DIAS
$$$
PAPINGO
TEL 0653 41257
Tiny, charming hotel in tiny, charming village off the beaten track, and built of stone with arched windows. Rooms are basic but clean, perfect for walkers exploring Vikos Gorge and Zagoria.
🛈 5 🅿 ➋ 🅢 🅢V

🏨 SAXONIS HOUSES
$$
DASKA 11, MEGALO PAPINGO
TEL 0653 41615
A cluster of traditional Zagorian mansions converted into elegant, if somewhat expensive, hotel accommodations, retaining some original features such as fireplaces and painted ceilings.
🛈 10 🅿 ➋ 🅢🅢No credit cards

🍴 KATERINA'S ART
$
NEA VIKOS GORGE
TEL 0653 61233
Impressive restaurant in old village mansion with some unusual Zagorian dishes, especially game.
🅢 🅢No credit cards

🍴 MONODENDRI PENSION & RESTAURANT
$
MONODENDRI
TEL 0653 61233
Caters to walkers and climbers exploring the region. No surprises on the menu (grills, moussaka, salads) but a pleasant place to eat.
🅢 🅢No credit cards

MACEDONIA & THRACE

ALEXANDROUPOLI

🏨 ALKYON
$
MOUDANION 1
TEL 0551 23593
Simple, inexpensive, friendly hotel, tastefully done up and with good sea views. Although modern in design, it has a traditional feel inside, with old-fashioned furnishings.
🛈 32 🅿 ➋ 🅢 🅢All major cards

🍴 KLIMATARIA
$
POLYTECHNIOU 18
TEL 0551 26288
On a busy square with a number of eating places, this is one of the best for fish. It also has an extensive menu of traditional Greek dishes and some more unusual ones, such as baked goat. Good choice of local wines, too.
🅢 🅢All major cards

CHALKIDIKI

🏨 EAGLES PALACE
$$$
OURANOPOLIS
TEL 0377 31047
Four-star luxury in large wooded grounds with a pool, tennis courts, bars, restaurants, and even its own luxury yacht.

Most rooms have superb views out to sea, across to the Agion Oros peninsula. One of the best hotels in the region.
🛈 167 🅿 ⬍ 🅢 🚇 📺 🌫 All major cards

🏨 SKITES
$$$
OURANOPOLIS
TEL 0377 71140
Tasteful, family-run, luxury but low-key hotel, with white-washed wooden-balconied cottages blending into the wooded grounds. Highly rated restaurant. Good for those who want peace and quiet.
🛈 21 🅿 🅢 🌫 All major cards

🍴 KOSTIS
$$
NEA FOKEA
TEL 0374 81379
Imaginative menu, with a tasty eggplant salad. Fresh fish is always available, with batter-fried cod in garlic sauce a specialty of the house.
🅢 🌫 All major cards

🍴 TA PEFKA
$
NEOS MARMARAS
WATERFRONT
TEL 0375 71763
Exquisite hilltop setting among pines and surprisingly good food given the reasonable prices. Seafood is popular, such as fresh sardines, octopus meze, or catch of the day, and more unusual dishes such as mussels in a red sauce or saganaki (deep-fried cheese).
🕒 Closed midwinter 🅢 🌫 All major cards

🍴 TORONEOS
$
PEFKOHORI
TEL 0374 61495
Eat bread made to a special recipe by the local baker, and unusual dishes, especially fish, such as squid stuffed with feta and coriander, fried peppers and pumpkins; friendly service.
🕒 Closed winter 🅢 🌫 All major cards

KASTORIA

🏨 ORESTION
$
PLATEIA DAVAKI 1
TEL 0467 22257
Small, inexpensive option in center of town, just below the Old Town. There's a bar and breakfast room, all rooms are well cleaned and comfortable, and the owners are friendly.
🛈 20 🅿 ⬍ 🅢 🌫 All major cards

🏨 TSAMIS
$
KOROMILA 3
TEL 0467 85334
Modern hotel but in old-fashioned style, a little out of the center in pleasant grounds and with good views of lake and town. All rooms have telephones, and there is a bar and restaurant, as well as water sports and other amenities.
🛈 80 🅿 ⬍ 🅢 📺 🌫 All major cards

🍴 OMONOIA
$
PLATEIA OMONOIA
TEL 0467 23964
Tables outside on busy little square, a good place to people-watch and to enjoy the basic, but well-prepared, Greek food. Try the fish soup made from lake-caught fish.
🅢 🌫 No credit cards

KAVALA

🏨 GALAXY
$$$
VENIZELOU 27
TEL 051 224521
Right by the port and therefore on the expensive side, this is a very good, modern hotel with spacious rooms. It is convenient for ferries and all Kavala's attractions, including its waterfront restaurants.
🛈 149 🅿 ⬍ 🅢 🌫 All major cards

🏨 LUCY
$$
KALAMITSA BEACH
TEL 051 242830
For those wanting a beach-front hotel this is the place, as it is right on the best beach in Kavala. It is modern and clean, and the rooms are well maintained. Prices are lower than in the center of town.
🛈 217 ⬍ 🅢 🚇 🌫 All major cards

🍴 PANOS ZAFIRA
$$
KARAOLI DIMITRIOU 20
TEL 051 227978
Of the many seafood restaurants in town this has established a superior reputation, serving unusual items as well as the catches of the day such as mullet or octopus. Near the harbor.
🅢 🌫 All major cards

KOMOTINI

🏨 RODOPI
$$
ETHN MAKARIOU 3
TEL 0531 35988
Named for the mountains it looks out on, the hotel has large, balconied rooms in a converted traditional Thracian

mansion. The place is full of character.

[i] 18 [P] [≡] [S] [S] No credit cards

LITOCHORON

🏨 MYRTO
$

AGIOS NIKOLAOS 5
TEL 0352 81398
Located close to the center of town, this modern hotel has good-sizze rooms, helpful staff, and a bright restaurant/breakfast room. Inexpensive for its standard and a good base for exploring the Olympus area.

[i] 31 [P] [≡] [S] [S] All major cards

🍴 DAMASKINIA
$

KONSTANTINOU 4
TEL 0352 81247
Good, bustling family taverna, packed with locals on weekends and serving no-frills Greek food for hearty appetites. Charcoal grill for fresh meat and fish in summer.

[S] [S] No credit cards

PRESPA LAKES

🍴 PARADOSI
$

PSARADES
One of several fish tavernas in the pretty fishing village of Psarades, with an idyllic setting and an offering of excellent seafood.

[S] [S] No credit cards

THESSALONIKI

🏨 MAKEDONIA PALACE
🍴 $$$$

MEGALOU ALEXANDROU 2
TEL 031 897197
The city's only deluxe hotel is the most comfortable in town, with excellent food, a quiet location a short walk from the center, all rooms with balconies and most with sea views.

[i] 287 [P] [≡] [S] [≋]
[≋] [Y] [S] All major cards

🏨 AMALIA
$

ERMOU 33
TEL 031 268321
Central but not too expensive, this modern hotel has large rooms, all with phones and some with balconies. Noise can be a problem.

[i] 66 [≡] [S] [S] All major cards

🏨 PARK
$

DRAGOUMI 81
TEL 031 524121
Small, modern hotel with helpful staff in a fairly quiet setting but close to the city's main sights. Typical clean, efficient, mid-range hotel.

[i] 56 [≡] [S] [S] All major cards

🍴 KAVOS
$$$

NIKIFOROS PLASTIRAS 81
TEL 031 430475
One of the best, if priciest, of the city's fish restaurants, with a good reputation among locals. Simple decor, but the best of the day's catch, impeccably prepared.

[S] [S] All major cards

🍴 ARISTOTELEOUS OUZERIE
$$

ARISTOTELEOUS 8
TEL 031 230762
Fashionable and tasteful ouzerie hidden down an arcade, serving some of the best Greek dishes you will find, usually with a difference: cuttlefish stuffed with feta, or a spicy dip of feta, hot pepper, tomato, and oil.

[🕐] Closed Sun. D [S]
[S] All major cards

🍴 TA NISSIA
$$

PROXENOU KOROMILAN 13
TEL 031 285991
This unmistakable blue-and-white house, one street back from the waterfront, has one of the most imaginative menus around, such as shrimp

with bacon, hare with onions, quince-and-walnut pie.

[S] [S] All major cards

🍴 TA KOUBARAKIA
$

EGNATIA 140
TEL 031 271905
Simple Greek grill with friendly waiters, limited menu, but generous helpings. Set back from busy Egnatia behind a Byzantine church.

[S] [S] No credit cards

🍴 TO MAKEDONIKO
$

GIORGIOU PAPADOPOULOU 32
TEL 031 627438
Good, popular, basic Greek taverna in the Eptapyrgiou area of the upper town, with limited choice but good daily specials.

[🕐] Closed Tues. [S] [S] No credit cards

🍴 STRATIS
$

NIKIS 19
TEL 031 279353
Modern seafront restaurant with good service, traditional food, extensive wine list, imported beers, generous helpings; especially popular for lunch on Sunday.

[S] [S] All major cards

🍴 THANASIS
$

MODIANO KOMNENOU 32
TEL 031 274170
There is no more authentic place than this long-established market taverna, usually packed with locals seeking the good home cooked food. A unique eating experience.

[S] [S] No credit cards

XANTHI

🏨 SISSY
$

LEFKIPOU 14
TEL 0541 23242
Very central but not too expensive, this is a well-maintained and roomy hotel

HOTELS & RESTAURANTS

with some rooms having good views over the town.

🛏 27 🅿 ⬍ 🚹 🚫 No credit cards

EVIA

🏨 APOLLON SUITES
$$$
KARYSTOS
TEL 0224 22045
This classy, stylish, and modern small hotel is made up of several suites spread over a large area, overlooking the sea and the hotel's own water-sports facilities. The area around is beautiful, and the hotel is a delightful retreat.

🛏 36 🚹 ⛱ 🚫 All major cards

🍴 O GOUVERIS
$$
BOUDOURI 22, HALKIDA
TEL 0221 25769
Right on the waterfront, this taverna has a tasty range of fish and seafood dishes, including bream, sole, or whatever else has been caught that day, along with lobster, crayfish, and other shellfish. Plenty of meat and vegetarian options too.

🚹 🚫 No credit cards

🍴 KAVO D'ORO
$$
PARAODOS SACHTOURI, KARYSTOS
TEL 0224 22326
Just off the main square, this taverna has been pleasing locals and visitors alike for many years. It serves local wine straight from the barrel and special Evian dishes known as *ladera* (cooked in olive oil). These include vegetable stews such as *briam* and meat stews.

🕒 Closed winter 🚹
🚫 No credit cards

🍴 PYROFANI
$
LIMNI
TEL 0227 31640

This ouzerie near the main square is especially noted for its fresh seafood and shellfish, including reasonably priced lobster. Baked shrimps are a specialty.

🚹 🚫 No credit cards

ARGO-SARONIC ISLANDS

EGINA

🏨 EGINITIKO ARCHONTIKO
$
EGINA TOWN
TEL 0297 4968
Restored traditional mansion, first built in 1820. Stronger on atmosphere than quality of rooms, but a perfectly acceptable economic option in the center of Egina town, with its two courtyards and a roof garden.

🛏 12 ⬍ 🚹 🚫 All major cards

🍴 KOSTAS
$
AGIA MARINA
TEL 0297 32424
If you're in Agia Marina to visit the nearby Temple of Aphea, seek out this taverna with its attractive garden seating, not far from the beach. Friendly service and standard menu, but very well done.

🕒 Closed winter 🚹
🚫 No credit cards

IDRA

🏨 BRATSERA
$$$
TOMBAZI, IDRA TOWN
TEL 0298 53971
For somewhere different, stay in this former sponge factory close to the main harbor. Excellent conversion of the 1860 building with traditional island decor, pool, garden, and dining area.

🛏 14 ⬍ ⛱ 🚹 🚫 All major cards

🍴 KONDYLENIA'S
$$
COAST ROAD W OF IDRA TOWN
TEL 0298 53520
A short walk of only half a mile (1 km) along the coast west of Idra is this wonderful taverna with terrific views across to the Greek mainland. It's a favorite place for watching the sunset. The menu is pretty impressive too, catering to the more sophisticated Idra palates with dishes such as spinach, squid, and shrimp casserole, although fresh fish simply grilled is also available.

🕒 Closed midwinter 🚹
🚫 No credit cards

🍴 O KIPOS
$$
NEAR THE STADIUM, IDRA TOWN
TEL 0298 52329
Popular spot with a shady garden, away from the pricier port area. Specializes in meat, including lamb in filo pastry, or goat, but also has fresh fish and vegetarian dishes, reflecting the island's more cosmopolitan nature.

🕒 Closed L & winter 🚹
🚫 All major cards

¶ TO STEKI
$$
MIAOULI, IDRA TOWN
TEL 0298 53517
This taverna is open all year so must satisfy the residents in winter as well as the tourists in summer. It does so in a pleasing setting with old murals on the walls, fresh fish on the menu, and a limited number of daily specials.
 No credit cards

¶ XERI ELIA
$
OFF MAIN SQUARE, IDRA TOWN
TEL 0298 52886
Down the narrow street near O Kipos is this tucked-away traditional taverna, which has a garden dining area. Simple menu of meats and fish, but beautifully prepared and friendly service.
No credit cards

POROS

¶ CARAVELLA
$
PARALIA
TEL 0298 23666
Very friendly, busy waterfront taverna with a typical Greek menu, prepared with care: moussaka, souvlaki, fish, octopus, *stifado*, vegetarian dishes.
All major cards

¶ MARIDAKI AEGINA
$
DIMOKRATIAS
TEL 0297 25869
Lively waterfront restaurant/café where you can dine cheaply on salads or omelettes, moderately on grilled octopus or moussaka, or expensively on fresh fish.
No credit cards

SPETSES

NISIA
$$$
DAPIA
TEL 0298 75000
The only Luxury-class hotel on the island, the Nisia has 20 rooms and 10 suites in what was originally a 19th-century factory. Now the facilities are superb, with well-tended gardens, a magnificent swimming pool, a children's play area, and a highly regarded restaurant.
30 All major cards

POSSIDONION
$$$
DAPIA WATERFRONT, SPETSES TOWN
TEL 0298 72308
Poseidon himself would enjoy this, overlooking the harbor and across to the mainland. Delightfully old-fashioned hotel with slightly fading grandeur but great charm.
52 All major cards

¶ EXEDRA
$$
PALEO LIMANI, SPETSES TOWN
TEL 0298 73497
Right on the Old Harbor; prices are a little high but the standard of the food makes it worth paying. They do many of the island's seafood specialties, such as *argo*, a casserole of shrimp, lobster, and feta cheese.
All major cards

¶ PANA'S
$
LIGONERI
TEL 0298 73030
This lively restaurant is in a village a few miles west of Spetses town. In the evening the owner may start playing his bouzouki, and when he does then you are guaranteed a good evening. Even if he doesn't, there is the sea view and the good food, including grills and vegetarian options.
No credit cards

¶ LIRAKIS
$
MAIN HARBOR, SPETSES TOWN
TEL 0298 72188
Above the Lirakis super-market with a fine view of the harbor, the Lirakis has an eclectic menu ranging from omelettes and vegetarian dishes such as *briam* (very like ratatouille) to more sophisticated but traditionally Greek meat and fish choices.
Closed winter
All major cards

SPORADES

ALONISSOS

¶ ASTROFENGIA
$
OLD ALONISSOS
TEL 0424 65182
Wonderful views at this popular restaurant, which is about as high as you can go in the Old Town. The evenings get lively with a festive atmosphere in summer. The food ranges from simple grilled fish steaks and stuffed tomatoes to the more sophisticated: artichoke hearts with a cream-and-dill sauce.
Closed L All major cards

¶ TO KAMAKI
$$
IKION DOLOPON, PATITIRI
TEL 0424 65245
This ouzerie is the best eating in town, a couple of streets away from the waterfront. An impressive menu of seafood includes baked mussels and stuffed squid. You can either have them as meze to whet the appetite with an early-evening ouzo, or even better, spend the night there and order several selections.
Closed Mon. L No credit cards

SKIATHOS

ATRIUM
$$$$
PLATANIAS
TEL 0427 49345
Stylish new hotel, in a wonderful setting on

a wooded hill and with an Olympic-size pool looking out over the Aegean. The rooms are large, and they, too, have good views from their balconies. Restaurant, bar, and water sports available.

(i) 75 🔲 🔲 🌊 🔲 All major cards

🍴 ASPROLITHOS
$$
MAVROYIALI, SKIATHOS TOWN
TEL 0427 23110
Taverna traditions are kept up here but in upscale style, and while they serve old favorites like moussaka, it's the lightest moussaka you've ever tasted. Specialties such as shrimp with artichokes are pricier.
🕐 Closed L 🔲 🔲 No credit cards

🍴 KAMPOURELI OUZERIE
$$
PARALIA, SKIATHOS TOWN
TEL 0427 21112
In the great bustling Greek ouzerie tradition, serving meze (the Greek answer to the Spanish *tapas*)—a range of nibbles to eat with your ouzo, such as octopus, squid, and olives. More substantial meals are also served.
🔲 🔲 No credit cards

🍴 WINDMILL
$$
SKIATHOS TOWN
TEL 0427 24550
Right at the top of the eastern hill in the main town, this chic restaurant serves food just as special as the setting. Chicken with bourbon and chili is just one example of the unusual combinations. Desserts include poached pears.
🔲 🔲 No credit cards

SKIROS

🏨 NEFELI
$$
SKIROS TOWN
TEL 0222 91964
This modern place, built in traditional fashion, is a mix of

hotel rooms and larger apartments. Located on the edge of town, it's fairly quiet, but ask for a room with a view and make advance reservations as it is extremely popular.
(i) 14 🔲 🔲 All major cards

🍴 KRISTINA'S RESTAURANT
$$
SKIROS TOWN
TEL 0222 91897
Austrian Kristina is trying to combine a more modern touch, such as a generous number of vegetarian dishes and a variety of breads, with Greek traditions. Her specialty is chicken fricassee.
🕐 Closed L 🔲 🔲 All major cards

SKOPELOS

🍴 ANATOLI OUZERIE
$
SKOPELOS TOWN
This is a place aimed at Greeks, with live music late at night. Dine on a selection of their exceptionally good meze. No phone, no address, so climb the hill and ask for Anatoli's. Locals will point the way.
🕐 Closed L & winter 🔲 🔲 All major cards

🍴 MOLOS
$
HARBOUR, SKOPELOS TOWN
TEL 0424 22551
There are several restaurants on the waterfront, offering good basic Greek food at inexpensive prices. Molos has fresh fish as well as grilled meats and excellent casserole dishes.
🕐 Closed midwinter 🔲 🔲 No credit cards

🍴 TAVERNA T'AGNANTI
$
GLOSSA, SKOPELOS
TEL 0424 33606
This little, family-run taverna is one of those unpretentious

places that are a delight to find in the islands. It has a great atmosphere, friendly hosts, inexpensive and well-prepared examples of standard Greek dishes: squid, grills, chops, moussaka.
🔲 🔲 No credit cards

HIOS

🏨 HOTEL KYMA
$
EVGENIOU CHANDRI 1, HIOS TOWN
TEL 0271 44500
A good, inexpensive, but lovely family-run hotel overlooking the beach, in a 1917 mansion tastefully renovated and provided with all modern amenities. Be sure to ask for a room with a sea view.
(i) 59 🔲 🔲 All major cards

🍴 APOLAISI
$$
AGIA ERMIONI
TEL 0271 31359
Residents of Hios town happily travel the 6 miles (10 km) or so to this fishing village and its excellent fish taverna, which overlooks the water. It's a romantic setting, and you'll get the best of what's been caught in the village that day.
🕐 Closed L 🔲 🔲 All major cards

🍴 TAVERNA HOTZAS
$
STEFANOU TSOURI 74, HIOS TOWN
TEL 0271 42787
The oldest taverna in town and one of the best loved, Hotzas is an island institution and not to be missed. It is tricky to find in the back streets, but everyone knows its name. It has a lovely garden eating area, which you share with the taverna's cats and hens, and the food is as wonderful as the rustic

atmosphere. Simple dishes such as grilled fish or fried eggplant can be washed down with retsina from the barrel. 🚭 🚫No credit cards

🍴 O MORIAS STA MESTA
$
MAIN PLATEIA, MESTA
TEL 0271 76400
It's well worth making the journey to this Mastic village to sample the traditional island fare at this simple taverna on the main square. The house specialty is pickled rock samphire (ask for *kritamo*). The local wine is made from raisins and has a sweet taste and thick consistency.
🚭 🚫All major cards

🍴 THEODOSIOU OUZERIE
$
PARALIA, HIOS TOWN
If you are in the mood for casual dining by the waterfront, then this ouzerie offers a good selection of meze dishes, which could make up a meal. Pastries and ice cream are on offer too.
🕐 Closed L 🚭 🚫No credit cards

LESVOS

🏨 OLIVE PRESS
$$
MITILINI
TEL 0253 71646
Mitilini is an essential part of any visit to Lesvos, and you should try to reserve rooms here if you can. A traditional building right on the seafront, it really is where olives were pressed. There's a beautiful private courtyard and gardens too. Ask for a sea-view room.
🛏53 🔌 🚭 🚫All major cards

🍴 VAFIOS
$$
VAFIOS, NEAR MITILINI
TEL 0253 71752
In the village of the same name, in the hills 3 miles

(5 km) southeast of Mitilini, the Taverna Vafios is a popular drive out in the evenings. Locals know it has a good range of pies and grills, with big helpings and low prices. Wine from the barrel too.
🕐 Closed winter 🚭 🚫No credit cards

🍴 AVEROF 1841 GRILL
$
KOUNDOURIOTOU, MITILINI
This simple little grill on the port is a safe bet if you are spending time in the island capital. Good souvlaki and other standard Greek dishes.
🚭 🚫No credit cards

🍴 CAPTAIN'S TABLE
$
HARBOR, MITILINI
TEL 0253 71241
Right on the harbor. The house special is a huge "Captain's Plate" of mixed seafood, but there are also simple grills, vegetarian dishes, Italian choices, and more exotic dishes too.
🕐 Closed winter 🚭 🚫 All major cards

🍴 ERMIS
$
KORNAROU 2, MITILINI
TEL 0251 26232
This venerable ouzerie certainly oozes atmosphere, the interior being like a cross between an antique store and a bar. It is a very popular local hangout, good for a quick drink or a full meal. Choose from the tasty meze dishes, such as fried cheese or squid.
🚭 🚫No credit cards

🍴 I SYKAMINIA
$
SKALA SYKAMINIAS
TEL 0253 55319
A taverna in a quiet setting, right on the picturesque harbor of this little fishing village. Take a table under the shade of the mulberry tree and sample the simple, delicious fish dishes such as squid or sardines. If there in

late summer, try the regional dish of stuffed squash flowers. 🚭 🚫No credit cards

LIMNOS

🏨 AKTI MYRINA
$$
MYRINA
TEL 0254 22310
This resort hotel is about half a mile (1 km) west of the main town, with its own private beach, three restaurants, water sports, and tennis. The well-equipped rooms are actually stone cottages set in the attractive surroundings.
🛏125 🚭 🏊 🏋 🚫All major cards

🍴 O PLATANOS
$
KYDHA, MYRINA
TEL 0254 22070
Beautifully located on a little square just off the main street, O Platanos gets its name from the two huge plane trees that it shelters beneath. The food is simple but very tasty country fare, such as meat casseroles, oven-baked lamb. Some vegetarian options, too.
🚭 🚫No credit cards

SAMOS

🏨 FITO BUNGALOWS HOTEL
$$
PITHAGORIA
TEL 0273 61314
A peaceful, low-level hotel, with its bungalows nestling in well-tended lawns and gardens crossed by shady paths. Whitewashed walls and pine furniture create an air of comfortable simplicity.
🛏87 🚭 🏊 🚫All major cards

🍴 VARKA
$$
PARALIA, PITHAGORIA
TEL 0273 61636
In this ouzerie, funded by the local community, the food is as good as the setting is

unusual. *Varka* means "boat," and this is indeed a former fishing boat that has been converted. Expect the best of the local fish, and steaks are also available, but go for the meze—they do a surprisingly good range of munchies.
🕒 Closed winter 🔧
🚫 No credit cards

🍴 STELIOS
$
KEPHALOPOULOU, SAMOS TOWN
TEL 0273 23639
This well-established taverna specializes in traditional Samian recipes, as well as other Greek favorites, such as the ever-popular *stifado* (beef cooked in wine).
🔧   🚫 All major cards

🍴 TAVERNA AVGO TOU KOKORA
$
KOKKARI
TEL 0273 92113
Fantastic waterfront location for this slightly more upscale eating place in Kokkari, 6 miles (10 km) west of Samos town. It offers a great variety of meze dishes that can be highly recommended.
🔧   🚫 All major cards

THASSOS

🏨 MAKRYAMMOS BUNGALOWS
$$$
MAKRYAMMOS
TEL 0593 22101
This resort hotel, with its own bar, restaurant, and tennis courts, is made up of cottages plus ten luxurious suites scattered around the lush green grounds. It has its own immaculate white sandy beach and one of the best settings on Thassos.
🛏 206   🅿   🔧   🏊
🚫 AmEx, MC, Visa

🍴 O GLAROS
$
ALYKI
TEL 0593 53047

On the hill to the north of Alyki, with lovely views across the bay, O Glaros has an excellent local reputation for serving the best fish in the area. Enjoy fresh fish simply grilled over charcoal, or go for one of the delicious meat grills or roast chicken dishes.
🕒 Closed winter 🔧
🚫 No credit cards

MIKONOS

🏨 CAVO TANGOO VILLAGE
$$$
NORTH OF MIKONOS TOWN
TEL 0289 23692
This stylish hotel has won architectural awards. It is designed in true Cycladic style with the brightest of blues and whites. In addition to the rooms there are five cottages, with lovely views of the harbor.
🛏 68   🔽   🔧   🏊   🚫 All major cards

SOMETHING SPECIAL

🍴 CHEZ KAT'RINE
In the Greek islands there are very few restaurants that can combine atmosphere and top-quality cooking, but this is one of those rarities. It brings French flair to Greek cooking, so while the menu may say coq au vin, it will be Greek chicken cooked in Greek wine with a result that would grace a Parisian restaurant. Be prepared to pay much more than average, and make a reservation ahead to guarantee a table in the intimate dining room.
$$$
NIKI AGIOS GERASIMOS, CHORA
TEL 0289 22169
🕒 Closed L 🔧   🚫 All major cards

PRICES

HOTELS
An indication of the cost of a double room without breakfast is given by **$** signs
$$$$$ Over $300
$$$$ $220–$300
$$$ $160–$220
$$ $80–$160
$ Under $80

RESTAURANTS
An indication of the cost of a three course dinner without drinks is given by **$** signs
$$$$$ Over $80
$$$$ $50–$80
$$$ $35–$50
$$ $20–$35
$ Under$20

🍴 NIKO'S
$
CHORA
If the island's relentless expensive sophistication is not to your taste, try this unpretentious but always busy little taverna, which serves fish, souvlaki, grills, and other conventional dishes. Low on cost, high on atmosphere.
🔧   🚫 No credit cards

🍴 SESAME KITCHEN
$
PLATEIA TRIA PIGADIA, CHORA
TEL 0289 24710
A welcome addition to the growing number of health-conscious and vegetarian restaurants in Greece. The Sesame isn't totally vegetarian, as their popular chicken pies demonstrate, but it does offer vegetarian moussaka, brown rice, and many other vegetarian delights. Try the delicious spinach pie.
🕒 Closed L 🔧   🚫 No credit cards

NAXOS

🍽 ONEIRO
$$$
PLATEIA BRADOUNA, NAXOS
TOWN
TEL 0285 23846
Probably the best restaurant in town, Oneiro commands wonderful views from its roof garden, the atmosphere enhanced by the candlelit tables and a peaceful courtyard setting. The food matches the mood, with a menu that leans to the international but does not exclude Greek dishes such as lamb stuffed with garlic and bacon and cooked very slowly in the oven.
🕐 Closed L & winter 🅢
🚫 No credit cards

🍽 FAROS
$$
PARALIA, CHORA
TEL 0285 23325
An example of a restaurant where foreign influence (in this case German) is combined with Greek tradition and ingredients to provide a wide menu. An old Greek standby, meatballs, is given a new lease on life with a goulash-style sauce.
🅢 🚫 All major cards

🍽 MANOLIS GARDEN TAVERNA
$
KASTRO, NAXOS TOWN
TEL 0285 25168
Right in the Old Town near the castle there are several restaurants catering to the tourist trade, but this delightful garden taverna maintains its reputation by serving traditional Greek dishes such as moussaka, deep-fried eggplant, and stuffed peppers and tomatoes.
🕐 Closed winter 🅢
🚫 No credit cards

🍽 NIKOS
$
PARALIA, CHORA
TEL 0285 23153
Nikos is owned by fisherman Nikos Katsayannis, so fish on the menu is guaranteed fresh, and there are generally some unusual varieties on offer. Plenty of other choices too, on a wide menu. The wine list concentrates on wines from Naxos and the other Cycladic islands.
🅢 🚫 No credit cards

PAROS

🏨 ASTIR OF PAROS
$$$$
KOLYMBITHRES BEACH, NEAR NAOUSSA
TEL 0284 51976
Paros's flagship hotel is almost a Cycladic village in its own right, with its own beach, small golf course, and an art gallery. The reception area displays modern Greek art. Well worth the outlay.
🛏 57 🅿 🔄 🅢 🏊
🎾 🚫 All major cards

🍽 LALULA
$$
NAOUSSA
TEL 0284 51547
Greek island cooking is being influenced by the many overseas visitors who take up residence. This stylish German-run place does just that, adding more vegetarian choices and a lighter touch to the traditional meat and fish dishes.
🕐 Closed L 🅢 🚫 All major cards

🍽 ALIGARIA
$
PLATEIA ALIGARI, PARIKIA
TEL 0284 22026
This delightful little place is run by a gifted cook, Elizabeth Nikolousou. She knows how to serve up old favorites such as moussaka or stuffed tomatoes with an attention to detail that reminds you how

good they can be when done properly.
🅢 🚫 No credit cards

🍽 TO KYMA
$
AYII ANARGHIRI BEACH
TEL 0284 52025
"The Wave" is run by two French women who serve up an international menu, including Thai, Chinese, French, and even Scottish dishes alongside Greek favorites such as squid, stuffed vegetables, and lobster.
🅢 🚫 All major cards

🍽 LEVANTIS
$
PARIKIA
TEL 0284 23613
The name of this friendly little taverna, with its tables beneath trailing vines, indicates a nod toward the flavors of the Middle East with the use of yogurt, apricots, and nuts, and tender chicken dishes.
🕐 Closed L & Tues. 🅢
🚫 All major cards

SANTORINI

🏨 EREVOS
$$$
IMEROVIGLI
TEL 0286 24250
A unique hotel actually built into the rock face in a position overlooking the crater of Santorini. It was built in the 18th century but has been lovingly maintained using traditional furnishings.
🛏 8 🅢 🚫 All major cards

🍽 1800
$$
NIKOLAOS NOMIKOS, OIA
TEL 0286 71485
One of the best restaurants in this dramatically set town where you can watch the sunset *and* eat good food. Try chicken in a walnut sauce or the best of the catch from the harbor down below.
🕐 Closed L 🅢 🚫 All major cards

HOTELS & RESTAURANTS

KATINA
$
OIA PORT
TEL 0286 71280
If you can face the trek down to the harbor at Oia—or rather face the climb back up again (though you can always phone for a taxi)—then Katina's is a great place for seafood, right by the sea.
🚭 🚫No credit cards

SIFNOS

TO LIOTRIVI
$$
ARTEMON
TEL 0284 32051
Sifnos is said to produce the best chefs in Greece, and the chef here, Yiannis Yiorgoulis, is said to be the finest one who has stayed on the island. Try a simple but unusual and delicious kaparosalata (caper salad), and you'll know why this place is so popular.
🚭 🚫All major cards

CAPTAIN ANDREAS
$
BY THE BEACH, KAMARAI
TEL 0284 32356
If your needs are simple—the best local fish, grilled—then this restaurant right on the beach is the place to come. The eponymous owner catches most of the menu himself, buys the best from his fellow fishermen, and the taste and setting don't come any better.
🚭 🚫No credit cards

SIROS

HOTEL OMIROS
$$
OMIROU 43, ERMOUPOLI
TEL 0281 84910
This elegant hotel in a pedestrianized street has a charming, quiet setting and large rooms tastefully done out with traditional furniture. The roof garden offers terrific views across the harbor.
🛏13 🔁 🚭 🚫No credit cards

TINOS

PERISTERIONAS
$
PAKSIMADI FRAISKOU 12, TINOS TOWN
TEL 0283 23425
Named after, and decorated in the style of, the Venetian dovecotes that Tinos and other Cycladic islands are famous for, this restaurant has indoor and outdoor seating in a quiet street. The menu has a few specialties, such as deep-fried eggplant and zucchini, as well as conventional meat and fish dishes.
🚭 🚫All major cards

DODECANESE

KALIMNOS

PANORAMA
$
AMMOUDARA
TEL 0243 23138
Slightly back from the busy waterfront at the top of a steep hill, this modern hotel has very welcoming owners. Some of the rooms have terraces, and all have stunning sea views and are beautifully maintained.
🛏13 🚭 🚫No credit cards

BARBA PETROS
$
PLATEIA DIAMANTIS, POTHIA
TEL 0243 29678
Full of character, this restaurant at the north end of the harbor offers fresh fish grilled on olive-wood charcoal, along with Greek island specialties such as squid stuffed with a delicious mix of spinach, cheese, and herbs.
🚭 🚫No credit cards

DOMUS ROOF GARDEN
$
KANTOUNI
TEL 0243 47959
The Domus has a splendid setting—at Kantouni on the west coast, overlooking the beach and the Aegean—and food to match. Ordinary dishes such as dolmades and moussaka are exceptionally well done, and there are plenty of surprising inclusions too, such as Armenian lamb cooked with yogurt. A very warm welcome too.
🚭 🚫All major cards

TAVERNA KSEFTERIS
$
CHRISTOS, POTHIA
TEL 0243 28642
This taverna is an island institution, handed down through several generations of the same family. You won't get nouvelle cuisine but you will get tasty dolmades, hearty stews, and a generous welcome.
🚭 🚫No credit cards

KOS

AFFENTOULIS HOTEL
$
EVRIPILOU 1, KOS TOWN
TEL 0242 25321
A friendly, family-run hotel, this is the kind of place that the Greek islands are all about. Simple but spotless, close to the center and to the beach but in a quiet location. All rooms have balconies with views of the harbor.
🛏23 🚭 🚫No credit cards

OLYMPIADA
$
KLEOPATRAS 2, KOS TOWN
TEL 0242 23031
In a town that is full of below-average tourist tavernas, here is a treat. It's a genuine no-nonsense Greek restaurant serving good food at cheap prices. Try a simple souvlaki or one of the many vegetable dishes.
🚭 🚫No credit cards

¶ PLATANOS
$
PLATEIA PLATANOS, KOS TOWN
TEL 0242 28991
With the best setting in town, the Platanos offers unusual Greek dishes such as octopus *stifado* and international variety such as Indonesian fillet steak. There's also live music on most summer evenings.

🚭   🐾 All major cards

¶ TAVERNA MAVROMATIS
$
PSALIDI BEACH, KOS
TEL 0242 22433
The Mavromati brothers who run this taverna take no easy options but cater to Greek palates as well as those of overseas visitors. The deep-fried cheese is delicious, as are the tender grilled meat dishes, and of course there is always fresh fish.

🕐 Closed winter   🚭
🐾 All major cards

PATMOS

⌂ AUSTRALIS
$
SKALA
TEL 0247 31576
This family-run hotel, owned by a couple who used to live in Australia, is in a very quiet location and surrounded by beautiful gardens. Breakfast is served on a terrace overlooking the harbor.

🛏 18   🚭   🐾 No credit cards

¶ PATMIAN HOUSE
$$
CHORA, PATMOS TOWN
TEL 0247 31180
The best restaurant on the island. A beautifully restored 17th-century building is the backdrop to fine food. Conventional hors d'oeuvres such as *taramosalata* and spinach pie are homemade and mouth-wateringly good, as are main dishes

such as rabbit *stifado* with juniper berries.

🕐 Closed L   🚭   🐾 All major cards

¶ OLYMPIA
$
PLATEIA THEOFAKOSTA, CHORA
TEL 0247 31543
Open year-round, the Olympia appeals more to locals than visitors, but provides some unusual choices such as octopus baked in the oven. For dessert, try their homemade walnut cake.

🕐 Closed Sun.   🚭   🐾 No credit cards

¶ TO PYROFANI
$
PARALIA, SKALA
TEL 0247 31539
This fish taverna buys direct from the local fishermen, so you may get lobster, swordfish, tuna, or mullet, depending on what's in season—but whatever it is it will be fresh and simply grilled.

🚭   🐾 All major cards

RHODES

⌂ LINDOS MARE
$$$
LINDOS BAY, LINDOS
TEL 0244 31130
A luxury hotel on several levels leading down to a wonderful beach. It is in the more expensive bracket because rooms are quoted at half-board rate (including breakfast and dinner), but as it is over a mile (2 km) outside Lindos itself, most guests prefer to eat in and enjoy the many facilities.

🛏 123   🅿   🚭   🌊
🐾 All major cards

⌂ RODOS IMPERIAL
$$$
LEOFOROS IALLYSOU, IXIA, RHODES TOWN
TEL 0241 75000
This excellent 5-star hotel, with its own splendid gardens

and beach, is a few miles away from the noise of Rhodes town. Rooms are spacious and all have marble bathrooms, while facilities include restaurant, bar, sauna, tennis court, and jacuzzi.

🛏 402   🅿   ⇕   🚭   🌊
   🐾 All major cards

⌂ ST. NIKOLIS HOTEL
$$
IPPODAMOU 61, RHODES OLD TOWN
TEL 0241 34561
An Old Town hotel that oozes history, incorporating stonework that goes back 800 years. Although some rooms are a little cramped, all of them are modern and have telephones, . The owners also have rooms to rent nearby.

🛏 10   🚭   🐾 All major cards

¶ ALEXIS
$$$
SOKRATOUS 18, RHODES TOWN
TEL 0241 29347
One of the best fish restaurants in the Dodecanese. You will encounter seafood here not commonly seen on other menus (sea urchins for one example), and the best of the catch from the harbor. All vegetables are also organically grown by the owners.

🕐 Closed Sun.   🚭   🐾 All major cards

¶ KIOUPIA
$$
TREIS VILLAGE, RHODES TOWN
TEL 0241 91824
Make sure you come here with an appetite. After a choice of soups you will be faced with a table full of tempting meze dishes and hearty main courses. Remember, too, that there is a big and mouth-watering dessert menu.

🕐 Closed L & Sun.   🚭
🐾 All major cards

HOTELS & RESTAURANTS

🍴 MAVRIKOS
$$
LINDOS
TEL 0244 31232
You get traditional Greek dishes here, such as oven-baked lamb or assorted meze, but prepared with a flair that originated with the restaurant's first chef, who cooked for many years in France. The flair and family tradition continue.
🅢 🅢 All major cards

🍴 PALIA ISTORIA
$$
MITROPOLEOS 108, AMMOS, RHODES NEW TOWN
TEL 0241 32421
This award-winning restaurant is one of the best in the town. Their meze dishes are renowned and include unusual dishes such as beets with walnuts, while main courses might range from a simple succulent roast pork to a pricier lobster spaghetti.
🅲 L 🅢 🅢 All major cards

🍴 CLEO'S
$
AGIOU FANOURIOU 17, RHODES OLD TOWN
TEL 0241 28415
There are many mediocre places in the Old Town, but slip away from the main street, Sokratous, and you will find this wonderful Italian restaurant. You can still sample the local fish—done Italian style—if you don't fancy pasta.
🅢 🅢 AmEx, DC, MC, V

🍴 YIANNIS
$
APPELOU 41, RHODES TOWN
TEL 0241 36535
It's a pleasure to find a cheap and cheerful place where Greek hospitality has not been lost. The same dishes feature here as elsewhere (moussaka, stuffed tomatoes, souvlaki) but the standard is good and the portions generous.
🅢 🅢 No credit cards

SIMI

🏨 ALIKI
$$$
YIALOS, SIMI TOWN
TEL 0241 71655
Although it has changed hands in recent years, this venerable hotel on a quiet part of the Simi waterfront retains its charm. A three-story neoclassic mansion, it was built in 1895, and rooms have been modernized so that they are comfortable without being stuffy. The best rooms are those upstairs at the front, with sea views and small balconies. Elegant simplicity and a warm welcome encourage many visitors to return year after year.
🅘 15 🅢 🅢 No credit cards

SOMETHING SPECIAL

🍴 GEORGIO'S
There is no restaurant in the whole of Greece quite like Georgio's. It manages to be chaotic yet produce mouth-watering food night after night. The eponymous owner glides from kitchen to front of house, sometimes waiting on diners, or maybe taking his bouzouki from the wall to entertain, as the mood takes him. Efficiency is not the strong point, so do not be slow to ask for service, or the bill. Wander into the kitchen and ask to see what's cooking, then grab a table and sit back and watch the nightly drama unfold, as in a theater.
$
CHORIO, SIMI
🅲 Closed L 🅢 🅢 No credit cards

🍴 MERAKLIS
$
YIALOS, SIMI TOWN
TEL 0241 71003
This family-run taverna is what the Greeks do best. The menu is limited to that morning's

catch from the harbor, tasty meze, and good versions of traditional Greek dishes such as stuffed peppers.
🅢 🅢 No credit cards

🍴 NERAIDA
$
YIALOS, SIMI TOWN
TEL 0241 71841
The Neraida looks no different from many other tavernas around Simi town harbor, but the standard of food is exceptional. Fresh fish is good, and the homemade spinach pies superb. Pop into the kitchen to see what's cooking.
🅢 🅢 No credit cards

TILOS

🏨 IRINI
$
LIVADIA
TEL 0241 44293
Impeccably run family hotel with attractive, well-maintained gardens and a peaceful location. Front rooms have good sea views, and the breakfasts are generous. Nothing is too much trouble for the owners.
🅘 23 🅢 🅢

CRETE

AGIOS NIKOLAOS

🍴 CRETAN RESTAURANT
$$
AKTI KOUNDOUROU 10
TEL 0841 28773
Slightly more formal than many of the restaurants down on the harbor, this long-established place also has a more wide-ranging and interesting menu, including perch, fresh fish, stews, and grills, but all excellently done.
🅲 Closed winter 🅢 🅢 All major cards

ELOUDA

SOMETHING SPECIAL

🏨 ELOUDA BEACH
Easily the most luxurious hotel on Crete, and one of the finest in Europe, with room rates you might expect to find in the center of New York or Paris. There are 301 rooms, some of which are actually private cottages with their own swimming pools, rented out to the mega-rich who value their privacy. For other guests there are a pool, beach, water sports, minature golf, sporting facilities, a sailing club, a health center, and an entertainment center.
$$$$$
ELOUDA (1.2 MILES, 2 KM NORTH OF CENTER)
TEL 0841 41412
🛈 301 P 🏊 🎾
🅰 All major cards

🏨 ELOUDA MARE
$$$$
ELOUDA (1.2 MILES/2 KM NORTH OF CENTER)
TEL 0841 41102
Exceptional gardens surround this resort hotel that has a superb setting overlooking the Aegean. Whitewashed cottages surround the main building. Public areas have antique furnishings, and combine tradition with modern comfort.
🛈 108 P 🚭 🚹 🏊
🅰 All major cards

🍴 VRITOMARTES
$
G. SFIRAKI WATERFRONT
TEL 0841 41325
An unsophisticated and excellent taverna right on the harbor, where you dine gazing out over the sea. The fish on the menu was caught here just a few hours earlier, perhaps even by the owner himself. Meat and vegetable dishes are also available, but go for the fish every time.
🕒 Closed in winter 🚭
🅰 MC, V

HANIA

🏨 VILLA ANDROMEDA
$$$
VENIZELOU 150
TEL 0821 28303
This delightful, intimate hotel is in a restored neoclassic mansion of 1870. Its marble floors and elegant furniture give a grand impression, and rooms have views over sea and town, but can be noisy.
🛈 6 🚭 🅰 All major cards

🏨 AMPHORA
$$
PARODOS THEOTOKOPOULOU 20
TEL 0821 93224
First built around 1300, this restored mansion combines Venetian elegance, Turkish style, and modern comforts. The roof terrace has a great view over Hania's beautiful harbor, and rooms are spacious, but there can be noise from the port.
🛈 21 🚹 🚭 🅰 All major cards

🍴 ANEMOS
$$
AKTI TOMBAZI
TEL 0821 58330
One of the best restaurants in Hania, with an upscale setting overlooking the harbor and attentive service. You'll find unusual dishes such as stuffed goat alongside Greek favorites and a range of good fresh seafood platters.
🕒 Closed Dec.–Jan. 🚭
🅰 MC, V

🍴 THE WELL OF THE TURK
$
KALINIKOU SARPAKI 1–3
TEL 0821 54547
Though there's no love lost between the Greeks and the Turks, this Middle Eastern restaurant thrives thanks to its imaginative cuisine, historic building, and stylish interior. Meatballs mixed with eggplant are one house specialty.
🚭 🅰 No credit cards

IRAKLIO

🏨 CANDIA MARIS
$$$
ANIODARA
TEL 0813 14632
This Luxury-class modern hotel was built in brick and marble using traditional Cretan styles, but the rooms (or rather cottages) all have modern facilities and sea views. The huge round swimming pool is an extra delight.
🛈 257 P 🚭 🏊 🎾
🅰 All major cards

🏨 LATO
$–$$
EPIMENIDOU 15
TEL 0812 28103
This attractive hotel is simple and modern, but its friendly atmosphere and central location make it one of the best bets in the city. Some rooms have balconies overlooking the Venetian harbor, and the Archaeological Museum is close by.
🛈 50 🚹 🚭 🅰 All major cards

🍴 KYRIAKOS
$$
LEOFOROS DIMOKRATIAS 53
TEL 0812 24649
Some of the best food in Iraklio, with traditional Cretan dishes served with great style and attention to detail. Formal dress preferred, although it's a remarkably friendly place. Try octopus with onions or the house specialty: snails.
🕒 Closed Wed. & sometimes in summer 🚭
🅰 All major cards

LIMENAS HERSONISOU

🏨 ROYAL MARE VILLAGE
$$$$
LIMENAS HERSONISOU
TEL 0897 25025
Greece's only thalassotherapy center is housed within this luxury resort hotel between Iraklio and Malia. In addition to the main rooms, there are a further 101 with direct access to the center, and 24 suites. Every comfort, lovely gardens, and private beach.
🛏 435 🅿 ⊟ ⊠ ⊟
🚫 All major cards

RETHIMNO

🏨 GRECOTEL CRETA PALACE
$$$$
MISIRIA BEACH
TEL 0831 55181
Surrounded by lush gardens, this modern resort hotel has been built simply but stylishly in traditional Cretan fashion. In addition to the rooms there are 204 cottages and villas, with every facility. Three restaurants, four bars, tennis court, scuba diving.
🛏 370 🅿 ⊟ ⊠ ⊟
🚫 All major cards

🏨 FORTEZZA
$$
MELISINOU 16
TEL 0831 55551
This modern hotel incorporates traditional Cretan architectural styles and is wonderfully located in a quiet street near the Venetian fortress, only a short stroll from the waterfront.
🛏 54 ⊟ ⊠ ⊟ 🚫 All major cards

🍴 CAVA D'ORO
$$
NEARCHOU 42
TEL 0831 24446
One of the better places on the Venetian Harbor, popular and always busy so reserve a table in season. Good views complement the food, which is simple with an emphasis on

fish of the day, lobster, and other seafood dishes.
⊕ Closed winter ⊟
🚫 All major cards

🍴 I VARDIA
$
OLD HARBOR
TEL 0812 23731
In a great setting right on the harbor, this simple little place is what Greek dining is all about. No frills, but good Cretan specialties lovingly prepared. Great atmosphere.
⊕ Closed in winter ⊟
🚫 No credit cards

IONIAN ISLANDS

CORFU

🏨 HOLIDAY PALACE CORFU
$$$$
NAUSICAA, KANONI
TEL 0661 36540
Luxury resort hotel close to the airport and a taxi (or bus) ride away from Corfu town. Two restaurants, several bars, snack bars, two pools, and a casino are among the facilities.
🛏 256 🅿 ⊟ ⊟ ⊠
⊠ ⊟ 🚫 All major cards

SOMETHING SPECIAL

🏨 BELLA VENEZIA
This is a very modest C-class hotel which has a charm and character all its own, belying its simple facilities. The building is a 19th-century neoclassic mansion that has been lovingly restored, with spacious, high-ceilinged rooms. There is also a beautiful garden. It is on a quiet street a few minutes walk from the center of town. Staff are noted for their friendliness.
$
ZAMPELI 4, CORFU TOWN
TEL 0661 46500
🛏 32 ⊟ ⊟ ⊟ 🚫 All major cards

🏨 CAVALIERI
$$$
KAPODISTRIOU 4, CORFU TOWN
TEL 0661 39041
This is almost on the seafront and upper front rooms have good views of the Old Fort and the sea. It's in an old mansion that has been restored without losing the old-fashioned style. The rooms are a little spartan but do have all modern conveniences.
🛏 48 ⊟ ⊟ 🚫 All major cards

🍴 DIMARXION
$$$
GUILDFORD 71, CORFU TOWN
TEL 0661 39031
The best and most expensive restaurant in town. Beautiful location near Town Hall Square, and food that ranges from the conventional (but superbly done) moussaka to island specialties such as *bourdetto* (fish in a tomato-garlic sauce).
⊟ 🚫 All major cards

⚟ AEGLI
$$
KAPODISTRIOU 23, CORFU TOWN
TEL 0661 31949
A great place on Corfu town's fashionable Liston, where people come to see and be seen. The location adds to the price, but the food is exceptionally good, and includes many island specialties. Try their *sofrito* (veal in a garlic sauce).
🅢 🅢 All major cards

⚟ SOSSI FISH TAVERNA
$$
MANDOUKI, CORFU TOWN
Whatever fish is in season, and in the fishermen's nets, will be here. You will have to elbow your way through local people, who know that this is the place for fish: bream, snapper, red mullet, whitebait, sardines, swordfish, squid, octopus.
🕒 Closed L 🅢 🅢 All major cards

⚟ VENETIAN WELL
$$
PLATEIA KREMASTI, CORFU TOWN
TEL 0661 44761
In a beautiful quiet square (allow time to find it!), this serves some of the most inventive food on the island, mixing Greek with Middle and Far Eastern dishes to great effect. Good wine list.
🕒 Closed Sun. 🅢 🅢 All major cards

⚟ GRILL ROOM CHRISSOMALIS
$
THEOTOKI 6, CORFU TOWN
TEL 0661 30342
Very basic, much frequented by locals, and you will get the best of grilled meals at reasonable prices with friendly service.
🅢 🅢 No credit cards

⚟ NIKOLAS
$
GIMARI, NEAR KALAMI
TEL 0663 91136
This traditional taverna is right on the beach in the quiet village of Gimari, 1 mile (2 km) west of Kalami. Busy at lunchtime with bathers and families, in the evening it is quieter as diners enjoy both its peaceful setting and its excellent fresh fish dishes, such as mullet, swordfish, or tuna.
🕒 Closed winter 🅢 🅢 No credit cards

⚟ TRIA ADELFIA
$
WATERFRONT, KASSIOPI
TEL 0663 81211
In a town where many restaurants cater unimaginatively for the tourist trade, the owners of "The Three Brothers" try to maintain standards and keep their place Greek rather than blandly "international." Although meat dishes such as souvlaki and roast chicken are good, the best option is fish, caught fresh each day by one of the brothers.
🕒 Closed winter 🅢 🅢 No credit cards

⚟ YIAYIA'S TAVERNA
$
GUILDFORD 16, CORFU TOWN
TEL 0661 37147
Authentically basic Greek taverna, where locals stop in for small talk and more adventurous visitors savor the atmosphere. Unpretentious food, mainly grills, but of the best quality and a terrific lively atmosphere.
🅢 🅢 No credit cards

ITHACA

⚟ FATOURO
$
STAVROS
TEL 0674 31385
Well worth the trek up to Stavros, this homely family taverna is on the main square, not far from the bust of Odysseus. The food is unpretentious with no surprises, but simple dishes such as moussaka, stuffed grape leaves, and stuffed tomatoes are prepared with the best local ingredients.
🕒 Closed L 🅢 🅢 No credit cards

⚟ GREGORY'S
$
PALEO KARABO, VATHI
TEL 0674 32573
Some way out of the island's capital, but you can get a boat to take you there to sample the daily catch—fresh fish and hearty local wine straight from the barrel.
🅢 🅢 All major cards

⚟ TREHADIRI TAVERNA
$
VATHI
TEL 0674 33066
Wonderful family-run place, where the wife cooks and the husband serves. Basic menu with such dishes as moussaka and grilled meats, but all are prepared with great care and are delicious.
🕒 Closed L 🅢 🅢 No credit cards

KEFALONIA

⌂ WHITE ROCKS
$$$$$
PLATYS YIALOS, LASSI, ARGOSTOLI
TEL 0671 28332
One of the best hotels on the island, with its own private beach and another public beach nearby. It has good facilities and is not too far

HOTELS & RESTAURANTS

from Argostoli. In addition to the rooms it has 60 cottages.
[i] 102 [P] [Closed] winter [Elevator] [S] [All major cards]

🍴 ANONYMOUS
$
ANTONI TRITSI 146, ARGOSTOLI
TEL 0671 22403
This little family-run place, right on the harbor, limits its menu to a few daily specials, plus the conventional grills and fresh fish. Friendly, relaxed service.
[S] No credit cards

🍴 DASOS
$$
HARBOR, FISKARDON
TEL 0674 41276
Fiskardon is not cheap, but at Dasos you get good quality food for your money and outdoor seating by the appealing harbor front. There is a good list of local wines, and the menu includes island specialties, most notably the Kefalonia meat pie whose pastry topping hides tender pieces of beef.
[Closed winter] [S] No credit cards

🍴 OLD PLAKA
$
METELAS, ARGOSTOLI
TEL 0671 24849
Typical open-all-hours Greek place, but a dressier clientele comes in the evenings for the reasonably priced but tasty Greek fare. Pork stuffed with garlic is a succulent house specialty.
[S] All major cards

🍴 PATSOURAS
$
IOANNOU METAXA 32, ARGOSTOLI
TEL 0671 22779
On busy days in Argostoli, it's a relief to retreat to the garden of this delightful and friendly little restaurant. The menu includes several island specialties, depending on the

season, but Kefalonia meat pie is usually available.
[S] No credit cards

LEFKADA

🏨 LEFKAS HOTEL
$$
PAPAGOU 2, LEFKADA TOWN
TEL 0645 23916
The best bet if staying in the island capital, this hotel is large, central, and of a good standard. Spacious comfortable rooms and very accommodating staff and management.
[i] 93 [Elevator] [S] All major cards

🍴 REGANTOS
$
DIMARHOU VERIOTI 17, LEFKADA TOWN
TEL 0645 22855
A restaurant that's popular in Lefkada town must be good, as there aren't too many foreign visitors around and the locals know what's what. Try the meat stews, sausages, and kebabs, for which Lefkada is noted.
[Closed L] [S] No credit cards

PAXI

🍴 REX
$
GAÏOS
TEL 0662 31268
If you want fresh fish then Rex has got it, simply grilled. The menu also includes basic Greek dishes such as moussaka and dolmades (stuffed grape leaves), but fish is the focus.
[S] No credit cards

🍴 TAKA-TAKA
$
GAÏOS
TEL 0662 31323
A long-established favorite specializing in grilled meat and fresh fish. Friendly owners and a lovely outdoor eating area, covered in vines.
[S] All major cards

🍴 VASSILI'S
$
WATERFRONT, LONGOS
TEL 0662 31587
Right on the picturesque little harbor at Longos, this restaurant looks very ordinary but serves up the best food on the island, backed up by an extensive wine list. Best to reserve a table at busy times of the year.
[Closed some days L] (phone to check) [S] All major cards

ZAKINTHOS

🏨 STRADA MARINA
$$$
LOMVARDOU 14, CHORA, ZAKINTHOS TOWN
TEL 0695 42761
Perfectly situated on the waterfront in the capital, this classy hotel has all the modern amenities and an attractive roof terrace with excellent views.
[i] 112 [Elevator] [S] All major cards

SOMETHING SPECIAL

🍴 MANTALENA
Arguably the best restaurant on the island, this is in a small village just south of the resort of Alikanas. It's family run, and the menu is made up of recipes collected from the owners' relatives over the years. Manager Tasos makes a charming maître d', with his good looks and impeccable English, while his mother produces delicious dishes from the kitchen. They serve water from their own well, wine from their own vineyards, and a complimentary glass of ouzo to every guest.
$
ALIKANAS
TEL 0695 83487
[S] All major cards

SHOPPING IN GREECE

Souvenir shops offer the usual knick-knacks, with a heavy emphasis on ceramics. By looking around it is possible to find more unusual items made by craftspeople rather than settling for mass-produced goods. Leather is a good buy, from tiny purses to thick coats. Wool blankets are easily found, along with *flokati,* the sheepskin rugs produced particularly in the northern mountains and in Thrace.

Among the best buys are gold and silver jewelry—for which the Greeks have a reputation. There are exquisite rings, earrings, and necklaces. Other delicate work is seen in embroidery and handwoven items, lace, cotton skirts, and blouses. Many towns have folk museums displaying traditional clothing and decorative work, most with a gift shop selling modern examples. If there's no shop, the curators will be able to tell you where to find the local specialists. Other good souvenirs are tapes of Greek music and the *koboloi* (worry beads) you see hanging in most tourist shops. Generally Greek food and wine doesn't travel well, although some brand-name spirits are good bargains and so is the virgin olive oil.

Where to Go

Different areas of Greece specialize in particular crafts. If you are keen on ceramics then the best examples are available in Rhodes, Sifnos, and Skiros, although you will find good work for sale almost anywhere in the country. For jewelry the place to go is Ioanina in Epiros, the traditional center of the silverworkers of Greece. Rhodes and Athens are both good for gold, but prices are high. Quality leatherwork is widely available, but the finest examples are available on Crete, and in particular the town of Hania. Wooden carvings and embroidery are especially good in Metsovon, and quality embroidery is also to be found in the Ionian islands, especially Kefalonia and Zakinthos.

Antiques

It is a criminal offense in Greece to buy, sell, own, or export any antique item. There is no clear definition of what is considered an antique item, but the law is aimed at protecting Greece's historical and cultural artifacts. If you are offered anything in an underhand manner that is obviously extremely old, then beware: If it is genuine, you could be in line for committing a criminal offense, and if it is not genuine then you are probably being ripped off. Better stick to obvious copies from museum shops.

That is not to say that you can't legally buy more recent antiques, such as books, paintings, engravings, and so on, and indeed you will see many such items for sale in markets such as at Monastiraki in central Athens and in Pireas on a Sunday morning, or in antique shops around the country. However, there are not too many of these as Greeks tend to hold on to their family heirlooms rather than trade in them, and shopping for antiques is not as popular a pastime in Greece as in, say, the U.S.A. or Britain.

Haggling

Haggling is acceptable in certain circumstances, notably in tourist areas such as the Plaka in Athens. Here store owners will start you off on the process anyway by immediately quoting you a price less than the one on the ticket ("special price for today only"). The gullible tourist then accepts this as a bargain, rather than wondering if the price might have come down further: It usually will. Jewelry and craft shops often have room for maneuver, although by no means as much as is common farther east or in North Africa.

ATHENS

ANTIQUES, ARTS, & CRAFTS

Artworks, old prints, and postcards can be bought in several good junk/antique shops at the very far end of Adhrianou: Keep walking and get beyond the souvenir shops of the Plaka.

A.D. Gallery
Pallados 3
Tel 01 360 2948
Tucked away in the newly fashionable Psirri district, this little gallery puts on changing exhibitions of contemporary art mixing painting, photography, and multimedia works. Opens lunchtimes and evenings only, closed Sunday and Monday.

Aidini
Nikis 32
Tel 01 323 4591/322 6088
An unusual basement craft shop/gallery located between Syntagma and the Plaka, where the owner makes distinctive metalwork sculptures, ranging from interesting fishes to pretty surreal objects.

Spiro Aravantinos
Adrianou 114
Tel 01 323 6363
This Plaka store is a treasure-trove inside, with superbly handcrafted children's toys, dolls, and puppets.

L'Atelier
Adrianou 116
Tel 01 323 3740
It is illegal to export genuine Greek antiquities, but here you can find good copies of vases, frescoes, and Cycladic statues. Many are genuinely beautiful, and you might be lucky enough to see these instant "antiques" being made.

Athens Gallery
Pandrossou 14
Tel 01 324 6942/894 0217
This stylish gallery is a cut above most of the surrounding Plaka

souvenir shops. It represents a handful of contemporary Greek artists, which include sculptors, painters, potters, and jewelers. Even if you cannot afford to buy the more expensive items, they are well worth looking at.

Gallerie Areta
Pandrossou 31
Tel 01 324 3397/894 0217
A small offshoot of the Athens Gallery selling mainly ceramics and paintings, including some delightful primitive artwork.

Center of Hellenic Tradition
Mitropoleos 59/Pandrossou 36
Tel 01 321 3023/3842
In an arcade between the main Plaka street of Pandrossou and Mitropoleos is a selection of small stores devoted to Greek arts and crafts, including paintings, ceramics, woodwork, painted postcards, and icons. It also has a very good café with a view down onto the passing throngs of the Plaka.

EOMMEX
Mitropoleos 9
Tel 01 323 0408
In this cooperative you can buy handmade rugs made by weavers from all over Greece, using traditional looms, materials, and techniques.

Greek Women's Institution
Ypatias 6
Tel 01 325 0524
This outlet highlights the Greek embroidery tradition, providing the more remote rural and island communities with some financial benefit from the country's popularity as a tourist destination—which they would not otherwise receive. A cause worth supporting.

Iakovos Antiques
Ifaistou 6
Tel 01 321 0169
Ceramics, paintings, and knick-knacks old and new, not just from Greece but from around the world.

Vassilios Kevorkian
Ifaistou 6
Tel 01 321 0024
Handmade guitars, bouzoukis, and other stringed instruments produced in a tiny workshop in the bazaar. The friendly owner doesn't mind if you merely want to look.

Karamikos Mazarakis
Voulis 31–33
Tel 01 322 4932
As well as traditional Greek *flokati* rugs and *kilims,* this large store between Syntagma and the Plaka sells wool and silk rugs from elsewhere in the world, and features unusual rugs using designs by Dali, Picasso, Magritte, and other artists.

Takis Moraytis
Adrianou 129
Tel 01 322 5208
Shop of a Plaka artist, with some good original Greek scenes. Expensive but good quality.

Motakis
Plateia Abyssinia 3
Tel 01 321 9005
Sprawling antique/bric-a-brac shop that has been doing business in its sizable Plaka basement for almost a century. Items on sale range from antiques to offbeat curios.

Museum of Greek Children's Art
Kodrou 9
Tel 01 331 2621
Delightful prizewinning paintings by Greek children are both on display and for sale. A chance to make an original purchase which will not only support the museum but bring a smile to the young artist's face.

Nasiotis
Ifaistou 24
Tel 01 321 2369
Look for the long display of old photos, engravings, books, magazines, and saucy postcards in this Aladdin's cave. Downstairs is a jumble of old books, mostly in Greek but some in other languages and worth a look.

National Welfare Organization
Ypatias 6
Tel 01 325 0524
This excellent cooperative offers for sale traditional craftwork and practical items made by rural communities throughout Greece: embroidery, rugs, ceramics, icons. There is an especially good array of kitchenware, including coffeemakers, breadboards, and pots and pans. They are all attractive yet sturdily made and typically Greek, and buying here helps keep the craft traditions alive.

Olive Wood Workshop
Mnisikleous 8
Tel 01 321 6145
Small family shop in a Plaka side street selling beautiful olive wood carvings, including breadboards, cheeseboards, and bowls. The friendly young owner also makes many of the items and is usually at work in the corner of the shop.

Panayiri
Kleomenous 25
Tel 01 722 5369
Kolonaki shop with a good range of craft items, paintings, books, and—its specialty—model ships, carved by the owner, in wood taken from old ships.

Pyromania
Kodrou 14
Tel 01 325 5288
Tasteful examples of handblown glass, ceramics, and olive wood carvings, with a small workshop at the rear where the affable and talented artist-owner works. On the edge of the Plaka and easily spotted by its strikingly lit window displays.

Riza
Voukourestiou 35
Tel 01 361 1157
Fine examples of handmade and machine-produced lace are displayed here for sale, also glassware and other contemporary Greek crafts.

Kostas Sokaras
Adrianou 25
Tel 01 321 6826
Embroidery, jewelry, Greek folk costumes, and puppets from the traditional Greek art of the shadow theater.

BOOKS, NEWSPAPERS, & MAGAZINES

The Booknest
Panepistimiou 25–29
Tel 01 323 1703
Great jumble of a bookstore covering hardbacks and paperbacks, old and new, guidebooks and fiction, in many languages.

Compendium
Nikis 28
Tel 01 322 1248
English-language books, magazines, guides, fiction, books about Greece, maps, and a large secondhand section for exchanging your used paperbacks. There are sometimes readings from local or visiting authors—check the notice board for details.

Pantelides
Amerikis 11
Tel 01 362 3673
This is the biggest English-language bookstore in Athens, with everything from popular blockbuster paperbacks to obscure specialist works. There is a good section of books about Greece, plus dictionaries, art books, cookbooks, and history. The English-speaking owner is always pleased to help.

Raymondos
Voukourestiou 18
Tel 01 364 8189
You will find a wide range of foreign magazines here, and it's a good source of magazines about Greece, as well as Greek fiction in English and guidebooks.

CLOTHES

The car-free Ermou Street has a range of international clothing stores such as Benetton, Lacoste, and Marks & Spencer, as well as many Greek equivalents. More exclusive designer stores can be found in the fashionable Kolonaki district, at the foot of Lykavittos.

Artisti Italiani
Kanari 5, Kolonaki
Tel 01 339 0254
Italian designs for women and men and appropriately priced.

Stavros Melissinos
Pandrossou 89
Tel 01 321 9247
Now a Plaka institution, Melissinos has been making sandals and writing poetry since the 1960s. He made sandals for John Lennon and will do the same for you.

FOOD & DRINK

Visit the **Central Market** south of Omonoia on Athinas to buy herbs, spices, nuts, olives, cheeses, and other delicacies.

Asimakopouli
Charilaou Trikoupi 82
Tel 01 361 0092
Renowned Athenian patisserie, for those with an extremely sweet tooth—Greeks like their desserts and pastries much sweeter than most.

Bachar
Evripidou 31
Tel 01 321 7225
Specialist store near the Central Market, with spices and herbs for both culinary and medicinal use.

Brettos
Kydathinaion 41
Tel 01 323 2110
Well-stocked and colorful liquor store in the Plaka, with own-brand spirits and liqueurs as well as numerous Greek drinks like ouzo and Metaxa brandy.

Katsarou
Liossion 89
Tel 01 821 1767
Slightly out of the center near the Larissis train station, but worth the effort if you want to stock up on reasonably priced Greek drinks, from apéritifs via wines to brandies.

JEWELRY

Athens has a long tradition of silversmiths, and a number of stores can be found in the district around Lekka and Praxitelous streets. Some of these have huge, garish silver displays, but there are still some smaller stores which include more tasteful items. Several of the more expensive jewelry stores are along the pleasant pedestrianized Voukourestiou shopping street.

Borell's
Ypsilandou 5
Tel 01 721 9772
Modern and some antique jewelry, just off Kolonaki Square.

Ilias Lalaounis Jewelry Museum
Karyatidon-Kallisperi 12
Tel 01 922 1044
See copies of works by this world-famous Greek jewelry designer, in a stylish museum showing his collections. Originals can be ordered, at a price. The Lalaounis store is at Panepistimiou 6, tel 01 361 2429.

Nisiotis
Lekka 28
Tel 01 324 4183
Excellent store specializing in upscale silverware.

Zolotas
Stadiou 9
Tel 01 322 1222
One of Greece's leading jewelers, with work worth seeing in its own right, whether you buy or not. Also has a store in the Plaka at Pandrossou 8.

MUSEUM REPRODUCTIONS

Several of the major museums in Athens sell copies of their most appealing items, and these can range from small and inexpensive to life-size reproductions. The standard is generally high. The main stores are at the National Archaeological Museum (see pp. 78–81), the Benaki Museum (see p. 70), and the Goulandris Museum of Cycladic Art (see pp. 74–75).

MUSIC

In the **Monastiraki flea market** there are several specialist record stores, with a particular emphasis on 1960s and 1970s music, from the popular to the obscure. Good selection of vinyl as well as CDs.

Museum of Greek Popular Musical Instruments
Diogenous 1–3
Tel 01 325 0198
The museum shop sells recordings of every type of musical tradition from all over Greece. Vast stock, plus books (mostly in Greek).

PELOPONNESE

NAFPLIO

The Great Store
Amalias 21
Tel 0752 25972
Well worth seeking out, as this gift shop stocks a wide range of items, including paintings and engravings, old books, old postcards, and other pieces that make for unusual souvenirs.

Odyssey
Plateia Syntagmatos
Tel 0752 23430
Good selection of books, newspapers, and magazines in several languages. Books include guidebooks and Greek fiction, or fiction set in Greece.

CENTRAL GREECE

IOANINA

Athanasias Daktylithos
Pirsinela 14
Tel 0651 28005
Good stock of Greek and foreign-language newspapers and magazines; newspapers usually available the day after publication.

Kasa Makis
Plateia Eleuthezotou 2
Tel 0651 22502
Wine merchant selling a worldwide range as well as many good-quality Greek wines, of the type that seldom make it onto the limited menus of many restaurants. Also sells a selection of Greek cakes and candy.

Nikos Xaritos
Anexartisias 2
Tel 0651 29200
There are plenty of stores selling silver in Ioanina, but only a handful of workshops remain. This one sells the young owner's handmade plates, cups, jewelry, and decorative items, mainly in silver and brass.

MACEDONIA & THRACE

THESSALONKI

Marina
Mitropoleos 62
Tel 031 238361
The eponymous Marina once worked for Greece's most celebrated jeweler, Ilias Lalaounis, whose work has influenced her own designs. Not cheap...but certainly cheaper than her former teacher.

Molho
Tsmiski 10
Tel 031 275271
If you want to find a book, newspaper, or magazine in English or any other foreign language in Thessaloniki, then this is the place to look. If you cannot find it here it probably cannot be found—from conventional

guides to archaeology, history, poetry, and fiction. A good selection of Greek titles too.

Terra Cotta
Smirnis 13
Tel 031 220191
Thessaloniki has a lively artistic scene, and this gallery displays some striking work by contemporary artists, both local and from elsewhere in Greece. Closed in midsummer.

ARGO-SARONIC ISLANDS

EGINA

Elefteris Diakoyiannis
Vas-Georgiou 39, Egina town
Tel 0297 24593
A good selection of ceramics from all over Greece. Also has a selection of jewelry and reproductions of Greek sculpture.

SPORADES

SKIATHOS/SKOPELOS

Archipelago
Skiathos town & Skopelos town
Tel 0427 22163 & 0424 23127
These two stores have a mix of antiques, unusual arts and crafts items, and clothing—well worth browsing through.

Galerie Varsakis
Plateia Trion Ierarchon, Skiathos town
Tel 0427 22255
Owned by an artist whose surreal paintings are for sale, this arts and crafts treasure trove includes jewelry, embroidery, carvings, and carpets.

SKIROS

Faltaïts Museum
Palaiopyrgos, Skiros town
Tel 0222 91232 (museum); 0222 92158 (Argo)
Small museum of folk art with a workshop and gift shop attached where you can buy the work of modern craftsmen and women,

keeping the island traditions alive. The museum has an outlet, called Argo, on the main street.

Stamatis Ftoulis
Skiros town
Tel 0222 91559
Retail outlet for traditional-style island ceramics, made at the owner's workshop at Magazia. Hand-painted plates, bowls, vases, and other items.

NORTHEASTERN AEGEAN ISLANDS

HIOS

The Art Cooperative
Kallimasia
Tel 0271 51180
Delightful little gift shop some 4 miles (7 km) south of Hios town, which helps the women of the area find an outlet for their work, specifically wonderful handmade dolls wearing traditional island costumes.

LESVOS

Athens School of Fine Arts
Krallis Mansion, Mitilini
This highly regarded school has occasional exhibitions of its students' work, with the chance to buy something original and at the same time help a young artist. Ask at the local visitor information center for details.

CYCLADES

ANDROS

Batsi Gold
Batsi
Tel 0282 41575
In this south coast resort, find a good collection of jewelry inspired by ancient Greek myths and legends: bracelets, earrings, necklaces, pins, rings.

Paraporti
Plateia Kairi, Andros town
Tel 0282 23777
Craft items, especially ceramics, from Andros, plus embroidery, some jewelry, and model ships.

MIKONOS

Center for Contemporary Art
Kouzi Yorgouli 43, Mikonos town
Tel 0289 26868
You could shop till you drop in Mikonos, as a great number of artists, producing quality arts, crafts, and clothing, have set up shop here. This center concentrates on modern Greek artists.

Ilias Lalaounis
Polykandrioti 14, Mikonos town
Tel 0289 22444
The most famous jeweler in Greece, with his own museum in Athens, has an outlet on Mikonos. His work is priced accordingly.

NAXOS

Tirokomika Proionia Naxou
Papavasiliou, Naxos town
Tel 0285 22230
Fantastic food and drink store on Naxos, an essential visit if you want to take anything home or simply prepare a fine picnic with local cheeses, all kinds of olives, and local wines.

PAROS

Studio Yria
Kostos
Tel 0284 29007
If you want to buy something modern made from the superb Parian marble, head for this artists' studio 3.5 miles (6 km) east of Parikia. The husband and wife team have distinctive island ceramics, embroidery, and metalwork too.

SANTORINI

Canava Roussos
Between Thira and Kamari
Tel 0286 31278
They make some good wine on Santorini, and here is a chance to sample at the source, and buy a few bottles at reasonable prices.

SIFNOS

Antonis Kalogirou
Harbor, Kamares
Tel 0284 31651
This potter sells his own distinctive work, in Sifnos style, and also sells paintings of island life, which are much better than many of the mass-produced prints on sale everywhere.

TINOS

Harris Prassas Ostria-Tinos
Evangelistrias 20, Tinos town
Tel 0283 23893
This jeweler has produced an eclectic collection of work, incorporating ancient and modern styles, in both silver and gold. Much of it has a religious theme, appropriate to Tinos as a pilgrimage site.

DODECANESE

There are many shops selling sponges in the Dodecanese, and almost all tourist shops will have at least a few on display. In order to know what you're buying, you should first visit a specialist center (see in the list below). Experts there will explain what to look for in a good sponge and allow you to test several types before making up your mind. Some points to remember are that naturally colored brown sponges are stronger than artificially colored yellow ones, smaller holes make better sponges, and cut sponges do not last as long as whole sponges.

KALIMNOS

Astor Workshop of Sea Sponges
Pothia
Tel 0243 29815
See the whole process of sponge production, then buy some of the best quality sponges on the island known for them throughout Greece.

PATMOS

Katoi
Chora
Tel 0247 31487
Good choice of jewelry, icons, and ceramics of the island.

RHODES

Ministry of Culture Museum Reproduction Shop
Ippitou, Rhodes Old Town
Official government shop selling top-quality reproductions of statuary and other items that are on display in museums throughout Greece.

SIMI

Aegean Sponge Center
Harbor, Yialos
Thousands of sponges for sale on an island that once made part of its wealth from sponge fishing. The owners will demonstrate how to tell quality sponges, and talk about the life of the sponge fishermen.

CRETE

Embroidery and weaving have both been long traditions on Crete, going back to Minoan times, and you can pick up some fine examples in the larger towns and especially in the villages on the Lasithi Plateau. Leatherwork is also good, and the rugged knee-length Cretan boots are very popular.

Eleni Kastrinoyanni
Ikarou 3, Iraklio
Tel 0812 26186
Exclusive store selling modern examples of many of the Cretan folk arts, such as weaving, embroidery, pottery, and jewelry.

Leather Alley
Odos Skridlof, Hania
Close to the market, the street known as Leather Alley is lined with stores selling all manner of leather goods, including sandals, boots, handbags, backpacks, belts, and wallets.

Maria Patsake
Sfakianakis 2, Agios Nikolaos
Tel 0841 22001
Good source for high quality—and not cheap—weaving, embroidery, and other Cretan craft items.

Petrakis Icon Workshop
Elouda 72053
Tel 0841 41669
A young married couple keep the Greek icon-painting tradition alive with superb skill. The owners also display conventional paintings and other craft work.

IONIAN ISLANDS

CORFU

Bizarre
Arseniou 25, Corfu town
Tel 0661 26384
Corfu town is good for buying clothes, from inexpensive T-shirts to upscale designer labels. Bizarre has some more outrageous designs, mainly from Greece but some from Asia, too.

Danilia Village
Near Gouvia
Tel 0661 91621
This attempt at reconstructing a 200-year-old Greek village includes workshops where artisans sell their work.

Elli
Theotki 88, Corfu town
Tel 0661 26283
An outlet for the hand-embroidered tablecloths and other items produced by the island women. Good quality work is expensive, but the shop's owner will explain how many months of work go into some of the items. Smaller items are also for sale, all exquisitely made.

Mavromatis Distillery
8 miles (13 km) from Corfu town on road to Palaiokastritsa
Tel 0663 22174
See the manufacturing process for the company's three main products: brandy, ouzo, and the

unique local liqueur made from kumquats. A chance to buy them, too, of course.

Terracotta
Filarmonikis 2, Corfu town
Tel 0661 45260
Good-quality outlet for arts and crafts items made only by Greek artists. These are excellent examples of work, such as sculptures and ceramics, and while it may be expensive, it is of the best quality.

Vassilakis
Opposite Achilleion Palace
Tel 0661 52440
One of the largest stocks of Greek wines, spirits, and liqueurs that you will find anywhere, with tastings before you buy.

KEFALONIA

Alexander's
Vergoti, Argostoli
Tel 0671 23057
Large and varied collection of Greek handicrafts, including jewelry handmade by the store's owner, plus ceramics, dolls in island costumes, embroidery, and unusual handmade glass items.

Gentilini Vineyard
Minies
Tel 0671 41618
This small-scale vineyard does not have organized tours so telephone to check before visiting. If it is convenient you will get a personal tour of the vineyard and a chance to sample and buy some of the very high-quality wine.

ZAKINTHOS

Handicraft Cooperative
Lombardou 42, Zakinthos town
On the waterfront at the harbor, this excellent store sells a range of island-made products including rugs, clothing, embroidery, and tablecloths.

ENTERTAINMENT

Entertainment is often impromptu: Someone is inspired to get up and sing or dance in a bar or taverna; there's a party to mark one of the many feast days scattered throughout the Greek calendar; or maybe it's someone's name day (the Greek equivalent of a birthday), when everyone sharing the same name will jointly host a party. However, there are also some more organized events and festivals to look for, details of which are given below.

ATHENS

ARTS FESTIVAL

An annual festival of music, dance, drama, and other arts is held in Athens every summer, throughout the months of June–October. Events take place at Herodes Atticus Theater (Tel 01 322 1459/323 2771).

FEASTS

January 6 is a national holiday, the Feast of the Epiphany, but is also the day for the **Blessing of the Waters,** to bring good fortune to this maritime nation for the forthcoming year. This is done at Pireas, and throughout the country. March 25 is **Independence Day,** when Athens hosts parades and other special festivities to celebrate the 1821 War of Independence against the Turks.

FOLK DANCE

Dora Stratou was a renowned dancer and enthusiast for Greek music and culture, and the dance troupe she founded performs nightly from May to the end of September in a delightful open-air theater, the **Dora Stratou Theater** on Philoppapou Hill (Tel 01 324 4395).

SOUND & LIGHT SHOW

Held on the Pnyx Hill opposite the Acropolis from April to October. There are different language shows each evening so check the current program (Tel 01 322 1459).

PELOPONNESE

ARTS FESTIVALS

A festival including classical music, drama, and other arts is held in the charming town of **Nafplio** every summer. For details call 0752 28607.

Each summer, **Patra** hosts a festival devoted to classical music, theater, and traditional music and dance.

DRAMA FESTIVAL

Held in conjunction with the Athens Arts Festival, this festival of drama in the stunning setting of the ancient theater at **Epidavros** runs throughout the summer. Performances are not held every night, so obtain a current program (Tel 01 322 1459/0753 22066).

FEASTS

July 18–20 is the **Feast of Profitis Ilias,** celebrated with services and festivities at many monasteries throughout the country bearing that name. The biggest celebration by far takes place on the high peak of **Mount Taygettus,** near the town of Sparti.

WINE FESTIVAL

Patra is renowned for its Carnival celebrations and for a big annual wine festival that runs from late August to mid-September (Tel 061 279866).

CENTRAL GREECE, THESSALY, & EPIROS

FEAST

On April 23, the **Feast of St. George** is celebrated with traditional music, dancing, and costumes in the mountain village of **Arachova,** near Delphi.

MACEDONIA & THRACE

ARTS FESTIVALS

A festival concentrating on **drama** is held in the ancient theater at **Philippi** during the summer months.

In **Thessaloniki,** the annual **Dimitria Festival** includes music, theater, and opera, and takes place at various venues around the town in late October and early November. The festival is timed to correspond with October 26, the feast day of the city's patron saint.

FEASTS

On May 21, at the **Feast of Agios Konstantinos,** there are fire-walking ceremonies in some of the villages near Thessaloniki, most notably at **Lagkadas.** October 26 is the **Feast of Agios Dimitrios** in **Thessaloniki** (see above).

In villages across **Thrace,** a tradition takes place on January 8 that turns this male-dominated society on its head: The men stay home and and do the house-work, and the women relax in the cafés.

ARGO-SARONIC ISLANDS

FEASTS

September 8 marks the **Battle of the Straits of Spetses,** a battle that is reenacted in the town's harbor each year. The same date is the **Feast of the Birth of the Virgin Mary,**

ENTERTAINMENT

celebrated all over Greece. The **Independence Day** celebrations of March 25 are celebrated with particular fervor and exuberance on **Idra.**

FEASTS

February 25 is celebrated on **Skopelos** as the **Feast of Agios Riginos,** the island's patron saint.

St. George is **Skiros's** patron saint, so his **festival** on April 23 is enthusiastically celebrated there with music and feasting.

DRAMA FESTIVAL

A festival devoted to the ancient drama of Greece takes place every July in **Thassos town.**

FEASTS

In the village of **Agia Paraskevi,** on Lesvos, there are festivities on the **feast day** of that name, which falls on July 26. On August 15 the **Feast of the Assumption** is best observed in **Ayiassos.**

On **Samos,** the **Feast of Agia Paraskevi** is especially celebrated in the village of that name on July 26.

There is a tradition on **Limnos** of horse racing to celebrate the **Feast of St. George,** on April 23.

FEASTS

There are big celebrations on **Tinos** on March 25, **Independence Day,** and August 15, the **Assumption of the Virgin.**

MUSIC FESTIVAL

A music festival is held on Santorini every August.

FEASTS

The mountain village of **Olympos,** near Karpathos, is a great place to be on August 15, the **Feast of the Assumption.**

The **Feast of Agia Marina** on July 17 is a big day in the village of that name on the island of **Kasos.**

On **Kos,** the **Feast of St George,** April 23, is traditionally celebrated with horse racing.

The **Feast of Agia Marina,** July 17, is a big celebration in the village of Agia Marina on **Leros.**

July 18–20 is when the **Feast of Profitis Ilias** is celebrated in the numerous monasteries named after the prophet. Celebrations are particularly colorful at the monastery on **Rhodes,** about half a mile (1 km) southeast of Kameiros.

The islanders of **Simi** travel to the offshore island of Agia Marina to celebrate the **Feast of Agia Marina** on July 17.

On **Tilos** on July 27, villagers travel to the monastery of Agios Pandelimon for the annual **feast** of food, music, and dancing.

FOLK DANCE

In **Rhodes Old Town** there are nightly performances during the week, from April to October (currently 9:20 p.m. Mon.–Fri.) by the **Nelly Dimoglou Company.** Find them at the Old Town Theater, near Plateia Arionos, Rhodes town, Tel 0241 20157.

SOUND & LIGHT SHOW

Held in **Rhodes's** Municipal Garden, next to the Palace of the Grand Masters, from April to October. Shows are in different languages, check for details (Tel 0241 21922).

ARTS FESTIVAL

A major **arts festival** takes place in **Iraklio** each August, with drama, dance, and music concerts featuring international names as well as Greek stars.

Every August/September the **Renaissance Festival** in **Rethimnon** includes lively music and theater events (Tel 0831 22245/53583).

WINE FESTIVAL

Rethimnon also holds an annual wine festival, usually held throughout most of July.

CRICKET

In **Corfu,** July is the time of the annual **Cricket Week,** the island's odd British sporting legacy. Matches take place on the Esplanade in Corfu town. Participants include island teams, visiting English village teams, and anyone else who cares to make up a team.

FEASTS

The **Unification of the Ionian Islands** on May 21 is celebrated throughout the island group, but especially in and around **Corfu town.**

SOUND & LIGHT SHOW

This is held in the Old Fortress, **Corfu town,** from May until the end of September. Check locally for details (Tel 0661 37520).

ACTIVITIES IN GREECE

Greece offers a wide array of activities, with water sports featuring prominently. Most resorts have a choice of sports available such as windsurfing, waterskiing, pedaling boats, jet skiing, and paragliding. Activities such as walking and cycling tend to be unorganized and left to the individual. Tennis, soccer, and basketball are popular, and there are a few golf courses.

GOLF

Avid golfers may be interested in the following courses:
Glyfada Golf Course
Konstantinou Karamanli, Glyfada, Athens
Tel 01 894 6820
A 150-acre (60-hectare), 18-hole, par 72 course. The best in Greece, with a clubhouse and full facilities.
Afantou Golf Course
Rhodes
Tel 0241 51255
An 18-hole, par 72 course. Not particularly good, but still enjoyable for its setting.
Corfu Golf Club
Ermones, Corfu
Tel 0661 94220
An 18-hole, par 72 course, suitable for all levels. Coaching is given, and there is a restaurant and a shop with equipment for rent.

HORSEBACK RIDING

Not very big in Greece, but for details of clubs in Athens, Thessaloniki, and around the country, contact:
Hellenic Riding Club
Maroussi, Athens
Tel 01 682 6128

MARATHON RUNNING

The original marathon route is run twice a year. Details from:
SEGAS
Syngrou 137, Athens
Tel 01 935 9302

MOUNTAINEERING

There are numerous mountaineering clubs around Greece that can provide information on activities, mountain trails, and the many mountain huts and refuges that can be reserved through them. For an up-to-date list contact:
Hellenic Federation of Mountaineering Clubs
Miloni 5, 10673 Athens
Tel 01 364 5904

SAILING

Sailing enthusiasts, whether experienced or not, will find the variety of sailing conditions in the Greek seas most satisfying. For general information contact:
Hellenic Professional Yacht Owners Association
A8–A0 Marina Zea, 18536 Piraeus

SCUBA DIVING

Diving is permitted only in certain areas during daylight hours, so check locally. The permitted areas are on or near Corfu, Kalimnos, Kos, Lefkada, Mikonos, Paxi, Rhodes, and Zakinthos. For details, contact:
Union of Greek Diving Centers
Tel 01 922 9532

SKIING

Information on skiing in Greece is available from the **Hellenic Federation of Skiing Clubs** Karayoryi tis Servias 7, 10563 Athens
Tel 01 323 0182
Skiing centers include:
Kalavrita Ski Resort
Xirokambos, Kalavrita
Tel 0692 22174/22661
In the Peloponnese, 12 runs totaling 15.5 miles (25 km) and covering all levels of ability, at altitudes between 5,578 and 7,700 feet (1,700 and 2,347 m). Restaurant, shop, clinic, mountain refuge.

And in Central Greece:
Metsovon Ski Center
Karakoli and Politses-Profitis Ilias Metsovon
Tel 0656 41312/41211
Open Christmas to Easter. Good facilities for Greece, but not up to Western European or U.S. standards.
Parnassos Ski Center
Fterolakka and Kellaria
Tel 0234 22693
Twelve runs ranging from two green to two black runs, at an altitude of 5,750 feet (1,750 m) at Kellaria and 5,900 feet (1,800 m) at Fterolakka. Store, ski school, chalet for meals. Open around December to Easter.
Pilion Ski Center
Agriolefkes, Pilion
Tel 0421 25696/73719
Usually open from late November to late April, with three main slopes, beginners' slopes, and cross-country trails.

SPECTATOR SPORTS

Soccer remains Greece's number one sporting obsession, but in recent years it has been caught up by basketball, since the Greek team won the 1987 European Championships. Don't be surprised if you find it hard to get served in a bar or taverna when all eyes are glued to sport on TV. An interest in soccer or basketball will certainly win you instant friends.

WATERSKIING

For general information on facilities in the Athens area contact:
Greek Water Skiing Federation
Posidonos Avenue, Elliniko, Athens
Tel 01 894 7413

WINDSURFING

Experienced windsurfers who want the best facilities and space away from beginners should look to the Ionian Islands (Corfu, Lefkada, and Zakinthos in particular), and to Kos, Lesvos, Naxos, and Samos.

MENU READER

GENERAL TERMS
the check o logariasmos
bottle boukali
glass potiri
water nero

BASICS
bread psomi
cheese tyri
eggs avga
fish psari(a)
honey meli
meat kreas
oil lathi
    without oil khoris lathi
pepper to piperi
salt alat
seafood thalassina
sugar zakhari
vegetables lakhanika
vegetarian khortofagos
yogurt yiaourti

HORS D'OEUVRES
cod roe pâté taramosalata
eggplant dip melitzanosalata
garlic dip skordalia
mixed hors d'oeuvres mezedes
olives elies
soup soupa
stuffed grape leaves dolmades
yogurt, cucumber, and garlic dip
    tzatziki

VEGETABLES
beans (green) fasolakia
beans (lima) koukia
beans (white) gigantes
cabbage khorta
cucumber ango'ri
eggplant melitzana
    eggplant (stuffed) papoutsakia
Greek salad khoriatiki
lentils fakes
lettuce marouli
okra bamies
peppers piperies
potatoes patates
    french fries patates tighanites
ratatouille briam
rice rizi/pilafi
salad salata
spinach spanaki
tomato domates
zucchini kolokithakia

FISH AND SEAFOOD
anchovy gavros
bream kefalas
clams kidonia
cod bakaliaros
crayfish karavides
cuttlefish soupia
lobster (Aegean variety) astakos
mackerel skoumbri
mussels mydhia
octopus oktapodi
oysters streidia
red mullet barbouni
sardines sardelles
sea bass lavraki
shrimp/prawns garides
sole glossa
squid kalamaria
    baby squid kalamarakia
swordfish xifias
tuna lakerda/tonnos
whitebait marides

MEAT
chicken kotopoulo
chop (pork or beef) brizola
hamburger bifteki
lamb arni
liver sikoti
meatballs keftedes
pork khirino
rabbit kounelli
veal moskhari

DESSERTS
custard krema
custard pie galaktoboureko
honey-and-nut pastries baklava
ice cream pagoto
rice pudding rizogalo
sesame-seed sweetmeat halva
walnut cake karydopita

FRUIT
apples mila
cherries kerasia
figs syka
grapes stafylia
kiwi fruit aktinida
lemon lemoni
melon peponi
oranges portokalia
peaches rodakino
pears akladia/krystalia
quince kydoni
strawberries fraoules
watermelon karpouzi

DRINKS
beer bira
chocolate milk galakakao
coffee kafes
lemonade limonada
milk gala
orangeade portokalada
tea tsai
water nero
    mineral water metaliko nero
wine krasi
    red wine kokkino/mavro
    rosé wine kokkinelli/roze
    white wine aspro

SOME COMMON DISHES/TERMS
kleftiko meat wrapped in thick
    parchment paper and baked in
    the oven with potatoes and
    vegetables
loukanika spicy sausage
loukoumades deep-fried
    doughnuts soaked in honey
moussaka baked layers of
    eggplant, potato, and meat
pastitsio macaroni baked with
    meat
scharas from the grill
souvlaki small pieces of meat
    grilled on a skewer
souzoukakia ground beef
    patties
stifado beef or other meat stew,
    with tomatoes and onions
youvetsi lamb or other meat
    baked in the oven with
    pasta or potatoes in a clay
    casserole dish or sometimes,
    aluminum foil

LANGUAGE GUIDE

TIME
in the morning *to proí*
in the afternoon *to mesiméri*
in the evening *to vrádhi*
at night *ti níchta*
this morning *símera to proí*
this afternoon *símera to mesiméri*
this evening *símera to apóyevma*
tonight *apópse*
last night *timberasméni níchta*
this week *avtí tin evdhomádha*
next month *ton epómeno mína*
What time is it? *Ti óra íne?*
What time? *Ti óra?*

NUMBERS
zero *midhén*
1 *éna*
2 *dhío*
3 *tría*
4 *téssera*
5 *pénde*
6 *éxi*
7 *eftá*
8 *ochtó*
9 *enyá*
10 *dhéka*
100 *ekató*
1000 *hílya*

DAYS OF THE WEEK
Monday *símera*
Tuesday *tríti*
Wednesday *tetárti*
Thursday *pémpti*
Friday *paraskeví*
Saturday *sávato*
Sunday *kiriakí*

USEFUL PHRASES
Could you help me, please? *Boríte na me voithísete, parakaló?*
Could I ask you something? *Boró na rotíso káti?*
Do you know..? *Xérete...?*
Where's the toilet? *Poo íne i twaléta?*
Who? *Pyós?*
Who's that? *Pyós íne?*
What? *Ti?*
Why? *Yatí?*
How? *Pos?*
How far is that? *Póso makriá íne?*
How long does that take? *Pósi óra dhiarkí/kratái?*
How long is the trip? *Póso kratái to taxídhi?*
Which? *Pyo? Pya?*
When? *Póte?*
Where are you from? *Apó poo érhesthe?*
I'd like a kilo of apples, please *Tha íthela éna kiló míla*
How much? *Pósos*

How much is this? *Póso káni?*
Can I take this? *Boró na to páro mazí moo?*
I'm just looking, if that's all right *Tha ríxo mya matyá, an epitrépete*
Could you giftwrap it, please? *Boríte na to tilíxete ya dhóro, parakaló?*

Yes, of course *Ne, vévea/vevéos*
No, I'm sorry *Óhi, lipáme*
All right *Kalá*
Okay *Endáxi*
I don't know *Dhen xéro*

Thank you *Efcharistó*
You're welcome *Parakaló*
Thank you very much *Efcharistó polí*
Very kind of you *Polí evyenikó ek méroos sas*
Thank you for your trouble *Efcharistó ya tongópo*

Sorry! *Sighnómi*
Excuse me *Me sinchoríte*
I do apologize *Me sinchoríte*
I'm sorry *lipáme*
Never mind *Endáxi étsi*
Do you like it? *Soo arési?*
Wonderful! *Thavmásio!*
It's really nice here! *Ti oréa poo íne edhó!*

I'm American *Íme amerikos*
Do you speak English? *Miláte angliká?*
I (don't) understand *(dhen) Katalavéno*
Do you understand me? *Me katalavénete?*
Could you repeat that, please? *Boríte na to epanalávete, parakaló?*
Could you speak more slowly, please? *Boríte na miláte pyo arghá, parakaló?*
How do you pronounce that? *Pos proférete aftó?*

Help! *Voítha!*
Could you call/fetch a doctor, please? *Parakaló, kaléste/idhopiíste ghríghora éna yatró?*
Call an ambulance! *Idhopiíste éna asthenofóro!*

DINING OUT
Is the restaurant open yet? *Íne anichtí i koozína?*
What time does the restaurant open/close? *Póte aniyí/klíni I koozína?*
I'd like a table for two, please. *Tha íthela éna trapézi ya dhío átoma.*
We've/we haven't made a reservation. *(dhen) Klísame trapézi.*
Can we wait for a table? *Boróome na periménoome ya éna trapézi?*
Is this seat taken? *Íne eléftheri aftí i thési?*
Could we sit here/there? *Boróome na kathísoome edhó/ekí?*
Can we sit by the window? *Boróome na kathísoome kondá sto paráthiro?*

Can we eat outside? *Boróome na fáme kyéxo?*
Do you have another chair for us? *Mas férnete akóma mya karékla?*

Waiter!/Madam!/Sir! *Garsóni!/Kiría!/Kírie!*
Could we see the menu/wine list, please? *Boróome na dhóome tongatálogho/tongatálogho krasyón?*
Do you have a menu in English? *Éhete éna katálogho sta angliká?*
Do you have a dish of the day?/tourist menu? *Éhete pyáto tis iméras/tooristikó menóo?*
What are the specialties of the region/the house? *Pyes íne i spesialité tis periohís/too maghazyóo?*
What's this? *Ti íne aftó?*
Is this a hot or a cold dish? *Aftó to fayitó íne krío i zestó?*
Is this sweet? *Aftó to fayitó íne ghlikó?*
Is this spicy/hot? *Aftó to fayitó íne pikándiko/piperáto?*
I'll/we'll have what those people are having *Théloome to ídhyo fayitó poo tróne ekíni i ánthropi, parakaló*
Could I have some more bread, please? *Parakaló, lígho psomí akóma?*
  a bottle of water/wine *Parakaló, éna bookáli neró/krasí akóma*
  some salt and pepper *Mas férnete to alatopípero, parakaló?*
  a napkin *Mas férnete mya chartopetséta, parakaló?*
  a spoon *Mas férnete éna kootaláki, parakaló?*
  some toothpicks *Mas férnete odhondoghlifídhes, parakaló?*
  a glass of water *Mas férnete éna potíri neró, parakaló?*
  a straw (for the child) *Mas férnete éna kalamáki (yu tu pédhi), parakaló?*
How much is this dish? *Póso káni aftó to fayitó?*
Could I have the bill, please? *To loghariazmó, parakaló?*

Do you have a highchair? *Mas férnete mya pedhiki karékla?*
Could you warm up this bottle/jar for me? *Boríte na moo zestánete avtó to biberó/vazáki?*
Is there somewhere I can change the baby's diaper? *Ipárhi kápyos chóros ópoo boró na aláxo to moró?*
The child will share what we're having *To pedhí tha fái lígho apó to dhikó mas fayitó*

ACCOMMODATIONS

Do you have a single/double room available? *Éhete éna eléfthero monó/dhiplό dhomátyo?*
Does that include breakfast/lunch/dinner? *Me to proinó/to mesimeryanó/to vradhinó?*
Could I see the room? *Boró na dho to dhomátyo?*
Could we have two adjoining rooms? *Boróome na échoome dhío dhomátya dhípla-dhípla?*

with/without toilet/bathtub/shower *me/chorís twaléta/bányo/doos*
(not) facing the street *(óhi) apó ti meryá too dhrómoo*
with/without a view of the sea *me/chorís théa pros ti thálasa*
Is there an elevator in the hotel? *To xenodhohío éhi asansér?*
Do you have room service? *To xenodhohío éhi exipirétisi dhomatíoo/room sérvis*
What time's breakfast? *Ti óra íne to proinó?*
Can I have breakfast in my room? *Boró na écho to proinó sto dhomátiómoo?*
Where's the emergency exit/fire escape? *Poo íne i éxodhos kindhínoo/i skála pirkayás?*
The key to room..., please *To klidhí too dhomatíoo..., parakaló*
Is there drinking water? *Ipárchi pósimo neró?*
Could you put in a crib? *Boríte na válete kyéna pedhikó kreváti sto dhomátiómas?*
Could you find a babysitter for me? *Boríte na moo vríte mya béibi-síter?*

Could you put it on my bill? *Boríte na to ghrápsete sto loghariazmómoo?*
Does this amount include the tip? *(Sto posó aftó) simberilamvánete i exipirétisi?*
Can I pay by credit card? *Boró na plíroso me pistotikí kárta?*
Can I pay with foreign currency? *Boró na plíroso me xéno sinálaghma?*
Could I have a receipt, please? *Boró na écho mya apódhixi/to loghariazmó?*

DIRECTIONS

Where? *Poo?*
here/there *edhó/ekí*
to the right/left *pros ta dhexyá/aristerá*
on the right/left of *dhexyá/aristerá apó*
straight ahead *ísya*
via *méso*
in *se*
opposite *apénandi*
next to/near *dhípla se/kondá se*
in front of *brostá*
in the center *sti mési*
down *(pros ta) káto*
up *(pros ta) páno*
inside *(pros ta) mésa*
outside *(pros ta) éxo*
behind *(pros ta) píso*
at the front *brostá*
at the back *píso-píso*
in the north *sto vorá*
to the south *pros to nóto*
from the west *apó ti dhísi*
from the east *tis anatolís*
north/south/west/east of *vórya/nótya/dhitiká/anatolitiká apú*
address (street/number) *idhiéfthinsi (odhós/arithmós)*

TRAVELING AROUND

Where does this train go to? *Poo piyéni aftó to tréno?*

Does this boat go to...? *Aftó to plío piyéni se ...?*

Can I take this bus to...? *Boró na páo se ... me to leoforío?*

Does this train stop at...? *Aftó to tréno stamatái se ...?*

Is this seat taken/free/reserved? *Aftí i thési íne pyazméni/eléftheri/klizméni?*

Could you tell me where I have to get off for...? *Moo léte poo prépi na katevó ya...?*

Could you let me know when we get to...? *Boríte na me proidhopiísete ótan tha ftánoome kondá se...?*

Could you stop at the next stop, please? *Boríte na stamtísete stin epómeni stási, parakaló?*

Where are we now? *Poo ímaste edhó?*

Can I come back on the same ticket? *Ine me epistrofí aftó to isitírio?*

Can I change on this ticket? *Boró na sinechíso maftó to isitírio?*

How long is this ticket valid for? *Ya póso kyeró ischíi aftó to isitírio?*

Where can I...? *Poo boró na...?*

buy a ticket? *Poo boró na aghoráso isitírio?*

make a reservation? *Poo boró na klíso thési?*

make a flight reservation? *Poo boró na klíso thési sto aeropláno?*

Could I have a...to..., please? *Thélo éna...ya...*

a one-way *Thélo éna apló isitírio ya...*

a round-trip *Thélo éna metepistrofís ya...*

business class *biznesklás*

first class *próti thési*

second class *dhéfteri thési*

tourist class *tooristikí thési*

Do you also have...? *Mípos éhete ke...?*

season tickets? *Mípos éhete ke kárta polaplón dhiadhromón?*

weekly tickets? *Mípos éhete ke kárta ya mya evdhomádha?*

I'd like to reserve a seat/sleeping berth/cabin *Thélo na klíso thési/kreváti/kabína*

by the window *sto paráthiro*

smoking/no smoking *kapnízondes/mi kapnízondes*

single/double *ya éna átomo/ya dhío átoma*

Where's...? *Poo íne...?*

Where's the information desk? *Poo íne to ghrafío pliroforyón?*

Do you have a city map with the bus/the subway routes on it? *Mípos éhete éna chárti tis pólis me to dhíktio leoforíon/too metró?*

Do you have a schedule? *Mípos éhete to orário ton dhromoloyíon?*

How much is a one-way/round-trip? *Póso káni éna apló isitírio/éna metepistrofís?*

Do I have to pay a supplement? *Prépi na pliróso simbliromatikó isitírio?*

How much baggage am I allowed? *Póses aposkevés boró na páro mazímoo?*

Do I have to change trains/buses/boats? Where? *Prépi naláxo tréno/leoforío/plío? Poo?*

Does the plane touch down anywhere en route? *To aeropláno káni endhiámeses prosyiósis?*

Does the boat call in at any ports on the way? *To plío pyáni skála ke sála limánya?*

Does the train/bus stop at...? *Káni stási se... to tréno/to leoforío?*

Is there a connection to...? *Ipárchi andapókrisi ya...?*

How long do I have to wait? *Pósi óra prépi na periméno?*

When does...leave? *Póte févyi...?*

Could you get me a taxi, please? *Boríte na kalésete éna taxí ya ména?*

Where can I find a taxi around here? *Poo boró na vro éna taxí edhó kondá?*

BANKS

Where can I find a bank/an exchange office around here? *Ipárchi edhó kondá kamyá trápeza/kanéna ghrafío sinalághmatos?*

Where can I cash this traveler's check? *Poo boró na exaryíroso aftí tin taxidhiotikí epitayí?*

Can I withdraw money on my credit card here? *Boró na páro leftá edhó me mya pistotikí kárta?*

I've had some money transferred here. Has it arrived yet? *Ékana éna tileghrafikó émvazma. Eftase to émvazma?*

I'd like to change some money *Tha íthela naláxo chrímata*

dollars into... *dholária ya...*

What's the exchange rate? *Pya íne i isotimía?*

Could you give me some small change with it? *Boríte na moo dhósete ke lígha psilá, parakaló?*

INDEX

GREEK ALPHABET

Alpha	A, α	a, as in rather
Beta	B, β	v, as in very
Gamma	Γ, γ	y, as in yes, before i or e; g, as in get, before o, a, ou
Delta	Δ, δ	th, as in that
Epsilon	E, ε	e, as in yes
Zita	Z, ζ	z
Eta	H, η	ee, as in meet
Theta	Θ, θ	th, as in thing
Iota	I, ι	i, as in lid
Kappa	K, κ	k
Lambda	Λ, λ	l
Mu	M, μ	m
Nu	N, ν	n
Xi	Ξ, ξ	ks
Omicron	O, o	o, as in pot
Pi	Π, π	p
Rho	P, ρ	rolling r
Sigma	Σ, σ (mid-word) ς (end of word)	s
Tau	T, τ	t
Upsilon	Y, υ	e, very (similar to eta)
Phi	Φ, φ	f
Chi	X, χ	h, as in loch
Psi	Ψ, ψ	ps, as in corpse
Omega	Ω, ω	o, as in bone

PRONUNCIATION

αι	e, as in met
αυ	av/af
ει	ee, as in reed
ευ	ev/ef
ου	ou, as in tour
γγ	ng, as in angel
γκ	g, as in goat, at beginning of a word; ng in the middle
μπ	b at beginning of a word; mb in the middle
ντ	d at beginning of word; nd in the middle
σι	sh, as in shelter
τζ	j, as in Johnny

ILLUSTRATIONS CREDITS

Abbreviations for terms appearing below: (t) top; (b) bottom; (l) left; (r) right

Cover (tl), World Pictures Ltd. (tr), T. Harris/Just Greece. (bl), Y. Travert/ Diaf. (br), Images Colour Library. (spine), T. Harris/Just Greece. 1, Studio Kontos/Photostock. 2/3, Ideal Photo. 4, G. Mooney/Corbis UK Ltd. 9, K. Schafer/Corbis UK Ltd. 11, M. Borchi/National Geographic Society. 12, Yiorgos Depollas. 14/15 J. L. Stansfield/National Geographic Society. 16/17, Y. Depollas. 19, T. Harris/Just Greece. 20/21, G. Mooney/Corbis UK Ltd. 24, Ashmolean Museum, Oxford, UK/Bridgeman Art Library, London. 25, J. L. Stansfield/National Geographic Society. 26/27, Mykonos Archaeological Museum, J. L. Stansfield/ National Geographic Society. 28/29, D. Lees/Corbis UK Ltd. 30, Photo © H. Palmer. 33, T. Gervis/Robert Harding Picture Library. 34, Hulton Getty Picture Collection Ltd. 35, Hulton-Deutsch Collection/Corbis UK Ltd. 36, Hulton-Deutsch Collection/Corbis UK Ltd. 37, Bettmann/Corbis UK Ltd. 39, Y. Nikiteas/ Eye Ubiquitous. 40, C. Perry. 40/41, P. Wilson. 42/43, J. L. Stansfield/National Geographic Society. 44/45, P. Partington/S. Cordaiy. 47, T. Harris/ Just Greece. 48, Bettmann/Corbis UK Ltd. 49, M. Southern/Eye Ubiquitous. 52/53, N. Setchfield/Powerstock/Zefa. 54, A. Gin/Powerstock/Zefa. 56, Brad Walker/Powerstock/Zefa. 57, Studio Kontos/Photostock. 58/59, M. Kouri/ World News. 59, D. Dailey. 60/61, Terry Harris/Just Greece. 62, M. Borchi/National Geographic Society. 64/65, V. Efthymiou/Ideal Photo. 65, P. Wilson/AA Photo Library. 66, James Davis Worldwide. 67, P. Wilson. 68, Studio Kontos/Photostock. 69, M. Borchi/National Geographic Society. 70, AKG—London. 71, Studio Kontos/Photostock. 72, C. Watson. 73, E. Lessing/AKG—London. 74, Spectrum Colour Library. 75, Studio Kontos/Photostock. 76, M. Borchi/ National Geographic Society. 77, M. Borchi Massimo/National Geographic Society. 78, National Archaeological Museum, Athens, Greece/ Bridgeman Art Library, London. 79, Spectrum Colour Library. 80, Studio Kontos/Photostock. 81, Powerstock/ Zefa. 82, C. Vegas/Ideal Photo. 85, Photo © H. Palmer. 86/87, Helga Lade Fotoagentur. 88/89, T. Harris/ Just Greece. 90, R. Reichenfeld/ Dorling Kindersley. 91, Schings/ Explorer. 92, R. Surman/AA Photo Library. 93, M. Holford. 95t, T. Harris/AA Photo Library. 95c, G. Tsafos. 95b, C. Watson. 97, N.l Bowen-Morris/Travel Ink. 98, Studio Kontos/Photostock. 99, Studio Kontos/Photostock. 100, World Pictures Ltd. 103, C. Vergas/ Ideal

Photo. 104, T. Gervis/Robert Harding Picture Library. 107, J. L. Stansfield/National Geographic Society. 108, N. Bowen-Morris/Travel Ink. 109, J. Sierpinski/Diaf. 110/111, T. Harris/Just Greece. 111, Spectrum Colour Library. 112l, Mary Evans Picture Library. 112r, AKG—London. 113, Ashmolean Museum, Oxford/ Bridgeman Art Library, London. 114, A. Gin/Powerstock/Zefa. 115, L. Janicek/Bildarchiv Steffens. 116, J. Smith/S. Cordaiy. 117, B. Davis/ Aspect. 118/119, Photo © H. Palmer. 120, B. Gibbons/Eye Ubiquitous. 121t, L. Janicek/Bildarchiv Steffens. 121b, C. Perry. 122/123, T. Harris/AA Photo Library. 123, V. Efthymiou/Ideal Photo. 124/125, Photo © H. Palmer. 126, Photo © H. Palmer. 127, Cl. Perry. 128/129, J. L. Stansfield/ National Geographic Society. 130, C. Vergas/Ideal Photo. 131t, National Archaeological Museum , Athens, J. L. Stans- field/National Geographic Society. 131b, Poseidon Pictures. 132/133, Mary Evans Picture Library. 133, Hulton Getty Picture Collection Ltd. 134, Ideal Photo. 135, Studio Kontos/Photostock. 137, C. Pickles/ Ffotograff. 139, Ideal Photo. 140/141, C. Vergas/Ideal Photo. 142, T. Harris/ Just Greece. 144/145, P. Wilson. 146, D. & J. Heaton/Spectrum Colour Library. 147t, Studio Kontos/Photo- stock. 147b, Studio Kontos/Photo- stock. 148/149, Ideal Photo. 150, C. Vergas/Ideal Photo. 151, C. Watson. 152, C. Pickles/Ffotograff. 153, P. Wilson. 154, V. Efithymion/Ideal Photo. 155, Kunz/Bilderberg Archiv der Fotografen. 156, K. Wothe/ Oxford Scientific Films. 157, T. Harris/Just Greece. 158/159, Photo © H. Palmer. 159, P. Wilson. 161, Photo © H. Palmer. 162, Ideal Photo, 163, T. Harris/AA Photo Library. 164, T. Harris/ AA Photo Library. 165, C. Perry. 166/167, T. Harris/Just Greece. 169, J. Heseltine. 171, P. Baker/Inter- national Photobank. 172/173, Cephas Picture Library. 174, National Archaeological Museum, Athens/Bridgeman Art Library, London. 174/175, Ideal Photo. 175, E. Lessing/AKG—London. 176, J. Heseltine. 177, M. Dubin/Travel Ink. 178, J. Heseltine. 179, J. Heseltine. 181, Spectrum Colour Library. 182/183, Bilderberg Archiv der Fotografen. 183, Spectrum Colour Library.185, Studio Kontos/ Photostock. 187, P. Baker/Inter- national Photobank. 188/189, J. L. Stansfield/National Geographic Society. 190, James Davis Worldwide. 191, T. Dassios/Ideal Photo. 192, F. York/Dorling Kindersley. 193, Studio Kontos/Photostock. 194/195, J. Heseltine. 196/197, G. Tsafos. 199, F. York/Dorling Kindersley. 200, D. Tipling/BBC Natural History Unit Picture Library. 201l, B. Glover/Bruce Coleman Collection. 201tr, F. Labhardt/Bruce Coleman Collection. 201br, A. Manzanares/Bruce Coleman Collection. 202/203, Y. Depollas. 205, Ecole Suisse d'Archéologie en Grèce.

207, R. Reichenfeld/Dorling Kindersley. 208/209, R. Moore/AA Photo Library. 211t, R. Moore/AA Photo Library. 211b, R. Moore/AA Photo Library. 212/213, R. Moore/AA Photo Library. 214, R. Moore/AA Photo Library. 216, R. Moore/AA Photo Library. 217, Studio Kontos/Photostock. 219, T. Harris/ Just Greece. 220, Images Colour Library. 221, S. Thorn/Powerstock/ Zefa. 223, F. Kyriakou/Ideal Photo. 224/225, Photo © H. Palmer. 225, L. Frost/Robert Harding Picture Library. 226/7, Travel Library. 227, James Davis Worldwide. 228, T. Harris/Just Greece. 229, C. Perry. 230, Robert Harding Picture Library. 231, James Davis Worldwide. 232, T. Harris/Just Greece. 233t, Terry Harris/ Just Greece. 233b, R. Lawrence/ Ffotograff. 234, A. Sattin/AA Photo Library. 235, T. Harris/Just Greece. 236/237, Ideal Photo. 238l, Archivo Iconografico, S.A./Corbis UK Ltd. 238r, A. Sattin/AA Photo Library. 239l, E/H Lessing/AKG—London. 239r, Keystone/Hulton Getty Picture Collection Ltd. 240, Photo © H. Palmer. 241, Photo © H. Palmer. 242, A. Sattin/AA Photo Library. 245, Images Colour Library. 246, T. Harris/AA Photo Library. 247, T. Harris/ Just Greece. 248, T. Harris/Just Greece. 249, Photo © H. Palmer. 250, A. Tovy Amsel/Eye Ubiquitous. 251, D. Forman/Eye Ubiquitous. 252, James Davis World- wide. 254, Photo © H. Palmer. 255, Studio Kontos/Photostock. 256, J. Sierpinski/Diaf. 257, Studio Kontos/Photostock. 258, D. Thierry/Diaf. 259, Hugh R./Eye Ubiquitous. 260, C. Perry. 262/263, S. Day/AA Photo Library. 264, T. Harris/Just Greece. 265, Images Colour Library. 266, N. Hall/R. Harding Picture Library. 267, S. Day/AA Photo Library. 268, Photo © H. Palmer. 269, Terry Harris/Just Greece. 270, P. Haloftis/ Ideal Photo. 271, James Davis Worldwide. 272, Ideal Photo. 273, Photo © H. Palmer. 274, S. Paine/Ffotograff. 275, Ideal Photo. 277, C. Pendle/Ffotograff. 279, Travel Library. 281, G. Mooney/Corbis UK Ltd. 283, R. Grant Archive. 284, Poseidon Pictures. 285, R. Harding/Robert Harding Picture Library. 286, Studio Kontos/Photostock. 287t, C. Pendle/ Ffotograff. 287b, Spectrum Colour Library. 289, Ashmolean Museum, Oxford/Bridgeman Art Library, London. 290, Clay Perry. 291, A. Belich/Helga Lade Fotoagentur. 292, T. Harris/Just Greece. 293, Travel Library. 294/295, T. Harris/Just Greece. 296, K. Paterson/AA Photo Library. 297, World Pictures. 298/299, Studio Kontos/Photostock. 299, R. Wood/Corbis UK Ltd. 300, Travel Library. 301, D. Bailey/Spectrum Colour Library. 302/303, Ideal Photo. 304, Zooid Pictures. 305, K. Paterson/ AA Photo Library. 306, L. Wilson/Robert Harding Picture Library. 307, Studio Kontos/Photostock. 308, Spectrum

Colour Library. 309, James Davis Worldwide. 310, World Pictures. 311, T. Harris/Just Greece. 312, T. Harris/Just Greece. 314, T. Harris/Just Greece. 316, James Davis Worldwide. 317, Ideal Photo. 318/319, H. Merten/Robert Harding Picture Library. 320, H. Merten/Robert Harding Picture Library. 321t, J. Tims/AA Photo Library. 321b, S. Outram/AA Photo Library. 322/323, Ideal Photo. 324/325, Photo © H. Palmer. 327, Photo © H. Palmer. 328, Photo © H. Palmer. 329 Photo © H. Palmer. 330, J. L. Stansfield/National Geographic Society. 331, British Museum, London, UK/Bridgeman Art Library. 332, Ideal Photo. 333, Photo © H. Palmer. 334, James Davis Worldwide. 335, James Davis Worldwide. 336, D. Ireland. 337, T. Harris/Just Greece

All credits © H. Palmer are from "The Most Beautiful Villages of Greece" by Mark Ottaway, published by Thames & Hudson Ltd, London.

The world's largest nonprofit scientific and educational organization, the National Geographic Society was founded in 1888 "for the increase and diffusion of geographic knowledge." Since then it has supported scientific exploration and spread information to its more than nine million members worldwide.

The National Geographic Society educates and inspires millions every day through magazines, books, television programs, videos, maps and atlases, research grants, the National Geographic Bee, teacher workshops, and innovative classroom materials.

The Society is supported through membership dues, charitable gifts, and income from the sale of its educational products. Members receive NATIONAL GEOGRAPHIC magazine—the Society's official journal—discounts on Society products, and other benefits.

For more information about the National Geographic Society, its educational programs, publications, or how to support its work, call 1-800-NGS-LINE (647-5463), or write to: National Geographic Society, 1145 17th Street, N.W., Washington, D.C. 20036 U.S.A.

Printed in the U.S.A

Published by the National Geographic Society

John M. Fahey, Jr., *President and Chief Executive Officer*

Gilbert M. Grosvenor, *Chairman of the Board*

Nina D. Hoffman, *Executive Vice President, President, Books and School Publishing*

William R. Gray, *Vice President and Director, Book Division*

Elizabeth L. Newhouse, *Director of Travel Publishing*

Barbara A. Noe, *Senior Editor and Project Manager*

Allan Fallow, *Senior Editor*

Caroline Hickey, *Senior Researcher*

Cinda Rose, *Art Director*

Carl Mehler, *Director of Maps*

Joseph F. Ochlak, *Map Coordinator*

Gary Colbert, *Production Director*

Richard S. Wain, *Production Project Manager*

Edited and designed by AA Publishing (a trading name of Automobile Association Developments Limited, whose registered office is Norfolk House, Priestley Road, Basingstoke, Hampshire, England RG24 9NY. Registered number: 1878835).

Rachel Alder & Marilynne Lanng, *Project Managers*

David Austin, *Senior Art Editor*

Ann Stonehouse, *Editor*

Ellie King, *Designer*

Inna Nogeste, *Senior Cartographic Editor*

Richard Firth, *Production Director*

Steve Gilchrist, *Prepress Production Controller*

Cartography by AA Cartographic Production

Picture Research by Zooid Pictures Ltd.

Drive maps drawn by Chris Orr Associates, Southampton, England

Cutaway illustrations drawn by Maltings Partnership, Derby, England

Library of Congress Cataloging-in-Publication Data

Gerrard, Mike.
    The National Geographic traveler. Greece / Mike Gerrard.
        p. cm.
    Includes index.
    ISBN 0-7922-7923-9
        1. Greece--Guidebooks. I. Title: Greece. II. Title.

DF716 .G48 2001
914.9504'76--dc21   00 069562

Printed and bound by R.R. Donnelly & Sons, Willard, Ohio.
Color separations by Leo Reprographic Ltd., Hong Kong.
Cover separations by L.C. Repro, Aldermaston, U.K.
Cover printed by Miken Inc., Cheektowaga, New York.

Visit the Society's Web site at http://www.nationalgeographic.com